Capturing Campaign Effects

Capturing Campaign Effects

Edited by Henry E. Brady and Richard Johnston

The University of Michigan Press   *Ann Arbor*

Copyright © by the University of Michigan 2006
All rights reserved
Published in the United States of America by
The University of Michigan Press
Manufactured in the United States of America
∞ Printed on acid-free paper

2009 2008 2007 2006   4 3 2 1

No part of this publication may be reproduced, stored in a retrieval system, or transmitted in any form or by any means, electronic, mechanical, or otherwise, without the written permission of the publisher.

A CIP catalog record for this book is available from the British Library.

Library of Congress Cataloging-in-Publication Data

Capturing campaign effects / edited by Henry E. Brady and Richard Johnston.
   p.   cm.
   Includes index.
   ISBN-13: 978-0-472-09921-4 (cloth : alk. paper)
   ISBN-10: 0-472-09921-3 (cloth : alk. paper)
   ISBN-13: 978-0-472-06921-7 (pbk. : alk. paper)
   ISBN-10: 0-472-06921-7 (pbk. : alk. paper)
   1. Political campaigns—United States. 2. Elections—United States.
   3. Voting—United States. I. Brady, Henry E. II. Johnston, Richard, 1948–

JK2281.C385   2006
324.70973—dc22   2005028455

To Patricia and Kathryn

Contents

Acknowledgments ix

The Study of Political Campaigns
Henry E. Brady, Richard Johnston, and John Sides 1

I Voter Decision Making and Campaign Effects
The Paradox of Minimal Effects *Stephen Ansolabehere* 29
The Impact of Campaigns on Discrepancies, Errors, and
  Biases in Voting Behavior *Patrick Fournier* 45
Priming and Persuasion in Presidential Campaigns
  Larry M. Bartels 78

II Research Designs and Statistical Methods for Studying Campaign Effects
Campaigns as Experiments *Stephen Ansolabehere* 115
Three Virtues of Panel Data for the Analysis of
  Campaign Effects *Larry M. Bartels* 134
The Rolling Cross-Section and Causal Attribution
  Henry E. Brady and Richard Johnston 164

III Campaign Effects in Congressional and Senatorial Races: Information and Issues
Measuring Campaign Spending Effects in U.S. House Elections
  Gary C. Jacobson 199
Informational Rhythms of Incumbent-Dominated
  Congressional Elections *Laurel Elms and Paul M. Sniderman* 221
Alternative Tests for the Effects of Campaigns and Candidates
  on Voting Behavior *Benjamin Highton* 242

IV	**The Rules of the Game and Election Results**	
	Do Polls Influence the Vote?	
	André Blais, Elisabeth Gidengil, and Neil Nevitte	263
	Strategic Learning in Campaigns with Proportional Representation: Evidence from New Zealand	
	Richard Johnston and Jack Vowles	280
V	**The Role of the Mass Media**	
	Studying Statewide Political Campaigns	
	R. Michael Alvarez and Alexandra Shankster	307
	Gender, Media Coverage, and the Dynamics of Leader Evaluations: The Case of the 1993 Canadian Election	
	Elisabeth Gidengil and Joanna Everitt	336
	Mass Media and Third-Party Insurgency *Richard Jenkins*	356
	Contributors	383
	Index	385

Acknowledgments

THIS BOOK has been a long time coming—too long, we admit. In part this reflects the rush of events, most critically the rapid spread of the very studies this book is intended to encourage. The editors got caught up in this happy evolution, as did several of the contributors. For the same reason, the introductory chapter seemed in a race against time: no sooner did we finish a draft than new studies demanded recognition and discussion. But we finally declared editorial closure, and here the book is. With the knife-edge results of recent American campaigns and the growing evidence that campaigns matter a lot, capturing campaign effects seems even more important to us than when we began this project. These effects are still more fugitive than we would like, but we believe that this book provides a field guide to those intent on identifying and pinning them down so that we can better understand and even improve political campaigns.

The book began life as a colloquium on campaign studies at the magnificent Green College, a graduate foundation in the University of British Columbia (UBC). Somehow, the participants resisted the distraction of the setting. The participants included not just the contributors to this volume but several UBC colleagues and students and others. Notable among these were John Zaller of UCLA, who gave us an early look at his work on media dynamics, and Kathleen Jamieson and Joe Capella of the Annenberg School for Communication at the University of Pennsylvania, who had much to say about the media backdrop to campaigns. In a sense, the Green College colloquium was also the genesis of the National Annenberg Election Study.

We acknowledge the help of the college and of its principal at the time, Richard Ericson, who turned the facility over to us virtually free of charge. Most of the bills were paid by the Social Sciences and Humanities

Research Council of Canada, under its small-conference grant program. Priceless administrative support was given at the Berkeley end by Lynn Civitello and at the Vancouver end by Dory Urbano. At Berkeley, the Survey Research Center and the Department of Political Science generously supported Henry Brady's research, and at UBC, the Department of Political Science provided the same generous support for Richard Johnston's work. It goes without saying that none of these persons or institutions bears any responsibility for errors or omissions in this volume.

Three graduate students were critical to logistics: Stuart Soroka, now at McGill University, took care of ground arrangements in Vancouver; John Sides, now at George Washington University, kept us abreast of subsequent developments in the literature as well as grounded the enterprise deeply in the older literature on campaigns and elections, to the point that the only honest choice left to us was to make him a coauthor of the introductory chapter; and Julia Lockhart reduced the diversity—some would say, perversity—in presentation formats to meet the standards of the University of Michigan Press.

The press has been unfailingly patient. The gestation of this book has taken us through three editors, Chuck Myers, Jeremy Shine, and Jim Reische. The greatest leap of faith was required of Jim, and we are deeply grateful for it. We trust that the volume vindicates that faith. We also thank the patient and attentive reviewers, who should recognize their handiwork in the ultimate product.

Once again, we thank our families. Each family seems to have acquired a certain fatalism about the manic and peripatetic nature of its respective husband and father. Each of us has camped out in the other's basement and bored the host family with political science arcana. Each of us extended trips designed for other purposes to stage furtive editorial meetings in hotel rooms. These years were tough ones for both of our families, and our editorial preoccupations only increased the burden on them. It may be small consolation that we believed in the editorial enterprise all along and that, at last, we have delivered the goods.

Henry E. Brady   Richard Johnston
Berkeley, California   Vancouver, British Columbia

The Study of Political Campaigns

Henry E. Brady, Richard Johnston, and John Sides

Do POLITICAL CAMPAIGNS MATTER? This question, like so many in political science, seems natural, important, and straightforward. Yet the answer founders on the difficulty of defining both the subject and the predicate. What do we mean by political campaigns? How might they matter? This essay attempts to organize the study of campaigns by marking its boundaries and by ordering questions and designs in relation to each other. In our view, the following questions must be addressed:

> *Defining a Campaign*—What *is* a campaign, and thus when is an effect a campaign effect?
> *Defining Campaign Effects*—How do campaigns affect the factors relevant to vote choice and vote choice itself?
> *Studying Campaign Effects*—What designs have been employed, and what are their relative merits for campaign effects?
> *Campaigns and Democratic Theory*—What is the place of the campaign in democratic theory and practice? Is the campaign a place for deliberation, manipulation, or both?

Defining a Campaign

The answer to the question "What is a campaign?" is not simple. To start, there are two conceptually distinct, but empirically linked, ways of looking at a campaign. One focuses on institutional or quasi-institutional conditions. The second considers campaigns as periods of uncommon intensity in the political order, which can either broaden the period identified as a campaign or narrow it.

We begin by delineating the institutional conditions. Usually, if the following are true, a campaign is under way:

> The date of the election is known.
> The identity of the candidates is known.
> Candidates are available to spend virtually all of their time getting (re)elected.
> Certain actions that are normally unregulated are now regulated and, in some cases, forbidden—for example, fund-raising and spending.

The first requirement, that the date of the election is known, not only defines a necessary condition for a campaign to be under way but also defines the end of a campaign. The beginning is harder to identify. If *all* these things are true, then a campaign is certainly under way. But a campaign may be under way if only some are true. Or it may not be. In the United States, the date of every election has been known since the ratification of the Constitution. If the incumbent is determined to seek reelection then that person may begin campaigning immediately. Does a transparently reelection-oriented speech delivered early in the incumbent's term qualify as part of the campaign for the next election? This point illustrates the difficulty of locating a campaign's inception.

However, we may learn more by considering that campaigns, whatever their formal institutional definition, are usually characterized by heightened *intensity*.[1] Intensity may not correspond to the formal period of the campaign, as it depends on the intentions of the players themselves. A campaign could easily begin "early" if the candidates take to the hustings well in advance of Election Day, though that is no guarantee that anyone would pay attention. The opposite scenario seems less likely but is possible. What then is intensity, and who can exhibit it?

Minimally defined, a campaign is the period right before citizens make a real political choice. This common knowledge typically heightens citizens' attention to politics in direct relation to the proximity of the event. Concomitantly, campaign activity is more likely to register on voters' minds as Election Day draws near. Thus there is an interaction between campaign effort and the approaching "deadline" of Election Day. Evidence of greater salience for voters could manifest itself in, for example, media attentiveness, campaign interest, political discussion, knowledge about candidates, and strength of vote intention.

Another indicator of intensity is the effort put into the campaign by parties and candidates, which usually increases as the campaign progresses. This increase may come in total outlays, such as a flurry of television advertising, or merely in a different distribution of the same overall amount of effort, such that the campaign seems more intense to (some) voters and the media. For instance, in the last month of a presidential campaign, candidates constantly travel to swing states with large Electoral College delegations. In the 1988 Canadian campaign, the parties focused their advertisements more closely on the central issue, the Canada–U.S. Free Trade Agreement, and on the respective credibility of the leaders in addressing this issue. The battle seemed more furious, even if expenditures did not increase much. Measuring campaign effort means attending to both time and money, as dollars and hours spent are the most fundamental indicators. Conventions, debates, appearances, voter mobilization, and television advertising are all manifestations of time and/or money.

A final indicator of intensity is mass media attention to the campaign. Without it, a campaign may be the proverbial tree falling unheard in the woods. Presumably media coverage reflects what will attract an audience, and this in turn reflects a judgment about the interest of the story and about the attentiveness of potential viewers or readers. Any campaign story should be more interesting if the audience is ready for it, and the audience may be more ready the closer is their moment of choice. We might then expect media attention to increase toward the end of the campaign. Even if it does not increase in total volume, it should, like party effort, become more focused, though not so much on the key elements of the electorate as on the key elements of the choice. Coverage might focus on the front-runners. If the winner seems clear early, coverage might shift to who will finish second or whether a minor player will clear some threshold. If none of the usual stories seems interesting, the media may be tempted to invent one.

The institutional definition of campaigns suggests that campaigns are like election dates—either they exist or they do not. But the move toward intensity suggests that campaigns can be graduated from those that barely exist to those that consume voters, parties, and the media. Scholars of Senate elections in particular have incorporated gradations of intensity

(Kahn and Kenney 1999a; Westlye 1983, 1991).[2] In his study of congressional races, Zaller (1989, 1996) pinpoints "information flow" as a key variable. The amount of information flow and the extent to which that flow is "two-sided" (that is, coming from both candidates) shape public opinion. Gradations of intensity can often be pinned to level of office. Presidential campaigns are more intense than many legislative races, which in turn are generally more intense than races for local offices, such as city council. Of course, there can also be variation over time within levels of office—for example, some presidential campaigns are more competitive or intense than others, and any given campaign is more intense in battleground states than in the others (Shaw 1999c). Arguably, when defining a campaign, the crucial thing is that all campaigns are not equal. The three pieces to the intensity puzzle—voters, candidates, and the media—must be studied carefully to see how they relate and how this matters for campaign effects.

Defining Campaign Effects

To gain initial purchase on campaign effects, we begin by reviewing five of the most important book-length treatments of the subject. Then we summarize their findings and those from other relevant literature into a typology of campaign effects.

The prevailing scholarly consensus on campaigns is that they have minimal effects. Minimal effects mean in essence minimal persuasion. Because of the existing information and prejudices that voters possess, campaigns rarely change their minds. Often, this view is said to originate with the early studies of the Columbia School (Berelson, Lazarsfeld, and McPhee 1954; Lazarsfeld, Berelson, and Gaudet 1948). For example, Lazarsfeld and his colleagues found that during the 1940 presidential campaign over half of their sample had decided on a candidate by June and only 8 percent actually switched their intention from one candidate to the other during the campaign.

However, this simple fact in no way encapsulates the findings of these two studies, as is sometimes implied. For example, Lazarsfeld, Berelson, and Gaudet (1948, 87) argue that even early deciders benefited from the reinforcing effect of campaign discourse: "political communication served the important purposes of preserving prior decisions instead of initiating new decisions. It kept the partisans 'in line' by reassuring them in their vote decision; it reduced defection from the ranks." Moreover, these two works emphasize how campaigns can "activate" preferences. A substantial fraction of voters who began the campaign undecided or unsure came to a vote choice consonant with their predispositions, namely, sociological facts such as occupational status and religious preference. For example, working-class and Catholic respondents came to support Roosevelt. Lazarsfeld, Berelson, and Gaudet (1948, 73) write that campaigns identify for the voter "a way of thinking and acting which he is already half-aware of wanting." The net result is the reconstitution of a preexisting party coalition. In their study of the 1948 campaign, Berelson, Lazarsfeld, and McPhee arrived at a similar conclusion.[3] The major trend among their sample of residents from Elmira, New York, was a Truman rally among traditionally Democratic groups such as union members and Catholics. Most interesting, they find that these initially uncertain Democrats came to support Truman as the campaign made certain issues salient, in particular issues that tapped working-class economic concerns. Though few scholars since have picked up on this finding, it is perhaps the prototypical empirical example of priming: the campaign may have converted only a few from Dewey to Truman or vice versa, but it did shape the dimensionality of issue conflict and make certain issues more salient for vote choice.[4] This finding has been largely overlooked and is not consonant with a minimal effects characterization.[5]

Book-length treatments of campaign effects were virtually unknown for decades after the Columbia School's initial forays.[6] This derived both from the emerging minimal effects view of both *Voting* (Berelson, Lazarsfeld, and McPhee 1954) and *The People's Choice* (Lazarsfeld, Berelson, and Gaudet 1948) and from political scientists' reliance on National Election Studies (NES) data and analyses in the tradition of Campbell et al. (1960), who tended to emphasize long-standing and fairly immutable factors such as party identification.[7] The NES constitute, to be sure, one of the most valuable collections of public opinion data on politics and elections. However, typically the NES entail only a pre- and postelection cross-sectional survey—an instrument that will not capture most campaign dynamics. There was thus no reason to believe that American elections had campaign effects and not much data to study those effects if one believed otherwise.

However, scholars who looked beyond presidential elections soon began to conclude differently.[8] Jacobson's (1983) work on congressional elections demonstrated the powerful effects of candidate spending on outcomes. This spending is essentially an indicator of campaign effort, since so much of it funds such things as television advertising and the daily expenses incurred while pressing the flesh. Moreover, Bartels's (1987, 1988) work on presidential primaries demonstrated that, in an arena where predispositions like party identification are useless, campaigns have substantial effects. In particular, campaign activity and its attendant media coverage confer viability on candidates. Voters respond accordingly: the more likely it seems that a candidate will win, the more voters gravitate to that candidate.

Most recently, scholars have discovered campaign effects even at the rarified presidential or executive level of government. Johnston et al.'s (1992) study of the 1988 Canadian campaign relied on a unique survey instrument, the rolling cross-section (discussed in more detail later), to explain how campaigns shape public opinion and vote choice. Their findings in many ways build on and elaborate those of the Columbia School. Johnston and his colleagues describe how candidates confront a menu of possible issues, from which they choose some and not others to emphasize. Most important, these strategic choices had direct consequences for voters. In this particular election, the Liberal leader John Turner decided he would stake his candidacy on opposition to the Free Trade Agreement (or FTA, the precursor to NAFTA). His major opponent, the Conservative Brian Mulroney, followed suit with the opposite argument. Because of the leaders' efforts, the FTA came to the fore while another issue, the Meech Lake Accord (which addressed the constitutional place of Quebec), receded. As the campaign progressed, the FTA became the voters' most important issue; voters grew more polarized on this issue (following the hardening positions of their respective parties); arguments intended to change voters' minds on this issue became less effective; and voters' positions on this issue became more important predictors of their vote preference.

The second important finding of this study was a renewed respect for campaign events. In particular, Johnston et al. (1992) track the impact of a seminal debate about midway through the campaign. This debate had a hand in most of the trends cited previously: it helped make the FTA the most salient issue; it polarized partisans on the FTA; it enhanced perceptions of the victor's (John Turner of the Liberal Party) competence; it shifted public opinion more toward the Liberal Party's position on the FTA; and it even boosted the Liberal Party's overall vote share. (Ultimately, however, this did not produce a Turner victory, as the Conservative Brian Mulroney prevailed.) Thus, this campaign had a striking effect on numerous facets of public opinion, an effect traceable in part to a specific campaign event and more generally to elite decision making.

Campaign events play an even greater role in Thomas Holbrook's (1996) book on recent American presidential campaigns. Holbrook situates his work amid the literature on elections forecasting, whose major finding is that election outcomes can be predicted quite well by a few fundamental variables measured well before the outset of the campaign (e.g., Bartels and Zaller 2001; Campbell and Garand 2000; Fair 1978; Hibbs 2000; Lewis-Beck 1992; Rosenstone 1983).[9] These variables typically include some measure of economic health, the popularity of the incumbent administration, and sometimes the breakdown of vote preference just after the primary season. The predictability of election outcomes is often taken to imply little role for campaigns. Holbrook incorporates these variables by arguing that they establish an equilibrium outcome but that public opinion may deviate from this equilibrium during the campaign due to events such as party conventions and debates. By and large, Holbrook finds that events do shift opinion. Presumably these shifts are manifestations of persuasion—or at least of voters' shifting from indecision to preference—and constitute on their face a refutation of the minimal effects model. However, these effects are dwarfed by the overall impact of national and economic conditions, and thus campaigns can only be influential when these conditions do not overwhelmingly favor one side.[10] The summation of Holbrook's argument might be this: campaigns matter but in limited ways.

Campbell (2000) arrives at much the same conclusion in his study of American presidential campaigns. He argues that presidential campaigns by and large have predictable effects because of several systematic conditions: the election-year economy strongly influences outcomes; incumbents have numerous electoral advantages; and the front-runner's margin of victory tends to narrow as the campaign progresses. However, Campbell emphasizes how campaigns bring about these effects. In other words, we could not predict elections so well if the campaign did not somehow translate objective conditions into an actual outcome.[11] Moreover, Campbell finds a potential for unpredictable and unsystematic campaign effects. Examining the deviation between the actual outcome and the outcome predicted by a forecasting model, he finds that, of the thirty-three presidential elections since 1868, an estimated four to six were likely decided by unsystematic factors. His conclusion echoes Holbrook's: "Perhaps the best characterization of campaign effects is that they are neither large nor minimal in an absolute sense, but sometimes large enough to be politically important" (188).[12]

How do these works inform a typology of campaign effects? A first and necessary component is undoubtedly *persuasion*. Regardless of how uncommon it may be, campaigns do change some voters' minds.[13] Moreover, there is reason to believe the existing minimal effects consensus is based somewhat shakily on only one type of elections, American presidential elections. Studies in other countries or at other levels of office within the United States have yielded different conclusions. Indeed, in his study of why people vote for the opposition party's candidate in congressional races, Zaller (1996, 36) finds that "very large campaign effects—effects of mass communication—do occur."[14] Furthermore, even if the ultimate vote choice does not change, campaigns can certainly shift other sorts of attitudes, such as voters' issue positions, where they locate parties and candidates on these issues, and how they evaluate candidates' characteristics and traits—all of which will still be related to the probability that a voter will support a given candidate. That said, we do not want to discount the role of long-standing predispositions and long-term structural forces. One's social background and party identification, as well as broader economic and political conditions, clearly influence individual vote choices and aggregate election outcomes. But a question lingers, one that we return to subsequently: do these predispositions and conditions always have the same effect? If not, does a campaign's ability to persuade voters change accordingly?

A second kind of campaign effect, one much less noticeable in the extant literature, is *priming*. As observed in the 1948 American presidential election and in the 1988 Canadian election, campaigns can shape public opinion by making certain issues or considerations salient to voters. This can occur with or without a concomitant change in vote choice. Both of these examples found that a particular candidate, Harry Truman in 1948 and John Turner in Canada, tended to benefit (though only temporarily in Turner's case) from attention to these issues. However, priming can also occur even as many people's vote preferences remain constant; as voters learn about the candidates and focus on certain considerations, the underlying structure of these preferences may change. Though the ability of events and the news media to prime is well known (Iyengar and Kinder 1987; Krosnick and Kinder 1990; Krosnick and Brannon 1993), this phenomenon is only now being rigorously investigated in the campaign effects literature (e.g., Carsey 2000; Johnston et al. 1992; Kahn and Kenney 1999a; Mendelberg 2001; Mendelsohn 1996; Simon 2002; Valentino, Hutchings, and White 2002).[15] This phenomenon may be all the more important if priming is indeed the mechanism by which voters are "enlightened" and, as Holbrook (1996), Campbell (2000), and Gelman and King (1993) suggest, fundamental conditions such as the state of the economy come to influence election outcomes so strongly.[16] If this is true, then particular attention should be paid to "valence" issues, such as the state of the economy, where there is general consensus on the end (prosperity in this case) but dissensus on who can get us there. To look at valence issues in this way is somewhat unorthodox, in that some scholars (Campbell 2000; Popkin 1991) argue that economic voting is "easy" because it involves easily available information about one's personal financial circumstance.[17] However, one cannot assume that such "easy" cues are automatic: one factor in Al Gore's loss in 2000 was his failure to "prime" voters' quite positive assessments of the national economy (Johnston, Hagen, and Jamieson 2004). This may explain why in 2000 so many forecasting models, which hinge on "fundamentals" like the economy, overestimated Gore's vote share. In this volume, Ansolabehere ("The Paradox of Minimal Effects") describes how economic voting might be swayed by public information provided by the campaign, and Bartels ("Priming and Persuasion in Presidential Campaigns") provides evidence that campaigns in fact prime economic considerations.[18]

We must also consider whether "position" issues, where there is actual disagreement over the end, may be even more susceptible to priming in that they tend to distinguish the two candidates more clearly and thus could be expected to polarize voters. A key consideration here is the dimensionality of issue conflict in a given political system. Where do the cleavages lie? Which are interparty and which are intraparty? For example, in the United States we commonly distinguish economic and social issues, since it is possible to be, for example, a pro-choice fiscal conservative. In this volume Highton ("Alternative Tests for the Effects of Campaigns and Candidates on Voting Behavior") demonstrates voter response to candidate position taking on abortion. Alvarez and Shankster ("Studying Statewide Political Campaigns") trace how campaign advertising in two 1994 California races directly shaped the issues voters considered in choosing a candidate.[19]

Priming is not only a process with consequences for voters. It also can affect the balance of partisan forces and, ultimately, the election as a whole. As voters come to weight certain considerations more heavily, the probability of their choosing the candidate who benefits from those considerations will increase. For example, a pro-choice voter will gravitate increasingly toward the pro-choice candidate as abortion becomes a salient election-year issue. Candidates thus have an incentive to structure the election's agenda as much as possible.[20] Priming will solidify the support of their partisans and potentially lure swing voters into their camp as well. Finally, priming has implications for how we interpret elections: its impact on the election's agenda will speak strongly to the perennial question, "What was this election about?"

Persuasion and priming are perhaps most prominent in this typology of campaign effects, but they are by no means exhaustive. In particular, we want to consider two others, one quite straightforward and the other much more subtle. First, campaigns obviously affect voters by *informing* and *mobilizing* them. Voters begin the campaign in a state of comparative ignorance. From a normative perspective, we hope that the campaign will capture their attention and inspire them to learn about and cogitate on the choice before them. Of course, the extent of that cogitation is always an open question. Nevertheless, a number of studies have shown that campaigns educate voters about the candidates and in particular about their stands on certain issues (Alvarez 1998; Conover and Feldman 1989; Dalager 1996; Franklin 1991; Holbrook 1999; Marcus 1982; see Jacobson and Fournier essays, this volume).[21]

As noted, informing is bound up with a host of other related effects—growing interest, attention to campaign news, and so forth—but perhaps the most important of these effects is the propensity to vote. That is, campaigns may help to mobilize voters (Patterson and Caldeira 1983; Caldeira, Patterson, and Markko 1985; Rosenstone and Hansen 1993; Gerber and Green 2000a, 2000b). Chief among these means is direct contact with voters, such as a phone call or a knock at the door. Acknowledging mobilization as a campaign effect also allows us to consider the opposite case, when campaigns could conceivably *demobilize* voters. The logic here, documented most thoroughly by Ansolabehere et al. (1994) and Ansolabehere and Iyengar (1995), is that "negative" campaigning alienates voters so much that they grow to dislike both candidates and therefore stay home on Election Day. Though, empirically speaking, the jury is still out on this thesis, it nonetheless draws our attention to the potentially deleterious effects of campaigns and, in particular, contemporary modes of campaign activity such as the "attack ad."[22] While these studies all deal with campaigns' secular effects on turnout, it is equally likely that mobilization could have partisan consequences as well. While it is a truism that candidates want to mobilize their followers and to encourage their opposition to stay home, political science has as yet failed to investigate this phenomenon.

Second, campaigns can alter voters' *strategic considerations*. We can imagine two kinds of strategic issues that a campaign may influence. One such issue is electoral viability, which seems especially relevant under the plurality formula but can also be relevant for threshold requirements under proportional representation (PR). The other is a coalitional signal, which seems most pertinent under PR.

Campaigns provide voters an opportunity to update their expectations of each candidate's or party's chances of success. In the American context, this notion is particularly relevant in primary elections. When there is an absence of partisan cues and a bewildering array of candidates, many of them strangers, viability becomes paramount. As discussed previously, voters prefer candidates who seem like they can win (Bartels 1987, 1988)—a tendency no doubt supported by media eager to cover the horse race among these candidates (Patterson 1980, 1994; Brady and Johnston 1987). In multiparty systems, party viability is also an important consideration for voters (see the Blais, Gidengil, and Nevitte and the Jenkins essays, this volume).

Under certain kinds of PR, a party's probability of meeting threshold requirements may be a factor in choice. In New Zealand, for instance, the main way for a party to win seats in the house is to win at least 5 percent of the national popular vote. In 1996, as it happened, the smaller parties of the Right were in particular danger of failing to achieve this level of support. There might thus have been an incentive for Rightist voters to shift from the largest conservative party to one or the other of two smaller ones. Campaign-period polls could factor into these considerations (see the Johnston and Vowles essay, this volume).

A campaign is also an obvious site for signaling by potential coalition partners. A party's willingness to take on certain partners may enhance or detract from its support. A party may alienate support by seeming too willing to embrace an unacceptable partner. Another possibility is this: if you wish to defect from your "usual" party to a "new" party it might help that this new party is willing to enter into a coalition with the one you traditionally support. None of this absolutely must happen in the campaign, but the campaign may be the most effective time to send the signal.

What Is the Scope for Manipulation?

When investigating campaign effects, we must avoid reductionist research questions such as "Do campaigns matter?" The research discussed previously demonstrates that a better question is this: When and how do campaigns matter? Campaign effects are themselves quite variable, and therefore we must identify which conditions narrow or broaden the scope for manipulation. One such factor is the *number of parties and candidates*. As noted already, primary election outcomes in the United States are often surprising and seem highly contingent on campaign activity. Similarly, an election featuring numerous minor and major parties can have both qualitatively and quantitatively different campaign effects than one with only two contenders for the throne. A related factor is the *dimensionality of issue conflict*. This concerns not only long-standing fissures in the party system but also new ones that might emerge during a campaign, perhaps thanks to the entrepreneurial efforts of a candidate. We need to also consider the *competitiveness* of the race at hand. A runaway victory usually requires no great campaign genius. But an equally matched race, with equal resources on and "messages flows" from both sides, could make campaign events and activity more meaningful. Fundamental *economic and political conditions* will themselves affect the degree of competitiveness and may dictate messages and strategies.

Besides these broader contextual considerations, there are those that pertain to candidates and voters themselves. For one, a *candidate's record* often comes into play. Candidates cannot create themselves de novo and thus may find that past words and deeds constrain their impact on voters. Parties face a comparable constraint in *issue ownership*: they often cannot credibly claim that they will act on an issue they had previously ignored.[23] The *novelty of issues* is similarly limiting. Voters tend to have firmer opinions on long-standing issues, opinions that remain steady amid campaign winds. However, new issues, whether raised by a candidate or arising from external events, may prove more amenable to campaign manipulation. Finally, we must account for heterogeneity among voters in terms of their attention and exposure to campaign activity. Perhaps the key variable here is *political awareness*. Voters will be most susceptible to persuasion in particular, at medium levels of awareness, as the well aware are too set in their ways and the least aware are not paying attention.[24] (See the Gidengil and Everitt essay in this volume for intriguing evidence that a voter's *gender* conditions how he or she responds to news coverage of candidates.)

A nuanced and promising scholarly agenda starts with the premise that there is more to campaigns than persuasion—priming, informing, mobilizing—and thus perhaps the minimal effects hypothesis misleads. This agenda should treat campaign effects not as dichotomies that do or do not exist but as variables or continua that depend on history, current circumstance, and the voters themselves.

Studying Campaign Effects

The hypothesis we want to explore is that political campaigns matter. We want to know the following: Do campaigns persuade voters, and, if so, which voters? Do campaigns prime certain issues or considerations? If so, which ones and for whom? Do campaigns stimulate voter interest and ultimately voter turnout? Do campaigns shape strategic considerations as well? The next logical question is, How do we investigate these questions? What research designs are useful for studying campaign effects? Next we identify the major ways that scholars have explored campaign effects and discuss each design's strengths and weaknesses.

Laboratory Experiments

The advantages of experiments are well known. Establishing causality is relatively unambiguous as long as the design possesses internal validity. Experiments eliminate competing causal explanations via random assignment and thereby isolate the causal impact of some treatment. In the case of campaign effects, experiments enable the researcher to create a very specific stimulus, which might be a television ad or printed material related to a candidate or race, and then to examine its impact (examples include Lodge, Steenbergen, and Brau 1995; Ansolabehere and Iyengar 1994, 1995; and Mendelberg 1997).

On the other hand, it may be hard to establish a laboratory context that is credible for subjects. Although Ansolabehere and Iyengar (1995) created such a context—in that subjects viewed campaign media in a casual setting that resembled the average living room—we wonder how much further their approach can be pushed (see Ansolabehere's other essay in this volume, "Campaigns as Experiments," for more discussion of the challenges facing experimental research). Even for credible setups, there remains the problem of external validity. Does "looking real" mean "being real"? At most the laboratory can establish potential, rather than actual, impact. Some treatments may never find campaign analogues. Moreover, in the laboratory, exposure is controlled and every subject receives the stimulus. In the field, exposure is a variable and those most persuadable may be least exposed.

Field Experiments

Until recently, field experiments in political science were quite rare, and experiments specifically about campaigns were more so. One kind of field experiment embeds the treatment within a survey questionnaire. Respondents then randomly receive question wording variations and so forth. Examples of this technique include the 1988 and 1992–93 Canadian Election Studies and the 1994 Missouri study by Paul Sniderman and his colleagues (see the Elms and Sniderman essay, this volume). A second kind of field experiment is the one employed by Gerber and Green (2000a, 2000b) in New Haven, Connecticut. In this case, New Haven voters were randomly assigned to receive various get-out-the-vote materials. The field experiment retains the advantages of random assignment and compensates for some of the disadvantages of the laboratory because it does not require an artificial setting. It can be even more effective if conducted during an actual campaign.

On the other hand, field experiments cannot create all manner of campaign stimuli. The New Haven study, for example, employed treatments involving leaflets, phone calls, and face-to-face contact. However, it may be more difficult to design a true field experiment that could capture a more complex stimulus, such as an advertising campaign. Most important, the field experiment shares the laboratory's limitation: it identifies a potential rather than an actual effect.[25]

Panels

The panel design seems the natural starting point for analyzing campaign-induced change in that it generates observations potentially straddling a "treatment." Only a panel permits characterization of individual trajectories. Change across waves cannot possibly derive from sampling error (although it can be a regression artifact). Given enough waves, the panel also allows the researcher to separate instability from unreliability; that is, it addresses the errors-in-variables problem directly. Bartels (1993) shows convincingly that measurement error in indicators such as media exposure attenuates their impact on political preferences and thus understates the potential effect of the campaign. Furthermore, if we know in advance the events and the periods we want to cover, for example, a debate and a specific period after the debate, the panel is the most effective way of identifying event-induced change. (See the Bartels essay, this volume, for further discussion of these and other advantages of panels. Extant empirical studies include, inter alia, Lazarsfeld, Berelson, and Gaudet 1948; Berelson, Lazarsfeld, and McPhee 1954; Patterson 1980; Markus 1982; Bartels 1993; Finkel 1993; Norris et al. 1999; Hillygus and Jackman 2003.)

With these great advantages come serious disadvantages. One is an instrument effect: an interview may affect subsequent responses so much that observed changes may result from nothing but previous interviews. Mortality in the panel raises questions about the representativeness of later waves, particularly in terms of their susceptibility to influence and change. Diligent pursuit of respondents across later waves can be expensive.

The biggest issue, however, may be the crudeness of the panel's "granularity." The greater the gap between waves, the harder it is to identify campaign effects as competing explanations accumulate. Even when a single event could explain shifts, as with a debate, identifying its impact necessitates conditioning on cross-sectional differences, for example, in exposure. Infrequent waves will reduce the residual effects of exposure. Consider the example of a debate that succeeds in changing people's minds. Right after the debate, differences between those who did and did not see the debate tend to be large. But as time passes, this difference will shrink as the broadly held interpretation of the debate permeates the population. If we are fortunate enough to be in the field right after the debate, we can at least capture the direct impact but will still miss the indirect effect, barring yet another wave. If the second wave is late, we will miss everything. The waves should register the net shift, of course, but how will it be pinned to the debate?

The Rolling Cross-Section

The rolling cross-section (RCS) addresses these concerns. Because it typically is composed of daily samples, its granularity is very fine. The design does not precommit researchers to timing, to events, or to a theory of dynamic form. For certain plausible models, for example, diffusion models with curvilinear trajectories, it may be the only design that can capture the hypothesized effect. And the design is cheap. It costs little more than an ordinary cross-section. Garnering adequate daily samples does require some micromanagement, and the response rate must be allowed to drop off at the very end, but these problems pose no fundamental difficulties. The RCS has been implemented in several Canadian Election Studies (see Johnston et al. 1992, inter alia) and most recently in the Annenberg National Election Studies of 2000 and 2004 (Johnston, Hagen, and Jamieson 2004).

In principle, the RCS can be married to a panel design, where the first wave precedes the campaign and the RCS component is, in effect, a "metered" panel. So long as the net partisan direction of impact from the campaign does not change mid-period, it suffices to interview each respondent only once during the campaign. Stretches of the campaign can be treated as subpanels. To capture the campaign's cumulative impact, however, it would be necessary to go into the field a third time, after Election Day. Arguably, making the RCS the first wave and then reinterviewing after the event can realize much of the advantage of marrying the RCS to a panel.[26] At the same time, the response captured during the campaign proper is uncontaminated by instrument effects.

A major disadvantage of the RCS is that the daily sample is small. Just how small is a function of the total target sample and the campaign's length in days. Describing aggregate trends over time requires smoothing to separate real change from sampling noise (see the Brady and Johnston essay in this volume for a discussion of smoothing). Second, the RCS simply cannot solve the errors-in-variables problem, unless it is joined to at least two more waves (but this is also true of a conventional cross-section). Finally, to interpret dynamic trends persuasively, contextual information about media coverage and events is necessary. This enables one to link, say, a sudden downturn in a candidate's fortune to breaking news about a scandal, a poor debate performance, and so forth. Collecting and analyzing contextual data is difficult in two senses. First, it is time-consuming, especially when these data must be coded in some fashion to generate interpretable quantities. Second, there is no strong theory to guide coding and to suggest the shape and duration of effects that may result from certain kinds of campaign events (see Brady and Johnston 1987 for one coding scheme and Shaw 1999a for a discussion of event effects). Of course, it is fundamentally a strength of the RCS that it can be so fruitfully married to contextual data of this kind.

Multiple Races

The 1978 NES was the prototype of this design, with random samples from a large number of congressional districts. The NES Senate Election Studies have continued in this same tradition. This is, in fact, the oldest form of systematic investigation of campaign effects, going back to Jacobson's (1983) work on congressional elections. The crucial aspect of this design is that it samples districts, not respondents (Stoker and Bowers 2002). This ensures greater variation across settings, in candidates, races, party effort, media attention, and voter characteristics. Where the dependent variable is measured from a survey, the design allows employment of the whole sample (but see the next paragraph). It is rich in possibilities for "naturalistic" controls—for example, in the case of the U.S. Senate, one can examine the same state in years with and without an election.[27] However, in the case of Senate elections, the sample must also be designed to capture variation in races across states (Westlye 1983). This is the chief advantage of the NES Senate Election Studies.

There is, of course, the danger that any independent variable of interest may be correlated with idiosyncratic or fixed effects across the races so that it mistakenly picks up these fixed effects. The design may not address selection problems, and certain measurable variables may not really be predetermined. For example, do debates build interest or are they more likely to be held in states where interest is already high? The design is as reliant as others on exogenous information, such as candidate spending.[28] Finally, dynamic effects will be missed by this purely cross-sectional design.

Same Cross-Section, Different Elections

This design gains leverage from the traditional cross-sectional design by analyzing the same respondents as they vote in different races (see the Alvarez and Shankster and the Elms and Sniderman essays, this volume). In a way, this design is like a panel on the cheap, in that it permits comparison of repeated behavior by the same respondents. The behavior is virtually simultaneous, of course, but this is actually a strength, for the respondent must be essentially the same person each time, however divergent the behavior. In principle, then, just estimating the same equation on the same respondents for different races can identify certain campaign effects. When variation across coefficients is married to exogenous data, for example, the content of advertising, the story can be quite powerful. The design does leave causal questions open. For example, what if people—candidates, voters, or both—*always* behave in characteristically different ways in different arenas? And in the end, the design is still not quite a panel, and so true dynamics cannot be captured.

These research designs draw attention to two key dimensions: time and space. Panel studies and RCSs tell dynamic stories, stories of how people's ideas and intentions change in the weeks and months preceding an election. When married with contextual data like events and advertising, one can tell even more nuanced stories about how the money and time that candidates and parties spend actually shape people's ideas and intentions. But even if data are not ordered over time, spatial variation can provide explanatory leverage. Examining multiple elections allows one to compare lopsided races where a heavily favored incumbent ran roughshod over some poor challenger with hard-fought races where two equally matched candidates slugged it out or to compare races where the campaign turned on the performance of the incumbent with races where it turned on a hot-button issue. The evolution of American presidential elections in particular may make the conjoint study of time and space easier: the increased concentration of campaign activity in battleground states is making the country into a giant natural experiment (see Johnston, Hagen, and Jamieson 2004). So far, however, the potential of expanding both time and space in campaign studies has only barely been explored.

Campaigns and Democratic Theory

That campaigns do influence citizens is fundamentally good news. Campaigns are the moments in political life when representatives and the represented interact most energetically. It would thus disappoint if voters largely tuned out and voted only in rote and ritualistic partisan ways. The recent research discussed herein suggests that, when candidates press the flesh and go on the air, voters are listening and learning. Campaigns can affect what voters know, whether they will vote, whom they will vote for, and why they will vote for that person. Ultimately, campaigns can affect who wins the election. Thus, the strategic decisions of candidates are not merely empty exercises in collective war-room intellect. Both the inputs and outputs of campaign processes can be consequential.

But this raises another, more disconcerting possibility. What if campaigns function not so much to enlighten voters as to manipulate them? Manipulation entails two things: a candidate must make an unseemly statement, and voters must believe it. The meaning of *unseemly* could be debated endlessly, but ultimately such debate is rendered at least somewhat moot if the second condition fails to hold true. We believe that two conditions militate against manipulation. First and foremost, voters do not believe everything they are told. New information is filtered first through existing partisan predispositions. Second, new information, when it speaks strongly for or against one party or candidate, will typically not go unchallenged. This is to say, campaign discourse is contested. Claims by one party are contradicted by another. Furthermore, the media scrutinizes and evaluates the claims of all parties. The very nature of campaigns prevents any one side from single-handedly manipulating the electorate. However, this works best when the campaign is competitive, when all parties and candidates have the resources to make themselves heard. Arguably, then, the best way to limit campaign manipulation is to have more of a campaign.

NOTES

1. Intensity is related to, but distinct from, competitiveness. A competitive election is one in which the outcome is in question. An intense campaign is one contested doggedly by the candidates or parties, regardless of whether any or all of them has a real chance of winning. Our guess is that all competitive elections have intense campaigns but that not all intense campaigns correspond to a competitive election.

2. Westlye (1983) distinguishes between "hard-fought" and "low-key" races, and he uses preelection descriptions of Senate contests in *Congressional Quarterly Weekly Report*'s biennial special election issue. Westlye notes, "The CQ descriptions usually focus on such matters as media coverage of the candidates, levels of public interest in the campaign, and candidate organization and campaigning skills" (259). Kahn and Kenney (1999a) argue for a single dimension of campaign intensity, operationalized as an index combining candidate activities, media reports, and competition. For our part, we believe that concrete indicators are generally preferable to the judgments of observers—especially because they can often be measured as continuous variables and not as dichotomies—and that intensity may in fact be multidimensional.

3. Finkel (1993) also arrives at this conclusion in his examination of panel data from the 1980 presidential election.

4. Berelson, Lazarsfeld, and McPhee (1954, 183) elaborate how campaigns shape issue dimensions: "the political process which finds its climax in the campaign is a system by which disagreements are reduced, simplified, and generalized

into one big residual difference of opinion. It is a system for *organizing* disagreements."

5. To our knowledge, only Popkin (1991, 108–10) and Johnston (1992, 313) have noted explicitly that the Columbia School's results constitute priming. Gelman and King (1993, 433–34) present a general case for this finding when they describe the process of "enlightenment": "The function of the campaign, then, is to inform voters about the fundamental variables and their appropriate weights."

6. A notable exception is Patterson (1980), who keeps the Columbia tradition alive by analyzing a panel survey conducted in two communities—Erie, Pennsylvania, and Los Angeles—during the 1976 presidential campaign. He does not, however, emphasize the same themes, focusing more on voters' exposure and reaction to media coverage than on "campaign effects" per se.

7. Some have argued, however, that even party identification, that "unmoved mover," can shift during a campaign (Allsop and Weisberg 1988; but see Johnston 1992).

8. To the credit of the NES, this work was facilitated in part by some innovative NES surveys, notably the 1978 Congressional Election Study and the 1984 Rolling Cross-Section Study.

9. Though he is not in the business of election forecasting per se, Bartels (1998) examines historical dynamics in presidential elections and concludes that there is a great deal more electoral continuity than volatility. Like predictability, continuity seems to imply a lesser role for campaigns.

10. Shaw (1999a) elaborates Holbrook's work by estimating the duration of event effects but reaches similar conclusions about the magnitude of these effects. Likewise, Shaw (1999b) examines two other forms of campaign activity, campaign appearances and television advertising, and finds that each tended to move voter support. However, he again reaches a qualified conclusion: "Too much should not be made of the campaign effects discovered here—no elections would have been reversed without implausible changes in the distribution of campaigning in several key states" (357).

11. Holbrook (1996, 157) acknowledges this possibility—"One of the important roles of the campaign is to help move public opinion toward the expected outcome"—but does not make it an explicit part of his theory. As yet, political scientists do not necessarily understand how this equilibrating process arises.

12. Wlezien and Erikson (2002) make a strong claim that campaigns really do move the vote. Their approach resembles Holbrook's in relying on compilations of polls, but they apply more sophisticated dynamic modeling to argue that the electorate's response to campaigns resembles a random walk: a campaign's impact at one point in time endures for some time, and further displacement requires another impulse. This seems to be the aggregate analogue to the "on-line processing" model of Lodge, McGraw, and Stroh (1989), in that campaign information is incorporated (more or less permanently) into the running tally constituted by the tracking poll. For all that, Wlezien and Erikson's findings can still be squared with the Holbrook-Campbell imagery of a campaign whose potential impact is constrained by foreordained external factors.

13. Indeed, given that candidates and their campaign operatives generally ignore

the unpersuadables and focus only on so-called swing voters or swing states, it appears that they are aware of their limited power to persuade. Bradshaw (1995, 37) makes this point: "The key to successful strategy is not to try to appeal to everyone on his or her particular flash point but instead to select the types of voters you can most easily persuade based on the contrasts presented by the candidates."

14. Lodge, Steenbergen, and Brau (1995) come to a similar conclusion, though they rely on experimental evidence and champion an entirely different model of information processing.

15. Priming is related to another process, agenda setting. Agenda setting concerns the problems citizens consider most important (see, e.g., Baumgartner and Jones 1993; Erbring and Goldenberg 1980; MacKuen and Coombs 1981; McCombs and Shaw 1972).

16. Holbrook and Campbell cannot really test the hypothesis that campaigns prime fundamental considerations because they rely on aggregate data, while priming is an individual-level phenomenon.

17. However, Hetherington (1996) shows that negative media coverage of the economy shaped economic evaluations in the 1992 presidential race and thereby contributed to George Bush's defeat. This suggests that this simple voting cue is actually malleable.

18. Candidate traits could also be considered a "valence issue," in the sense that everyone agrees that candidates should be honest, intelligent, and so on. Johnston, Hagen, and Jamieson (2004) identify changing perceptions of Gore's honesty as the key dynamic in the 2000 election. Johnston et al. (1992) demonstrate that campaigns can prime candidate traits as well (see also Mendelsohn 1996).

19. We do not address here possible emotional responses to candidates, as documented by Marcus and MacKuen (1993) and Marcus, Neuman, and MacKuen (2000).

20. The strategic benefits of priming, as contrasted to a Downsian convergence on the median voter, are discussed by Riker (1983) as "heresthetics" and by Hammond and Humes (1993) and Carsey (2000).

21. Moreover, contrary to Shepsle (1972) and Page (1976), who argue that it benefits a candidate to be obfuscatory and vague about issues, Alvarez (1998) finds that reducing voters' uncertainty improves candidates' standing.

22. Participants in the ongoing debate include Bartels (1996); Finkel and Geer (1998); Freedman and Goldstein (1999); Ansolabehere, Iyengar, and Simon (1999); Kahn and Kenney (1999b); Wattenberg and Brians (1999); Lau et al. (1999); Jamieson (2000); Lau and Pomper (2002); and Clinton and Lapinski (2004).

23. See Petrocik 1996 for evidence of how consonance among voters' and parties' agendas shapes preferences.

24. This argument is, of course, Zaller's (1992). He builds on the work of McGuire (1968, 1969).

25. There is also the possibility that the actual campaign may render an experimental manipulation ineffective. For instance, for the 1988 Canadian election, Johnston et al. (1992) discuss the effect of giving or withholding Brian Mulroney's name as the agent implicitly responsible for negotiating the FTA. This effect, which

became evident only through experimental manipulation within a survey questionnaire, did not persist after the key debate primed the issue once and for all.

26. Johnston and Brady (2002) show the precise conditions under which a post-election reinterview can capture most of the relevant, preelection cross-sectional variation.

27. Franklin (1991) draws upon another natural experiment, comparing perceptions of senators up for election to those of senators not up for election.

28. A noteworthy development in campaign advertising data deserves mention here. Advances in satellite tracking now produce precise information about when and where specific television advertisements appear. For example, these data could tell you that, during the 2000 election, Al Gore aired an advertisement that discussed his education policy on October 24 at 4:47 p.m. on the ABC affiliate in Fresno, California, during an episode of *Oprah*. Freedman and Goldstein (1999) and Goldstein and Freedman (2000) were the first to exploit these data. The Wisconsin Television Advertising Project continues to collect, compile, and release these data.

REFERENCES

Allsop, Dee, and Herbert F. Weisberg. 1988. "Measuring Change in Party Identification in an Election Campaign." *American Journal of Political Science* 32:996–1017.

Alvarez, R. Michael. 1998. *Information and Elections*. Rev. ed. Ann Arbor: University of Michigan Press.

Ansolabehere, Stephen, and Shanto Iyengar. 1994. "Riding the Wave and Claiming Ownership over Issues: The Joint Effects of Advertising and News Coverage in Campaigns." *Public Opinion Quarterly* 58:335–57.

———. 1995. *Going Negative: How Political Advertisements Shrink and Polarize the Electorate*. New York: Free Press.

Ansolabehere, Stephen D., Shanto Iyengar, and Adam Simon. 1999. "Replicating Experiments Using Aggregate and Survey Data: The Case of Negative Advertising and Turnout." *American Political Science Review* 93:901–10.

Ansolabehere, Stephen, Shanto Iyengar, Adam Simon, and Nicholas Valentino. 1994. "Does Attack Advertising Demobilize the Electorate?" *American Political Science Review* 88:829–38.

Bartels, Larry M. 1987. "Candidate Choice and the Dynamics of the Presidential Nomination Process." *American Journal of Political Science* 31:1–30.

———. 1988. *Presidential Primaries and the Dynamics of Public Choice*. Princeton: Princeton University Press.

———. 1993. "Messages Received: The Political Impact of Media Exposure." *American Political Science Review* 87:267–85.

———. 1996. Review of *Going Negative: How Political Advertisements Shrink and Polarize the Electorate*. *Public Opinion Quarterly* 60:456–61.

———. 1998. "Electoral Continuity and Change, 1868–96." *Electoral Studies* 17: 301–26.

Bartels, Larry M., and John Zaller. 2001. "Presidential Vote Models: A Recount." *PS: Political Science and Politics* 34:9–20.

Baumgartner, Frank R., and Bryan D. Jones. 1993. *Agendas and Instability in American Politics*. Chicago: University of Chicago Press.

Berelson, Bernard R., Paul F. Lazarsfeld, and William N. McPhee. 1954. *Voting: A Study of Opinion Formation in a Presidential Campaign.* Chicago: University of Chicago Press.

Bradshaw, Joel. 1995. "Who Will Vote for You and Why: Designing Strategy and Theme." In *Campaigns and Elections American Style,* ed. James A. Thurber and Candice J. Nelson. Boulder: Westview Press.

Brady, Henry E., and Richard Johnston. 1987. "What's the Primary Message: Horse Race or Issue Journalism?" In *Media and Momentum: The New Hampshire Primary and Nomination Politics,* ed. Gary R. Orren and Nelson W. Polsby. Chatham, NJ: Chatham House.

Caldeira, Gregory A., Samuel C. Patterson, and Gregory A. Markko. 1985. "The Mobilization of Voters in Congressional Elections." *Journal of Politics* 47:490–509.

Campbell, Angus, Philip E. Converse, Warren E. Miller, and Donald Stokes. 1960. *The American Voter.* New York: Wiley.

Campbell, James A., and James C. Garand, eds. 2000. *Before the Vote: Forecasting American National Elections.* Thousand Oaks, CA: Sage.

Campbell, James E. 2000. *The American Campaign: U.S. Presidential Campaigns and the National Vote.* College Station: Texas A&M Press.

Carsey, Thomas M. 2000. *Campaign Dynamics: The Race for Governor.* Ann Arbor: University of Michigan Press.

Clinton, Joshua D., and John S. Lapinski. 2004. "Targeted Advertising and Voter Turnout: An Experimental Study of the 2000 Presidential Election." *Journal of Politics* 66 (1): 69–96.

Conover, Pamela Johnston, and Stanley Feldman. 1989. "Candidate Perception in an Ambiguous World: Campaigns, Cues, and Inference Processes." *American Journal of Political Science* 33:912–40.

Dalager, Jon K. 1996. "Voters, Issues, and Elections: Are the Candidates' Messages Getting Through?" *Journal of Politics* 58:486–515.

Erbring, Lutz, and Edie N. Goldenberg. 1980. "Front-Page News and Real-World Cues: A New Look at Agenda-Setting by the Media." *American Journal of Political Science* 24:16–49.

Fair, Ray. 1978. "The Effect of Economic Events on the Vote for President." *Review of Economics and Statistics* 60:159–72.

Finkel, Steven E. 1993. "Reexamining the 'Minimal Effects' Model in Recent Presidential Campaigns." *Journal of Politics* 55:1–31.

Finkel, Steven E., and John Geer. 1998. "A Spot Check: Casting Doubt on the Demobilizing Effect of Attack Advertising." *American Journal of Political Science* 42:573–95.

Franklin, Charles H. 1991. "Eschewing Obfuscation? Campaigns and the Perception of U.S. Senate Incumbents." *American Political Science Review* 85:1193–214.

Freedman, Paul, and Ken Goldstein. 1999. "Measuring Media Exposure and the Effects of Negative Campaign Ads." *American Journal of Political Science* 43:1189–208.

Gelman, Andrew, and Gary King. 1993. "Why Are American Presidential Election Polls So Variable When Votes Are So Predictable?" *British Journal of Political Science* 23:409–51.

Gerber, Alan S., and Donald P. Green. 2000a. "The Effects of Personal Canvassing,

Telephone Calls, and Direct Mail on Voter Turnout: A Field Experiment." *American Political Science Review* 94:653–64.

———. 2000b. "The Effect of a Non-Partisan Get-Out-The-Vote Drive: An Experimental Study of Leafletting." *Journal of Politics* 62:846–57.

Goldstein, Ken, and Paul Freedman. 2000. "New Evidence for New Arguments: Money and Advertising in the 1996 Senate Elections." *Journal of Politics* 62:1087–108.

Hammond, Thomas H., and Brian D. Humes. 1993. "The Spatial Model and Elections." In *Information, Participation, and Choice,* ed. Bernard Grofman. Ann Arbor: University of Michigan Press.

Hetherington, Marc J. 1996. "The Media's Role in Forming Voters' National Economic Evaluations in 1992." *American Journal of Political Science* 40:372–95.

Hibbs, Douglas A., Jr. 2000. "Bread and Peace Voting in U.S. Presidential Elections." *Public Choice* 104:149–80.

Hillygus, D. Sunshine, and Simon Jackman. 2003. "Voter Decision Making in Election 2000: Campaign Effects, Partisan Activation, and the Clinton Legacy." *American Journal of Political Science* 47 (4): 583–96.

Holbrook, Thomas M. 1996. *Do Campaigns Matter?* Thousand Oaks, CA: Sage.

———. 1999. "Political Learning from Presidential Debates." *Political Behavior* 21:67–89.

Iyengar, Shanto, and Donald Kinder. 1987. *News That Matters: Television and American Opinion.* Chicago: University of Chicago Press.

Jacobson, Gary C. 1983. *The Politics of Congressional Elections.* Boston: Little, Brown.

Jamieson, Kathleen Hall. 2000. *Everything You Think You Know about Politics . . . And Why You're Wrong.* New York: Basic Books.

Johnston, Richard. 1992. "Party Identification and Campaign Dynamics." *Political Behavior* 14:311–31.

Johnston, Richard, André Blais, Henry E. Brady, and Jean Crête. 1992. *Letting the People Decide: Dynamics of a Canadian Election.* Montreal: McGill-Queens University Press.

Johnston, Richard, and Henry Brady. 2002. "The Rolling Cross-Section Design." *Electoral Studies,* 21:283–95.

Johnston, Richard, Michael G. Hagen, and Kathleen Hall Jamieson. 2004. *The 2000 Presidential Election and the Foundations of Party Politics.* Cambridge: Cambridge University Press.

Kahn, Kim Fridkin, and Patrick J. Kenney. 1999a. *The Spectacle of U.S. Senate Campaigns.* Princeton: Princeton University Press

———. 1999b. "Do Negative Campaigns Mobilize or Suppress Turnout? Clarifying the Relationship between Negativity and Participation." *American Political Science Review* 93:877–90.

Krosnick, Jon A., and Laura R. Brannon. 1993. "The Impact of the Gulf War on the Ingredients of Presidential Evaluations: Multidimensional Effects of Political Involvement." *American Political Science Review* 87:963–75.

Krosnick, Jon A., and Donald R. Kinder. 1990. "Altering the Foundations of Support for the President through Priming." *American Political Science Review* 84:497–512.

Lau, Richard R., and Gerald M. Pomper. 2002. "Effectiveness of Negative Campaigning in U.S. Senate Elections." *American Journal of Political Science* 46:47–66.

Lau, Richard R., Lee Sigelman, Caroline Heldman, and Paul Babbitt. 1999. "The Effectiveness of Negative Political Advertising: A Meta-Analysis." *American Political Science Review* 93:851–75.

Lazarsfeld, Paul F., Bernard Berelson, and Hazel Gaudet. 1948. *The People's Choice: How the Voter Makes Up His Mind in a Presidential Campaign*. New York: Columbia University Press.

Lewis-Beck, Michael. 1992. *Forecasting Elections*. Washington, DC: Congressional Quarterly Press.

Lodge, Milton, Kathleen M. McGraw, and Patrick Stroh. 1989. "An Impression-Driven Model of Candidate Evaluation." *American Political Science Review* 83:399–419.

Lodge, Milton, Marco R. Steenbergen, and Shawn Brau. 1995. "The Responsive Voter: Campaign Information and the Dynamics of Candidate Evaluation." *American Political Science Review* 89:309–26.

MacKuen, Michael B., and Steven L. Coombs. 1981. *More than News: Media Power in Public Affairs*. Beverly Hills: Sage.

Marcus, George E., and Michael B. MacKuen. 1993. "Anxiety, Enthusiasm, and the Vote: The Emotional Underpinnings of Learning and Involvement during Presidential Campaigns." *American Political Science Review* 87:672–85.

Marcus, George E., W. Russell Neuman, and Michael B. MacKuen. 2000. *Affective Intelligence and Political Judgment*. Chicago: University of Chicago Press.

Markus, Gregory B. 1982. "Political Attitudes during an Election Year: A Report on the 1980 NES Panel Study." *American Political Science Review* 76:538–60.

McCombs, Maxwell E., and Donald L. Shaw. 1972. "The Agenda-Setting Function of the Mass Media." *Public Opinion Quarterly* 36:176–87.

McGuire, William J. 1968. "Personality and Susceptibility to Social Influence." In *Handbook of Personality Theory and Research*, ed. E. F. Borgatta and W. W. Lambert. Chicago: Rand-McNally.

———. 1969. "The Nature of Attitudes and Attitude Change." In *Handbook of Social Psychology*, ed. G. Lindzey and E. Aronson, 2d ed. Reading, MA: Addison-Wesley.

Mendelberg, Tali. 1997. "Executing Hortons: Racial Crime in the 1988 Presidential Campaign." *Public Opinion Quarterly* 61:134–57.

———. 2001. *The Race Card: Campaign Strategy, Implicit Messages, and the Norm of Equality*. Princeton: Princeton University Press.

Mendelsohn, Matthew. 1996. "The Media and Interpersonal Communications: The Priming of Issues, Leaders, and Party Identification." *Journal of Politics* 58 (1): 112–25.

Norris, Pippa, John Curtice, David Sanders, Margaret Scammell, and Holli A. Semetko. 1999. *On Message: Communicating the Campaign*. London: Sage.

Page, Benjamin I. 1976. "The Theory of Political Ambiguity." *American Political Science Review* 70:742–52.

———. 1978. *Choice and Echoes in Presidential Elections*. Chicago: University of Chicago Press.

Patterson, Samuel C., and Gregory A. Caldeira. 1983. "Getting out the Vote: Participation in Gubernatorial Elections." *American Political Science Review* 77:675–89.

Patterson, Thomas E. 1980. *The Mass Media Election: How Americans Choose Their President*. New York: Praeger.

———. 1994. *Out of Order*. New York: Vintage.
Petrocik, John R. 1996. "Issue Ownership in Presidential Elections, with a 1980 Case Study." *American Journal of Political Science* 40:825–50.
Popkin, Samuel L. 1991. *The Reasoning Voter: Communication and Persuasion in Presidential Campaigns*. Chicago: University of Chicago Press.
Riker, William. 1983. "Political Theory: The Art of Heresthetics." In *Political Science: The State of the Discipline*, ed. Ada Finifter. Washington, DC: American Political Science Association.
Rosenstone, Steven. 1983. *Forecasting Presidential Elections*. New Haven: Yale University Press.
Rosenstone, Steven, and John Mark Hansen. 1993. *Mobilization, Participation, and Democracy*. New York: MacMillan.
Shaw, Daron R. 1999a. "A Study of Presidential Campaign Event Effects from 1952 to 1992." *Journal of Politics* 61:387–422.
———. 1999b. "The Effect of TV Ads and Candidate Appearances on Statewide Presidential Votes, 1988–96." *American Political Science Review* 93:345–61.
———. 1999c. "The Methods behind the Madness: Presidential Electoral College Strategies, 1988–1996." *Journal of Politics* 61:893–913.
Shepsle, Kenneth A. 1972. "The Strategy of Ambiguity: Uncertainty and Electoral Competition." *American Political Science Review* 66:555–69.
Simon, Adam F. 2002. *The Winning Message: Candidate Behavior, Campaign Discourse, and Democracy*. Cambridge: Cambridge University Press.
Stoker, Laura, and Jacob Bowers. 2002. "Designing Multi-level Studies: Sampling Voters and Electoral Contexts." *Electoral Studies* 21:235–67.
Valentino, Nicholas A., Vincent L. Hutchings, and Ismail K. White. 2002. "Cues that Matter: How Political Ads Prime Racial Attitudes during Campaigns." *American Political Science Review* 96:75–90.
Wattenberg, Martin P., and Craig Leonard Brians. 1999. "Negative Campaign Advertising: Demobilizer or Mobilizer?" *American Political Science Review* 93:891–900.
Westlye, Mark Christopher. 1983. "Competitiveness of Senate Seats and Voting Behavior in Senate Elections." *American Journal of Political Science* 27:253–83.
———. 1991. *Senate Elections and Campaign Intensity*. Baltimore: Johns Hopkins University Press.
Wlezien, Christopher, and Robert S. Erikson. 2002. "The Timeline of Presidential Election Campaigns." *Journal of Politics* 64 (4): 969–93.
Zaller, John R. 1989. "Bringing Converse Back In: Modeling Information Flow in Political Campaigns." *Political Analysis* 1:181–234.
———. 1992. *The Nature and Origins of Mass Opinion*. Cambridge: Cambridge University Press.
———. 1996. "The Myth of Massive Media Impact Revived: New Support for a Discredited Idea." In *Political Persuasion and Attitude Change*, ed. Diana C. Mutz, Paul M. Sniderman, and Richard A. Brody. Ann Arbor: University of Michigan Press.

1 Voter Decision Making and Campaign Effects

The Paradox of Minimal Effects

Stephen Ansolabehere

CENTRAL TO THE STUDY OF campaigns and elections lies a paradox. Voters rely heavily on the information conveyed by campaigns in order to form judgments about who should govern. By most accounts, citizens in modern democracies know little about and feel distant from public affairs. Most people tune in during political campaigns, and what they see and hear can influence their opinions considerably, as shown by recent research on individual voting behavior (Ansolabehere and Iyengar 1995; Bartels 1993; Jacobson 1990; Johnston et al. 1992; Popkin 1991; Zaller 1992) and on aggregate voting patterns (Bartels 1987; Brady and Johnston 1987; Jacobson 1980, 1990). It should, thus, be hard to anticipate the outcomes of elections without knowing how the media cover the elections, what themes the candidates stress, which candidates advertise the most, and what is said during conventions and debates. Election outcomes are strongly predicted, however, by forces outside of campaign politics. Evidence from an extensive literature on economics and elections shows that the governing party's reelection depends overwhelmingly on whether the country is prosperous at home and at peace abroad.[1] Campaigns seem to be inessential to understanding who wins and who loses.

The 1988 presidential election perhaps best exemplifies this puzzle. To many political scientists the 1988 presidential election represented an analytical triumph. George Bush won with nearly exactly the vote predicted by a simple model in which the vote is predicted by the percentage change in real personal disposable income.[2] The lots of George Bush and Michael Dukakis, it seems, were drawn by the economic fates.

But Bush did not win with ease. Throughout the campaign the polls fluctuated dramatically, suggesting that large fractions of the electorate made up their minds in the months, even days, leading up to Election Day (Gelman and King 1993). Michael Dukakis even held a substantial lead in the polls late in the summer of 1988. Observers of the campaigns argue that Dukakis was brought down not by the sudden realization of many voters that the economy was doing well but by the themes and strategies of the competing campaigns. The Republicans' messages of crime, patriotism, and conservatism resonated well with the public, while the Democratic campaign lost its focus after the primaries. Bush used attack advertisements and the free media with cunning and success, while Dukakis refused to slug back (Germond and Witcover 1989; Jamieson 1992). Such factors are nowhere to be found in the macropolitical models. Even still, those models worked smashingly well, though in the end they looked a lot like voodoo political economics.

How is it that elections are highly predictable when voters rely heavily on what they see and hear in a particular campaign? The obvious, most common, and probably correct response is that the public discourse observed during campaigns confirms what most people privately believe about the state of the country and the political parties and candidates. Beginning with Paul Lazarsfeld's important studies of the elections of 1944 and 1948, social scientists have argued that campaigns reinforce the political orientations of voters and mobilize them to vote rather than convert large segments of the population to new ways of thinking or new patterns of behavior (Berelson, Lazarsfeld, and McPhee 1954; Key 1966; Campbell 1960).

Recent social science research has further refined our understanding of reinforcement. The stylized facts that emerge from this research are that campaign communications are reinforcing for different groups within the electorate, depending on their partisan orientation and prior levels of information and interest (Zaller 1992). Partisans, especially low information partisans, seem to be particularly susceptible to messages from their own party's candidates. Partisans seem resistant to messages that are sponsored by the opposing party or that favor the opposing party. Nonpartisans seem to behave somewhat differently. Low information nonpartisans seem to tune out political messages of all sort, but the high information nonpartisans seem to be particularly influenced by political communications.[3]

But there is a fundamental problem with reinforcement arguments. People seem to throw away the public information that campaigns produce, or they use it inefficiently or not at all. Why would people use information this way? Do people just fool themselves?

Two sorts of explanations of the reinforcing effects of campaigns are commonly expressed. First, political psychologists argue that these effects arise because people use cognitive shortcuts, such as priming, cognitive dissonance, and acceptability biases. As a result, individuals believe information that agrees with their beliefs and ignore information dissonant with their beliefs (Iyengar and Kinder 1987; Popkin 1991; Zaller 1992). By this account, elections are predictable because individuals hear what they want to hear, which is consistent with their private assessments of the economy. Second, political economists and many political scientists argue that people use their private information and discount publicly provided information, such as news and ads, because it is not as credible or as reliable as each individual's personal and private experiences (Downs 1957; Key 1966; Fiorina 1981). By this account elections are predictable because aggregate indicators of national well-being are the sum of many individual experiences, and the political campaigns matter little to those judgments.

Each explanation has complementary strengths and weaknesses. Psychological accounts emphasize the importance of public information, such as ads and news, that all people see. These arguments arise out of attempts to understand the ups and downs that occur during elections, as many of the essays in this volume attest. Psychological explanations, though, have difficulty explaining the behavior of key groups within the electorate. In the advertising case, it is hard to think of a priming or framing story that explains the behavior of both partisans and independents and in particular why high information independents appear to move in the direction of the sponsor of the ads. Finally, these stories imply an eventual convergence of beliefs that is rarely observed. If all information were truly public and common, then over time we would observe complete consensus in public opinion on topics where all people agree about the objectives, such as greater economic growth or presidential job approval.

Economic explanations emphasize private information and provide a coherent way to understand why people have different beliefs and preferences. Individuals' beliefs and preferences are rooted in their disparate experiences in the economy and with the government, parties, and specific politicians. However, such explanations discount the publicly conveyed information. This hardly seems consistent with the basic conjectures of rational choice, namely, that individuals make decisions in the most efficient (lowest cost) way or with empirical reality (Erikson et al. 2003). Economic man seems consistent with the observed predictability of elections but not with the variation that occurs during campaigns.

This essay offers a simple theory of campaign information and learning that is entirely consistent with the basic observations made in empirical research. I build on the insights of political psychologists that campaigns fundamentally involve public information and of political economists that individuals' beliefs and preferences derive considerably from their private experiences and information. I assume that people use all information and that they value it equally. It is the mix of the public information from campaigns and the private information from personal experiences that creates the dynamics social scientists have observed. Private information generates heterogeneity in people's beliefs; public information creates coordinated shifts in those beliefs, which look identical to the patterns observed in survey data and experiments.

The account offered here raises what I consider to be a very important set of methodological concerns in the study of campaigns. What is an adequate model of voter reasoning and behavior? The intellectual move made here is to introduce public as well as private information into a simple model of economic voting and to show that many of the basic individual-level behavioral changes can be understood in these terms. The challenge for political economists, then, is to develop models that incorporate more subtle notions of information. Several empirical studies have done so and have found that both the information in the mass media and private information matter (Erikson et al. 1993). Little attention has been given to establishing the differential effects that these factors have on the total vote.

The challenge for political psychologists is much greater—to show that specific psychological phenomena actually influence electoral behavior. The important possibility exists that much of what cognitive psychologists have uncovered simply averages out in the process of counting votes. In short, many of the subtle processes of cognition and learning noted by survey and experimental researchers may be inessential to understanding election outcomes. To judge the importance of such factors requires that political psychologists have a clear standard or null model against which to judge the cumulative effects of psychological factors. The political economic model offered here provides a baseline against which to measure the importance of such effects.

In the first section of this essay, I develop an economic model of election. In the second section I introduce campaign information as public information and consider the possible effects that it may have. The concluding section offers some thoughts on how this model might be used to integrate questions of strategic voting, issue voting, and other topics touched on in other essays in this volume.

A Model of Economic Voting

Models of economic voting (e.g., Downs 1957; Kramer 1973; Fiorina 1981; Alesina, Londregan, and Rosenthal 1995) make four assumptions about individuals: (1) individuals pursue their self-interest, (2) they rely on private information, (3) they make judgments about the comparative competence of the parties or candidates rather than about policies, and (4) they use rules to update information.

The first assumption holds that individuals pursue their self-interest. They act in ways that will make them better off economically. A single indicator best captures the economic voter's interest: real personal disposable income. Kramer (1973) and subsequent researchers have shown that changes in real personal disposable income predict election outcomes best. Folded into this measure, of course, are inflation (real), taxes (disposable), wages, growth and employment (income), and other factors that the government may influence. Whatever the factors involved, all people are assumed to want and to benefit from the same thing: income growth.

How citizens pursue their interests in the electoral arena is more difficult to formulate. Economic voting usually implies that the electorate assesses the abilities or competence of the competing parties or politicians more than the policies they promise. People do not control the policy levers directly, nor do they appear to know much about the policies pursued by the government. Even if the candidates and parties could clearly promise specific policies, it is not evident that policies that make sense today, such as minimum wages or low interest rates, would be appropriate in two or four years. As a result, it is often supposed that economic voters really want the most able governance of the economy (DiIullio and Stokes 1993; Alesina, Londregan, and Rosenthal 1995).[4]

The second assumption holds that people rely on private information, their own experiences in the economy and with the government, to form electoral judgments. Forecasting models simplify this further: people simply vote their pocketbooks, their personal finances (Kramer 1973; Tufte

1975). Pocketbook voting is surely a strong version of this assumption. More generally, private information consists of information that each individual observes independent of what others observe. Political economists commonly model private information as a signal, the realization of a random variable, that an individual receives (Alesina, Londregan, and Rosenthal 1995). Different people see different signals, different features of the economy. Some people are highly attentive to wages, others to fluctuations in the stock market. Importantly, unlike information that all people see, such as the unemployment rate, private information leads people to hold different beliefs about which party or politician governs best.

This assumption is subtly at odds with notions of information found in much political psychology and survey research. To most political scientists, an individual is informed if he or she knows a lot of facts about the candidates involved in a race, follows current affairs closely, or has weighed the issues carefully. Measures of knowledge include the number of correct identifications of prominent politicians, newspaper readership, and the number of answers to survey questions. Such measures capture the heterogeneity in levels of factual information within the electorate. By this metric, the public does not stack up well against the classical image of a democratic citizenry.

Private information, as it is formulated in economic models of voting, implies that each person receives the same amount of information. All persons live under the government for the same amount of time and, thus, draw inferences about politics and public affairs on the same amount of personal experiences. Am I better off now than I was four years ago? Or last year? The sorts of experiences people have is a different matter.

The third assumption defines the nature of the signal or private information that people receive. Private information may indicate that (1) the incumbent candidate or party governs well, (2) the incumbent candidate or party governs badly, or (3) public affairs are irrelevant to the person's life or there is insufficient information to make a judgment. In Kramer's original model of economic voting, an individual judges the incumbent party favorably if the individual's income increases substantially; he or she judges the incumbent party unfavorably if personal income decreases substantially. Modest changes in income give ambiguous information about the government's performance.[5]

The fourth assumption holds that people update their beliefs over time. Following Fiorina (1981), I assume that individuals keep a running tally of their information. People express support for a party or politician if the sum of their past experiences with that party or politician is favorable. More sophisticated models suppose that voters revise their beliefs using Bayes's rule (Calvert 1985; Bartels 1993) or some other more complicated learning model. Such models lead to more subtle predictions than those offered here. The assumption of a simple moving average of information has the strength of simplicity. People try to reduce the effort they put into making decisions, and more sophisticated learning strategies require more information and effort.

These four assumptions describe voters as narrowly focused on their own interests and their own experiences. These are not the citizens of classical democratic theory. But the beauty of democracy is that it adds up these disparate experiences pretty effectively. Each individual doesn't have to know what others think and feel or how the entire macroeconomy works in order to reach a decision and voice his or her own preference.

The final piece to economic models of voting shows that public decisions indeed aggregate individuals' private information and judgments. In the terms developed in social choice theory, theories of economic voting describe a situation in which people have the same preferences (economic growth) but disparate beliefs. Condorcet's 1787 jury theorem addresses precisely this problem: majority rule will accurately measure the private information of jurors the larger the size of the jury. Contemporary political scientists have developed a rich literature relating to this theorem, applying it not only to juries but also to elections (Austen-Smith and Banks 1996; Fedderson and Pessendorfer 1997). Under the assumptions discussed here, the vote of the majority will accurately reflect the extent to which the population has prospered, as claimed by forecasting models.

A simple model helps us appreciate how information aggregates over time and into public decisions. One may think of the private information that people receive as draws from a deck of cards. Each card may have one of three faces, corresponding to the three sorts of evaluations that each person may reach about public affairs. A card marked "G" means information favors the government; a card marked "O" means information favors the opposition; and a card marked "N" means information favors neither or no one. The incidence of Gs, Os, and Ns in a deck reflects the overall prosperity of the country.

To give some richness to people's beliefs, suppose that each individual is dealt two cards, corresponding to a two-year term of office. Six pairs of cards are possible: GG, OO, NN, GO, GN, ON. These pairs describe different types of people. The frequency of each type depends on the frequency of Gs, Os, and Ns. Table 1 displays the possible pairings.

The extent to which the cards that an individual receives point to either G or O reveals which party, if either, the individual supports. A person with GG strongly supports the government; a person with OO strongly opposes the government. A person with NG or NO leans weakly in the direction of the government or opposition, respectively. Independents are those with either GO or NN.

The incidence of Ns captures the individual's level of interest in government. Importantly, interest in politics is an outcome of this model. It stems from the degree to which people see that public affairs affect their well-being. Individuals with no Ns have the highest levels of interest; individuals with NN have no interest in public affairs.

This simple accounting may describe whether someone votes and how they vote. An individual's level of interest, whether they feel they have a stake in the election outcome, determines whether he or she votes. People with NN definitely do not vote; people with GG or OO definitely vote. People with NG or NO are indifferent between voting and not; they flip a coin. Given that a person does vote, he or she will chose the party for whom they have the larger number of Gs or Os. High interest independents will definitely vote, but they are indifferent between the choices.

Condorcet's jury theorem states that the share of the votes won by each party will reflect the relative frequency of Gs and Os. The intuition stems from the law of large numbers. The private information resembles the unknown parameter in a Bernoulli trial (for example, p is the probability of G occurring). The average of a large number of independent Bernoulli trials will approximate the true but unknown parameter from the Bernoulli extremely well. Several contemporary authors have proved more general versions of this result and derived conditions when it fails to hold, as when people vote strategically (Austen-Smith and Banks 1996). Such conditions

TABLE 1. Types of Private Information Held by Individuals

Levels of Interest	Partisanship		
	G Supporters	Independents	O Supporters
High	GG	GO	OO
Low	GN	NN	NO

might be especially important in electoral systems like New Zealand and Canada, where voters seem to cast their ballots with an eye to not "wasting" votes or to preventing their least preferred candidate from winning.

The stylization presented here remains faithful to the basic decision theoretic models of economic voting. In particular, it captures the main empirical prediction of such models, namely, that personal income forecasts election results. If there is sufficient economic growth, then people's private information will indicate that the incumbent party governs well (that is, Gs outweigh Os). In this context, we also understand more clearly how campaigns affect voting behavior and even appear to cement people's privately held beliefs.

Elections with Campaigns

As a statistical matter, economic voting, as described previously, offers an extremely parsimonious model of elections. Income growth explains two-thirds of the variation in congressional and presidential election results (Kramer 1973). Income growth and presidential popularity combined explain over 80 percent of the variability in election returns (Tufte 1975; Lewis-Beck and Rice 1992). The inclusion of debates, conventions, and other election-related events adds little to the predictive power of economic models (Holbrook 1993). As a theoretical matter, though, the omission of campaigns from formal analyses introduces an inconsistency. A rational, effort-minimizing citizen who faces a complex and uncertain choice should use all information at hand. Pocketbook voting is justified on the grounds that people know their own situations well and with little additional effort can draw inferences from this about the economy and the incumbent party. In other words, the marginal cost of personal financial information is essentially zero. By the same reasoning, analytical models should include campaign information. In modern democracy, where citizens have little incentive to inform themselves, competing politicians bear the costs of informing voters. Candidates and party leaders must package their message into accessible formats and distribute it widely and free of charge.

What is distinctive about information generated by campaigns is that it is *public* information. All people see the same spectacle, or, in the language of the model described previously, they see the same signal. The technologies of communication make it difficult to say one thing to one audience and quite another thing to a different audience. Once a message is broadcast or printed in a newspaper or magazine, the candidate has no control over who happens to tune in or where it may be reproduced. In fact, politicians often look for reversals in their opponent's campaign materials and then advertise the occasional flip-flop. Reliance on mass media only heightens the public nature of campaign information. Competition for votes drives candidates to make their case as efficiently as possible. That means making the information as accessible as possible, which in turn requires broadcasting messages over the most popular media available.

Whether all people interpret the information the same way is another matter. I assume that they do: all people receive exactly the same signal. In doing so, this treatment breaks with much political psychological research that emphasizes the importance of selective perceptions. For example, John Zaller argues in *The Nature and Origins of Mass Opinion* (1992) that people's preferences influence the sorts of information they are willing to believe and receive. In this model the probability that someone is receptive to a signal is an increasing function of his or her underlying interest in politics. Given that an individual has received a signal, the probability that that person believes or accepts the information is a decreasing function of their interest in politics. People most influenced by new information, then, are those with moderate levels of interest. Such effects will certainly produce patterns of reinforcement. Selective perception along the lines described by Zaller (1992), Popkin (1992), and others cannot explain the pattern of reinforcement found in our experimental studies. In particular, given that they have received the information (a situation that we created in the laboratory), low interest independents should be more strongly moved by campaign news and advertising than high interest independents, but they are not. Such behavior, it turns out, is consistent with the simple economic model presented here, once public information is added to the mix. This is not to deny the existence or importance of the phenomena describe by cognitive psychologists. These forces may magnify the effect described here, but they do not appear sufficient to account for reinforcement.[6]

Public information adds to an individual's cache of signals in the same way that private information does. People take away from the campaign a message about the capacity of the candidate or party to govern. To update their beliefs, people simply add that message to the private information that the individuals have received. From this tally they infer whether politics are of much interest and whom they support.

In the simple schematic using cards, campaign information represents a third card that each person receives. Unlike private information, though, each individual receives identical information. Public information will, of course, carry a unique signal, and, depending on the nature of the signal, campaigns will produce varying patterns of political loyalty and defection.

Here I consider two extreme types of signals. In the first case, the public information favors one party entirely; in the second case the public information conveys a balanced signal. Zaller (1992) calls these one-sided and two-sided flows of information. Most U.S. House elections look like the first case: House incumbents completely dominate the flow in information (see Jacobson, this volume; Elms and Sniderman, this volume). The experiments that Shanto Iyengar and I performed involving exposure to a single campaign ad are also of this sort. Presidential general elections look more like the second case, because both presidential campaigns usually muster equal resources.

A one-sided campaign, as might occur in a House race, sends all people the same signal. Suppose that the information favors the government, so everyone receives a G card. How does behavior change? Consider the pattern displayed in table 1. If we give each person an additional G, then we get the pattern of information displayed in panel A of table 2. What has happened to each of the people in table 1? Everyone has more information, but not everyone has changed their allegiances to G or even away from O. Three types of voters will keep their old behavioral patterns; three types will change. The high information partisans remain partisans. Those whose private information made them strong supporters of the government (that is, GG) are now GGG. They vote, and they vote for G. Those whose private information made them supporters of the opposition

TABLE 2. Types of Information Held by Individuals in Campaigns

Levels of Interest	Partisanship		
	G Supporters	Independents	O Supporters
A. One-Sided Campaign			
High	GGG, GOG		OOG
Low	GNG	NNG, NOG	
B. Two-Sided Campaign			
High	GGGO	GOGO	OOGO
Low	GNGO	NNGO	NOGO

(that is, OO) are now OOG. They vote, and they vote for O, because their net information still favors O. One other type of voter remains unmoved by such a campaign, the low interest independents. They start out highly unlikely to vote and favoring neither party (that is, NN). The information that they get may improve their opinions of the government, but they began sufficiently disconnected from politics that they remain nonvoters and lean toward neither party.

Three types of voters adopt new behaviors in response to a one-sided campaign. First, low interest or weak supporters of the government become strong partisans. This group began indifferent between not voting and voting for the government (that is, GN). The campaign reinforces their leanings and mobilizes them to vote. Second, low interest or weak supporters of the opposition abandon their party. They begin the campaign season indifferent between not voting and voting for the opposition party (that is, NO). They learn favorable information about the governing party that creates even greater dissonance (that is, NOG). They now have a sufficiently high interest to vote, but they are unsure for whom. Finally, high interest independents vote for the government. They begin interested in the outcome of the election but indifferent between the two parties (that is, GO). What they learn tips them toward the government (that is, GOG).

This is precisely the pattern observed experimentally. Low interest partisans move in the direction of the candidate whose message they see, regardless of the person's identification, but low interest nonpartisans are unmoved by campaign messages. High interest partisans do not vote differently as a result of campaign information, but high interest independents move in the direction of the government.

A two-sided campaign, or a perfectly balanced news story, produces no movement in political preferences, though it does mobilize people to vote. Suppose that every person receives two bits of information from a two-sided campaign, one G and one O. Panel B of table 2 shows the resulting types of people, derived by adding GO to the tallies of each of the types in table 1. The net balance of partisan information remains the same for each person. Not surprisingly, such a campaign produces reinforcement of people's voting preferences across the board. It also mobilizes the low interest individuals to vote.

This pattern reflects the argument sometimes made that the campaigns cancel each other out. Even still, the candidates and parties must run vigorous campaigns. If one side chooses not to campaign, then the resulting behavior follows the one-sided case. Candidates who do not campaign may lose by not energizing their base and not moving enough of the other types of voters.

Conclusions

In this essay I have sought to resolve what I perceive to be a fundamental tension between the study of elections and the study of campaigns. Many social scientists analyze elections as regular phenomena that are predictable on the basis of factors determined outside of the campaigns, such as economic performance; others think of elections as highly dependent on the debate that is waged throughout the campaigns. I assume that both are right: elections are predictable and campaigns matter.

One driving assumption underlies this analysis: people use the lowest cost information to make electoral judgments. This assumption means that people use both the private information that they observe during daily life (this is the chief assumption behind retrospective voting) and the public or common information conveyed throughout the campaigns. Before the campaign begins, though, people's political beliefs are rooted in their personal experiences. Have they prospered? Are they secure? Private information creates heterogeneous beliefs about which party, if any, governs best. Public information can create coordinated movements in opinions. But such movements in opinion are constrained by the private beliefs that people hold. As a result, the interplay between public information and private information produces patterns of reinforcement that *make* elections regular and predictable.

This model contains also the potential for change. Cataclysmic events such as the Great Depression certainly fit the general pattern described by economic models of elections. Severe economic dislocations created by depressions shake people's core political beliefs. More troubling are the notable shifts that occur in response to seemingly minor economic changes, like the elections of 1994. Surprisingly, Tufte's simple forecasting model predicted this election within a percentage point of the overall vote. The framework sketched here suggests why. Dramatic changes in voting patterns of this sort generally reflect long-term and gradual shifts in people's deeply held beliefs. Support for a party will erode as individuals observe successive periods of weak performance in office; likewise, support for a party may strengthen as people see capable administration of the economy. Such seems to have been the case with the Democrats, who lost votes in each successive election from 1988 to 1994. Sufficient erosion of a party's base may create the conditions for a seemingly sudden collapse. Against such a background, a campaign can produce sufficient movement in the same direction so as to tip the electoral balance.

NOTES

1. Much of this research has been done in the U.S. context in the presidential and congressional elections. Notable studies include Kramer 1973; Tufte 1975; Rosenstone 1985; Hibbs 1987; and Lewis-Beck and Rice 1992. Similar patterns hold elsewhere; see Crewe 1987.

2. This is the model due to Tufte (1975). This model performs remarkably well. In Tufte's original analysis, he reports an R-squared of over .9 and a forecast error smaller than the final Gallup Poll. The model has since held up well against other forecasting models. Most notably, it forecast the Democrats' share of the vote in the 1994 midterm election within a percentage point.

3. A number of studies document such effects. On a wide variety of specific issues, see Zaller 1992; on the issue of race, see Sniderman and Piazza 1993; on the case of political advertising, see Ansolabehere and Iyengar 1995.

4. Voters might also have distributional preferences. In other words, they may prefer that their relative well-being in society matters rather than the absolute improvement in their standard of living. In this case politicians may wish to redistribute economic goods rather than grow the economy (Hibbs 1987). This complicates the analysis considerably.

5. Another interpretation of the third assumption is that each signal that an individual receives privately contains two pieces of information. One piece of the information is whether the government and public affairs bear on the individual's life at all. For many Americans, public affairs simply seem irrelevant. But others' experiences lead them to feel that they have a stake or interest in what the government does. A second piece of information in each signal indicates whether the incumbent administration or politicians govern ably or not.

6. A much stronger critique of the social psychological models is that the description of how people perceive public information and events should extend to private information as well as public information. So if a person is Republican and he or she does well under a Democratic administration, then that person gives the Democrats no credit. If that same person does well under a Republican regime, then he or she gives the GOP all of the credit. In such a world, there is never change in beliefs, once they exist, and therefore in preferences.

REFERENCES

Alesina, Alberto, John Londregan, and Howard Rosenthal. 1995. "A Model of the Political Economy of the United States." *American Political Science Review* 87:12–33.

Ansolabehere, Stephen, and Shanto Iyengar. 1995. *Going Negative*. New York: Free Press.

Austen-Smith, David, and Jeffrey Banks. 1996. "Information Aggregation, Rationality, and the Condorcet Jury Theorem." *American Political Science Review* 90: 34–45.

Bartels, Larry. 1987. *Presidential Primaries*. Princeton: Princeton University Press.

———. 1993. "Messages Received: The Political Impact of Media Exposure." *American Political Science Review* 87:267–85.

Berelson, Bernard, Paul Lazarsfeld, and William McPhee. 1954. *Voting*. Chicago: University of Chicago Press.

Brady, Henry E., and Richard Johnston. 1987. "What's the Primary Message?" In *Media and Momentum*, ed. Gary Orren and Nelson Polsby. Chatham, NJ: Chatham House.

Calvert, Randall. 1985. "The Value of Biased Information: A Rational Choice Model of Political Advice." *Journal of Politics* 47:530–55.

Campbell, Angus. 1960. "Surge and Decline: A Study of Electoral Change." *Political Opinion Quarterly* 24:397–418.

Cramer, Richard Ben. 1992. *What It Takes*. New York: Vintage.

Crewe, Ivor. 1987. "What's Left for Labour?" *Public Opinion* 10:52–56.

Dilullio, John, and Donald Stokes. 1993. "Valence Politics." In *The Election of 1992*, ed. Gerald Pomper. Chatham, NJ: Chatham House.

Downs, Anthony. 1957. *An Economic Theory of Democracy*. New York: Harper and Row.

Erikson, Robert, Michael MacKuen, and James Stimson. 2002. *The Macro Polity*. New York: Cambridge University Press.

Fedderson, Timothy, and Wolfgang Pessendorfer. 1997. "Voting Behavior and Information Aggregation in Elections with Private Information." *Econometrica* 65:1029–58.

Fiorina, Morris. 1981. *Retrospective Voting in American National Elections*. New Haven: Yale University Press.

Germond, Jack, and Jules Witcover. 1989. *Whose Broad Stripes and Bright Stars?* New York: Warner Books.

Gelman, Andrew, and Gary King. 1993. "Why Are American Presidential Election Polls So Variable When Votes Are So Predictable?" *British Journal of Political Science* 23:409–51.

Hibbs, Douglas. 1987. *The American Political Economy*. Cambridge, MA: Harvard University Press.

Holbrook, Thomas. 1994. "Campaigns, National Conditions, and U.S. Politics." *American Journal of Political Science* 38:973–98.

Iyengar, Shanto, and Donald Kinder. 1987. *News That Matters*. Chicago: University of Chicago Press.

Jacobson, Gary. 1980. *Money and Congressional Elections*. New Haven: Yale University Press.

———. 1990. "The Effects of Campaign Spending in House Elections: New Evidence for Old Arguments." *American Journal of Political Science* 34:334–62.

Jamieson, Kathleen Hall. 1992. *Dirty Politics*. New York: Oxford University Press.

Johnston, Richard, André Blais, Henry E. Brady, and Jean Crête. 1992. *Letting the People Decide: Dynamics of a Canadian Election*. Montreal: McGill-Queens University Press.

Key, V. O. 1966. *The Responsible Electorate.* New York: Vintage.

Kramer, Gerald. 1973. "Short-Term Fluctuations in the U.S. Voting Behavior, 1896–1964." *American Political Science Review* 65:131–43

Lewis-Beck, Michael, and Tom Rice. 1992. *Forecasting Elections.* Beverly Hills: Sage.

MacKuen, Michael, Robert Erikson, and James Stimson. 1992. "Peasants or Bankers? The American Electorate and the U.S. Economy." *American Political Science Review* 86:597–611.

Popkin, Samuel. 1991. *The Reasoning Voter.* Chicago: University of Chicago Press.

Rosenstone, Steven. 1985. *Forecasting Presidential Elections.* New Haven: Yale University Press.

Sniderman, Paul M., and Thomas Piazza. 1993. *The Scar of Race.* Cambridge, MA: Harvard University Press.

Tufte, Edward. 1975. "Determinants of the Outcomes of Midterm Congressional Elections." *American Political Science Review* 69:812–26.

Zaller, John. 1992. *The Nature and Origins of Mass Opinion.* New York: Cambridge University Press.

The Impact of Campaigns on Discrepancies, Errors, and Biases in Voting Behavior

Patrick Fournier

THERE ARE VARIOUS WAYS BY which political campaigns can be relevant. One can look at the impact of political campaigns on vote intentions, on opinions about leaders and issues, on perceptions of candidates' issue positions, and on the determinants of decisions (Bartels 1988, 1992; Franklin 1991; Johnston et al. 1992, 1996b; Johnston, Hagen, and Jamieson 2004; Gelman and King 1993; Norris et al. 1999; Nevitte et al. 2000; Blais et al. 2002). However, one terrain for campaign influence remains to be explored: what happens to interpersonal diversity in behavior during a campaign?

Previous research has identified two forms of heterogeneity in political behavior: diversity in the process of decision making and diversity in the outcome of decision making. First, there is evidence that people of different information or sophistication levels do not reason the same way about politics: they rely on different considerations, or they give different weight to similar considerations (Stimson 1975; Sniderman, Brody, and Tetlock 1991; Johnston et al. 1996b; Fournier 2000). Second, low political information ultimately leads to individual and aggregate choices that deviate from informed decisions: less knowledgeable citizens have opinions that differ from those they would have had they been fully informed (Bartels 1996; Delli Carpini and Keeter 1996; Althaus 1998; Luskin, Fishkin, and Jowell 2002; Sturgis 2003).

The dynamics of these two types of interpersonal heterogeneity during political campaigns have not been investigated. We do not know whether the differences between very and less informed citizens are minimized or compounded by the progress of a campaign or whether they remain intact, unaffected by the unfolding of campaigns. Yet, such an investigation is crucial, as it informs us about the impact of the democratic process on the quality of voters' decisions. We need to ascertain whether campaigns help people make more enlightened choices. Never mind learning and persuasion, this is arguably the most socially important effect that a campaign can have.

This study tackles an important but neglected issue by analyzing the impact of campaigns on both diversity in decision making and diversity in decision outcome. Three separate campaigns are examined: the 1988, 1993, and 1997 Canadian federal elections. The goal is to determine whether campaigns increase, decrease, or do not influence the differences between information groups in the determinants of vote choice on one hand and the individual and aggregate deviations in vote choice attributable to low information on the other hand.

Heterogeneity and Political Campaigns

There are two types of interpersonal heterogeneity in models of individual political behavior: heterogeneity in the process of decision making, and heterogeneity in the outcome of decision. Heterogeneity in decision making refers to relationships between independent and dependent variables that are not uniform across the entire population, that differ in strength across segments of the population. For instance, in a model of voting behavior, partisan identification, ideology, issues, and leader evaluations may not have the same impact on the vote of all citizens. Ideology may be more closely linked to the decision of some individuals (perhaps the more informed), while leader evaluations are stronger determinants of the choice of other citizens (possibly the less informed). Such results are generally understood as a sign of differing decisional or reasoning rules: people with differing levels of expertise think differently about politics, relying on different considerations or giving different weight to similar considerations (Rivers 1988; Sniderman, Brody, and Tetlock 1991).[1] Sniderman, Brody, and Tetlock (1991) found interpersonal diversity between individuals of different education levels among a myriad of political decisions. An expanding number of studies have uncovered evidence of this type of heterogeneity between citizens of different levels of political information (Zaller

1992; Lupia 1994; Delli Carpini and Keeter 1996; Johnston et al. 1996b; Krause 1997; Fournier 2000).[2]

There is also evidence of heterogeneity in decision outcome. Studies demonstrate that the information deficiencies of the electorate seriously affect individual choices and collective preferences (Bartels 1996; Delli Carpini and Keeter 1996; Althaus 1998; Luskin, Fishkin, and Jowell 2002; Sturgis 2003). First, at the individual level, lack of information leads to opinions that differ from informed opinions. For instance, uninformed voters do not mimic the choices of informed voters with similar sociodemographic profiles: they do not vote the way they would have had they been fully informed (Bartels 1996). So all the means reportedly available to citizens to overcome informational disparities (polls, cues, and shortcuts) do not perform perfectly (Kuklinski and Hurley 1994; Kuklinski and Quirk 2000). These results severely undermine the low information rationality claims (McKelvey and Ordeshook 1986; Popkin 1991; Sniderman, Brody, and Tetlock 1991; Lupia 1994). Furthermore, at the aggregate level, these individual "errors" are not random; they do not cancel each other out; they are systematic. This means that actual collective preferences do not correspond to hypothetical preferences of the same population if it were fully informed. For example, American presidential incumbents receive about 5 percentage points more, on average, than they would under full information, while Democrat presidential candidates do about 2 percentage points better (Bartels 1996).[3] Thus, the aggregationist claims are not vindicated (Miller 1986; Lahda 1992; Page and Shapiro 1992).

The evidence concerning heterogeneity in decision outcome is congruous. Statistical simulations that apply the behavior of the most informed to all individuals (Bartels 1996; Althaus 1998) and quasi-experiments that deliberately increase subjects' level of information (Luskin, Fishkin, and Jowell 2002) both yield informed political preferences that differ from real preferences in comparable ways. Moreover, one study that uses both techniques on the same data uncovered similar "biases" in public opinion attributable to information deficiency (Sturgis 2003).

Beyond their common focus on interpersonal diversity, there is, I believe, a strong link between the two types of heterogeneity. People of identical profiles except for their levels of political information do not have the same opinions *because* they rely on different considerations that do not all lead as effectively to the same judgment. Heterogeneity in the process of decision making is a necessary (but not sufficient) condition for heterogeneity in the outcome of decision. Thus, similar citizens who reason differently about politics will not necessarily reach different decisions; they may still get to the same choice. However, divergent decisions cannot occur without the presence of heterogeneity in process. The causal sequence follows the following form: reliance on considerations of varying efficiency encourages the emergence of individual deviations from informed behavior, which, in turn, are generally not nullified by the aggregation of opinions and translate into collective preferences that differ from hypothetical fully informed preferences.[4]

Two questions emerge at this point: (1) What happens to the level of heterogeneity in process during electoral campaigns? and (2) What happens to the level of heterogeneity in outcome during campaigns? I now ponder each of these questions, potential answers, and plausible explanations.

Heterogeneity in Decision Making

Postelection data reveal that citizens with differing levels of information do not end up with the same structures of vote determinants (Johnston et al. 1996b). Preelection data also indicate a significant quantity of heterogeneity (Rivers 1988). However, these studies use different methods to document the existence of heterogeneity, so their results are not comparable.[5] Thus, we know that different decision rules exist before and after the election, but whether any movement occurs in the level of heterogeneity in process during the campaign remains to be determined. Three scenarios are possible: divergence, convergence, and stability.

First, in the divergence scenario, differences in decision rules may be magnified by political campaigns. Disparities in exposure or sensitivity to campaign messages may prompt groups of contrasting levels of information to move away from one another. The literature on agenda setting, framing, and priming, by establishing a relationship between political information and the susceptibility to mass media influence, contains evidence that suggests that increasing heterogeneity is a viable scenario. Survey and experimental studies indicate that politically sophisticated citizens are more prone to modify their priorities and considerations according to the attention allocated to the issues by the media (MacKuen 1984; Hill 1985; Krosnick and Brannon 1993; Nelson, Oxley, and Clawson 1997; Miller and Krosnick 2000).[6] If the dominant coverage points to issues and considerations that diverge from the structure of vote determinants used by the less informed, then the gaps between informed and uninformed individuals should accentuate.

The literature on the dissemination of information also lends credence to the divergence scenario. Most notably, Tichenor and his associates (1970) found empirical support for the knowledge gap hypothesis: "As the infusion of mass media information into a social system increases, segments of the population with higher socioeconomic status tend to acquire this information at a faster rate than the lower status segments, so that the gap in knowledge between these segments tends to increase rather than decrease" (159–60). The knowledge gap hypothesis has also been validated, to a limited extent, in the political realm (Moore 1987; Holbrook 2002). However, unequal levels of motivation to acquire the information appear to be a necessary condition for broadening gaps (Tichenor et al. 1973; Ettema, Brown, and Luepker 1983; Kwak 1999). The question is therefore whether the electoral process generates equal levels of motivation. Studies indicate that citizens experience varying levels of interest in and attention to political activities and that campaigns have little aggregate impact on these attitudes (Lazarsfeld, Berelson, and Gaudet 1944; Berelson, Lazarsfeld, and McPhee 1954). Thus, widening political knowledge gaps are possible. Would they translate into increasingly divergent structures of vote determinants? There are indications that the learning, discussion, and thought induced by a deliberative poll increase the attitude constraint advantage of the more informed over the less informed (Sturgis, Roberts, and Allum 2003). Thus, widening knowledge gaps during a campaign could translate into widening differences in decision rules.

In the second scenario—convergence—political campaigns reduce the level of heterogeneity. There are three plausible paths to convergence. (1) Everybody learns what the election is about, what the driving issues are, and on what considerations their voting decision should be based. This path is consistent with the idea that mass communications, most notably television, have a "mainstreaming" effect on public opinion: uniform coverage cultivates common outlooks (Morgan and Signorielli 1990; Gerbner et al. 1994). In this case, simplified and consensual media coverage of campaigns could serve to minimize the differences between groups, leading them to move toward one another, converging on a more unified decisional process. (2) The less informed learn with the unfolding of the campaign what others already know (about issue positions, leader evaluations, and so forth), and they zero in on the consensual decision process. This path could be labeled a sophistication-dependent Gelman and King conception (1993) where only a portion of the public, the less knowledgeable, experiences the activation of enlightened preferences. (3) Campaign events and coverage push the most informed, since they are more attentive to new information (Zaller 1992; Price and Zaller 1993) and more sensitive to media effects (Nelson, Oxley, and Clawson 1997; Miller and Krosnick 2000), toward a structure of vote ingredients already adopted by the less knowledgeable.

Finally, in the stability scenario, the level of heterogeneity in process might be unaffected by political campaigns. If campaigns do not carry much information to anyone, or similar amounts of information to everyone, and if they do not modify the public's electoral agenda, two quite improbable assertions in light of the research cited previously, then the level of heterogeneity may remain the same.

Heterogeneity in Decision Outcome

People of different information levels do not think similarly about politics and do not reach the same voting decision. These individual "errors" translate into "biased" collective preferences (Bartels 1996; Luskin, Fishkin, and Jowell 2002). But what is the role of campaigns in this process? Classical democratic theory expects campaigns to be a forum for debate about policies, ideas, and leadership, a debate that exposes the electorate to the major alternatives competing for government, that allows voters to learn about them, compare them, and deliberate on their respective value. In fact, previous evidence of learning is vast and somewhat diverse. During campaigns, citizens gain knowledge about parties, candidates, and intervenors, notably their stance on the major issues of the day; about the nature of referendum proposals; and about the electoral viability of competitors (Bartels 1988; Johnston et al. 1992, 1996b). Furthermore, campaigns activate citizens' political predispositions, indicating that knowledge acquired is related to long-standing preferences and rendered relevant (Bartels 1988; Finkel 1993; Finkel and Schrott 1995; Gelman and King 1993; Johnston et al. 1992, 1996b).

Extending Bartels's work on the deviations from informed vote choice to a dynamic perspective provides another way to determine whether respondents exhibit behavior consistent with a conception of campaigns as a context of deliberation. Two questions are central. First, does the level of individual deviations from informed decisions move during the progress of campaigns? Second, do campaigns affect the "biases" in aggregate preferences? If campaigns were conducive to substantial learning and reflection about political parties, candidates, and issues, then we would expect early vote intentions to be marked by much more individual "errors" than Election Day choices. If the uninformed people's capacity to emulate the decision of the more informed improves with the progress of a campaign, individual deviations from informed decisions should decline. Apart from reducing individual deviations, learning may also translate, at the aggregate level, into less significant deviations from full information collective preferences.

The Study

To compare the levels of interpersonal diversity in decision making and in decision outcome present at each stage of the campaign, I need to measure these phenomena. By my count, there are three methods one can employ to expose heterogeneity. First, Douglas Rivers (1988) recommends the use of an econometric specification that uses complete preference orders to correct for the presence of interpersonal heterogeneity in the estimation of the influence of ideology and partisanship on vote choice. This method accounts for the presence of heterogeneity, but it does not easily provide assessments of the magnitude of heterogeneity in decision making, nor does it enable estimation of individual and aggregate deviations from informed decisions.

The second method, the most frequently used, involves splitting the population into separate subgroups according to information and estimating a separate explanatory model for each group.[7] Since it produces a different set of coefficients for each subgroup, this method allows us to directly exhibit differences in parameter strength and to examine any movement in the level of heterogeneity in process during the campaign. However, since the effects of information are not integrated into a single model, this method cannot estimate the total impact and significance of heterogeneity nor individual and aggregate deviations from informed opinions.

The third method is proposed by Bartels (1996): an interactive form where the information scale and its reverse interact with every explanatory variable, thereby producing high and low information sets of coefficients in the same model. This technique allows us to measure the differences in model fit between a heterogeneity-sensitive setup and a traditional homogeneous design and the individual and aggregate consequences of low information. Unfortunately, due to the less than straightforward specification (each respondent's behavior is a weighted function of the high and low information sets of coefficients), analysis of movement in the magnitude of heterogeneity in process is quite difficult. Moreover, this method restricts the effects of information to be linear, an assumption that is theoretically and empirically problematic (Zaller 1992). Bartels acknowledges this point but argues that experimentation with alternative monotonic and nonmonotonic specifications did not improve the fit of the model in the case of presidential voting in the United States (1996, 207–8). I believe that a more flexible setup that permits the coexistence of linear and nonlinear effects eliminates the necessity to test alternative specifications by allowing information effects to take various forms in the same model.

I propose a fourth method where three information dummy variables (low, medium, high) interact with all independent variables. This specification is illustrated by the following equations:

Homogeneous model:

$$Y = a + b_1(I_f) + b_1(X_a) + b_2(X_s) + b_3(I_1) + b_4(I_3) + e \qquad (1)$$

Heterogeneity in decision making:

$$Y = a + b_1(I_1 \cdot X_a) + b_2(I_2 \cdot X_a) + b_3(I_3 \cdot X_a) + b_4(X_s)$$
$$+ b_5(I_1) + b_6(I_3) + e \qquad (2)$$

Heterogeneity in decision outcome:

$$Y = a + b_1(I_1 \cdot X_s) + b_2(I_2 \cdot X_s) + b_3(I_3 \cdot X_s) + b_4(I_1)$$
$$+ b_5(I_3) + e, \qquad (3)$$

where Y is either vote intention or reported vote; where I_1, I_2, and I_3 are three dummy variables (low, medium, and high information); where X_a is a set of attitudinal independent variables (such as party identification, leader evaluations, and issues positions); and where X_s is a set of sociodemographic independent variables.[8] Because of the binary nature of the dependent variables, the functional form is logistic.

This method combines the advantages of the previous two techniques. First, it estimates a distinct parameter structure for each information group, hence replicating the straightforwardness of the sample-splitting technique in identifying differences in decision rules.[9] Second, by integrating all effects into a single model, this method allows us to measure the significance of the contribution of the heterogeneous specification over the homogeneous design and to calculate variants of Bartels's individual and aggregate deviations from full information. Furthermore, it permits nonlinear effects to coexist with linear ones. The decision to divide the distribution into three tiers simplifies the presentation and interpretation of results, and it allows multiple types of nonlinear effects to manifest themselves.

These equations will be used here to assess the level of heterogeneity in three different ways: two of them dealing with heterogeneity in process and one relating to heterogeneity in outcome. First, I examine the heterogeneity captured by the total gaps between the parameters of each attitude (b_1–b_3 of equation (2)). If homogeneity prevails, if every citizen relies on the same considerations similarly, then the gaps between parameters should be small, even nonexistent. In contrast, if there are important interpersonal differences in decision making, then large parameter gaps should be encountered. Since logistic coefficients use a noninterpretable scale, I rely on first differences—the gain in the probability of voting for X produced by a variable as it moves from one end of its scale to the opposite end. Each first difference was calculated as the difference between two predicted values: one where the manipulated variable is set at its lowest level and all other variables remain unchanged and another where the manipulated variable is set at its highest level and all other variables are unchanged. To assure that all forms of interpersonal differences in parameter strength are captured by the measure, I estimate the gaps between all group pairings. For instance, to measure the variation in the impact of party identification on vote choice, I tally the gaps in party identification (PID) first differences between the low and medium information groups, between the low and high, and between the medium and high. The absolute values of the gaps were then summed for all independent variables in each model. Finally, in order to compare the gaps across different campaign period samples, I adjust for variation in the mean of the dependent variable by dividing each model's total gaps by the period's average vote share.[10]

Second, I look at the improvement in model fit provided by the interactive model (equation (2)) over the basic homogeneous model (equation (1)). There should be a relationship between the level of heterogeneity in a model and the power of the homogeneous explanatory model (where the impact of each independent variable is constrained to be uniform). Ceteris paribus, high heterogeneity should lead to low model fit. An average parameter that does not accurately reflect the behavior of two different groups should lead to inefficient predictions for both groups. Of course, a heterogeneity-sensitive specification would correct for the interpersonal variation and generate more accurate predictions. So, the greater the differences in decision rules, the larger the model improvement of the interactive setup should be over the homogeneous specification. A log-likelihood ratio test is employed to ascertain the significance of the contribution of the information interactive terms. To compare across different campaign period samples, the standardized difference in log-likelihood is also reported (where each log-likelihood is divided by the number of cases and the mean of the dependent variable).

The third analysis concerns diversity in decision outcome. It determines whether individuals' actual voting preferences coincide with the preferences they would have possessed had they been fully informed. Following Bartels's lead (1996), high information behavior is applied to the entire population on the grounds of similar sociodemographic variables only. Two statistics are produced for each model: an individual and an aggregate deviation from informed opinions. Individual and aggregate deviations are operationalized as the difference between each respondent's predicted value from the complete sociodemographic model (equation (3)) and the corresponding predicted value computed from the high information set of coefficients (b_3 of equation (3)). Instead of calculating deviations from a hypothetical condition where all the electorate is perfectly informed (Bartels 1996), I estimate deviations from a hypothetical situation where everybody behaves as the top third of the information distribution, a less dramatic but more plausible scenario. An average deviation (the mean of all absolute deviations) exposes the average individual difference in behavior attributable to low information, while an aggregate deviation (the mean of all signed deviations) reveals the departure of the entire electorate's actual preference from the hypothetical high information preference. Since information is a valuable resource that "assists citizens in discerning their individual and group interests, in connecting their interests to broader notions of the public good, and in effectively expressing these views through political participation," then informed opinions constitute more enlightened opinions (Delli Carpini and Keeter 1996, 1; Bartels 1996; Fishkin 1991, 1997; Luskin,

Fishkin, and Jowell 2002). Consequently, individual and aggregate deviations from informed opinions can be considered individual errors and aggregate biases attributable to low information.

There are problems with comparing people based only on their sociodemographic characteristics. Two individuals with similar sociodemographic profiles could still have different priorities and different interests. However, using attitudes would be even more problematic. As Bartels notes, attitudes "may themselves be affected by levels of political information, rendering problematic any imputation of vote choices from more informed people to less informed people with the same measured attitudes. By contrast, since demographic and social characteristics . . . are essentially fixed, they provide a firmer base for imputing the hypothetical 'fully informed' voter choices of less informed people from the observed choices of more informed people with similar characteristics" (1996, 208).

The analyses rely on the Canadian Election Studies of the 1988, 1993, and 1997 federal elections. Each of these is a two-wave panel study: one campaign rolling cross-section telephone interview and one postelection telephone reinterview. Since the analysis requires the production of several voting models, identical in structure, each spanning a distinct portion of the campaign, the campaign rolling cross-section surveys are essentially treated as a series of three cross-sectional surveys covering different periods of the campaign. Because each day's sample is a separate replicate, this is totally justified. Each campaign was simply divided into three equal portions.[11] I can therefore compare the levels of heterogeneity present at four points in time: in each third of the campaigns and in the postelection data.

The models contain a wide range of independent variables: partisan identification and leader evaluations, along with an election-specific set of political values and issue positions.[12] Based on the variables used by the co-investigators of the Canadian Election Studies (Johnston et al. 1992, 1996a; Nevitte et al. 2000), these lists were limited to items measured during the campaign in order to avoid postelectoral rationalization. Besides PID and leader ratings, the 1988 set includes the free trade agreement, feelings toward the French, ties with the United States, the power of unions, the level of taxation and services, the Meech Lake constitutional agreement, government honesty, immigration, and abortion. The 1993 models contain feelings toward racial minorities, feelings toward the French, moral traditionalism, the power of unions, continentalism, macroeconomic policy, and the welfare state. The 1997 set incorporates regional alienation, feelings toward Quebec, feelings toward racial minorities, political cynicism, moral traditionalism, tax cuts, deficit reduction, government job creation, young offenders, and immigration. The array of independent variables will allow various forms of interpersonal variation in parameter strength to shine through. The list of sociodemographic characteristics is constant across models: region, gender, age, ethnic background, marital status, religion, education, income, union membership, employment status, and public sector employment.

The central concept, political information, is operationalized by a different indicator in each data set. I sought measures of general factual knowledge about politics (Luskin 1987; Fiske, Lau, and Smith 1990; Zaller 1990; Delli Carpini and Keeter 1993). The 1988 election models rely on a seven-item index of knowledge of party placements and local candidates.[13] For 1993, a six-item index of awareness of the major parties' main election stands is employed.[14] For 1997, I use a seven-item index of information about four general facts and three party campaign promises.[15] From each index, a dummy variable was created for each third of the resulting distributions (low, medium, and high information). These three dummy variables interact with all attitudes in equation (2) and all sociodemographic variables in equation (3).

Finally it should be noted that the analyses of 1993 and 1997 are limited to the non-Quebec sample.[16]

The Results

Heterogeneity in Decision Making

First tackled is movement of heterogeneity in process during campaigns. Table 1 reports the results of both equation (1) (homogeneous model) and equation (2) (heterogeneity in decision making model) at each time point for one of the models: support for the incumbent Liberal Party in our most recent data set (1997). First differences based on the logistic regressions are presented. Each first difference indicates the actual effect of the independent variable on that information subgroup's vote choice. There is no need to take into account the other parameters (as is the case when interactive terms are coupled with main effects). When the three first differences of an attitude are identical, then that variable has the same impact among all levels of information.

Table 1 contains plenty of examples that the presumption of homogeneity often leads to inaccurate explanatory models that, by estimating the behavior of the "average" citizen, systematically misconceive the behavior of informed and uninformed citizens. Most subgroups' parameters are weaker, stronger, or contrary to the parameters of the conventional homogeneous estimation. And many differences between information subgroups are statistically significant.[17] In some cases, the relationships simply vary linearly in strength across the groups. For instance, in the first portion of the campaign, the impact of party identification increases as information climbs: the effect is strongest among the more informed and weakest among the less informed.[18] But some variables suffer from even greater inconsistency, and the averaging effect of homogeneous parameters can completely mask the subgroups' true relationships. If two correlations of similar strength work in opposite directions, one positive and one negative, then the homogeneous parameter estimate can overestimate the relationship of some voters, underestimate the relationship of other voters, and effectively apply to very few individuals. Even worse, the average parameter can lead to the conclusion that there is no relationship at all. For instance, in the first third of the campaign (period 1), regional alienation, feelings toward Quebec, and feelings toward racial minorities all have contrary effects among some groups that are obscured by the homogeneous design. Attitudes toward minorities are strongly and positively related to the choice of the less informed (.29) but slightly negatively correlated to the decision of the medium and high information subgroups (.03, .06). This variable's homogeneous parameter cancels out these reverse patterns and delivers a barely positive and not statistically significant effect (.02).

Is there any change in the level of heterogeneity in decision making over the campaign? There are large parameter differences at each time point. So the information subgroups clearly possess different structures of vote determinants both at the beginning and the end of the campaign, indicating that the campaign did not create heterogeneity out of thin air. There is support for convergence (for example, regional alienation), divergence (for example, tax cuts), and stability (for example, immigration). The differences in reliance on regional alienation were substantially reduced during the course of the campaign. In contrast, the tax cut issue displays

TABLE 1. Homogeneous and Heterogeneous Models, 1997 Liberal Support (first differences of logistic coefficients)

		Homogeneous Models				Heterogeneous Models			
		Period 1	Period 2	Period 3	Vote	Info.	Period 1	Period 2	Period 3	Vote
Party identification		.52***	.40***	.48***	.34***	Low	.33***	.47***	.49***	.37***
						Med	.51***	.30***	.50***	.24***
						High	.60***	.27***	.24***	.29***
Leader evaluation		.61***	.56***	.42***	.38***	Low	.37***	.45***	.35***	.42***
						Med	.65***	.72***	.24**	.36***
						High	.58***	.49***	.64***	.52***
Regional alienation		−.02	−.06	−.06	−.03	Low	.11	−.10	−.13	−.06
						Med	−.10*	−.18***	−.07	−.02
						High	.08	.00	.03	−.04
Feeling for Quebec		−.07	−.03	.04	.04	Low	.01	−.14*	.14	−.03
						Med	−.05	−.09	−.07	.10**
						High	−.14*	.13	.05	.02
Feeling for minorities		.02	.04	−.02	.05	Low	.29***	.21**	−.14*	.11
						Med	−.03	−.09	.08	−.01
						High	−.06	.02	.02	.07
Cynicism		−.12	−.29***	−.12*	−.18***	Low	−.15	−.30***	−.15	−.16**
						Med	−.13	−.24**	.06	−.15**
						High	−.13	−.11	−.25**	−.09

Moral traditionalism	.02	.04	.02	−.03	Low	.09	−.02	.05	−.04
					Med	−.02	−.03	.01	−.04
					High	−.03	.14*	−.06	−.02
Tax cuts	−.14***	−.06	−.07	−.04	Low	−.18**	−.04	.02	.11*
					Med	−.05	−.06	−.21***	−.10*
					High	−.28**	−.03	−.04	−.06
Deficit reduction	.00	.06	.06	.09***	Low	−.01	−.01	−.16**	−.04
					Med	−.07	.13	.04	.13**
					High	.12	.06	.36***	.20***
Government job creation	.07	−.02	−.04	−.02	Low	.04	−.05	−.05	−.20***
					Med	−.04	.09	−.05	.11
					High	.26	−.06	−.06	−.03
Tough with young offenders	.05*	.06**	−.01	.05**	Low	.00	−.01	−.02	.02
					Med	.06	.06	−.03	.10***
					High	.12	.10*	.08	.00
More immigration	.04	.00	.02	.00	Low	−.01	.05	.16*	−.05
					Med	.09	.01	−.03	.00
					High	.00	−.02	.03	.07
Number of cases	728	855	889	1,991		728	855	889	1,991
Log-likelihood	560.6	639.7	731.4	1,784.7		524.5	598.9	661.6	1,742.6
Total parameter gaps						4.7	4.1	5.4	3.2

Note. Constant and sociodemographic controls not reported.
***p < .01   **p < .05   *p < .1

greater interpersonal differences in parameter strength after the election than earlier in the campaign. Finally, immigration was marked by similar amounts of heterogeneity both in period 1 and after the election. All in all, however, the main story seems to be one of modest convergence. An eyeball estimate suggests that about half of the variables experience convergence and close to half of the others encounter stability. Rare are the occurrences where parameter diversity is actually accentuated by the progress of the campaign.

To examine this evidence more systematically for all decision models, the analysis only concentrates on summary results of the three empirical tests introduced earlier. Table 2 reports the total gaps in first differences for all models.[19] If information is irrelevant for decisional processes, if voting structures are homogeneous, the gaps in parameter strength should exhibit very small values. Inversely, the presence of heterogeneity should be marked by gaps of significant size. Although this is a crude summary measure, it corroborates the subjective interpretation of table 1. The total of all parameter gaps for 1997 Liberal support and the more appropriate measure that controls for size of the vote share also manifest a decrease in the level of heterogeneity. The postelection measure is lower than at any point in the campaign. The other decisions tend to exhibit a similar pattern: heterogeneity exists early and late but declines as the campaign unfolds. As the average adjusted gaps illustrate (at the bottom of the table), there are differences between the less, the moderately, and the more informed in the strength of decision determinants throughout the campaign, and movement in the level of heterogeneity is generally toward convergence. Thus, the campaign diminished, though it did not eradicate, the gaps in decision rules between information groups.

Sometimes, the decrease is not linear. For instance, Liberal support in 1993 shows no decrease in adjusted gaps during the first three periods. A real drop in heterogeneity only occurs in the postelection data. In some cases, there are large jumps in heterogeneity during certain periods of the campaign. Notably, Liberal support in 1997 displays a leap in parameter gaps during the third period. But, ultimately, in all cases except for 1993 Conservative support, the magnitude of diversity in decision rules is lower after the election than at any other point. I will return to this issue of nonincremental convergence in the next section.

Next, I examine movement during the campaigns in the relevance of heterogeneity in decision making by analyzing the model fit improvement

TABLE 2. Dynamics of Total and Adjusted Gaps in Parameter Strength during Campaigns

	Campaign Vote Intentions			Postelection Reported Vote
	First Third	Second Third	Last Third	
1988 Conservative support				
Total gaps	3.5	2.9	3.9	2.1
Adjusted gaps	8.9	8.8	10.5	5.0
1988 Liberal support				
Total gaps	5.2	2.8	3.4	2.1
Adjusted gaps	27.8	9.4	11.8	8.5
1988 NDP support				
Total gaps	3.6	3.2	2.5	1.2
Adjusted gaps	19.5	17.8	15.3	7.3
1993 Conservative support				
Total gaps	4.1	3.3	3.2	2.6
Adjusted gaps	15.5	16.3	17.8	20.6
1993 Liberal support				
Total gaps	2.8	3.2	3.8	2.1
Adjusted gaps	7.9	8.2	9.8	5.2
1993 NDP support				
Total gaps	3.3	7.1	2.5	1.9
Adjusted gaps	41.6	88.3	38.8	27.2
1993 Reform support				
Total gaps	4.0	4.1	2.8	2.4
Adjusted gaps	31.2	23.0	11.2	10.4
1997 Conservative support				
Total gaps	6.7	4.9	5.3	3.3
Adjusted gaps	43.0	29.8	32.8	24.5
1997 Liberal support				
Total gaps	4.7	4.1	5.4	3.2
Adjusted gaps	12.8	12.7	16.0	10.4
1997 NDP support				
Total gaps	5.1	4.6	4.1	2.7
Adjusted gaps	46.4	44.7	38.0	26.0
1997 Reform support				
Total gaps	4.9	5.0	4.0	3.7
Adjusted gaps	33.2	27.9	20.3	16.0
Average total gaps	4.3	4.1	3.7	2.5
Average adjusted gaps	26.2	26.1	20.2	14.7

provided by the interactive model (equation (2)) over the basic model where all independent variables have a homogeneous impact for all citizens (equation (1)). Table 3 reports the difference in log-likelihood of each decision's two models (the homogeneous and the heterogeneous) for each period of the campaigns. The statistical significance of the differences was obtained from log-likelihood ratio tests. The table also presents the adjusted measure that permits comparison of each model across the four periods. The adjusted statistic is the difference between log-likelihoods that were divided by the average vote share and the number of cases of the period.

These results confirm the conclusions of the preceding test: convergence in voting decision rules. As campaigns proceed, the usefulness of political information's interactions to explain individual political behavior declines in all models. Significant differences in model fit are present within each period, but the standardized differences tend to get smaller over time (see the average adjusted differences at the bottom of the table).

The decline is not always steady and uniform. Again, there is stability or even slight increases in heterogeneity for certain models during the first three periods of the campaign. For example, 1997 Liberal and New Democratic Party (NDP) support shows a peak in model fit improvement during the third period of the campaign. But, again, the smallest level of heterogeneity is found after the election among all models' adjusted difference.

Heterogeneity in Decision Outcome

Campaigns produce decline in the level of heterogeneity in the decision-making process, as indicated by the movement in parameter gaps and model fit improvement. Does the level of heterogeneity in decision outcome move as well during campaigns? Does the relative homogenization of decision rules translate into smaller discrepancies from informed opinions? Does campaign learning and deliberation contribute to reduce the individual error and collective biases in voting preferences? Table 4 reports the individual and aggregate deviations from high information behavior for all models at each point of the campaigns. Here, in keeping with the logic of knowledge gap analyses and allowing campaign dynamics to have meaningful influences, actual behavior is compared to informed behavior of the same period (rather than the alternative: postelection informed behavior). Our focus is to ascertain whether the less informed are able to catch up to the more knowledgeable and improve their ability to express

TABLE 3. Dynamics of Model Improvement by the Heterogeneous Specification during Campaigns

	Campaign Vote Intentions			Postelection Reported Vote
	First Third	Second Third	Last Third	
1988 Conservative support				
Difference in log-likelihood	27.4***	24.9***	39.4***	45.5***
Adjusted difference	8.7	8.1	11.1	4.3
1988 Liberal support				
Difference in log-likelihood	57.5***	27.1***	31***	34.3***
Adjusted difference	38.1	9.5	11.3	5.3
1988 NDP support				
Difference in log-likelihood	27.3***	23.2***	19.4**	13.9
Adjusted difference	18	13.7	12.7	3.3
1993 Conservative support				
Difference in log-likelihood	29***	27.4***	31.3***	28.6***
Adjusted difference	16.6	18.1	22.5	10.4
1993 Liberal support				
Difference in log-likelihood	24.7***	27***	32.4***	27***
Adjusted difference	10.8	9.4	10.7	3.1
1993 NDP support				
Difference in log-likelihood	27.8***	42.8***	24.6***	20.9***
Adjusted difference	53.5	71.4	49.2	13.8
1993 Reform support				
Difference in log-likelihood	23.5***	28.8***	16.1**	20.3***
Adjusted difference	27.8	21.5	8.4	4.1
1997 Conservative support				
Difference in log-likelihood	59.9***	57.2***	52.6***	45.1***
Adjusted difference	51.2	41.2	35.3	16.7
1997 Liberal support				
Difference in log-likelihood	36.1***	40.8***	69.8***	42.2***
Adjusted difference	13	14.8	22.4	6.7
1997 NDP support				
Difference in log-likelihood	40***	42.4***	52.4***	31.2***
Adjusted difference	48.2	48.8	53.5	14.9
1997 Reform support				
Difference in log-likelihood	40.8***	37.7***	51.9***	65.3***
Adjusted difference	36.7	25	28.5	13.9
Average difference	35.8	34.5	38.3	34.0
Average adjusted difference	29.3	25.6	24.2	8.8

Note: Statistical significance of difference based on log-likelihood ratio test.
***$p < .01$ **$p < .05$ *$p < .1$

their underlying interests. Evidence based on comparison with the postelection informed opinions would not directly speak to such concerns. Any observed weakening of deviations from postelection informed behavior could have been due to the most informed driving improvement in the quality of decisions and the less informed falling even further behind. Nevertheless, both reference points yield very similar dynamics of individual and aggregate deviations.

Individual deviations, the summary indicator of individual differences between actual and informed behavior, have a propensity to decrease in all campaigns. Uninformed people tend to match the position of similar informed people more effectively as time goes on. For instance, at the beginning of the 1988 campaign, being more informed changed each respondent's probability of voting for the incumbent Conservative Party by an average of over 16 percentage points.[20] After the campaign, that value had been cut in half. The trend of average individual deviations at the bottom of the table points to an overall decline of individual deviations as the election draws nearer. These data do not actually say people are getting to the right position with regards to their predispositions and beliefs. But, if we assume that informed preferences are more accurate, then the declining individual deviations from high information are indicating that voters are making, on average, more enlightened choices as campaigns proceed.

In some cases, again, the evidence does not exhibit a steady reduction in heterogeneity. The individual deviations experience sudden increases among the models of 1993 Liberal, 1997 NDP, and 1997 Reform support during the second or third campaign period. However, among each model, the postelection individual deviation is always lower than at any other moment.

The aggregate deviations, also in table 4, speak of the collective biases of actual preferences with respect to hypothetical high information preferences. For instance, the Conservative score of 4.5 for the first third of the 1988 campaign signifies that the actual level of support for this party (50.8 percent) was 4.5 percentage points higher than it would have been in a hypothetical outcome where all voters behave like similar individuals with high levels of information (46.3 percent). If we assume that informed behavior is more consistent with people's latent interests, then hypothetical high information preference could be labeled the more enlightened collective preference.

The results show that, in any election, some political parties are

TABLE 4. Dynamics of Individual and Aggregate Deviations from Informed Preferences during Campaigns

	Campaign Vote Intentions			Postelection Reported Vote
	First Third	Second Third	Last Third	
1988 Conservative support				
Individual deviation	16.5	13.7	10.8	7.7
Aggregate deviation	4.5	7.3	−5.2	3.7
1988 Liberal support				
Individual deviation	14.2	14.6	12.7	7.2
Aggregate deviation	0.7	−3.1	7.0	−0.4
1988 NDP support				
Individual deviation	11.3	11.2	8.4	6.1
Aggregate deviation	−5.2	−4.2	−1.9	−3.3
1993 Conservative support				
Individual deviation	17.5	12.7	9.3	7.3
Aggregate deviation	−3.4	−5.1	1.2	−4.5
1993 Liberal support				
Individual deviation	18.7	13.3	17.1	10.0
Aggregate deviation	5.7	0.8	−2.7	3.5
1993 NDP support				
Individual deviation	12.3	8.7	8.9	5.6
Aggregate deviation	−2.8	4.4	1.2	0.0
1993 Reform support				
Individual deviation	13.7	13.3	11.7	7.6
Aggregate deviation	0.5	−0.1	0.3	1.1
1997 Conservative support				
Individual deviation	13.3	12.4	9.2	4.8
Aggregate deviation	4.4	0.6	3.8	−0.3
1997 Liberal support				
Individual deviation	16.5	16.5	11.9	10.5
Aggregate deviation	−1.8	6.1	4.4	5.7
1997 NDP support				
Individual deviation	9.4	9.5	11.7	5.5
Aggregate deviation	−1.5	−0.5	−4.7	−2.0
1997 Reform support				
Individual deviation	9.2	10.8	11.2	7.9
Aggregate deviation	−1.1	−6.1	−3.5	−3.4
Average individual deviation	13.9	12.4	11.2	7.3
Average absolute aggregate deviation	2.9	3.5	3.3	2.5

advantaged by the public's lack of information, while others are disadvantaged. These parties vary from one election to another. And, most important, the collective biases are relatively consistent over the course of the campaigns.

In 1988, the aggregate deviations of the incumbent party, the Conservatives, are positive in most periods. That party's actual support is greater than the support of a more informed electorate. The positive bias is slightly smaller in the postelection data (3.7 percentage points), but it is essentially the same size as when the campaign started. The incumbent's gains from low information were at the expense of the NDP. The left-of-center party that finished third in the race was systematically getting less support than the enlightened preferences. On Election Day, it obtained 3.3 percentage points fewer than what an informed citizenry would have conferred. The Liberal model exhibits inconsistent aggregate deviations during the campaign. But it concluded with a practically nil aggregate deviation: authentic election preferences for the Liberals coincide with the hypothetical high information preferences.

In 1993, the party that benefited from low knowledge five years earlier—the Conservatives—now had an unpopular incumbent whose fortunes dwindled dramatically during the campaign; it lost over half its vote share and the election (Johnston et al. 1992). Throughout these events, the uninformed were supporting the party less than they would have had they been informed. Despite the great volatility in vote intentions during the campaign, low knowledge consistently led people to punish the Conservatives more than the knowledgeable in three periods out of four. They ended up with 4.5 percentage points below what they would have received under high information. It was the Liberals, who had established themselves as the government in waiting, that benefited. Ultimately, they garnered 3.5 percentage points more than the informed hypothetical scenario. Such a positive deviation was already evident in the first third of the campaign. The NDP and Reform aggregate deviations in the reported vote are basically nonexistent. Some movement toward convergence may have taken place with the NDP, but not with the Reform Party.

Had the population been more informed in 1997, the Liberal Party would have won fewer votes than it did in reality (5.7 percentage points less). The incumbent governing party reaped the rewards of low information to the detriment of the two small off-center parties (left-wing NDP and right-wing Reform). Both of these parties would have fared better under high information. They would have captured an extra 2 and 3.4 percentage points, respectively. There is no clear indication that the aggregate deviations significantly decreased during this campaign. Throughout the campaign periods, actual support for these parties does not correspond to their hypothetical support under high information.

Incumbency seems to help take advantage of the public's lack of information, but only if the government is in good standing. In fact, the positive aggregate biases of uninformed electorates appear to coincide with a bandwagon conception rather than a blind incumbency advantage.[21] Negative biases tend to hurt the small parties.

These aggregate deviations reveal quite large departures of the actual election outcomes from the hypothetical high information outcomes. But they do not signal that "illegitimate" election results have occurred. None of the hypothetical scenarios would have meant a reversal of the outcome. With a more informed electorate, the same government would have been elected in each election. Even the rankings of parties would have remained the same in each case. However, their potential significance for the balance of power and for close races should not be underestimated.

More to the point, the evidence does not substantiate the claim that campaigns allow aggregation to perform more effectively in canceling individual errors and generating the fully informed preferences. Each model's results along with the summary average absolute aggregate deviations do not display a clear decline pattern. In contrast with the evolution of individual deviations, the collective biases in electoral preferences do not dwindle importantly during campaigns.

Discussion

Although the trend toward the reduction of heterogeneity in decision making during campaigns is clear, many party models exhibit a sudden surge in interpersonal diversity at one point or another. These bumps appear simultaneously in parameter gaps and model improvement statistics (tables 2 and 3). While this simultaneity provides validation that the indicators tend to measure the same basic phenomenon, it also suggests that these bumps are meaningful and deserve an explanation.

Most notably, we see the jumps in heterogeneity among 1988 Conservative and Liberal support during the last third of the campaign; among the Conservatives, Liberals, and NDP during the second and third periods of 1993; and among Conservative and Liberal support in the last portion of the 1997 campaign. Such instances demonstrate that campaigns often do not bring about a steady and uniform decline in heterogeneity. How can we account for the nonincremental nature of the decrease of interpersonal diversity in these cases?

One thing is certain: these temporary surges in heterogeneity do not happen during flat periods of the campaigns. They generally coincide with instances of great volatility in vote intentions (see campaign dynamics in Johnston et al. 1992, 1996a; Nevitte et al. 2000). However, it is not just a question of increased variance in the dependent variable, since the surges also appear in the measures that control for the size of the vote share. Moreover, some jumps in heterogeneity take place while a party is losing support. One could argue that levels of heterogeneity temporarily escalate when there is an intense period of conversion and reevaluation of voting intentions among numerous parties, when uncertainty, doubt, and possibly anxiety seize citizens. During such times of heightened attention and sensitivity, the correlates of vote choice could become scrambled by various stimuli. I cannot verify the validity of this speculation with the present evidence.

Another puzzle concerns the postelection data. In all tables, heterogeneity measures fall sharply when the reported vote is the dependent variable. Why are the post results so different from those of the end of the campaign? Could it be post hoc rationalization (Rahn, Krosnick, and Breuning 1994); that is, people adjust their answers to the postelection wave questions about the vote correlates to match how they marked their ballot? Because all independent variables were captured in the campaign wave, this account is not viable. Could it be panel attrition (Bartels 2000); that is, those who choose to take part in the second interview are different (they have a more similar set of decision correlates) from those who don't? Actually, nonpanel participants in the campaign models are rare, and analyses limited to panel participants show the same heterogeneity dynamics. Could it be panel conditioning (Bartels 2000); that is, panel participants were influenced by the fact that they responded to an election survey to adopt a more homogeneous structure of vote correlates? Could it be that postelection reported vote is fraught with misreporting (due to fading memory, the wish to support a winner, or the intervention of events since the vote took place) and that this misreporting is somehow correlated to initial heterogeneity? Or could a true reduction of interpersonal diversity in decision making really have occurred between the last third of the campaign and Election Day? Although unlikely, the last three accounts are possible. There is no way of determining with the data used here.

Thus, the exact source of the late plunge in interpersonal diversity in behavior remains ambiguous. Nevertheless, the conclusions of this study hold regardless of whether the postelection data are reliable, since the decline in heterogeneity is apparent within the campaign data.

Conclusions

The analysis reveals that all three campaigns significantly reduced the level of heterogeneity among the electorate but that considerable amounts of interpersonal diversity still subsist after the campaigns. As campaigns proceed, the discrepancies in decision rules between information groups diminish; the usefulness of a heterogeneity-sensitive specification in explaining individual voting behavior declines; and the ability of uninformed voters to make decisions analogous to those of informed citizens with similar sociodemographic profiles increases. On most counts, the evidence supports the notion that campaigns matter and that they do so by curtailing, but not eradicating, differences between voters with contrasting levels of political information. Only the evidence about aggregate deviations does not follow the same story; the collective biases in preferences are essentially unaffected by the unfolding of campaigns.

The significant reduction in individual deviations from informed opinions highlights the critical importance of the democratic process. Individuals would not have made the same choices had they not experienced these campaigns; they would have made more "erroneous" choices. Therefore, campaigns promote the expression of more enlightened preferences.

How do political campaigns generate these declining trends of heterogeneity? Obviously, patterns of learning and priming about contenders and issues could allow citizens to cut through the complex and conflicting rhetoric, to figure out what the election and the competing options are about, to connect each option to their own preferences and predispositions, to decide in similar ways, and to gradually improve the quality of their decisions.

Alternatively, campaigns may simply be about overcoming voter apathy and inattentiveness and activating predispositions. Early on, people may simply answer survey questionnaires indifferently and carelessly, thereby introducing errors in responses (attitudes and intentions), errors that affect the relationships between independent and dependent variables, and the precision of explanatory models. As the deadline for decision approaches and as parties and candidates increase their activity, citizens may become more seriously involved in the campaign, and their responses and behavior may accordingly appear more thoughtful and more similar.

Although the evidence I gathered cannot totally disconfirm either of these explanations, it seems to conform with a "campaigns matter because they activate certain predispositions and not others and they provide some kinds of information and not others" approach rather than a "campaigns matter only in activating predispositions" approach. Examination of all the models' parameters (not reported here) suggests that all voters tend to move toward a particular structure of vote choice determinants (some less efficiently than others) rather than one or two information groups catching up to other groups that had already figured things out. The decline in heterogeneity therefore seems to follow the particular and unique dynamics of campaign events and coverage rather than simply falling in line with an unavoidable underlying pattern or an inexorable simplification of things, as the choice becomes imminent, that operates regardless of the length of the campaign. Furthermore, the convergence is more consistent with the expectations drawn from mass media "mainstreaming" than those extrapolated from the widening knowledge gap literature or the agenda-setting/framing/priming research.

APPENDIX: Variables in the Models

The 1988, 1993, and 1997 Canadian Election Studies questionnaires and data can be obtained from the Canadian Election Study (www.ces-eec.umontreal.ca) and from the Inter-university Consortium for Political and Social Research (www.icpsr.umich.edu).

1988

Political information (h2b, h2c, h2d, h4b, h4c, h4d, xm2, xm3, xm4); campaign vote intentions (b1, b2, b3); reported vote (xb1, xb2); leader evaluations (d1a, d1b, d1c, d2a, d2b, d2c); party identification (i1, i2); free trade agreement (l2); Meech Lake constitutional agreement (14a); government honesty (j1); feelings toward French (h1a); ties with United States (h2a); power of unions (h3); level of taxation and services (h4a); immigration (l3); abortion (16a); region (province); gender (rsex); age (n1); ethnicity (n15);

marital status (n2); religion (n11); education (n3); income (n19); union membership (n9); retired (n5); public sector employment (n5).

1993

Political information (pese17a, pese18a, pese19a, pese20a, cpsg3a1, cpsg31b); campaign vote intentions (cpsa3, cpsa4); reported vote (pesa4); leader evaluations (d2a, d2b, d2c, d2d); party identification (cpsm1, cpsm2); feelings toward racial minorities (cpsk3a); feelings toward French (antf_f1a); moral traditionalism (cpsg6a, cpsg6b, cpsg6c, cpsg7a, cpsg7b, cpsg7e); power of unions (cpsk1a); continentalism (cpsf2a, cpsl1, cpsl3); macroeconomic policy (cps16a, cps19a, cps19b); welfare state (cps15a, cps15b, cps17b, cps17d, cps17e); region (cpsprov); gender (cpsrgen); age (cpsage); ethnicity (cpso13, refn13); marital status (cpso2); religion (cpso9); education (cpso3, refn2); income (cpso18, cpso18a); union membership (refn, cpsjob6); retired (cpsjob1); public sector employment (cpsjob1, cpsjob5).

1997

Political information (cps16, cpsf13, cpsf14, cpsf15, cpsl11, cpsl12, cpsl13); campaign vote intentions (cpsa4); reported vote (pesa4); leader evaluations (cpsd1a, cpsd1b, cpsd1c, cpsd1d, cpsdr1, cpsdr2, cpsdr3, cpdsr4); party identification (cpsk1, cpsk2); regional alienation (cpsj12); feelings toward Quebec (cpse3a, cpsj3); feelings toward racial minorities (cpsf1, cpsj9, cpsj10); political cynicism (cpsb10d, cpsb10e, cpsb10a); moral traditionalism (cpsf2, cpsf3); tax cuts (cpsa2d); deficit reduction (cpsa2b, cpsf5, cpsf8); government job creation (cpsf6, cpsf4, cpsa2c); young offenders (cpsj21); immigration (cpsj18); region (province); gender (cpsrgen); age (cpsage); ethnicity (cpsm13); marital status (cpsm2); religion (cpsm10); education (cpsm3); income (cpsm16a); union membership (cpsm9); retired (cpsm4); public sector employment (cpsm4, cpsm7).

NOTES

This study benefited from the financial support of the Fonds Québécois de la Recherche sur la Société et la Culture (FQRSC) and the Social Sciences and Humanities Research Council of Canada (SSHRC). I thank Michael Alvarez, André Blais, Henry Brady, Larry Bartels, Richard Jenkins, Richard Johnston, Simon McDougall, Paul Sniderman, and Stuart Soroka for their valuable comments and suggestions. The author is solely responsible for errors of analysis or interpretation.

1. While heterogeneity in decision making is generally interpreted as diversity

in decisional processes, it could also result from interpersonal differences in the levels of measurement error, in the susceptibility to survey effects (wording, ordering, and so forth), in the propensity to rationalize, and in the capacity to recall accurate information. However, it is beyond the scope of this essay to examine such alternative explanations. I will therefore accept, for the purpose of this study, the common interpretation and treat process heterogeneity in voting models as an indication of divergent decision rules.

2. Some dissenting opinions exist. For instance, Wendy Rahn and her colleagues argue that "the rich and often redundant flow of political information in a presidential election year, combined with the relative simplicity of a choice between two presidential candidates, leads to relatively similar assessment and decisional processes for most individuals" (Rahn et al. 1990, 137). Their model of candidate appraisal showed only a few signs of heterogeneity: partisanship had a slightly greater impact on the decision of the less sophisticated, while ideology had a slightly greater impact for the more sophisticated. Goren (2004) also found that information does not systematically enhance the impact of domain-specific beliefs and values on policy preferences.

3. Although the margins of victory would have been different, no winner would have lost under full information in the six presidential elections (1972–92) examined by Bartels.

4. This conjecture about the relationship between heterogeneity in process and heterogeneity in outcome will receive some credence if the analyses conducted herein show that the campaign dynamics of both types of heterogeneity follow the same pattern.

5. In the other major study of heterogeneity (Sniderman, Brody, and Tetlock 1991), the temporal location of the heterogeneity detected in voting models is not stipulated.

6. Some research shows that the effects of agenda setting and priming are greater among the least informed or the least educated (Iyengar et al. 1984; Iyengar and Kinder 1987; Krosnick and Kinder 1990). However, these results may be due to the fact that exposure and attention to media content were not controlled (Krosnick and Brannon 1993; Miller and Krosnick 2000).

7. Notable examples of this practice include Sniderman, Brody, and Tetlock 1991 and Johnston et al. 1996b.

8. Two of the three dummy variables are included to capture the direct effect of information on vote choice.

9. In fact, the estimates of this interactive design are almost equivalent to those produced by three separate estimations where the sample is split according to the three dummies. Slight differences are due to the single constant and the direct effects of information in the interactive design.

10. Otherwise, change in the variance of the dependent variable between periods could artificially modify the level of heterogeneity.

11. For the 1988 models: October 4–19; October 20–November 4; November 5–20. For the 1993 models: September 10–24; September 25–October 9; October 10–24. For the 1997 models: April 27–May 8; May 9–20; May 21–June 1.

12. All variables and original data sources are found in the appendix.

13. That is, the parties' relative positions regarding ties with the United States, the parties' relative positions concerning the level of taxation and services, the local Conservative candidate, the local Liberal candidate, and the local NDP candidate.

14. That is, the party that promised to spend more on public works (Liberal), the party that promised to eliminate the deficit in three years (Reform), the party that promised to eliminate the deficit in five years (Conservative), the party that opposes NAFTA (NDP), the party that opposes the goods and services tax (GST) (Liberal/Reform), and the party that supports the GST (Conservative).

15. That is, the current president of the United States (Clinton), the current provincial premier, the first woman prime minister of Canada (Campbell), the current federal minister of finance (Martin), the party that promised to lower income tax by 10 percent (Conservative), the party that promised to cut unemployment in half by 2001 (NDP), and the party that is against distinct society status for Quebec (Reform).

16. That province would require separate analyses (Johnston et al. 1996a, 1996b; Nevitte et al. 2000; Blais et al. 2002). However, the number of Quebec cases cannot support the interactive specification on three campaign period subsamples.

17. The differences in parameter strength that are statistically significant are not reported here. These can be revealed by variants of equation (2), where one group's interactions are replaced by the regular variables.

18. Note that, in the latter portions of the campaign, the weight of party identification tends to be greater among the less knowledgeable.

19. Again this is the sum of the absolute values of the gaps in first differences between the low/medium, low/high, and medium/high information groups.

20. Since the most informed cannot move (they are the reference point for the simulations), this number is an underestimation of the true effect among the less informed.

21. On the notion of bandwagon, see Gallup and Rae 1940; Simon 1954; Bartels 1988; McAllister and Studlar 1991; Nadeau, Cloutier, and Guay 1993; Goidel and Shields 1994.

REFERENCES

Althaus, Scott L. 1998. "Information Effects in Collective Preferences." *American Political Science Review* 92:545–58.

Bartels, Larry. 1988. *Presidential Primaries and the Dynamics of Vote Choice*. Princeton: Princeton University Press.

———. 1992. "The Impact of Electioneering in the United States." In *Electioneering: A Comparative Study of Continuity and Change*, ed. D. Butler and A. Ranney. Oxford: Clarendon Press.

———. 1996. "Uninformed Votes: Information Effects in Presidential Elections." *American Journal of Political Science* 40:194–230.

———. 2000. "Panel Effects in the American National Election Studies." *Political Analysis* 8:1–20.

Berelson, Bernard R., Paul F. Lazarsfeld, and William N. McPhee. 1954. *Voting: A*

Study of Opinion Formation in a Presidential Campaign. Chicago: University of Chicago Press.

Blais, André, Elisabeth Gidengil, Richard Nadeau, and Neil Nevitte. 2002. *Anatomy of a Liberal Victory: Making Sense of the Vote in the 2000 Canadian Election.* Peterborough: Broadview Press.

Delli Carpini, Michael X., and Scott Keeter. 1993. "Measuring Political Knowledge: Putting First Things First." *American Journal of Political Science* 37:1179–206.

———. 1996. *What Americans Know about Politics and Why It Matters.* New Haven: Yale University Press.

Ettema, James S., James W. Brown, and Russell V. Luepker. 1983. "Knowledge Gap Effects in a Health Information Campaign." *Public Opinion Quarterly* 47:516–27.

Finkel, Steven E. 1993. "Reexamining the 'Minimal Effects' Model in Recent Presidential Campaigns." *Journal of Politics* 55:1–21.

Finkel, Steven E., and Peter R. Schrott. 1995. "Campaign Effects on Voter Choice in the German Election of 1990." *British Journal of Political Science* 25:349–77.

Fishkin, James S. 1991. *Democracy and Deliberation: New Directions for Democratic Reform.* New Haven: Yale University Press.

———. 1997. *The Voice of the People: Public Opinion and Democracy.* New Haven: Yale University Press.

Fiske, Susan, Richard Lau, and Richard Smith. 1990. "On the Varieties and Utilities of Political Expertise." *Social Cognition* 8:31–48.

Fournier, Patrick. 2000. "Heterogeneity in Political Decision-Making: The Nature, Sources, Extent, Dynamics, and Consequences of Interpersonal Differences in Coefficient Strength." PhD diss., University of British Columbia.

Franklin, Charles. 1991. "Eschewing Obfuscation? Campaigns and the Perceptions of U.S. Senate Incumbents." *American Political Science Review* 85:1193–214.

Gallup, George, and Saul Forbes Rae. 1940. "Is There a Bandwagon Vote?" *Public Opinion Quarterly* 4:244–49.

Gelman, Andrew, and Gary King. 1993. "Why Are American Presidential Election Campaign Polls So Variable When Votes Are So Predictable?" *British Journal of Political Science* 23:409–51.

Gerbner, George, Larry Gross, Michael Morgan, and Nancy Signorielli. 1994. "Growing Up with Television: The Cultivation Perspective." In *Media Effects: Advances in Theory and Research,* ed. J. Bryant and D. Zillmann, 17–41. Hillsdale, NJ: Lawrence Erlbaum Associates.

Goidel, Robert, and Todd Shields. 1994. "The Vanishing Marginals, the Bandwagon, and the Mass Media." *Journal of Politics* 56:802–10.

Goren, Paul. 2004. "Political Sophistication and Policy Reasoning: A Reconsideration." *American Journal of Political Science* 48:462–78.

Hill, David. 1985. "Viewer Characteristics and Agenda Setting by Television News." *Public Opinion Quarterly* 49:340–50.

Holbrook, Thomas M. 2002. "Presidential Campaigns and the Knowledge Gap." *Political Communication* 19:437–54.

Iyengar, Shanto, and Donald Kinder. 1987. *News That Matters.* Chicago: University of Chicago Press.

Iyengar, Shanto, Donald Kinder, Mark D. Peters, and Jon A. Krosnick. 1984. "The

Evening News and Presidential Evaluations." *Journal of Personality and Social Psychology* 46:778–87.
Johnston, Richard, André Blais, Henry E. Brady, Elisabeth Gidengil, and Neil Nevitte. 1996a. "The 1993 Canadian Election: Realignment, Dealignment, or Something Else?" Paper presented at the annual meeting of the American Political Science Association, San Francisco.
Johnston, Richard, André Blais, Elisabeth Gidengil, and Neil Nevitte. 1996b. *The Challenge of Direct Democracy: The 1992 Canadian Referendum.* Montreal: McGill-Queen's University Press.
Johnston, Richard, Henry Brady, André Blais, and Jean Crête. 1992. *Letting the People Decide: Dynamics of a Canadian Election.* Kingston: McGill-Queen's University Press.
Johnston, Richard, Michael G. Hagen, and Kathleen Hall Jamieson. 2004. *The 2000 Presidential Election and the Foundations of Party Politics.* Cambridge: Cambridge University Press.
Krause, George A. 1997. "Voters, Information Heterogeneity, and the Dynamics of Aggregate Economic Expectations." *American Journal of Political Science* 41:1170–200.
Krosnick, Jon A., and Laura A. Brannon. 1993. "The Impact of the Gulf War on the Ingredients of Presidential Evaluations: Multidimensional Effects of Political Involvement." *American Political Science Review* 87:963–75.
Krosnick, Jon A., and Donald R. Kinder. 1990. "Altering the Foundations of Popular Support for the President through Priming." *American Political Science Review* 84:497–512.
Kuklinski, James H., and Norman L. Hurley. 1994. "On Hearing and Interpreting Political Messages: A Cautionary Tale of Citizen Cue-Taking." *Journal of Politics* 56:729–51.
Kuklinski, James H., and Paul J. Quirk. 2000. "Reconsidering the Rational Public: Cognition, Heuristics, and Mass Opinion." In *Elements of Reason: Cognition, Choice, and the Bounds of Rationality,* ed. A. Lupia, M. D. McCubbins, and S. L. Popkin. New York: Cambridge University Press.
Kwak, Nojin. 1999. "Revisiting the Knowledge Gap Hypothesis: Education, Motivation, and Media Use." *Communication Research* 26:385–413.
Lahda, Krishna K. 1992. "The Condorcet Jury Theorem, Free Speech, and Correlated Votes." *American Journal of Political Science* 36:617–34.
Lazarsfeld, Paul F., Bernard R. Berelson, and Hazel Gaudet. 1944. *The People's Choice.* New York: Duell, Sloane, and Pierce.
Lupia, Arthur. 1994. "Shortcuts versus Encyclopedias: Information and Voting Behavior in California Insurance Reform Elections." *American Political Science Review* 88:63–76.
Luskin, Robert C. 1987. "Measuring Political Sophistication." *American Journal of Political Science* 31:856–99.
Luskin, Robert, James Fishkin, and Roger Jowell. 2002. "Considered Opinions." *British Journal of Political Science* 32:455–87.
MacKuen, Michael. 1984. "Exposure to Information, Belief Integration, and Individual Responsiveness to Agenda Change." *American Political Science Review* 78:399–419.

McAllister, Ian, and Donley Studlar. 1991. "Bandwagon, Underdog, or Projection? Opinion Polls and Electoral Choice in Britain, 1979–1987." *Journal of Politics* 53: 720–41.

McKelvey, Richard D., and Peter C. Ordeshook. 1986. "Information, Electoral Equilibria, and the Democratic Ideal." *Journal of Politics* 48:909–37.

Miller, Johanne M., and Jon A. Krosnick. 2000. "News Media Impact on the Ingredients of Presidential Evaluations: Politically Knowledgeable Citizens Are Guided by a Trusted Source." *American Journal of Political Science* 44:295–309.

Miller, Nicholas R. 1986. "Information, Electorates and Democracy: Some Extensions and Interpretations of the Condorcet Jury Theorem." In *Information Pooling and Group Decision Making*, ed. B. Grofman and G. Owen. Greenwich: JAI Press.

Moore, David W. 1987. "Political Campaigns and the Knowledge-Gap Hypothesis." *Public Opinion Quarterly* 51:186–200.

Morgan, Michael, and Nancy Signorielli. 1990. "Cultivation Analysis: Conceptualization and Methodology." In *Cultivation Analysis: New Directions in Media Effects Research*, ed. N. Signorielli and M. Morgan, 13–34. Newbury Park: Sage.

Nadeau, Richard, Édouard Cloutier, and Jean H. Guay. 1993. "New Evidence about the Existence of a Bandwagon Effect in the Opinion Formation Process." *International Political Science Review* 14:203–13.

Nelson, Thomas E., Zoe M. Oxley, and Rosalee A. Clawson. 1997. "Toward a Psychology of Framing Effects." *Political Behavior* 19:221–46.

Nevitte, Neil, André Blais, Elisabeth Gidengil, and Richard Nadeau. 2000. *Unsteady State: The 1997 Canadian Federal Election.* Toronto: Oxford University Press.

Norris, Pippa, John Curtice, David Sanders, Margaret Scammel, and Holli A. Semetko. 1999. *On Message: Communicating the Campaign.* London: Sage.

Page, Benjamin I., and Robert Y. Shapiro. 1992. *The Rational Public.* Chicago: University of Chicago Press.

Popkin, Samuel. 1991. *The Reasoning Voter.* Chicago: University of Chicago Press.

Price, Vincent, and John Zaller. 1993. "Who Gets the News: Measuring Individual Differences in Likelihood of News Reception." *Public Opinion Quarterly* 57: 133–64.

Rahn, Wendy M., John H. Aldrich, Eugene Borgida, and John L. Sullivan. 1990. "A Social-Cognitive Model of Candidate Appraisal." In *Information and Democratic Processes*, ed. J. Ferejohn and J. Kuklinski, 136–59. Urbana: University of Illinois Press.

Rahn, Wendy, Jon Krosnick, and Marijke Breuning. 1994. "Rationalization and Derivation Processes in Survey Studies of Political Candidate Evaluations." *American Journal of Political Science* 38:582–600.

Rivers, Douglas. 1988. "Heterogeneity in Models of Electoral Choice." *American Journal of Political Science* 32:737–57.

Simon, Herbert. 1954. "Bandwagon and Underdog Effects and the Possibility of Election Predictions." *Public Opinion Quarterly* 18:245–53.

Sniderman, Paul M., Richard A. Brody, and Philip E. Tetlock. 1991. *Reasoning and Choice: Explorations in Political Psychology.* Cambridge: Cambridge University Press.

Stimson, James A. 1975. "Belief Systems, Constraint and the 1972 Election." *American Journal of Political Science* 19:393–417.

Sturgis, Patrick. 2003. "Knowledge and Collective Preferences: A Comparison of Two Approaches to Estimating the Opinions of a Better Informed Public." *Sociological Methods and Research* 31:453–85.

Sturgis, Patrick, Caroline Roberts, and Nick Allum. 2003. "A Different Take on the Deliberative Poll: Information, Deliberation and Attitude Constraint." Paper presented at the annual meeting of the American Association of Public Opinion Research, Nashville, Tennessee.

Tichenor, P. J., G. A. Donohue, and C. N. Olien. 1970. "Mass Media and Differential Growth in Knowledge." *Public Opinion Quarterly* 34:158–70.

Tichenor, P. J., J. M. Rodenkirchem, C. N. Olien, and G. A. Donohue. 1973. "Community Issues, Conflict and Public Affairs Knowledge." In *New Models for Communication Research*, ed. P. Clarke. Beverly Hills: Sage.

Zaller, John R. 1990. "Political Awareness, Elite Opinion Leadership, and the Mass Survey Response." *Political Cognition* 8:125–53.

———. 1992. *The Nature and Origins of Mass Opinion.* Cambridge: Cambridge University Press.

Priming and Persuasion in Presidential Campaigns

Larry M. Bartels

IN EVERY ELECTION CYCLE, the major parties and their presidential candidates spend vast sums of money and prodigious amounts of energy on the campaign for the White House. Thousands of journalists, campaign operatives, pollsters, and media consultants derive their livings from this yearlong spectacle. Every day, interested citizens can read and watch detailed accounts and analyses of the candidates' strategies, speeches, and issue stands. As soon as the election is over, star reporters and star campaigners race to produce best-selling inside accounts of the decisions and events that led to victory or defeat.

But is it all sound and fury, signifying nothing?

After more than half a century of academic election studies, the surprising reality is that political scientists still understand relatively little about how presidential campaigns affect the vote. Even more surprisingly, much of what they do understand seems to provide good grounds for doubting that campaigns significantly affect the vote at all, at least in the most straightforward sense of determining who wins and who loses. Finkel's (1993, 14) analysis of survey data suggests that "for all the presidential elections in the 1980s, the outcomes were essentially predictable from the electorate's spring or early summer dispositions." Moreover, statistical forecasts based upon historical relationships between presidential election outcomes and economic and political "fundamentals" measured before the fall campaign have even begun to match actual election outcomes about as well as opinion polls conducted just before Election Day (Rosenstone 1983; Lewis-Beck and Rice 1992; and many others). If, as Gelman and King (1993, 412) assert, summarizing this evidence, "the outcome of recent elections can be predicted within a few percentage points in the popular vote, based on events that have occurred before Labor Day," we are left to wonder how the millions of dollars and hours expended by candidates, campaign workers, and political journalists in the two months *after* Labor Day could possibly be well spent.

One obvious answer is that even highly effective campaign efforts on both sides may cancel each other out, leaving the election result essentially similar to what it would have been if neither side campaigned at all. This sort of stalemate seems especially plausible in presidential general election campaigns, since both major parties typically draw from roughly similar pools of candidates, spend roughly similar amounts of money, and adopt roughly similar campaign strategies. As I have put it elsewhere,

> In a world where most campaigners make reasonably effective use of reasonably similar resources and technologies most of the time, much of their effort will necessarily be without visible impact, simply because every campaigner's efforts are balanced against more or less equally effective efforts to produce the opposite effect. (Bartels 1992, 267)

Such countervailing effects are clearly an important part of the story. But they do nothing to account for the fact that campaigns sometimes do produce substantial shifts in the relative standings of the competing candidates, at least as measured in presidential trial heats in commercial opinion polls. Journalists and campaigners point to these substantial shifts to support their assertions that campaign strategies and campaign events are often significant and sometimes decisive.

At least in retrospect, the judgments underlying such assertions seem to reflect a good deal of consensus regarding the important turning points of each campaign season. But if these day-to-day campaign events really cause substantial shifts in vote intentions, we are left with the question of how eventual election outcomes could be so predictable in advance. To turn Gelman and King's (1993) apt question on its head, how are election outcomes so predictable when campaign polls are so variable?

A partial resolution of this apparent paradox may be provided by the notion that campaigns matter *because* they tend to produce congruence between fundamental political conditions and predispositions on the one hand and vote intentions on the other. This supposition is supported by survey-based findings on political activation (Berelson, Lazarsfeld, and McPhee 1954; Bartels 1988; Finkel 1993) and by aggregate-level analysis of poll results and election outcomes (Bartels 1992; Gelman and King 1993; Holbrook 1996). Most strikingly, Holbrook (1996) has observed that the net effects of campaign events in the 1984, 1988, and 1992 presidential elections were strongly correlated with the discrepancy between early poll results and the "expected" election outcome based upon a typical political science model including presidential popularity, party tenure, and economic conditions. In 1984, when the relative standing of the candidates in June already corresponded closely with the expected election outcome based upon these fundamental factors, campaign events had little net impact; perhaps not coincidentally, one prominent journalistic account of the 1984 campaign (Germond and Witcover 1985) was titled *Wake Us When It's Over.* In 1988, when George H. W. Bush began the summer well below his expected level of support, he gained substantial ground during the campaign. In 1992, when Bush began the summer well above his expected level of support, he lost substantial ground during the campaign. In effect, each campaign seems to have produced predictable changes (or stability) in candidate standings, more or less regardless of the specific strategies adopted by the competing candidates and their political skill in implementing those strategies.

This view admits the possibility of significant campaign effects that do not simply cancel each other out; but it is a far cry from the view of most journalists and campaigners that campaign strategies and day-to-day campaign events—and by extension the political skills of the candidates and campaigners who produce those strategies and events—have a substantial independent impact on presidential election outcomes. For example, if almost any Clinton television ad would have been effective in the political circumstances prevailing in 1992 and almost any Bush television ad would have been ineffective, as Holbrook's (1996) analysis implies and as Rosenstiel's (1993, chap. 10) account suggests, then the political circumstances would seem to be more important than the specific content or impact of the ads (or speeches or debates or editorials) themselves. Thus, this view is closer to representing an elaboration of the statistical modelers' perspective than a genuine reconciliation of the statistical and journalistic accounts of election outcomes.

The difficulty of evaluating the statistical and journalistic accounts is exacerbated by the fact that they are based upon very different sorts of evidence. Aggregate-level data of the sort employed in political science forecasting models seem useful for discerning patterns across campaigns, but much less useful for distinguishing the impact of campaign activities and events from other idiosyncratic factors and background noise within a given campaign season, or for specifying how the impact of campaign activities and events is conditioned by the political context of a particular election year. Impressionistic evidence of the sort offered by journalists and campaigners seems useful for generating hypotheses connecting specific campaign activities and events to eventual election outcomes but unlikely to be of much help in evaluating or generalizing from more or less plausible post hoc explanations of specific observed election outcomes. Neither sort of evidence by itself seems sufficient to shed clear light on the nature or magnitude of campaign effects.

Survey data gathered during presidential campaigns may provide a useful basis for resolving some of the persistent disparity between the (possibly exaggerated) generality of aggregate statistical analyses and the (possibly exaggerated) specificity of journalistic accounts. On the one hand, they can systematically reflect factors that aggregate statistical analyses must treat as random noise, such as campaign-related changes in specific aspects of the candidates' images. On the other hand, they can provide a fairly detailed picture of the nature and magnitude of significant shifts in vote intentions—and thus a check on the plausibility of impressionistic accounts of how those shifts were produced.

Unfortunately, most survey-based analyses of how campaigns matter—from the classic Columbia studies of the 1940 and 1948 elections (Lazarsfeld, Berelson, and Gaudet 1944; Berelson, Lazarsfeld, and McPhee 1954) to the more recent studies of Patterson and McClure (1976), Markus (1982), Bartels (1993), Finkel (1993), and Just et al. (1996)—focus on single presidential campaigns.[1] Studies of campaigns in other electoral systems (e.g., Johnston et al. 1992; Finkel and Schrott 1995) are similarly limited. Given inevitable differences in survey design, measurement, and data analysis among these various studies, we know relatively little about the consistency or variability of campaign effects across campaigns and relatively little about how the circumstances and events of particular campaigns either reflect or transcend the more fundamental political factors emphasized in aggregate-level statistical analyses.

My goal here is to provide a more general analysis of how campaigns matter, based on evidence from parallel surveys conducted in the midst of the six most recent U.S. presidential election campaigns. By examining these six campaigns both individually and collectively, I aim to evaluate and elaborate hypotheses drawn from statistical analyses of aggregate voting patterns on the one hand and journalistic accounts of specific presidential campaigns on the other.

Potential Campaign Effects

The question of how campaigns matter is obviously too broad to be exhaustively addressed in a single essay. In order to keep things manageable—and in keeping with the limitations imposed by the availability of data—I adopt a variety of more or less arbitrary limits on the scope of my analysis.

First, my analysis consists of a systematic search for two specific types of potential campaign effects, *priming* and *persuasion*. I use the term *priming* to refer to any systematic change in the weights attached to prospective voters' attitudes and perceptions in the formulation of vote intentions over the course of the campaign. *Persuasion*, in the sense adopted here, refers to any systematic change in the mean values of electorally relevant attitudes and perceptions over the course of the campaign.

Second, I focus only on presidential campaigns and only in the two months between Labor Day in early September and Election Day in early November. These restrictions allow me to tap the wealth of data about prospective voters' political attitudes and evaluations provided by the comprehensive preelection surveys conducted as part of the American National Election Studies (NES). The NES surveys employ much more representative samples than commercial polls conducted for the candidates or the news media, and they measure a much richer variety of potentially relevant political attitudes and perceptions in consistent form throughout each two-month campaign.

The earlier stages of presidential election campaigns, in which the candidates are less well known, may well produce more significant campaign effects (Bartels 1988), but they are less susceptible to systematic comparative analysis because relevant survey data are less plentiful and less uniform. Campaigns for elections to state and local offices may likewise produce more significant campaign effects, but here, too, high-quality survey data are in short supply.[2]

Third, I focus on presidential campaigns since 1980 because the range of relevant questions repeated in consistent form in NES surveys before 1980 is considerably less rich. Using questions asked consistently in several different years facilitates systematic comparisons across campaigns and also makes it possible to pool the data from several years in a single analysis. My temporal restriction has the additional virtue of minimizing heterogeneity in the political context of presidential elections, since I have argued elsewhere (Bartels 1998) that presidential elections in the 1960s and 1970s were less partisan and more volatile than at any other time in the last century but that elections since 1980 have seen a return to more typical historical patterns.

My analysis is based upon data from 6,926 respondents in the 1980, 1984, 1988, 1992, 1996, and 2000 NES surveys who reported in a postelection interview that they voted for a major-party candidate for president. Nonvoters and those who voted for Ross Perot, John Anderson, Ralph Nader, or other minor candidates are omitted to simplify the analysis and to facilitate comparison across campaigns. However, some of the 6,926 respondents who did eventually vote for a Republican or Democratic candidate were undecided, intended not to vote, or intended to vote for a minor candidate at the time of their preelection interview. Grouping these various intentions into a single intermediate category produces an ordinal dependent variable with three possible values: +1 for respondents who intended to vote for the incumbent party candidate; 0 for respondents who were undecided, intended not to vote, or intended to vote for a minor candidate; and −1 for respondents who intended to vote for the major-party challenger.

Fourth, I focus on changes in the mean values and in the electoral significance of four specific sets of potential explanatory factors: partisanship, issue preferences, candidate images, and economic perceptions. Together, these factors reflect the most important elements in most political scientists' models of voting behavior. Partisanship is measured by the familiar NES seven-point party identification scale. Issue preferences are measured by respondent self-placements on general ideology and three more specific issues: abortion, aid to minorities, and defense spending.[3] Candidate images are measured by relative evaluations of the competing candidates as "inspiring," "knowledgeable," and "moral."[4] Economic perceptions are measured by respondents' assessments of whether the national economy got better, got worse, or stayed about the same in the preceding year. A more detailed description of the data is contained in the appendix.

Fifth, I focus on changes in political attitudes and vote intentions that appear to be sustained over the course of an entire fall campaign. It seems quite likely that campaign events produce a substantial number of real but ephemeral changes in vote intentions (Shaw 1993; Holbrook 1994). In some sense all of these "bumps and wiggles" represent campaign effects; but since our real interest is presumably in voting behavior and election outcomes rather than in fluctuations in poll standings, it behooves us to identify changes that actually get reflected in the voting booth. The fact that NES has routinely reinterviewed respondents after the election to ascertain whether and how they voted makes it possible to limit an analysis of preelection vote intentions to respondents who actually reported voting in the postelection interview and to examine the consistency of preelection vote intentions and postelection vote reports.

I focus on changes over the course of the fall campaign that can be captured, at least to a first approximation, by linear trend terms. Of course, there is no good reason to believe that all sustained campaign-related changes will be precisely linear. But neither is there any obvious theoretical reason to prefer some more complicated specification; and the available data are not sufficiently plentiful to warrant much confidence in any non-linearities that they may reveal.

Thus, for present purposes, campaigns will be considered to matter to the extent that they produce linear changes over the two months between Labor Day and Election Day either in the mean values of partisanship, issue preferences, candidate images, or economic perceptions or in the weights attached to those attitudes and perceptions by prospective voters. For my analysis of persuasion, this formulation implies regression models with issue preferences, candidate images, and the like as dependent variables and the date of each respondent's preelection interview as an explanatory variable. For my analysis of priming, it implies comparing regression models with preelection vote intentions and postelection vote reports as dependent variables and simple interactions between the date of each respondent's preelection interview and other relevant explanatory variables.

Priming

One familiar and theoretically plausible story about how campaigns matter is that they remind prospective voters of the electoral relevance of preexisting political attitudes and perceptions. Systematic increases in the weights voters attach to particular political considerations as a result of campaign activities and arguments would be an example of what social psychologists refer to as priming. Apparent priming effects have been identified in a variety of political settings using both experimental data (Iyengar and Kinder 1987; Mendelberg 2001, chap. 7) and survey data (Berelson, Lazarsfeld, and McPhee 1954, chap. 12; Krosnick and Kinder 1990; Johnston et al. 1992, chap. 8; Mendelberg 2001, chap. 6). In presidential campaign settings, Petrocik (1996) and Vavreck (1997) have argued that candidates consciously strive to prime specific issues that, for historical or structural reasons, favor their cause. More generally, Gelman and King (1993) suggest campaign priming of political and economic "fundamentals" as one possible source of increasing congruence between trial heats and eventual election outcomes.

Most analyses of campaign priming have employed longitudinal survey data to measure the apparent weight attached to specific considerations in determining vote intentions at various points in the campaign. To the extent that any particular consideration is "primed" by the campaign, its impact on vote intentions should increase over time. Thus, in a previous version of the analysis reported here I compared regression coefficients representing the effects of partisanship, issue preferences, candidate images, and economic perceptions on preelection vote intentions as measured at the beginning of each fall campaign (on Labor Day) and at the end of the campaign (on Election Day), interpreting increases in those regression coefficients as evidence of priming.

Lenz (2004) has pointed out that this analytic strategy relies too uncritically on the notion that specific political attitudes and perceptions are causes rather than consequences of vote intentions. If, instead, prospective voters gradually adjust their views about issues, candidates, or national conditions to conform with their vote intentions, the cross-sectional correlation between specific considerations and vote intentions may increase over the course of the campaign for reasons having nothing to do with priming. Prospective voters may be persuaded by the arguments of their favorite candidate to change their specific views (or gradually come to learn which specific views are consistent with their vote intentions); or they may simply feel increasing psychological pressure to rationalize their vote choice as Election Day approaches. The resulting patterns of opinion adjustment may reflect the relative *salience* of different considerations in the campaign, but they shed no real light on the relative *importance* of different considerations in the evolution of vote intentions.

Lenz's (2004) reanalyses of a variety of well-known priming studies suggest that much of what previous analysts have interpreted as priming probably reflects opinion adjustment or rationalization. His evidence is most convincing in cases where panel data make it possible to disentangle the reciprocal effects of specific opinions on broad evaluations such as vote intentions or vote choices and of those broad evaluations on specific opinions. For example, being able to sort out the reciprocal effects of issue preferences and vote intentions over the course of a campaign would make it possible to tell whether an increasing correlation between issue preferences and vote intentions was attributable to issue priming or to issue opinion adjustment.

In the case of my analysis here, crucial leverage is provided by the fact that NES surveys in presidential years routinely include postelection reinterviews with more than 90 percent of the preelection respondents. Thus, it is possible not only to compare the apparent effects of issue preferences on vote intentions at various points in the campaign but also to compare the apparent effects of issue preferences at various points in the campaign on vote intentions and postelection vote reports. To the extent that issue preferences are "primed" by the campaign, the same issue preferences measured well before Election Day should have a larger effect on postelection vote reports than on preelection vote intentions. Conversely, processes of issue learning or rationalization would have no effect on precampaign measures of issue preferences and thus no impact on the relationship between these early issue preferences and postelection vote reports.

This reasoning suggests that the crucial comparisons for the purpose of detecting campaign priming are between the estimated effects of partisanship, issue preferences, candidate images, and economic perceptions as measured in the NES preelection surveys on vote intentions and on postelection vote reports. However, any differences between these estimated effects should diminish systematically over the course of the fall campaign, disappearing for respondents interviewed just before Election Day (since for those respondents the ingredients of vote intentions and actual vote choices should be virtually identical).[5] Thus, it is necessary to build interactions into the models from which the effects are estimated to reflect the point in the campaign at which each respondent was interviewed.

The effects of campaign time could, of course, be represented in a variety of more or less complicated ways. Given my interest here in sustained changes over the course of each fall campaign, I employ a simple interaction between each explanatory variable and the date of each respondent's preelection interview. With the date-of-interview variable rescaled to run from 0 on Labor Day to 1 on Election Day, the main effects of the various explanatory variables in this interactive model reflect the estimated impacts of partisanship, issue preferences, candidate images, and economic perceptions on the vote intentions and actual votes of respondents interviewed at the beginning of the campaign, while the interaction terms capture changes in the weights attached to specific electoral considerations over the course of the campaign.[6]

The parameter estimates reported in the first row of table 1 represent the main effects of partisanship, issue preferences, candidate images, and economic perceptions from this sort of interactive model of vote intentions; thus, they represent the effects of these explanatory variables on the vote intentions of NES respondents interviewed at the beginning of each fall campaign. The parameter estimates are from an ordered probit analysis with vote intentions categorized as pro-incumbent (+1), other or undecided (0), and pro-challenger (−1). In addition to these main effects, the probit model included interactions between each explanatory variable and the dates of respondents' preelection interviews as well as election-specific intercepts and interactions between these election-specific intercepts and the dates of respondents' preelection interviews. The full set of parameter estimates appears in table A3 in the appendix.

The parameter estimates reported in the second row of table 1 are from a parallel probit analysis of postelection vote reports, categorized as pro-incumbent (+1) or pro-challenger (−1). As in the first row of the

TABLE 1. Campaign Priming of Labor Day Attitudes, 1980–2000

	Incumbent Partisanship	Issue Preferences	Candidate Images	Economic Perceptions
Effect on preelection vote intentions	1.164	.527	2.536	.250
	(.057)	(.120)	(.159)	(.076)
Effect on postelection vote reports	1.364	1.088	3.188	.292
	(.073)	(.159)	(.223)	(.097)
Difference	.200	.561	.652	.042
	(.093)	(.200)	(.274)	(.123)
Change (%)	+17	+107	+26	+17

Note: Parameter estimates from probit analyses of preelection vote intentions and postelection vote reports reproduced from the first and third columns, respectively, of table A3. Standard errors in parentheses.

table, these main effects represent the impacts of partisanship, issue preferences, candidate images, and economic perceptions as measured on Labor Day at the beginning of the fall campaign. As with the parameter estimates for vote intentions in the first row of the table, election-specific intercepts and interactions between all of these variables and the date of each respondent's preelection interview are not shown in table 1 but are reported in table A3.

The third row of table 1 shows the difference between the estimated Labor Day effect of each variable on postelection vote reports and preelection vote intentions. These differences measure the extent to which Labor Day attitudes and perceptions were primed by the subsequent campaign. All of these estimated priming effects are positive, as one would expect if campaigns serve to highlight the electoral relevance of the corresponding political attitudes and perceptions. Moreover, three of the four estimates—for partisanship, issue preferences, and candidate images—are statistically significant by conventional standards. Thus, there is clear evidence of campaign priming in these results. However, three of the four priming effects are small by any reasonable substantive standard, implying increases on the order of 20 to 25 percent in the weights attached to the corresponding attitudes and perceptions over the course of recent fall campaigns. Only the estimate for issue preferences suggests a substantial priming effect, with early issue preferences getting more than twice as much weight in the formulation of eventual vote choices as in the formulation of Labor Day vote intentions.

The parameter estimates in table 1 are based upon a pooled analysis of survey data from all six recent campaigns. Table 2 reports the corresponding estimates of priming for each campaign separately. Each entry in table 2 corresponds to a difference between the estimated effects of a given explanatory variable, measured as of Labor Day, on preelection vote intentions and postelection vote reports, respectively. Thus, the entries are equivalent to the corresponding entry in the "Difference" row of table 1, but for a single campaign. The complete statistical results on which these entries are based appear in tables A4 through A9 in the appendix.

Most of the campaign-specific estimates of priming presented in table 2 are too imprecise to be very informative. Indeed, only two of the twenty-four estimates in the table differ sufficiently from the corresponding pooled estimates in table 1 to be worthy of real note. The first of these is the estimate for issue preferences in 1988, which accounts for more than half of the total priming of issue preferences evident in table 1. Setting aside this anomalous case—in which the estimated impact of Labor Day issue preferences on vote intentions was actually slightly *negative*—reduces the apparent magnitude of issue priming from more than 100 percent to a bit less than 40 percent.[7]

The other striking deviation in table 2 from the typical patterns of priming reported in table 1 is the estimate for economic perceptions in 2000, which suggests that the economy actually became a substantially *less* important electoral consideration over the course of the 2000 campaign. By comparison, the estimated economic priming effects in three of the five other election years in table 2 are large and positive. None of these estimates is close to being statistically significant by conventional standards. Nevertheless, omitting the 2000 election from the pooled analysis in table 1 would leave substantial evidence of economic priming in the remaining five election years, with an increase of almost 90 percent in the average weight attached to economic perceptions between Labor Day vote intentions and postelection vote reports.[8]

The latter estimate, omitting the anomalous 2000 data, is consistent with aggregate-level evidence suggesting that "prosperity gives the incumbent party a significant 'ace in the hole'" during general election campaigns, over and above the advantage reflected in Gallup trial heats conducted just before the party conventions (Bartels 1992, 264–65).[9] Thus, the 2000 elec-

TABLE 2. Campaign Priming of Labor Day Attitudes by Election Year

	Incumbent Partisanship	Issue Preferences	Candidate Images	Economic Perceptions
1980	.095	.639	.310	.333
	(.271)	(.547)	(.705)	(.380)
1984	.308	−.095	.889	.027
	(.223)	(.472)	(.688)	(.274)
1988	.157	1.504	1.090	.225
	(.210)	(.431)	(.843)	(.323)
1992	.316	.145	.093	−.046
	(.210)	(.441)	(.620)	(.295)
1996	−.195	.955	1.479	.347
	(.282)	(.662)	(.815)	(.407)
2000	.453	−.115	.910	−.407
	(.233)	(.538)	(.590)	(.251)

Note: Entries are differences between the estimated effects of Labor Day attitudes on postelection vote reports and preelection vote intentions in each election year, calculated from probit parameter estimates in tables A4 through A9. Standard errors in parentheses.

tion appears to be a striking exception to a general pattern of substantial priming of economic perceptions between Labor Day and Election Day. However, this striking case of nonpriming appears to have had rather modest electoral consequences: if economic perceptions had had the same impact on vote choices in 2000 that they had in the five previous presidential elections, Al Gore's share of the popular vote would have been less than 1 percentage point greater than it actually was.[10] Thus, it does not seem likely that Gore's failure to emphasize economic prosperity on the campaign trail can account for the fact that his vote share fell so far below most political scientists' forecasts based on historical patterns of retrospective economic voting (Campbell 2001; Fiorina, Abrams, and Pope 2002).

This calculation illustrates the more general point that the electoral consequences of the priming effects reported in table 2 depend crucially on the partisan balance of the attitudes and perceptions being primed. Economic perceptions at the beginning of the 2000 campaign were positive on balance but only modestly so (with an average value of +.158 on a scale running from −1 to +1); thus, increasing the weight of those perceptions would have increased Gore's vote only modestly. By comparison, economic perceptions in 1980 were much more strongly negative (with an average value of .625); thus, the fact that those perceptions were significantly primed by the fall campaign was much more damaging to incumbent Jimmy Carter, costing him more than 3 percent of the popular vote.

Table 3 presents estimates of the electoral impact of priming for each explanatory variable in table 2 in each election year. These estimates were computed by comparing the simulated probability of a pro-incumbent vote for each major-party voter in the NES sample using the weights relating Labor Day attitudes to postelection vote reports (from tables A4

TABLE 3. Electoral Impact of Campaign Priming by Election Year (in percentages)

	Incumbent Partisanship	Issue Preferences	Candidate Images	Economic Perceptions
1980	+0.51	−1.44	+0.24	−3.29
1984	−1.30	+0.11	+0.65	+0.01
1988	−0.16	+0.77	−0.58	−0.33
1992	−0.13	+0.03	+0.12	+0.33
1996	+0.11	−0.81	−2.22	+0.59
2000	+0.10	+0.05	+0.57	−0.73
Average (absolute values)	0.38	0.54	0.73	0.88

Note: Entries are simulated changes in incumbent vote shares attributable to the estimated election-specific priming effects reported in table 2.

through A9 in the appendix) with the probability computed by replacing one of the "primed" weights with the corresponding "unprimed" weight relating Labor Day attitudes to Labor Day vote intentions. (In both cases, I adjust the attitudes and perceptions on which the simulated probabilities are based to remove the effects of post–Labor Day shifts in average values reported in tables 4 through 6.) Thus, the reported value of -3.29 percent for economic perceptions in 1980 in the first row of table 3 represents the estimated decline in Carter's vote share attributable to the priming of economic perceptions over the course of the fall campaign, by comparison with how he would have fared if the weight voters attached to economic perceptions had remained unchanged from Labor Day to Election Day.

As it happens, the priming of economic perceptions in 1980 appears to have been a good deal more consequential than any other instance of priming in the past six presidential elections. Indeed, only one of the twenty-three other estimates in table 3 is even half as large, reflecting a substantial increase in the electoral salience of Bill Clinton's low ratings for "morality" over the course of the 1996 campaign. Fewer than half of the remaining estimates are larger (in absolute value) than one-third of a percentage point. The average effects for partisanship, issue preferences, and candidate images across all six campaigns are on the order of half a percentage point, while the average effect for economic perceptions is less than one percentage point. Moreover, it is not uncommon for positive and negative priming effects to appear for different dimensions of evaluation in the same election, making their net electoral impact a good deal smaller than the sum of these average effects might suggest.

In short, while presidential campaigns do appear to succeed in priming the crucial electoral considerations emphasized in academic analyses of voting behavior, the magnitude of that priming is often modest. Moreover, given the relatively even partisan balance of opinion with respect to most of these crucial electoral considerations in most election years, the impact of priming on election outcomes is even more often modest. Occasionally, campaign events do seem to prime an electoral consideration where one party or the other enjoys a marked advantage in the distribution of opinion in the electorate. However, only two such instances are evident in the past six presidential campaigns: priming of economic perceptions probably cost incumbent Jimmy Carter about 3.3 percent of the vote in 1980, while priming of candidate images probably cost incumbent Bill Clinton about 2.2 percentage points in 1996. (Of course, Clinton won anyway, and Carter would have lost anyway.) For the most part, campaign priming seems to be a matter of academic interest to political psychologists, not a major factor in determining the outcome of presidential elections.

Partisan Activation

Perhaps the most famous single instance of an apparently consequential presidential campaign was one of the first campaigns subjected to detailed scholarly study: the 1948 campaign analyzed by Berelson, Lazarsfeld, and McPhee in *Voting*. In 1948, they wrote,

> the psychologically most interesting (and, at the same time, the politically most relevant) phenomenon was the last-minute return of many voters to an earlier disposition. These were persons who had voted for Roosevelt in 1944 and often had many demographic characteristics or past political allegiances which would predispose them to a Democratic vote. In June, 1948, however, they expressed little confidence in Truman and intended to vote for Dewey. Yet just before election day they changed in their intentions. Their final Democratic vote was thus the reactivation of a previous tendency. (1954, 291–92)

Berelson, Lazarsfeld, and McPhee's findings on the "reactivation" of standing partisan loyalties fit nicely with the emphasis of Campbell et al. (1960) and other subsequent analysts on party identification as a psychological filter shaping prospective voters' reactions to more immediate political events. Although the Michigan surveys were never used to examine directly the role of political campaigns in this process, they seem to support the inference that partisan activation is a central element in campaigns and a primary source of campaign effects.

There are at least three different ways in which partisan activation could be manifested in the survey data analyzed here. First, and most directly, the impact of party identification on vote intentions could increase over the course of the campaign; in that case, partisan activation would be an instance of the more general phenomenon of priming considered in the previous section of this essay. As I have already indicated, the parameter estimate capturing this direct effect of partisan activation (in the first column of table 1) is quite small, implying that the impact of party identification on vote intentions probably increased by less than 20 percent over the two months of recent fall campaigns. Given the relatively even balance of partisan attachments in the electorate in recent years, it should not be surprising that priming of this magnitude has had only a very modest impact on election outcomes; indeed, only one of the six election-specific estimates of the electoral impact of partisan priming in table 3 exceeds about half a percentage point in magnitude. At least in this most direct sense, partisan activation does not appear to be a significant element of the fall campaign.

Alternatively, partisan activation might involve polarization of prospective voters into increasingly distinct partisan camps over the course of the campaign. Even if a given degree of partisan attachment had essentially similar effects throughout the campaign season, prospective voters' partisan attachments might themselves be strengthened by the campaign process, producing stronger partisan effects from the same coefficients. As it happens, there is no evidence in the data for this form of partisan activation either: the strength of partisan attachment (measured by the absolute value of the incumbent party identification variable) actually declined slightly between Labor Day and Election Day.[11]

Finally, the evaluations of candidates, issues, and economic conditions included as additional explanatory variables in table 1 could, over the course of the campaign, come increasingly to reflect more basic partisan dispositions. However, there is little or no evidence for this sort of partisan activation in the past six presidential campaigns. The estimated impact of party identification on economic perceptions increased by less than 7 percent between Labor Day and Election Day, while the estimated impact of party identification on issue preferences and candidate images declined by 2 percent and 5 percent, respectively.[12] These results are even less supportive of the hypothesis of partisan activation than the result for the direct effect reported in table 1.

Taken together, these three sets of results provide remarkably little evidence of partisan activation in recent general election campaigns. Obviously, this is not to suggest that partisan predispositions are politically insignificant. On the contrary, party identification has both very strong direct effects on vote choices and very strong indirect effects by virtue of shaping prospective voters' attitudes about the candidates, the issues, and the economy. The surprising point is that these effects are about as strong on Labor Day as they are on Election Day. Thus, while there is a good deal of evidence (e.g., from Conover and Feldman 1989; Bartels 1993, 2002; Finkel 1993) suggesting that partisan loyalties play a significant role in shaping developing perceptions of presidential candidates, this process appears from the present analysis to be essentially complete by the time the fall campaign is under way.

Persuasion

By *persuasion* I refer to any systematic change in prospective voters' electorally relevant attitudes and perceptions. Here, I treat any sustained change over the course of the fall campaign in average evaluations of the candidates' characters, the issues, or the state of the national economy as evidence of persuasion. I do not propose to address the question of who is doing this persuading or how. Moreover, I shall not explore a variety of potentially interesting changes in the distributions of attitudes and perceptions that leave the average values unchanged; nor shall I consider changes in the subjective uncertainty of prospective voters' attitudes and perceptions (Bartels 1986; Franklin 1991; Alvarez and Franklin 1994; Vavreck 1997).

Evidence of persuasion in the sense proposed here appears in table 4 (for issue preferences), table 5 (for candidate images), and table 6 (for economic perceptions). In each case, the table presents average values for

TABLE 4. Campaign Season Changes in Issue Preferences

	Labor Day	Election Day	Difference	Impact (%)
1980	−.1607	−.1320	.0286	−0.06
	(.0171)	(.0171)	(.0294)	
1984	−.0371	−.0152	.0219	+0.18
	(.0163)	(.0185)	(.0302)	
1988	.0383	−.0216	−.0599	−1.35
	(.0160)	(.0194)	(.0307)	
1992	−.0027	−.0911	−.0884	−0.83
	(.0164)	(.0169)	(.0284)	
1996	−.0719	−.0247	.0472	+0.57
	(.0165)	(.0183)	(.0300)	
2000	−.0547	.0301	.0849	+1.00
	(.0150)	(.0174)	(.0272)	
Average (absolute values)	.0609	.0524	.0552	0.66
Incumbent Partisanship	.1698	.1663	−.0035	—
	(.0089)	(.0099)	(.0162)	

Note: Regression analysis of Issue Preferences index for major-party voters only. Labor Day and Election Day coefficients are based on preelection interview dates assuming linear trends through each fall campaign. Standard errors in parentheses. Standard error of regression = .296; $R^2 = .18$; $N = 6{,}926$ (1980–2000).

the beginning and end of each fall campaign, derived from a regression model with indicator variables for each election year and interactions between the indicator variables and the date of each respondent's preelection interview. (Each regression model also includes partisanship and an interaction between partisanship and the date of each respondent's preelection interview to capture potential partisan activation.) In each case, the table also reports differences between the Labor Day and Election Day average values, as well as the estimated impact of these differences on each election outcome.

Of the eighteen possible instances of persuasion in tables 4, 5, and 6 (one for each of the six election years in each of the three tables), only three appear to have had electoral effects in excess of 2 percentage points. All three of those were instances of changing candidate images. In 1988, challenger Michael Dukakis's image eroded substantially while George Bush's improved, increasing Bush's vote share by an estimated 3.7 percentage points. In 1984, on the other hand, challenger Walter Mondale's image improved while incumbent Ronald Reagan's became less favorable, reducing Reagan's vote share by about 2.3 percentage points. Finally, in 1980 Reagan's image improved over the course of the fall campaign, reducing Jimmy Carter's vote share by about 2.2 percentage points.

Table 7 provides more detailed evidence about the nature of these

TABLE 5. Campaign Season Changes in Candidate Images

	Labor Day	Election Day	Difference	Impact
1980	−0.148	−.0460	−.0311	−2.18%
	(.0150)	(.0150)	(.0257)	
1984	.0970	.0509	−.0461	−2.26%
	(.0143)	(.0162)	(.0264)	
1988	−.0180	.0522	.0702	+3.71%
	(.0140)	(.0170)	(.0270)	
1992	.0913	.0538	−.0376	−1.62%
	(.0144)	(.0148)	(.0249)	
1996	−.1073	−.0830	.0243	+1.16%
	(.0144)	(.0161)	(.0263)	
2000	.0511	.0239	−.0272	−1.01%
	(.0131)	(.0153)	(.0239)	
Average (absolute values)	.0632	.0516	.0394	1.99%
Incumbent Partisanship	.2755	.2606	−.0149	—
	(.0078)	(.0087)	(.0142)	

Note: Regression analysis of Candidate Images index for major-party voters only. Labor Day and Election Day coefficients are based on preelection interview dates assuming linear trends through each fall campaign. Standard errors in parentheses. Standard error of regression = .259; R^2 = .38; N = 6,926 (1980–2000).

and other changes in candidate images in recent fall campaigns. The entries in the table represent changes over the course of each campaign in each of the specific character assessments that make up the candidate image scale employed in my analysis. Many of these changes are rather imprecisely estimated, but a handful are large enough to be both statistically

TABLE 6. Campaign Season Changes in Economic Perceptions

	Labor Day	Election Day	Difference	Impact (%)
1980	−.6250	−.6447	−.0197	−0.29
	(.0260)	(.0260)	(.0447)	
1984	.1049	.1929	.0880	+0.91
	(.0249)	(.0282)	(.0459)	
1988	−.0731	−.0538	.0193	+0.14
	(.0244)	(.0295)	(.0469)	
1992	−.5069	−.4885	.0184	+0.15
	(.0250)	(.0257)	(.0432)	
1996	.1581	.1737	.0156	+0.17
	(.0251)	(.0279)	(.0457)	
2000	.1580	.0802	−.0779	−0.26
	(.0228)	(.0265)	(.0415)	
Average (absolute values)	.2710	.2723	.0398	0.32
Incumbent Partisanship	.1970	.2102	.0132	—
	(.0136)	(.0151)	(.0246)	

Note: Regression analysis of Economic Perceptions index for major-party voters only. Labor Day and Election Day coefficients are based on preelection interview dates assuming linear trends through each fall campaign. Standard errors in parentheses. Standard error of regression = .451; R^2 = .41; N = 6,926 (1980–2000).

TABLE 7. Changes in Specific Candidate Images by Election Year

	1980	1984	1988	1992	1996	2000
Incumbent inspiring	.0228	−.0411	.0803	.0172	.0580	—
	(.0610)	(.0504)	(.0483)	(.0446)	(.0553)	
Incumbent knowledgeable	.0460	−.0635	.0629	.0171	.0675	−.0062
	(.0573)	(.0505)	(.0418)	(.0378)	(.0478)	(.0429)
Incumbent moral	−.0177	.0109	−.0357	−.0353	.0003	−.1519
	(.0608)	(.0438)	(.0474)	(.0423)	(.0502)	(.0489)
Challenger inspiring	.0890	.0956	−.1814	.0474	−.0342	—
	(.0642)	(.0458)	(.0475)	(.0423)	(.0533)	
Challenger knowledgeable	.0991	.0654	−.0963	.1113	−.0020	−.0192
	(.0618)	(.0396)	(.0405)	(.0371)	(.0420)	(.0468)
Challenger moral	.0363	.0240	−.0078	.0077	−.0075	−.0169
	(.0535)	(.0392)	(.0418)	(.0410)	(.0469)	(.0444)

Note: Entries are differences between Election Day and Labor Day values for each component of the Candidate Images index derived from separate regression analyses of candidate images in each campaign, assuming linear trends through the fall campaign. Coefficients for partisanship and interaction between partisanship and date of interview not shown. Standard errors in parentheses.

and substantively significant. In 1988, it is clear that prospective voters' assessments of Dukakis as "knowledgeable" and (especially) "inspiring" eroded substantially over the course of the fall campaign. In 2000, assessments of Al Gore as "moral" declined equally precipitously. In 1992, challenger Bill Clinton was increasingly viewed as "knowledgeable" over the course of the campaign, as was challenger Reagan in 1980.

Allowing for some canceling out of electoral effects for countervailing shifts in specific candidate images, the average net impact of changing candidate images in the past six general election campaigns amounted to about 2 percentage points. The corresponding effects of changes in issue preferences were even smaller, averaging about two-thirds of a percentage point, while the effects of changes in economic perceptions averaged about one-third of a percentage point. Of course, these shifts, too, sometimes had countervailing effects on election outcomes. In 2000, for example, Al Gore appears to have lost 1 percent of the vote due to erosion in prospective voters' assessments of his character but gained 1 percent of the vote due to a leftward shift in issue preferences over the course of the fall campaign. Taking such countervailing shifts in different dimensions of evaluation into account, the average net impact of persuasion in the past six presidential campaigns appears to have been about 1.8 percentage points.

While persuasion effects of this magnitude are clearly large enough to be electorally significant under the right circumstances, they are also clearly small enough to be roughly consistent with aggregate-level evidence that "the outcomes of recent elections can be predicted within a few percentage points in the popular vote, based on events that have occurred before Labor Day" (Gelman and King 1993, 412). Allowing for some exaggeration in the apparent fit of aggregate-level forecasting models (Beck 1994; Bartels 1997) and some additional persuasion effects associated with specific issues and character assessments beyond those included in my analysis, the survey-based and aggregate-level evidence seem to be in reassuring agreement regarding the likely magnitude of campaign effects in recent presidential elections.

Campaign Effects and Conventional Wisdom

The pattern of scattered persuasion effects documented in tables 4 through 7 suggests three general observations regarding the role of persuasion in recent presidential campaigns.

First, these effects do not seem susceptible to any straightforward explanation in terms of the nature of the explanatory factors at work, the identities of the candidates, or the political circumstances of each campaign. Thus, while systematic comparative analysis may highlight the desirability of a general theory of campaign persuasion, it does not seem at first glance to present promising raw material for such a theory. The road from journalism to science in this field may turn out to be winding and strewn with potholes.

Second, there is in any case little evidence here to support the general view of journalists and campaigners that effective or ineffective advertising campaigns, speeches, debate performances, and the like are the most important elements of contemporary electoral politics. Even if the persuasion effects estimated in tables 4 through 7 were clearly attributable to campaign events in the way journalists and campaigners seem to suppose, they would not be large enough to justify the great weight given to campaign events in conventional journalistic accounts of presidential elections. The campaigners' herculean efforts to shape and reshape the competing candidates' personal images seem to have moved election outcomes by about 2 percentage points in a typical election year, while persuasion effects with respect to issues and economic perceptions are on the order of half a percentage point. Effects of this magnitude may obviously be decisive in a close election—but they certainly are not routinely decisive. And while they are large enough and potentially important enough to warrant scientific investigation, they are probably small enough to be reliably identified only with a great deal of high-quality data and painstaking analysis.[13]

Third, and perhaps even more disconcertingly, there seems to be only modest correspondence between the specific campaign effects documented here and conventional accounts of recent presidential campaigns offered after the fact by journalists and campaigners. Both kinds of evidence are hard enough to interpret and evaluate in their own right—the statistical results because they involve a good deal of imprecision and display little in the way of intelligible pattern, the journalistic accounts because they are unsystematic and post hoc and clearly seem to exaggerate the overall importance of day-to-day campaign events. Convergence between these two disparate sources of evidence would go a long way toward mitigating the limitations of each considered in isolation, but the lack of convergence evident here further muddles the picture by highlighting uncertainties in the very raw material from which political scientists might begin to theorize productively about how campaigns matter.

Only one of the six campaigns considered here produced an estimated persuasion effect that seems clearly consistent with the conventional wisdom of journalists and campaigners. That was in 1988, when the most consequential opinion changes in any of the four election years—the striking decline in Dukakis's image as "inspiring" and "knowledgeable" and the less striking improvement in Bush's image on the same dimensions, reported in table 7—produced an apparent vote shift of 3.7 percentage points over the two months of the fall campaign. This shift seems plausibly attributable to the events emphasized in journalistic accounts of the 1988 campaign, including Bush's Willie Horton and Boston Harbor attack ads and visits to flag factories and Dukakis's hapless tank ride and lackluster debate performance. Moreover, it was almost large enough to have decided the outcome of the election, since Bush's winning margin amounted to only 7.9 percentage points.

On the other hand, nothing in conventional accounts of the 1988 campaign explains the almost equally striking shift to the left in prospective voters' issue positions during the course of the campaign (reported in table 4) or the remarkably strong priming of those issue preferences (reported in table 2). Indeed, these apparent campaign effects stand in marked contradiction to Germond and Witcover's (1989) characterization of the 1988 campaign as "the trivial pursuit of the presidency." Thus, even in 1988, the match between conventional wisdom and the specific campaign effects estimated here must be considered a good deal less than perfect.

For the other presidential campaigns considered here the match between conventional wisdom and my parameter estimates is even less obvious. For example, conventional accounts of the 1984 campaign suggest that "Reagan's brand of emotional advertising" (Kern 1989), with its "Morning in America" theme, lulled the electorate into an essentially nonideological endorsement of the status quo (Germond and Witcover 1985). While the statistical results presented here tend to confirm that the electorate's assessment of economic conditions became more optimistic over the course of the 1984 campaign, the contribution of that change to Reagan's landslide seems to have amounted to less than 1 percentage point. Meanwhile, despite Reagan's much-touted acting skills and the purported genius of his image makers, he appears to have lost more than twice that many votes due to a significant erosion over the course of the campaign in his advantage over Mondale on the candidate image dimensions considered here.

In 1992, James Carville and his "War Room" colleagues earned fame and fortune for their apparent success in keeping the electorate's collective mind off Bill Clinton's perceived character flaws and on the long recession then just ending—as Carville's famous campaign headquarters sign reminded them, "It's the Economy, Stupid." However, the data analyzed here suggest that prospective voters' economic perceptions did not change significantly over the course of the 1992 campaign, that the impact of those perceptions on vote intentions was no greater in 1992 than in other recent campaigns, and that the 1992 campaign probably did less, not more, than most other recent campaigns to increase the electoral relevance of economic perceptions. Instead, the most significant effects of the 1992 campaign evident in the NES data are a noticeable shift to the left in prospective voters' issue preferences and a noticeable improvement in ratings of Clinton as "knowledgeable," neither of which corresponds in any obvious way to any prominent theme in journalistic accounts of the 1992 campaign.

What accounts for such striking mismatches between conventional accounts of recent campaign effects and the "reality" reflected in my parameter estimates? In part, of course, the mismatches are attributable to the limitations of my own analysis, which focuses on a small (albeit important) set of potential campaign effects and utilizes data from a single (albeit high-quality) survey in each of the six most recent presidential campaign seasons. Some of the specific apparent campaign effects (and noneffects) estimated here are no doubt due to small survey sample sizes and the limitations of the simple statistical models employed here. But I suspect that there is more to it than that.

Most of the important discrepancies I have noted between statistical results and conventional wisdom share a common characteristic: the conventional wisdom attempts to "explain" why the winning candidate won, whereas the statistical results are equally likely to "explain" why the winning candidate did not win by even more. Thus, in 1988, changing candidate images—which contributed to Bush's victory—received a great deal of attention from the press, whereas changing issue preferences—which cost Bush votes—received very little. Conversely, in 1984, increasing economic optimism—which contributed to Reagan's victory—captured the attention of campaign observers, whereas changing candidate images—which cost Reagan votes—did not.

Elsewhere I have complained that

> much less is known in general about the impact of modern election campaigns on voters than one might gather from a superficial reading of the literature. Breathless accounts of brilliant campaign operatives manipulating the electorate are often based upon no better evidence than the claims of the operatives themselves. . . . When more substantial evidence is offered for the effectiveness of a particular campaign strategy, it is usually evidence of the simplest and least trustworthy sort: Campaign A did X and won. (Bartels 1992, 263)

It should not be surprising that political journalists are susceptible to the fallacy of *post hoc, ergo propter hoc*. Their primary aim is to construct a compelling narrative account of the election outcome, and their primary sources are often the winning campaign operatives whose enthusiastic (and self-interested) claims are most likely to give that account the flavor of a "just so" story. What is more surprising is that political scientists have done relatively little to improve upon journalists' accounts of how campaigns matter. Doing so will require much more systematic, comparative, and theoretically grounded analysis of campaign effects. The result will probably be less dramatic than the journalists' accounts but truer to the realities of contemporary electoral politics.

APPENDIX

This appendix provides a description of the data on which the statistical analyses described in the text are based, more detailed statistical results, and a comparison of the ingredients of vote intentions and postelection vote reports for respondents interviewed close to Election Day.

Data

The variables from the American National Election Studies Cumulative Data File utilized in my analysis are identified and described in table A1. The analysis includes 6,926 respondents in 1980, 1984, 1988, 1992, 1996, and 2000 who reported in the postelection survey that they voted for one or the other of the major-party candidates. Minor-party voters, nonvoters, and preelection respondents who were not reinterviewed after the election are excluded from the analysis. The 1992 and 1996 data are weighted to compensate for panel attrition using the "general weight" constructed by the NES staff (v009). In addition, all of the data are weighted to equalize the effective sample sizes for the six election years.

All of the variables are coded to range from −1 for extreme anti-incumbent responses through 0 for neutral responses to +1 for extreme pro-incumbent responses. Thus, the postelection "Incumbent Vote" variables is coded +1 for incumbent party voters and −1 for out-party voters; the preelection "Incumbent Vote Intention" variable is coded +1 for those intending to vote for the incumbent party candidate, 0 for those intending not to vote or to vote for a minor-party candidate, and −1 for those intending to vote for the out-party candidate.

The "Issue Preferences" variable represents an unweighted averages of self-placements on four separate issue scales: liberal-conservative ideology, abortion, aid to minorities, and defense spending. Conservative positions on these issues are classified as anti-incumbent positions in 1980, 1996, and 2000 and as pro-incumbent positions in 1984, 1988, and 1992. The "Candidate Images" variable represents an unweighted average of the differences between incumbent and out-party candidate ratings on three separate character traits: "inspiring," "knowledgeable," and "moral."[14] The mean values and standard deviations of the resulting variables are shown in the last two columns of table A1, and the separate mean values for each election year are shown in table A2.

Probit Analyses of Vote Intentions and Postelection Vote Reports
The estimated effects of priming reported in the body of this essay are derived from a series of probit analyses relating vote intentions and postelec-

TABLE A1. Descriptive Statistics for National Election Study Survey Data

	NES Variable(s)	Range	Mean	Standard Deviation
Incumbent Vote (postelection)	v705	−1 to 1	.0212	.9998
Incumbent Vote Intention	v713	−1 to 1	.0507	.9397
Incumbent Partisanship	v301	−1 to 1	.0119	.7390
Issue Preferences	v803, v830, v838, v843	−1 to 1	−.0437	.3243
Candidate Images	v353, v354, v355, v365, v366, v367	−1 to 1	.0158	.3293
Economic Perceptions	v871	−1 to 1	−.1255	.5746

Note: Incumbent Partisanship is the seven-point NES party identification scale, with endpoints reversed in years with Democratic incumbents (1980, 1996, and 2000). Issue Preferences are an unweighted average of self-placements on four issue scales: liberal-conservative ideology, abortion, aid to minorities, and defense spending. (Conservative positions are classified as anti-incumbent in 1980, 1996, and 2000 and as proincumbent in 1984, 1988, and 1992.) Candidate Images are an unweighted average of the differences between incumbent and challenger ratings on three character traits: "inspiring," "knowledgeable," and "moral" (in 2000, "knowledgeable" and "moral" only). Economic Perceptions reflect whether "over the past year the nation's economy has gotten better, stayed the same or gotten worse," with "much better" = 1, "somewhat better" = .5, "stayed the same" = 0, "somewhat worse" = −.5, and "much worse" = −1. Data from American National Election Studies Cumulative Data File. Total N = 6,926 major-party voters, weighted to equalize election years (and, in 1992 and 1996, for panel attrition).

tion vote reports to prospective voters' partisanship, issue preferences, assessments of the candidates' images, and economic perceptions. Table A3 presents the results of probit analyses employing all 6,926 major-party voters in the six most recent presidential campaigns. The results are from two separate but parallel probit analyses, one of preelection vote intentions (classified as pro-incumbent or pro-challenger, with an intermediate category consisting of respondents who said they were undecided or intended

TABLE A2. Survey Data Average Values by Election Year, 1980–2000

	1980	1984	1988	1992	1996	2000
Incumbent Vote (postelection)	−.1398	.1642	.0577	−.1700	.1632	.0536
Incumbent Vote Intention	−.0415	.1751	.0653	−.1583	.1920	.0732
Incumbent Partisanship	.1157	−.0438	−.0151	−.1245	.0763	.0634
Issue Preferences	−.1269	−.0345	.0096	−.0670	−.0372	−.0062
Candidate Images	.0007	.0641	.0087	.0396	−.0754	.0560
Economic Perceptions	−.6114	.1363	.0678	−.5233	.1807	.1362
N	844	1,376	1,195	1,357	1,034	1,120

TABLE A3. Probit Analyses of Vote Intentions and Postelection Vote Reports, 1980–2000 (N = 6,926)

	Preelection Vote Intentions		Postelection Vote Reports	
	Labor Day Attitudes	Election Day Attitudes	Labor Day Attitudes	Election Day Attitudes
Incumbent Partisanship	1.164	1.112	1.364	1.159
	(.057)	(.064)	(.073)	(.078)
Issue Preferences	.527	.717	1.088	.945
	(.120)	(.143)	(.159)	(.178)
Candidate Images	2.536	3.060	3.188	2.995
	(.159)	(.184)	(.223)	(.234)
Economic Perceptions	.250	.539	.292	.538
	(.076)	(.086)	(.097)	(.106)
1980 Pro-Incumbent Bias	.021	.066	−.254	−.190
	(.098)	(.104)	(.127)	(.129)
1984 Pro-Incumbent Bias	.267	.351	.335	.338
	(.089)	(.103)	(.112)	(.123)
1988 Pro-Incumbent Bias	−.074	.513	.196	.115
	(.080)	(.101)	(.100)	(.119)
1992 Pro-Incumbent Bias	−.207	.079	−.251	.052
	(.096)	(.104)	(.122)	(.129)
1996 Pro-Incumbent Bias	.594	.582	.541	.500
	(.098)	(.107)	(.124)	(.128)
2000 Pro-Incumbent Bias	−.048	−.202	−.134	−.279
	(.080)	(.094)	(.100)	(.113)
Ordered probit thresholds	+/−.352		—	
Log-likelihood; pseudo-R^2	−3,510.4; .48		−1,828.4; .62	

not to vote or to vote for a minor-party candidate) and the other of postelection vote reports (classified as pro-incumbent or pro-challenger, with nonvoters and minor-party voters excluded from the analysis). The explanatory variables in each case consist of relevant attitudes and perceptions plus an indicator variable for each election year. To allow for the possibility of campaign-related changes in the weights attached to each of these variables, I estimated separate coefficients representing the weight attached to each variable on Labor Day and on Election Day.[15]

The parameter estimates presented in table A3 are the basis for my analysis of priming in table 1. The campaign-specific analyses of priming in tables 2 and 3 are based on the results of separate parallel probit analyses for each election year. Those results appear in tables A4 through A9.

Vote Intentions and Votes

The analysis of priming reported in the body of this essay is based upon a comparison of the preelection vote intentions and postelection vote reports of respondents interviewed near the beginning of the fall campaign. But that comparison is only sensible if differences between vote intentions and postelection vote reports reflect the impact of the intervening campaign rather than peculiarities in one or the other of these dependent variables. The possibility of systematic discrepancies between vote intentions and postelection vote reports is not to be taken lightly, since there are potentially significant differences both in the social contexts of these two dis-

TABLE A4. Probit Analyses of Vote Intentions and Postelection Vote Reports, 1980 (N = 844)

	Preelection Vote Intentions		Postelection Vote Reports	
	Labor Day Attitudes	Election Day Attitudes	Labor Day Attitudes	Election Day Attitudes
Incumbent Partisanship	1.064	.778	1.159	1.039
	(.163)	(.160)	(.216)	(.209)
Issue Preferences	.358	−.119	.997	1.147
	(.330)	(.358)	(.436)	(.462)
Candidate Images	2.893	3.696	3.203	2.988
	(.421)	(.487)	(.565)	(.604)
Economic Perceptions	.188	.772	.521	.492
	(.235)	(.244)	(.299)	(.308)
Pro-Incumbent Bias	−.020	.173	−.069	−.155
	(.186)	(.186)	(.236)	(.233)
Ordered probit thresholds	+/−.464		—	
Log-likelihood; pseudo-R^2	−505.7; .42		−263.3; .54	

tinct responses and in the response options. (More than 10 percent of the major-party voters in my analysis said in their preelection interview that they were undecided or would not vote for president or would vote for a minor-party candidate.)

Fortunately, any systematic discrepancies of this sort should be evident in a comparison of the vote intentions and postelection vote reports of respondents interviewed close to Election Day, since for those respondents there is little or no intervening campaign to produce genuine shifts

TABLE A5. Probit Analyses of Vote Intentions and Postelection Vote Reports, 1984 (N = 1,376)

	Preelection Vote Intentions		Postelection Vote Reports	
	Labor Day Attitudes	Election Day Attitudes	Labor Day Attitudes	Election Day Attitudes
Incumbent Partisanship	.932	1.136	1.240	.967
	(.139)	(.161)	(.174)	(.187)
Issue Preferences	.854	.515	.759	.603
	(.291)	(.349)	(.372)	(.412)
Candidate Images	2.661	3.225	3.550	2.715
	(.399)	(.482)	(.560)	(.563)
Economic Perceptions	.320	.669	.347	.898
	(.172)	(.213)	(.213)	(.250)
Pro-Incumbent Bias	.239	.314	.268	.238
	(.093)	(.108)	(.116)	(.123)
Ordered probit thresholds	+/−.311		—	
Log-likelihood; pseudo-R^2	−681.5; .47		−382.8; .59	

TABLE A6. Probit Analyses of Vote Intentions and Postelection Vote Reports, 1988 (N = 1,195)

	Preelection Vote Intentions		Postelection Vote Reports	
	Labor Day Attitudes	Election Day Attitudes	Labor Day Attitudes	Election Day Attitudes
Incumbent Partisanship	1.078	1.363	1.235	1.161
	(.133)	(.170)	(.163)	(.190)
Issue Preferences	−.150	1.618	1.354	.940
	(.251)	(.358)	(.350)	(.432)
Candidate Images	2.748	3.770	3.838	3.724
	(.491)	(.592)	(.685)	(.735)
Economic Perceptions	.033	.486	.258	.343
	(.201)	(.237)	(.253)	(.278)
Pro-Incumbent Bias	−.082	.569	.194	.075
	(.083)	(.113)	(.101)	(.122)
Ordered probit thresholds	+/−.306		—	
Log-likelihood; pseudo-R^2	−621.9; .46		−336.1; .59	

in the weights they attach to specific electoral considerations. Such a comparison is provided in table A10. The first row of the table presents the estimated effects of partisanship, issue preferences, candidate images, and economic perceptions on the vote intentions of NES respondents interviewed near the end of each campaign, reproduced from the second column of table A3. The second row of the table presents the corresponding estimates for postelection vote reports, reproduced from the fourth column of table A3. The third row of the table presents the differences between

TABLE A7. Probit Analyses of Vote Intentions and Postelection Vote Reports, 1992 (N = 1,357)

	Preelection Vote Intentions		Postelection Vote Reports	
	Labor Day Attitudes	Election Day Attitudes	Labor Day Attitudes	Election Day Attitudes
Incumbent Partisanship	.981	1.185	1.297	1.303
	(.129)	(.140)	(.166)	(.179)
Issue Preferences	1.258	.591	1.403	.850
	(.270)	(.303)	(.349)	(.407)
Candidate Images	2.860	2.701	2.953	3.324
	(.373)	(.396)	(.495)	(.546)
Economic Perceptions	.372	.499	.326	.511
	(.180)	(.191)	(.234)	(.248)
Pro-Incumbent Bias	−.173	.081	−.217	.023
	(.131)	(.137)	(.166)	(.176)
Ordered probit thresholds	+/−.385		—	
Log-likelihood; pseudo-R^2	−666.9; .49		−326.8; .65	

TABLE A8. Probit Analyses of Vote Intentions and Postelection Vote Reports, 1996 (N = 1,034)

	Preelection Vote Intentions		Postelection Vote Reports	
	Labor Day Attitudes	Election Day Attitudes	Labor Day Attitudes	Election Day Attitudes
Incumbent Partisanship	1.504	1.028	1.308	1.140
	(.182)	(.199)	(.215)	(.225)
Issue Preferences	.474	1.086	1.429	.998
	(.388)	(.409)	(.536)	(.503)
Candidate Images	1.771	4.269	3.250	3.999
	(.432)	(.544)	(.691)	(.710)
Economic Perceptions	.223	.942	.570	.542
	(.251)	(.292)	(.321)	(.353)
Pro-Incumbent Bias	.509	.700	.523	.600
	(.129)	(.146)	(.156)	(.164)
Ordered probit thresholds	+/−.319		—	
Log-likelihood; pseudo-R^2	−388.9; .58		−208.1; .70	

the preelection and postelection estimates, while the fourth row presents these differences in percentage terms. The structure of table A10 is thus exactly parallel to the structure of table 1, but with the "Labor Day" parameter estimates from table A3 replaced by the corresponding "Election Day" parameter estimates.

The comparisons presented in table A10 provide rather little evidence of systematic discrepancies between the bases of preelection vote intentions and postelection vote reports. For respondents interviewed close enough to Election Day that we can discount the possibility of genuine, campaign-related shifts in the bases of choice from preelection to postelection, partisanship, candidate images, and economic perceptions all had

TABLE A9. Probit Analyses of Vote Intentions and Postelection Vote Reports, 2000 (N = 1,120)

	Preelection Vote Intentions		Postelection Vote Reports	
	Labor Day Attitudes	Election Day Attitudes	Labor Day Attitudes	Election Day Attitudes
Incumbent Partisanship	1.465	1.309	1.918	1.416
	(.134)	(.151)	(.191)	(.193)
Issue Preferences	.573	.678	.458	1.241
	(.329)	(.411)	(.426)	(.508)
Candidate Images	2.069	2.159	2.979	1.945
	(.331)	(.370)	(.488)	(.486)
Economic Perceptions	.329	.194	−.078	.410
	(.151)	(.169)	(.201)	(.209)
Pro-Incumbent Bias	−.053	−.123	−.083	−.251
	(.090)	(.101)	(.115)	(.122)
Ordered probit thresholds		+/−.348		—
Log-likelihood; pseudo-R^2		−559.1; .48		−274.2; .65

TABLE A10. Determinants of Vote Intentions and Postelection Vote Reports for Election-Day Interviews

	Incumbent Partisanship	Issue Preferences	Candidate Images	Economic Perceptions
Effect on preelection vote intentions	1.112	.717	3.060	.539
	(.064)	(.143)	(.184)	(.086)
Effect on postelection vote reports	1.159	.945	2.995	.538
	(.078)	(.178)	(.234)	(.106)
Difference	.047	.228	−.066	−.001
	(.101)	(.228)	(.298)	(.136)
Change (%)	+4	+32	−2	−0

Note: Parameter estimates from probit analyses of preelection vote intentions and postelection vote reports reproduced from the second and fourth columns, respectively, of table A3. Standard errors in parentheses.

virtually identical effects on preelection vote intentions and postelection vote reports. Issue preferences seem to have received about one-third more weight in postelection vote reports than in preelection vote intentions; but even this difference is much smaller than the corresponding difference in table 1 for respondents interviewed close to Labor Day, and it is far from being statistically significant by conventional standards. Thus, it does not seem imprudent to interpret the differences in the apparent bases of Labor Day vote intentions and postelection vote reports in tables 1 and 2 as reflecting genuine priming rather than some merely artifactual difference between vote intentions and actual votes.

NOTES

This essay is a significantly revised and updated version of a paper originally presented at the conference "Capturing Campaign Effects" in Vancouver in 1997 and subsequently presented in seminars at the University of California, Los Angeles, and Columbia University. I am grateful to participants on those occasions for helpful comments and especially to Stanley Kelley, Lynn Vavreck, and John Zaller for detailed reactions and advice. I also thank Gabriel Lenz, whose ongoing dissertation research has greatly clarified my thinking about priming. The Woodrow Wilson School of Public and International Affairs at Princeton University, the John Simon Guggenheim Memorial Foundation, and the Pew Charitable Trusts provided generous financial support for the work reported here. The data were collected by the American National Election Studies project at the Center for Political Studies, University of Michigan; funded by the National Science Foundation; and made available through the Inter-university Consortium for Political and Social Research.

1. A notable exception is Sanders's (1996) analysis of the 1984 and 1988 campaigns, which utilizes some of the same survey data I employ here but focuses on a different set of potential campaign effects.

2. The most ambitious systematic survey focusing on statewide elections, the NES 1988-90-92 Senate Study, only interviewed respondents after Election Day. Kahn and Kenney's (1999) comparative analysis of U.S. Senate campaigns made extensive use of the resulting data but obviously sheds little light on the phenomena of priming and persuasion as I have defined them here. All of the congressional election-related items in regular NES surveys conducted before 1996 were also carried only in postelection surveys.

3. I do not consider directly whether campaigning produced changes in respondents' perceptions of the candidates' issue stands but assume that the political significance of such changes would be reflected either in prospective voters' own issue preferences or in the weight they attached to those preferences in arriving at vote choices.

4. I make no use of more general candidate evaluations reflected in thermome-

ter ratings or open-ended "likes" and "dislikes," because these seem too proximate to vote intentions to add much to the analysis.

5. A test of whether they are, in fact, identical is reported in table A10 in the appendix. That table compares the parameter estimates relating preelection vote intentions and postelection vote reports, respectively, to partisanship, issue preferences, candidate images, and economic perceptions for respondents first interviewed at the end of each fall campaign. Only one of the estimated weights for postelection vote reports differs by more than a few percent from the corresponding weight for preelection vote intentions, and that difference is not statistically significant (with a t-statistic of 1.0).

6. In effect, each respondent's preelection vote intention and postelection vote report are modeled as weighted averages of "Labor Day" and "Election Day" effects, with the weights depending upon when the respondent was interviewed. So, for example, respondents interviewed in early October, halfway through the fall campaign, are assigned approximately half the Labor Day effect plus half the Election Day effect for each explanatory variable. Respondents interviewed in late September are assigned approximately three-quarters of the Labor Day effect plus one-quarter of the Election Day effect, while respondents interviewed in late October would be assigned approximately one-quarter of the Labor Day effect plus three-quarters of the Election Day effect and so on.

7. With the 1988 campaign excluded from the analysis, the parameter estimates for the effect of Labor Day issue preferences on Labor Day vote intentions and postelection vote reports are .714 (with a standard error of .138) and .994 (with a standard error of .179), respectively.

8. With the 2000 campaign excluded from the analysis, the parameter estimates for the effect of Labor Day economic perceptions on Labor Day vote intentions and postelection vote reports are .212 (with a standard error of .089) and .402 (with a standard error of .113), respectively.

9. The aggregate-level evidence comes from a regression of eventual incumbent vote margins in eleven presidential elections (1948–88) on preconvention polls and election-year income changes. Each 1 percent change in real income produced a corresponding change of 2.7 percentage points (with a standard error of 1.0 percentage points) in the incumbent party's vote margin on Election Day, over and above the incumbent's margin in the last preconvention Gallup poll. Adding relative campaign spending to the regression increased the estimated impact of income growth slightly, to 3.2 percentage points (with a standard error of .6).

10. The probit parameter estimate in table A9 representing the impact of Labor Day economic perceptions on postelection vote reports is −.078. The corresponding parameter estimate for the five previous elections is .402. Simulating the probability of a Gore vote for each major-party voter in the 2000 NES sample (with adjustments to remove the effects of post–Labor Day changes in average values of partisanship, issue preferences, candidate images, and economic perceptions) produces average probabilities of .5399 using the former value and .5484 using the latter value. Since the Democratic advantage in economic perceptions also declined substantially over the course of the fall campaign, the difference of .85 percentage points actually overstates how many votes Gore would have gained

on Election Day if economic perceptions had had the same effect in 2000 as in other recent election years.

11. This calculation is based on a regression analysis relating the strength of partisanship (measured by the absolute value of the -1 to $+1$ party identification variable) to the date of each respondent's preelection interview plus indicator variables for each election year. The average strength of partisanship declined from .674 on Labor Day to .663 on Election Day; the difference of $-.011$ has a standard error of .013. Similar regression analyses for each campaign separately produced differences of $-.050$ (with a standard error of .031) in 1996, $+.043$ (.036) in 1980, and $-.036$ (.030) in 2000.

12. These calculations are based on parameter estimates for incumbent partisanship and an interaction between partisanship and the date of each respondent's preelection interview in the regression analyses reported in tables 4, 5, and 6.

13. For an interesting analysis of the power of typical election surveys to detect campaign effects, see Zaller 2002. For a description (including data and codebooks) of a recent much larger than typical election survey, the 2000 National Annenberg Election Survey, see Romer et al. 2004.

14. The "inspiring" questions were not included in the 2000 survey; thus, the "Candidate Images" variable for 2000 is constructed from the "knowledgeable" and "moral" ratings only.

15. The separate "Labor Day" and "Election Day" estimates are derived from interaction terms reflecting the date of each respondent's preelection interview. The NES surveys include a variable indicating how many days before the election each respondent was interviewed. I recoded that variable to create a date-of-interview variable ranging from 1 at the beginning of the fall campaign to 0 on Election Day. I then reversed the coding to create a second date-of-interview variable ranging from 0 at the beginning of the fall campaign to 1 on Election Day. The parameter estimates in the "Labor Day" columns of table A3 are based on interactions between the relevant explanatory variables and the first date-of-interview variable, while those in the "Election Day" columns are based on interactions between the relevant explanatory variables and the second date-of-interview variable. In effect, each respondent's vote intention and postelection vote report are represented as weighted averages of these "Labor Day" and "Election Day" parameter estimates, with the weights depending on when the respondent was interviewed. Conversely, the "Labor Day" and "Election Day" estimates for each explanatory variable are both based on the full set of survey respondents, but with early respondents weighted relatively heavily in the "Labor Day" estimate and less heavily in the "Election Day" estimate and late respondents weighted relatively heavily in the "Election Day" estimate and less heavily in the "Labor Day" estimate.

REFERENCES

Alvarez, R. Michael, and Charles H. Franklin. 1994. "Uncertainty and Political Perceptions." *Journal of Politics* 56:671–88.

Bartels, Larry M. 1986. "Issue Voting under Uncertainty: An Empirical Test." *American Journal of Political Science* 30:709–28.

———. 1988. *Presidential Primaries and the Dynamics of Public Choice.* Princeton: Princeton University Press.

———. 1992. "The Impact of Electioneering in the United States." In *Electioneering: A Comparative Study of Continuity and Change*, ed. David Butler and Austin Ranney. Oxford: Clarendon Press.
———. 1993. "Messages Received: The Political Impact of Media Exposure." *American Political Science Review* 87:267–85.
———. 1997. "Econometrics and Elections." *Journal of Economic Perspectives* 11: 195–96.
———. 1998. "Electoral Continuity and Change, 1868–1996." *Electoral Studies* 17: 301–26.
———. 2002. "Beyond the Running Tally: Partisan Bias in Political Perceptions." *Political Behavior* 24:117–50.
Beck, Nathaniel. 1994. "We Should Be Modest: Forecasting the 1992 Presidential Election." *Political Methodologist* 5:19–24.
Berelson, Bernard R., Paul F. Lazarsfeld, and William N. McPhee. 1954. *Voting: A Study of Opinion Formation in a Presidential Campaign*. Chicago: University of Chicago Press.
Campbell, Angus, Philip E. Converse, Warren E. Miller, and Donald E. Stokes. 1960. *The American Voter*. New York: Wiley.
Campbell, James E. 2001. "The Referendum That Didn't Happen: The Forecasts of the 2000 Presidential Election." *PS: Political Science and Politics* 34:33–38.
Conover, Pamela Johnston, and Stanley Feldman. 1989. "Candidate Perception in an Ambiguous World: Campaigns, Cues, and Inference Processes." *American Journal of Political Science* 33:912–40.
Finkel, Steven E. 1993. "Reexamining the 'Minimal Effects' Model in Recent Presidential Campaigns." *Journal of Politics* 55:1–21.
Finkel, Steven E., and Peter R. Schrott. 1995. "Campaign Effects on Voter Choice in the German Election of 1990." *British Journal of Political Science* 25:821–49.
Fiorina, Morris, Samuel Abrams, and Jeremy Pope. 2002. "The 2000 U.S. Presidential Election: Can Retrospective Voting Be Saved?" *British Journal of Political Science* 33:163–87.
Franklin, Charles H. 1991. "Eschewing Obfuscation? Campaigns and the Perceptions of U.S. Senate Incumbents." *American Political Science Review* 85:1193–213.
Gelman, Andrew, and Gary King. 1993. "Why Are American Presidential Election Campaign Polls So Variable When Votes Are So Predictable?" *British Journal of Political Science* 23:409–51.
Germond, Jack W., and Jules Witcover. 1985. *Wake Us When It's Over: Presidential Politics of 1984*. New York: Macmillan.
Germond, Jack W., and Jules Witcover. 1989. *Whose Broad Stripes and Bright Stars? The Trivial Pursuit of the Presidency 1988*. New York: Warner Books.
Holbrook, Thomas M. 1994. "Campaigns, National Conditions, and U.S. Presidential Elections." *American Journal of Political Science* 38:973–98.
———. 1996. *Do Campaigns Matter?* Beverly Hills: Sage.
Iyengar, Shanto, and Donald R. Kinder. 1987. *News That Matters: Television and American Opinion*. Chicago: University of Chicago Press.
Johnston, Richard, André Blais, Henry E. Brady, and Jean Crête. 1992. *Letting the People Decide: Dynamics of a Canadian Election*. Montreal: McGill-Queen's University Press.

Just, Marion R., Ann N. Crigler, Dean E. Alger, Timothy E. Cook, Montague Kern, and Darrell M. West. 1996. *Crosstalk: Citizens, Candidates, and the Media in a Presidential Campaign.* Chicago: University of Chicago Press.

Kahn, Kim Fridkin, and Patrick J. Kenney. 1999. *The Spectacle of U.S. Senate Campaigns.* Princeton: Princeton University Press.

Kern, Montague. 1989. *30-Second Politics: Political Advertising in the Eighties.* New York: Praeger.

Krosnick, Jon A., and Donald R. Kinder. 1990. "Altering the Foundations of Support for the President through Priming." *American Political Science Review* 84:497–512.

Lazarsfeld, Paul, Bernard Berelson, and Hazel Gaudet. 1944. *The People's Choice.* New York: Columbia University Press.

Lenz, Gabriel. 2004. "A Reanalysis of Priming Studies Finds Little Evidence of Issue Opinion Priming and Some Evidence of Issue Opinion Change." Manuscript, Department of Politics, Princeton University.

Lewis-Beck, Michael S., and Tom W. Rice. 1992. *Forecasting Elections.* Washington: Congressional Quarterly Press.

Markus, Gregory B. 1982. "Political Attitudes during an Election Year: A Report on the 1980 NES Panel Study." *American Political Science Review* 76:538–60.

Mendelberg, Tali. 2001. *The Race Card: Campaign Strategy, Implicit Messages, and the Norm of Equality.* Princeton: Princeton University Press.

Patterson, Thomas E., and Robert D. McClure. 1976. *The Unseeing Eye: The Myth of Television Power in National Elections.* New York: Putnam.

Petrocik, John R. 1996. "Issue Ownership in Presidential Elections, with a 1980 Case Study." *American Journal of Political Science* 40:825–50.

Romer, Daniel, Kate Kenski, Paul Waldman, Christopher Adasiewicz, and Kathleen Hall Jamieson. 2004. *Capturing Campaign Dynamics: The National Annenberg Election Survey.* New York: Oxford University Press.

Rosenstiel, Tom. 1993. *Strange Bedfellows: How Television and the Presidential Candidates Changed American Politics, 1992.* New York: Hyperion.

Rosenstone, Steven J. 1983. *Forecasting Presidential Elections.* New Haven: Yale University Press.

Sanders, Mitch S. 1996. "Beneath Stormy Waters: The Evolution of Individual Decision Making in the 1984 and 1988 Presidential Elections." PhD diss., Department of Political Science, University of Rochester.

Shaw, Daron R. 1993. "Strong Persuasion: The Effects of Campaigns in U.S. Presidential Elections." PhD diss., Department of Political Science, University of California, Los Angeles.

Vavreck, Lynn. 1997. "More Than Minimal Effects: Explaining Differences between Clarifying and Insurgent Campaigns in Strategy and Effect." PhD diss., Department of Political Science, University of Rochester.

Zaller, John. 2002. "The Statistical Power of Election Studies to Detect Media Exposure Effects in Political Campaigns." *Electoral Studies* 21:297–329.

II Research Designs and Statistical Methods for Studying Campaign Effects

Campaigns as Experiments

Stephen Ansolabehere

EVERY ELECTION YEAR, the traffic rotaries around Boston clog with people carrying brightly colored signs bearing the names of candidates. Kennedy. Kerry. Weld. Menino. Celucci. Swift. The sign bearers come from all walks of life. Some are clad in business suits and look like they took the afternoon off from brokering deals; others wear overalls and union jackets and look like they may have been on the other side of the bargaining table. There are retirees, students, families, and often the candidates themselves. Traffic slows, sometimes to a standstill, as motorists gawk at the spectacle, honking and waving to express their common cause, sometimes gestering to signal their opposition.

This is electioneering in Boston. For those of us who live here, it is an entertaining spectacle and, at times, a nuisance. For visitors caught in a traffic rotary with one hundred screaming bricklayers, Young Republicans, and city workers, it is as strange a ritual as anything Clifford Geertz discovered in New Guinea. Why are these people distracting the already appallingly bad Boston drivers? What could anyone possibly learn about the election from just a sign? Is this what democracy has come to?

While the form may seem unusual, Boston's traffic-circle campaigns raise questions that one may ask of any campaign. What does any of the hoopla that accompanies elections in America signify? There is certainly endless commentary in newspapers and on television programs interpreting the nuances of the competition—the critical importance of the man in the chicken suit who dogged George Bush in 1992, Ed Muskie's and Pat Schroeder's tears, or Gary Hart's 37 percent showing in the New Hampshire primary. Still, the question nags at anyone caught in a traffic circle or deprived of their favorite TV show or just curious. Does any of this matter for who governs and how they govern? Or are campaigns just part of our culture—the stuff of best-sellers and blockbusters?

Driven by the big questions about the relevance of democracy, or perhaps out of a fundamental need to justify our own significance, social scientists have put campaigns under the microscope. In the last half century, we have developed subtle survey research methods that allow us to track the ebbs and flows of public opinion and to tie those to fluctuations in the information that voters receive. We have developed experimental techniques that allow us to isolate the effects of a single bit of information—an advertisement, a news story, an endorsement. We have developed fairly complex statistical methods in order to tease out the subtle relationship between the campaigns and the public's opinions.

A common analytical approach unites this research. Social scientists treat campaigns as experiments. Information—often in the form of advertisements, debates, and conventions—is the *stimulus*. The opinions and the intended and actual behaviors of people are the *responses*. The target of our research is to measure the differences among various treatment groups: those exposed to specific messages and those not exposed. At the grandest level, political scientists treat the entire campaign season as a stimulus, and sometimes democracy itself.

My aim, in this brief essay, is to outline what I see as the methodological challenges that this research program faces. I do not provide a comprehensive survey of the many excellent studies that have been done but instead draw very selectively on research in this area.

The essays in this volume attest to the pervasiveness of experimental thinking about elections and democracy. Nearly every essay in this volume asks what the effects are of different facets of campaign information: the volume of information, the content of information, the timing of information, and the qualities of the candidates who are running. The approach in nearly all of the work here is quasi-experimental, which involves treating our observations of the world as if they were natural experiments. Our discipline has also moved toward more real experiments. The most notable examples are the works of Donald Kinder and Shanto Iyengar; Paul Sniderman and his colleagues; and Charles Plott, Richard McKelvey, and their colleagues. Kinder and Palfrey (1992) present an excellent survey of experimental methods and their applications to political science.

Practitioners more and more treat campaigns as experiments too.

Politicians and their strategists often float ideas and see if they catch on. If a theme resonates with the electorate, it gets more emphasis; if not, it is dropped. The decision about what to use and what not to use is shaped more and more by the tools that social scientists have developed, such as tracking polls and focus groups.

Although experimental reasoning predominates, observation remains the modal approach to the scientific study of elections and democracy. And there is a strong tension between experimentation and observation in social sciences. Unlike physicists and biologists, our "nature" does not perform all possible experiments. Politicians, journalists, consultants, and voters try to anticipate what is the best course and try to avoid actions that might cost them dearly. Consequently, when we look at the world it is always with an eye toward the actions that were not taken, as well as toward the events that did occur. In order to understand to what extent and how campaigns matter, we must imagine worlds with different sorts of campaigns or no campaign at all. This is, I think, one of the greatest challenges for social scientists, and it is one that experimental thinking can help to understand and solve, possibly.

Experimental Reasoning: A Simple Example

To fix what I mean by "experimental thinking," consider a simple example drawn from my research with Shanto Iyengar. We wished to know whether negative advertisements produce lower participation. In other words, we wanted to know whether people who see negative ads are less likely to vote than people who see positive ads. We began by breaking the problem into three components: (1) design of the treatments or stimuli, (2) experimental control, and (3) measurement of responses.

Step 1 requires that we define both the stimulus of interest (exposure to a negative advertisement) and a contrast group. In our study we contrasted exposure to a negative ad with exposure to a positive ad. Call these treatments N (negative) and P (positive).

Skipping ahead to step 3, we wanted to measure whether there were any differences between those who saw a negative ad and those who did not. We measured participatory attitudes many ways using a battery of questions about confidence in government and voting developed by the National Election Studies (NES). We were most interested in intentions to vote; call this dependent or response variable Y. In our final analysis we wanted to compare the responses of those exposed to negative ads (i.e., $Y(N)$) and those exposed to positive ads (i.e., $Y(P)$). The dependent variable Y took a value of 1 if the person intended to vote and 0 if not. The average value of Y (call it y) for each group, then, equaled the percent of people in each group, that is, $y(P)$ and $y(N)$, that intended to vote. The estimated effect of negativity on participation was simply the differences between the average vote intentions of these two groups, that is, $y(P) - y(N)$. This is just the definition of a difference of means, sometimes casually called an effect. It means something more to say that the effect is causal.

The power of experimental reasoning comes from control. Control allows the researchers to conclude that any statistically important differences in responses to the two treatments are due solely to the experimental manipulation. In the simple example here, we grappled with two problems of control: what do people see (the treatments) and who should see what?

The choice of the two treatments P and N was fundamentally an issue of control. We could contrast (and actually did) the negative ads with a neutral ad, a nonpolitical ad. The problem with such a contrast is that there are actually many differences between the neutral and negative ads: one is about politics and the other is not; one comes from a specific candidate and the other does not; one raises a public policy issue and the other does not; one is negative and the other is not. To conclude unambiguously that it is the negativity of the message that turns people off, we had to eliminate those differences. So we created a positive version of the same ad, using the same video, the same candidate, and the same issue, but changed the negative words in the script to positive ones. In the end, we could be confident that the only difference between the treatments stemmed from the negativity of the message. One could also imagine more elaborate experiments that vary the lengths of the messages or that combine negative and positive messages to make even more refined measures of the effects of the amount of negative and positive information.

The second place where we exerted experimental control was in who saw what ad. More generally, this is an issue of sample selection. If the assignment of people to treatments is at all related to the dependent variable, then there will be biases in the estimated effect of the treatment on the dependent variable. The experimental approach allowed us to measure precisely who watched a negative ad and who watched a positive ad. This is a very important advantage. Surveys and other techniques must rely on reported or recalled exposure to ads. As discussed later, those measures can be highly inaccurate and produce serious biases in data analyses.

At this point in the experiments we introduced a further guard against other factors confounding our conclusion. We randomly assigned advertisements to participants. Another significant problem with simply measuring the difference between those who saw a negative ad and those who saw a positive ad is that the contrast might reflect who is in each group. We might, for example, let people choose which ad they wanted to see. If people sorted such that likely voters chose tape A and likely nonvoters chose tape B, then there would be a bias toward finding no effect, even where an effect is present. If the opposite occurred, and people unlikely to vote a priori chose tape A and likely voters chose B, then we would overestimate the effect of negativity. Similarly, almost any assignment rule might introduce biases. To prevent some unanticipated confounding factor from emerging, we randomly assigned (using a random number generator, not an arbitrary rule) tape numbers for participant identification numbers.

Randomization does not remove the features of individual participants that can create biases, such as their inherent likelihood of voting or not or their taste for certain kinds of advertisements. Rather, it provides a statistical safeguard against those dispositions generating biases in the comparison of the two experimental groups. Randomization allows researchers to state that we expect in the statistical sense that any differences between the groups likely did not arise by chance, even though we did not control for their possible causes in the initial design of the experiment. The advantages of control are equally significant. Control allows researchers to say that some specific causes could not have accounted for any differences between the experimental groups that might have emerged. In addition, experimental control is a precondition of randomization. Without control over who sees what, randomization is not possible.

A simple algebraic example helps to clarify these two key advantages to experimentation. This example is based on a very insightful paper by Donald Rubin (1974). Suppose again that we wish to measure the effect of negative ads on participation. Suppose also that we have two individuals we would like to examine, person i and person j. Many factors that affect political behavior will shape these individuals' responses to our study. Indeed, there are so many factors that we could not possibly design an experiment that would hold every one of them fixed through experimental control. What Rubin elegantly explains is how a controlled and randomized experiment can *eliminate from statistical conclusions* the influence of the myriad factors that shape behavior.

To begin with, it is important to understand that complete experimental control is an impossibility. Complete experimental control would mean that we show person i the same two treatments, P and N, and that we show person j the same two treatments, under exactly the same conditions. Suppose that we could set up the experiment so that the conditions of each showing of the videotapes are identical. Index the showings with the letter t. We would then measure the difference in person i's participatory intentions between the two treatment conditions and the difference in person j's intentions. Finally, we could average the two viewers' responses to measure what Rubin calls an Average Causal Effect:

$$Y(P) - Y(N) = (1/2) \{[Y_{it}(P) - Y_{it}(N)] + [Y_{jt}(P) - Y_{jt}(N)]\}.$$

It is physically impossible to observe this quantity. An experimenter may be able to set up very similar viewing conditions for the two persons, holding day, time, and so forth, the same. But an individual can never be exposed to two different treatments at exactly the same time. At this point, a solution to the problem of control seems hopeless.

Controlled and randomized experiments allow us to get around this impossibility. Instead of trying to see everything at once, we construct some alternative (counterfactual) situations and then construct a rule to decide which situation we will observe. Continuing with our example, we begin by constructing two hypothetical situations. In situation 1, we determine that person i watches tape P and person j watches tape N. In situation 2, we determine that person j watches tape P and person i watches tape N. We cannot, I have said, observe both of these situations.

The beauty and power of experimentation come at the next step. The experimenter plays God and determines which of these two situations will occur. We may choose which world will occur on the basis of any arbitrary rule. However, there is a very strong reason for selecting by random assignment, such as a coin toss. If we use an arbitrary rule, such as which person comes through the door first, we might inadvertently introduce another reason that any observed differences exist. With the coin toss we know that we can expect that any differences that emerge are due to chance variation, not to systematic differences.

In the advertising experiments, suppose that we tossed a fair coin to determine which of these situations we should observe. So, with probability 1/2 we observe the outcome of situation 1 and with probability 1/2 we observe the outcome of situation 2. Whichever we observe we take to be the estimate of the average causal effect. The key result is that the expected value of the experimentally derived estimate of the effect of advertising tone equals

$$E[y(P) - y(N)] = (1/2) [Y_{it}(P) - Y_{it}(N)] + (1/2) [Y_{jt}(P) - Y_{it}(N)].$$

Collecting the terms with P and the terms with N reveals that this quantity is identical to the Average Causal Effect: $Y(P) - Y(N)$. In statistical parlance, the observed outcome of the experiment provides an unbiased estimate of the Average Causal Effect.[1]

Five Challenges in the Study of Campaigns

The structure of a simple experiment helps to clarify the challenges that confront researchers who wish to measure the effects of political information using observational data. There are five: the size of the study, the construction of treatments (for example, P and N), the measurement of exposure (who sees what), the assignment of treatments (why did people see what they saw), and the measurement of responses.

Setting Our Sights

What are the possible effects of campaigns on elections and government? The campaign period is not the only time when people learn about their government, and during the campaigns the public discussions and mass media messages are not the only information that people draw on. Rather, campaigns are just one of the ways that people relate to their government, and this fact must temper our assessment of them.

Often journalists prime us to believe that the latest news is so very important. That is their job: to sell the news. That is also why commentaries in the popular press are so often the starting point of social science inquiries. Although journalists are some of the major consumers of what we discover, it is probably best that we get away from journalistic beliefs about the importance of campaigns, at least as the starting point of any inquiry.

Instead, in thinking about how to study campaigns and whether their effects are big or small, we must determine what a big effect would be in political terms. To my thinking, moving the public opinion polls by 5 to 10 percentage points, which is perhaps an optimistic estimate of the edge gained by congressional incumbents through their campaigns, is a very big effect. Campaigns probably matter a whole lot less than fluctuations in the economy or the ideologies of the parties and people's preferences about the size and extent of government activity. This does not mean that campaigns are unimportant and that we should direct our research elsewhere. Unlike people's preferences about the size of government or fluctuations in the economy, candidates control their campaign messages. Here is the politics of democracy.

The lesson for researchers, though, is that it is hard to measure the effects of campaigns with much confidence. To reliably measure many modest campaign effects at once and the subtle interactions among them requires an excessively large sample. For example, the postconvention bounce enjoyed by the party's standard-bearer is one of the strongest and most reliable campaign effects. The convention bounce averages 6 percentage points. One needs a sample of at least twelve hundred to reliably detect such an effect. Most media polls have samples of five hundred to one thousand. It is harder still to measure the size of effects of this size within particular subgroups, such as among people who identify with one party or another.

What is needed in the study of campaigns is a very focused approach that attempts to isolate a phenomenon of particular importance and then designs the instrument around it. In this volume, I think the best example is the study reported by Johnston and Vowles of strategic voting in New Zealand.

Defining Treatments

Campaigns are important because they are times of intense, focused public discourse. Politicians, parties, and interest groups present the choices to the electorate. For their part, many citizens tune in because they must make a judgment on Election Day about who should govern. Of course, intense public discourse arises at other times, such as the debates over national health insurance and over NAFTA during the first Clinton administration. Indeed, campaigns should be viewed as a continuation of the dialogues that occur throughout the duration of a government. For social scientists, though, they are an ideal time to measure the effects of information because the volume and complexity of the information increase during campaigns and because many more people seek information.

That discourse and information are the real concerns with campaigns suggests that there are two features of campaigns that we may analyze: what is said and how it is said.

The "what" of campaigns are facts. Political scientists, drawing on their Progressive roots, want people to cast informed votes, and our standards of information are high. Voters certainly use a wide range of facts, even if they do not always seem to do so. Indeed, not having heard anything about the candidates is a "fact." A crude, workable typology of facts undergirds most communications and elections research. First, voters need basic information about the election: when is the election and how do you vote? Second, voters use labels, including party, incumbency, group endorsements, race, and gender. Such facts seem necessary for some of the basic sorts of voting that social scientists have shown to exist, especially party voting, retrospective economic voting, incumbency voting, and racial bloc voting. Third, facts about the candidates as persons are also important. Do I know this person? Where does he or she come from? Finally, information about the issues is vitally important to many voters. The twentieth-century ideal of democracy is one based on deliberation about "the issues" facing the country. At the very least, people must have some familiarity with those issues, either at a personal level or at the rarefied level of public debates about specific laws. What is at stake in this election? What are the problems that the nation faces or that I face? What policies do each of the candidates and parties plan to pursue? What might be the consequences of those policies?[2]

To assess the effects of different sorts of information we must draw contrasts between situations where the information is available and where it is not. For example, most ballots are partisan ballots—they have the labels of the parties next to the candidates' names. This bit of information (a simple label provided in the campaign booth) matters quite a lot. I, for one, would be lost without it when voting for lesser offices like city council, sheriff, and judge. The extent to which these labels matter, though, can only be measured by contrasting elections where the labels are present and where they are not. One way to capture such effects is to contrast states with partisan and nonpartisan ballots. Another possible experiment is to consider states that change their ballot form. Minnesota in the early 1960s, for example, experimented with nonpartisan ballots. One can measure the effects of ballot form in this case by contrasting the partisan vote in years when the nonpartisan ballot was used with the partisan vote in the years when the partisan ballot was used.

Significant events, such as debates, conventions, and even the campaign season itself, are often viewed as treatments. Gelman and King (1993), for example, measure a variety of campaign effects, such as convention bounces, by pooling the media polls in the 1988 U.S. presidential election and then testing for the effects of events deemed important by the press coverage of that election. In a similar vein, Thomas Holbrook (1994) measures the effects of the presidential campaigns of the 1980s on election outcomes by contrasting the average presidential popularity and support in the months before the campaign began with the average presidential popularity and support registered throughout the campaign season. This approach gives us a crude assessment of the campaigns—did any movement in opinion occur?

There is an important limitation to such studies. The "treatments" or events may not be comparable. One party's convention might convey less information than the other party's convention. For example, the 1968 Democratic convention is often described as showing a party in disarray, but no one remembers the 1968 Republican convention, nor did it attract nearly as much commentary at the time. One way to adjust for comparability of events is to measure the strength of the signal with television ratings for conventions, advertisements, and other "events." To continue the convention example, researchers might count the number of minutes of issue discussion that occurred during prime time. Even still, it is hard to assay an entire campaign season. How we measure the "treatments" at the aggregate level remains a tricky problem, with few obvious solutions.

In studying the "what" of campaigns, the typology of basic facts, labels, personal traits, and issues offers a primitive but robust guide. But we need better measures of these treatments, especially at the aggregate level. Most of the study of campaigns is conducted at the micro level, largely with survey data. Survey data suffer from measurement errors, as noted later. We need a check on conclusions drawn from surveys, and, short of doing experiments, that means aggregate data. The only standard aggregate data that are available measure the volume of the campaigns, and these are the data reported by the Federal Elections Commission and state agencies on the candidates' campaign expenditures. There are no measures of candidates' expenditures for themselves and against others or of expenditures on different issues or traits.

The "how" of campaigns opens a much wider field for inquiry. By "how" I mean how campaigns are conducted. How many candidates and parties participate? Who controls access to the mass media? At their core, campaigns involve deliberation. Campaigns are protracted events in which the parties, candidates, and electorate attempt to engage in a discourse about what is the best direction for the future government. Indeed, one of the fundamental assumptions of democracy is that there is value in hearing many voices and in interacting among them. This theme was central to the research on political communication following World War II. Control of the mass media seemed necessary for the sustenance of the regimes in Germany and Italy. Social scientists have worked extensively to measure the effects of specific facts and events on opinions and election outcomes. However, we know very little about how the dialogue of campaigns works.

The extent of deliberation has reasserted itself in contemporary research in three important areas. The literature on transitions to democracy has emphasized telecommunications reform as one of the focal points for democratic reforms. The literature on presidential power has focused on the ability of the president to get his way in the Washington establishment by "going public" and on the limitations of this power when Congress is also able to go public (Kernell 1986; Brody 1992). Finally, the popular critiques of the American media and proposals for reform of it often focus on the effects of concentration of ownership and of commercialization on the quality of discourse. I know of no studies that establish such a link in any objective way, but the BBC is often heralded as the model for dragging U.S. politics out of the muck.

While questions of access to media may seem far removed from campaign politics, they are in fact quite central. In 1996, the U.S. Presidential Debate Commission chose to exclude H. Ross Perot from the nationally televised debates. Similar debates four years earlier reinvigorated his campaign and helped him win nearly 20 percent of the vote. In 1998, Reform Party candidate Jesse Ventura was allowed to participate in the Minnesota gubernatorial debate, in part because Democratic nominee Skip Humphrey felt that Ventura (with only 11 percent in the polls) had no shot of winning and would only draw support from the Republican nominee,

Norm Coleman. Ventura was the clear winner in the debates and, one month later, in the election.

The number of voices is certainly an important feature of deliberation. Beyond that, though, communications research still lacks an adequate framework for thinking about deliberation and measuring its effects. Three models of deliberative democracy in campaigns have currency. First, one might view voters as jurors, weighing the evidence laid before them by adversaries. Here the normative standards are fairness and truthfulness, and at times an arbiter must intervene. Often, journalists take the role of judge. Second, one might view deliberative democracy as a marketplace. Free and open competition (in our case for elected office) is the best test of any idea or politician. This rationale lies behind many of the Supreme Court opinions relating to campaign finance, broadcasting regulation, and censorship. Finally, one might think of democracy as an extensive town meeting, where ordinary citizens can openly put questions before their fellow citizens, criticize or praise their government, and challenge leaders directly.

How we measure deliberation and discourse poses an even greater research challenge. The very dimensions of the subject have yet to be distinctly defined. Perhaps the best starting point is the vantage of comparative politics, and that is to measure the openness of the media in different societies.

Complexity of Effects

One of the clearest lessons of media research over the last two decades has been the complexity and variety of responses that any message can elicit. Much early social science research on communications emphasized that modern democracy involved the behavior of the masses. Fear drove this research: fear that democracy could fall to the machinations of demagogic dictators. Such fears proved unfounded, mainly because the public is not a single entity easily moved in one direction or another, but consists of many publics.

Any message may have varied effects on the electorate as a whole. Some information may lead to convergence in people's beliefs and voting behaviors, but some information may create greater heterogeneity. Responses to campaign messages vary along at least three significant dimensions.

First, voters differ in their levels of sophistication and knowledge of politics, and this mutes the effects of new information on the public as a whole. More sophisticated voters are more attuned to politics, more likely to pick up new information, and more critical in their use of such information. John Zaller, in his book *The Nature and Origins of Mass Opinion* (1992), develops a parsimonious model that describes how new information can have very uneven effects in such an electorate. A very sophisticated voter is likely to learn new information but is unlikely to be influenced by it, since the new information adds little to the voter's existing cache of knowledge. An unsophisticated voter is very likely to be influenced by new information but is very unlikely to learn it. Voters with moderate levels of information—those who follow public affairs occasionally—are the most susceptible to new messages.

Second, voters differ in their political dispositions and preferences, and people's preferences can shape what information they seek, believe, and respond to. Paul Lazarsfeld and his colleagues (Berelson, Lazarsfeld, and McPhee 1954) discovered in their studies of Elmira, New York, that people learned about politics very selectively. For example, if an individual was unemployed, he or she sought information about how the candidates would get the economy moving again. A politician could sway such a voter by talking about the economy, but the candidates could not sway voters by talking about something else or by promising policies markedly against the individual's interests. Taking party and ideology as manifestations of people's underlying preferences, Shanto Iyengar and I (Ansolabehere and Iyengar 1995a) found a very similar pattern in television viewers' responses to advertising. People were most receptive to candidates who talked about the issues most important to them. They were also most receptive to politicians who were of their same party and who were thus likely to take actions that they would most approve of.

Third, voters face coordination problems, which they at times may be able to overcome. Rather than waste their votes on the candidate who they prefer best but who will certainly lose, voters may switch to their second choice in order to avoid the worst-case candidate. Voters may even choose not to collect information about candidates who have no chance of winning. Calculations of wasted votes will tend to favor moderate candidates, though not always. There is considerable debate in British political science about the extent of sophisticated or strategic voting, which in the 1980s may have hurt the Liberal-Democratic/Alliance party. There are many related phenomena in different electoral systems, such as bandwagons in American presidential primaries and momentum gained from coalition partners in New Zealand (see Johnston and Vowles, this volume; see also Cox 1996).

Social scientists have developed good models for each of these forms of behavior. The challenge for empirical research is one of scale. The number of possible campaign effects is staggering, as the electorate can vary along each of these dimensions, and these dimensions might even have interactive effects. To examine any one of these effects adequately or to detect important interactions among them requires studies that are focused on measuring the effects of campaigns and carefully designed to measure these effects. Only a handful of such studies have really ever been executed.

Measurement of Treatment Exposure

Perhaps the least appreciated problem in the study of campaigns is measuring actual exposure to a message. The great advantage of experiments is that the experimenter observes (and controls) who sees what message. Studies using survey and aggregate data do not measure this directly. In surveys, we may ask whether someone recalled seeing an ad or a story or whether they regularly watch certain programs. In aggregate data analysis, we know the dates that events happen on and can associate those with the time trend in the public opinion polls. These measures do not capture actual exposure.

Determining who actually saw or heard a message has proven a very thorny problem. Schuman and Presser's (1981) novel question-wording experiments show how fragile survey responses can be to slight changes in wording, timing of questions, and sensitivity of the subject. They conclude their research with a preference for using open-ended and uncoached or prefaced questions. In media research, even these forms of questions fail to get at actual exposure.

In our own study, Shanto Iyengar and I tested the advertising exposure question used by NES (Ansolabehere and Iyengar 1995b). About a half hour following the viewing of the videotape we asked participants, "Do you recall seeing any political commercials during the video? If so could you briefly describe the ad?" Using a generous coding, just over half (55 percent) of the people who actually saw an ad could remember that they did. If we required that they could say anything about the ad, that fraction fell to just above a quarter (28 percent). This is a very severe downward bias in the actual exposure rate reported by such a question.

To make matters worse, we found that recall did not mediate the effects of actual exposure. We measured the effects of actual exposure on vote preferences using an ordered probit predicting party preference in the vote on the party of the candidate whose ad was seen, plus many control variables. The effect of the ad was to move vote intentions about 7 percentage points toward the sponsor of the ad. We then measured the effect of recall on vote intentions. People who recalled the ad were only 2 percentage points more likely to vote for the sponsor than those who did not, an insignificant effect. The difference could be due to measurement error, which would bias the coefficient on recall downward, or to a significant mediating effect of recall, which would mean that there is a significant interaction between recalled and actual exposure.

The culprit is measurement error. As the third step in this analysis, we broke the treatment variable into two groups: those who were exposed to and recalled the ad and those who were exposed to the ad and did not recall it. The coefficients were nearly exactly the same. Those who recalled the ad were as strongly affected as those who did not recall the ad. In other words, recall seems to be nothing more than a very bad measure of actual exposure, which strongly influences opinions.

What to do with a measure like this? Perhaps the question should be discarded. Before doing so, though, researchers need to examine whether a valid correction for these measurement errors can be constructed. Are valid instruments available? Can multiple measures fix these problems? The work of Achen (1978) on representation and Bartels (1993) on media exposure generally seem like promising starting points.

Assignment of Treatments

The granddaddy of all media studies problems is the assignment of treatments. When we conduct experiments, randomization allows us to estimate the effects of a specific treatment without bias, eliminating statistically the effects of the many other factors that influence behavior.[3]

In a campaign, what is said and how it is said are dictated by the logic of political strategy, not by the roll of the experimenters' dice. Strategic behavior of candidates and other players will introduce bias into any study if the choice of strategy depends on the expected effect that such actions might have on the vote. For example, in a presidential race, the mathematics of the Electoral College lead candidates to focus their campaign efforts on the swing states. Heavily Democratic states like Massachusetts, New York, and Rhode Island and heavily Republican states like Utah, Alaska, Kansas, and Idaho will see few if any presidential advertisements, while the swing states of Illinois, Michigan, Florida, and Ohio will be inundated with campaign commercials.

The problem this creates for researchers can be seen by considering the hypothetical experiment sketched previously. Now we will choose who sees what by tossing a weighted coin rather than a fair coin. The weight on the coin will be determined by the likely response. Suppose that in the pretest questionnaire we determine that person i is more likely to participate than person j. In our mathematical symbols given previously, this means that $Y_{it}(P) > Y_{jt}(P)$ and $Y_{jt}(N) > Y_{it}(N)$. Now let us toss a weighted coin where the weights are such that the probability that i sees tape P is $q > 1/2$. The expected outcome of the equation now becomes

$$q [Y_{it}(P) - Y_{jt}(N)] + (1 - q) [Y_{jt}(P) - Y_{it}(N)].$$

This is larger than the Average Causal Effect. If the weight made j more likely to see the positive ad, then the estimated effect would be too small.

Of course, if we knew the value of q we could fix this quantity with the appropriate weights. Unfortunately, in survey research and analyses of aggregate data, we do not know this quantity. It depends on the behavior of voters, politicians, journalists, and others who produce and demand political information. If we are to reduce the biases that come from nonrandom treatment assignments, we must try to analyze the process that determines who sees what in politics. Three approaches have been used.

First, we may model the cognitive process described earlier. This is another take on John Zaller's model of mass opinion. In his formulation, the probability that someone is exposed to a message is an increasing function of his or her attentiveness to politics and the responsiveness to new information is a decreasing function of his or her attentiveness to politics. Zaller assumes that if a person doesn't receive a message he or she can't be influenced by it, and this allows him to estimate q as a function of attentiveness and Y as a function of attentiveness. The basic structure of this model can be applied to many other problems, such as the content of messages.

Second, we may use a conventional psychometric solution, which involves multiple measures for each individual and assumptions about the cumulative effects of those measures over time. Bartels (1993) uses such a model to estimate the effects of media exposure, measured using the NES panel data, on opinion formation. Bartels finds modest effects where negative or no correlations existed before. Achen (1983), though, documents the sensitivity of these models to assumptions. Looking at the Miller-Stokes representation data, Achen shows that one model converts correlations between candidates and voters preferences that are in the range of .4 to over .9. But another, equally plausible model pushes those correlations down to .10 or .05. I suspect that, in the end, these psychometric techniques using cross-sectional data or short panels will not prove terribly useful. Estimates are not very robust to specification assumptions, and testing assumptions is extremely difficult and usually impossible. Zaller's approach seems more fruitful, as does the third approach.

Third, we may use the conventional econometric solution of instrumental variables. Instrumental variables estimation requires that researchers measure variables that influence media exposure but not directly political behavior, such as turnout or vote preference. Within political science, these methods have been most widely applied to the study of campaign spending in congressional elections, and there is considerable debate over which sets of variables can be used to make valid instruments (see, e.g., Jacobson 1990; Gerber 1992). The sorts of variables that likely work for campaign spending are factors that affect the cost of raising campaign money, such as the willingness of interest groups to give to members on valuable committees, but do not affect other electoral advantages that incumbents possess. Research on campaign finance is unique in the development of instrumental variables in the study of campaigns, and this approach has considerable promise for other subjects. Needed, though, are systematic measures of factors that affect the volume and content of media coverage of politics.

Conclusions

Strange though many campaign practices may seem, political science has taken a decidedly nonanthropological approach to the study of campaigns. Instead, our field has been informed more and more by the rigors of experimental thinking. We understand the politics of campaigns as causes and effects rather than as its many cultures.

I have sketched, and this essay is surely just a sketch, the main tenets of experimental thinking in the study of campaigns. The strength of experiments is that they offer the most powerful way to observe how the world works under alternative scenarios; they allow us to compare the counterfactuals. Real experiments, though, are relatively rare and often not feasible. Even still, the logic of experimentation clarifies the difficulties of other ways of seeing the world. Analyses of surveys and aggregate data are ideal for mapping the contours of the political landscape. However, when we use surveys, aggregates, and simple observation to measure the effects of information on behavior, we immediately encounter the limitations outlined here. Fixing these problems is difficult but not impossible. And many of the essays in this volume offer innovative attempts to overcome these difficulties.

NOTES

1. With a weighted coin, we would devise an unbiased estimate by using the weights appropriately in the formula given previously.

2. It is tempting to throw many different ideas into this category of facts, including emotions and evaluations of candidates. These are not themselves facts. They are outcomes of the process, and calling them facts fundamentally muddies the enterprise.

3. This problem has long been extensively studied by econometricians and statisticians (Heckman 1978; Imbens, Angrist, and Rubin 1996).

REFERENCES

Achen, Christopher. 1978. "Measuring Representation." *American Journal of Political Science* 22:475–510.

———. 1983. "Toward Theories of Data." In *Political Science: The State of the Discipline*, ed. Ada Finifter. Washington, DC: American Political Science Association.

Ansolabehere, Stephen, and Shanto Iyengar. 1995a. *Going Negative: How Political Advertisements Shrink and Polarize the Electorate*. New York: Free Press.

———. 1995b. "Messages Forgotten." In *Campaigns and Elections American Style*, ed. Candice Nelson and James Thurber. Boulder: Westview.

Bartels, Larry. 1993. "Messages Received: The Political Impact of Media Exposure." *American Political Science Review* 87:267–85.

Berelson, Bernard R., Paul F. Lazarsfeld, and William N. McPhee. 1954. *Voting: A Study of Opinion Formation in a Presidential Campaign*. Chicago: University of Chicago Press.

Brody, Richard, 1992. *Assessing the President*. Palo Alto: Stanford University Press.

Cox, Gary. 1996. *Making Votes Count*. New York: Cambridge University Press.

Gelman, Andrew, and Gary King. 1993. "Why Are American Presidential Election Polls So Variable When Votes Are So Predictable?" *British Journal of Political Science* 23:409–51.

Gerber, Alan. 1992. "Measuring the Effects of Spending in U.S. Senate Elections." Manuscript, Department of Political Science, Yale University.

Heckman, James. 1978. "Dummy Endogenous Variables in a Simultaneous Equation System." *Econometrica* 96:931–59.

Holbrook, Thomas. 1994. "Campaigns, National Conditions, and U.S. Politics." *American Journal of Political Science* 38:973–98.

Imbens, Guido, Joshua Angrist, and Donald Rubin. 1996. "Identification of Causal Effects Using Instrumental Variables." *Journal of Econometrics* 71:145–60.

Jacobson, Gary. 1990. "The Effects of Campaign Spending in House Elections: New Evidence for Old Arguments." *American Journal of Political Science* 34:334–62.

Kernell, Samuel. 1986. *Going Public: New Strategies of Presidential Leadership.* Washington, DC: Congressional Quarterly Press.

Kinder, Donald, and Thomas Palfrey. 1992. *Experimental Foundations of Political Science.* Ann Arbor: University of Michigan Press.

Rubin, Donald. 1974. "Estimating Causal Effects of Treatments in Randomized and Nonrandomized Studies." *Journal of Educational Psychology* 66:688–701.

Schuman, Howard, and Stanley Presser. 1981. *Questions and Answers in Attitude Surveys.* New York: Academic Press.

Zaller, John. 1992. *The Nature and Origins of Mass Opinion.* New York: Cambridge University Press.

Three Virtues of Panel Data for the Analysis of Campaign Effects

Larry M. Bartels

THE PRIMARY AIM OF PARTICIPANTS in election campaigns is to produce politically significant changes in the attitudes and perceptions of prospective voters. The primary aim of scholarly observers of election campaigns is to measure and explain those politically significant changes. Because campaigns are dynamic phenomena, good campaign studies must be dynamic too. Time must enter the analysis either directly or indirectly (as a proxy for campaign activities and events). Survey researchers can incorporate time most simply by interviewing different respondents at different times and incorporating the date of the interview in their analyses as a potential explanatory variable (or incorporating variables describing campaign events keyed to dates of interview). The result is a species of *longitudinal* study or (in the quasi-experimental design literature) *interrupted time-series design* (Cook and Campbell 1979, chap. 5). In the specific setting of survey research—especially within the compass of a single survey spanning days or weeks rather than years—it has come to be known as a *rolling cross-section design* (Johnston and Brady 2002).

The rolling cross-section design's primary virtue is its simplicity. It exploits the leverage for scientific inference of a brute fact about the logistics of (at least most academic) survey research: interviews take time to conduct. By treating variation in the date of interview as a potential explanatory variable, this administrative nuisance becomes an opportunity to learn something about the substance of the political or social processes underlying survey responses.

Of course, a rolling cross-section survey may be timed to coincide with especially interesting political or social processes, as with the American National Election Studies (NES) 1984 Continuous Monitoring Survey, which was designed to capture the effects of primary campaigns, conventions, and other political events outside the time frame of the traditional NES preelection surveys (Bartels 1988). Moreover, artifactual differences in the characteristics of respondents interviewed at different times may be minimized by conscious attention to sampling procedures in the course of data collection, as with the 1988 Canadian Election Study's daily release of fresh sample replicates (Johnston et al. 1992, appendix A). But even in the absence of conscious attention to the implications of temporal variation in the course of data collection, analysts may come to realize that they are analyzing rolling cross-sections in more or less the same way that speakers come to realize that they are speaking prose. Thus, for example, Sanders (1996), Vavreck (1997), and Bartels (2000c; essay in this volume) have treated the traditional NES preelection surveys as two-month rolling cross-sections, and Wright (1990, 1993) has used the date of NES postelection interviews to examine the deterioration of accuracy in vote reports, despite the fact that these surveys were designed and conducted with neither purpose in mind.

The other most common way to incorporate a dynamic element in survey design is to interview the same individuals at two or more points in time and attribute *changes* in their attitudes or perceptions to the effects of intervening events. This so-called *panel design* can provide more direct evidence of campaign effects than the rolling cross-section design, in the sense that change is observed in the responses of the same individuals rather than being inferred from comparisons of different survey respondents. On the other hand, the problem of attributing observed changes to *specific* intervening events is often more difficult with panel data, since many different events may intrude in the period between successive panel waves—from a few weeks to several months or much longer, as in the four-year panel studies conducted by NES in 1956-58-60, 1972-74-76, and 1992-94-96 or the even longer political socialization panels analyzed by Jennings and Niemi (1981).

Panel designs have been especially prominent in the field of electoral studies. Significant campaign studies based primarily upon election-year panel surveys include the classic Columbia studies of the 1940 and 1948 presidential campaigns (Lazarsfeld, Berelson, and Gaudet 1948; Berelson, Lazarsfeld, and McPhee 1954), the parallel television-era panel studies of Patterson and McClure (1976) and Patterson (1980), and several studies based upon the 1980 NES election-year panel (Markus 1982; Bartels 1993; Finkel 1993). The recent efforts of Just et al. (1996) suggest that panel designs continue to appeal to scholars interested in capturing campaign effects.

The variety of significant campaign analyses based upon rolling cross-section surveys on the one hand and panel surveys on the other should be sufficient to demonstrate that neither approach represents an exclusive path to scientific progress in the field of electoral studies. Both will, no doubt, continue to provide important insights regarding the reactions of prospective voters to campaign events. However, scholarly assessments of the advantages and disadvantages of the two approaches seem to me to have been skewed—and scholarly exploitation of existing panel data seems to me to have been hampered—by insufficient appreciation of some of the specific analytic virtues of panel designs. Thus, my aim here is to outline what I consider to be the three primary advantages of panel data for the analysis of campaign effects.

(1) Panel data facilitate adjustments for measurement error in survey responses using Wiley and Wiley (1970) or other measurement models. Given the embarrassingly low reliability of typical measures of political attitudes and perceptions, adjustments for measurement error are essential for achieving plausible estimates of the magnitudes of many campaign effects.

(2) Panel data permit analyses of opinion change in which prior opinions appear as explanatory variables. Given the stability of typical political opinions and their modest correlations with relevant explanatory variables, direct measurement of prior opinions substantially increases the efficiency of statistical estimation and provides crucial perspective on the relative political importance of precampaign and campaign events.

(3) Panel data facilitate analyses in which relevant explanatory variables are measured outside the immediate campaign setting. Given the susceptibility of political attitudes to rationalization in terms of causally irrelevant themes prominent in campaign discourse, prior measurement of potential explanatory variables provides important insights regarding the causal priority of specific political attitudes and perceptions in the evolution of candidate evaluations.

In addition to rehearsing these three advantages of panel data, I briefly address the two most distinctive inferential problems posed by panel designs: panel attrition and panel conditioning. I also consider possibilities for melding panel and rolling cross-section elements in a single survey design. Although such mixed designs raise significant unresolved problems of model specification and estimation, they offer the very attractive prospect of combining the best features of panel and rolling cross-section designs and thus of contributing further to our understanding of opinion change in campaign settings.

Allowances for Measurement Error

Analysts of opinion dynamics typically ask two kinds of questions: First, how stable are opinions over time? And second, to the extent that opinions change, what produces those changes?

Thanks primarily to the efforts of Achen (1975, 1983), the effects of measurement error on inferences about opinion stability are now widely recognized. In particular, it is clear that the low levels of apparent opinion stability in mass publics observed by Converse (1964) and others are attributable in large part to the effects of random fluctuation in survey responses. Although the nature and significance of this "measurement error" are a matter of vigorous theoretical debate (Achen 1975; Feldman 1990; Zaller and Feldman 1992; Zaller 1992; Brady 1993), analysts of political attitudes and belief systems now at least know better (or *should* know better) than to mistake opinion responses in surveys for the real political opinions underlying those responses.

Curiously, the same level of methodological sophistication that has become fairly commonplace in analyses of opinion stability is much less commonplace in analyses of opinion change. It is by no means unusual for analysts to regress opinion variables on prior opinions plus some other variables intended to capture potential causes of opinion change, making no allowance for error either in measured prior opinions or in the other measured variables associated with potential opinion change. Unfortunately, such an approach cannot, in general, lead to reliable inferences about the nature and causes of opinion change; nor does data analytic experience give us good reason to believe that the resulting biases are likely to be so minor that we can safely ignore them in practice.

The key to correcting the biases created by measurement errors in explanatory variables is to obtain estimates of the magnitudes of those measurement errors. Panel data facilitate corrections for measurement error because repeated measurement of the same opinion or behavior provides a check on the statistical *reliability* of observed responses. In two-wave panels, an obvious measure of reliability is the "test-retest" correlation of individual responses. However, it would be imprudent to interpret instability as measurement error in contexts where underlying "true" opinions may also be changing. The primary advantage of three-wave panels is that they provide leverage for distinguishing between random measurement errors and changes in underlying true opinions.

Although specific models of measurement error in panel data may be complex (Heise 1969; Wiley and Wiley 1970; Jöreskog 1979; Achen 1983), the intuition underlying this leverage is simple: to the extent that "we can predict t_3 issue positions of individuals fully as well from a knowledge of their t_1 positions alone as we can from a knowledge of their t_2 positions alone" (Converse 1964), the apparent changes between t_1 and t_2 are interpreted as random measurement error rather than changes in underlying true positions. Conversely, to the extent that observed response instability varies inversely with the temporal proximity of the responses, the instability is attributed to real opinion change rather than to random measurement error.

My own work on the political impact of media exposure (Bartels 1993) provides a useful illustration of the importance of allowing for measurement error in analyses of campaign effects. My aim was to estimate the effects of television news exposure, newspaper exposure, and partisan predispositions on a variety of politically relevant attitudes and perceptions during the 1980 presidential campaign, using data from the NES election-year panel survey. The data consisted of a variety of opinion readings for 758 panel respondents (the survivors from a first-wave sample of 1,008) at three points in the 1980 campaign. The first wave of interviews was conducted in late January and February (before the first primary voting in New Hampshire), the second wave in June (between the end of the primary season and the national nominating conventions), and the third wave in September (during the first month of the general election campaign).

The dependent variables in the analyses summarized here include "thermometer" ratings of the competing candidates, assessments of Carter's performance as president, and ratings on a battery of trait items tapping the candidates' character, leadership, and competence.[1] To facilitate comparison, all of the original responses were recoded to range from 0 to 100, with 0 denoting the most negative possible opinion and 100 denoting the most positive possible opinion. For each perception, I estimated the effects of prior opinions, partisan predispositions, television news exposure, and newspaper exposure separately in each half of the election-year panel (February to June and June to September).[2]

I estimated the magnitudes of measurement errors using a variant of the Wiley and Wiley (1970) model.[3] The measurement error estimates calculated from the modified Wiley and Wiley model indicated that about 25 percent of the observed variance in thermometer ratings and about 40 percent of the observed variance in the job approval and trait ratings represented random noise. The estimated measurement reliabilities for the media exposure variables were somewhat higher—.75 for television news exposure and .78 for newspaper exposure—and the apparent measurement reliability of party identification was higher still, at .88.

The inferential consequences of these measurement errors are highlighted in table 1, which summarizes the estimated effects of television news exposure reported by Bartels (1993). The first and third columns of

TABLE 1. Impact of Measurement Error on Estimates of Television News Effects in the 1980 Presidential Campaign

	OLS June	EV June	OLS September	EV September
Carter thermometer rating	1.0	−2.6	2.3	2.4
	(2.4)	(3.1)	(2.2)	(2.9)
Reagan thermometer rating	3.4	5.2	1.4	1.2
	(2.2)	(3.0)	(2.4)	(3.3)
Carter job approval (5 items)	−0.7	−5.2	1.6	2.0
	(3.8)	(5.2)	(3.6)	(5.3)
Carter character (3 items)	0.5	−0.1	2.9	4.1
	(2.9)	(4.1)	(2.9)	(4.2)
Carter leadership (3 items)	0.5	−2.7	2.2	1.4
	(2.9)	(3.9)	(2.7)	(4.1)
Carter competence (3 items)	0.9	−2.9	3.8	4.5
	(2.7)	(3.9)	(2.7)	(4.1)
Reagan character (3 items)	2.4	0.2	3.2	1.4
	(2.6)	(3.7)	(2.8)	(4.1)
Reagan leadership (3 items)	0.3	0.2	−3.6	−8.5
	(2.6)	(3.6)	(2.9)	(4.3)
Reagan competence (3 items)	2.8	3.5	−4.5	−9.6
	(2.5)	(3.4)	(2.7)	(4.0)
Average (absolute values)	1.4	2.5	2.8	3.9
	(2.7)	(3.8)	(2.8)	(4.0)

Note: Average OLS and EV parameter estimates with average standard errors in parentheses, calculated from Bartels 1993. $N = 753$.

the table show ordinary least squares (OLS) parameter estimates for the effects of television news exposure in the period from February through June and from June through September, respectively. The second and fourth columns of the table show the corresponding errors-in-variables (EV) parameter estimates of the same effects.

As the average standard errors presented in table 1 make clear, most of the individual parameter estimates summarized in the table are too imprecise to be "statistically significant." However, the number and magnitude of "significant" effects—most notably, the negative impact of television news exposure between June and September on Reagan's "leadership" and "competence" ratings—are too large to be due to chance and suggest that television news coverage of political campaigns does sometimes produce large, politically consequential shifts in prospective voters' perceptions and evaluations of the candidates.[4]

For purposes of the present argument, what is most worth noting in table 1 is that these media effects are seriously underestimated in the OLS analysis, which takes no account of measurement error in the explanatory variables. The average magnitude of the OLS estimates is 2.1 points on the 100-point attitude scales; the corresponding average of the EV estimates, which allow for measurement error in the explanatory variables, is 50 percent larger.[5]

Table 2 shows a similar comparison of estimated effects of preexisting partisan loyalties on campaign season opinion changes. Here, in contrast to the case of media exposure, the OLS estimates significantly *overstate* the impact of partisan predispositions on opinion change during the campaign period, by an average of more than 50 percent. Although the EV estimates of the impact of party identification are still quite substantial, they suggest that partisan bias in campaign-season opinion changes is markedly less pervasive than naive analysis would suggest. This example illustrates Achen's (1983) warning that measurement error does *not* necessarily bias ordinary regression parameter estimates toward zero, making them "conservative" estimates of the corresponding true effects, as analysts sometimes seem to assume. In most cases of practical interest, the direction of biases produced by measurement error is simply not predictable a priori.

If the comparisons presented in tables 1 and 2 are typical—and there is no obvious reason to suppose they are not—then many estimates of campaign effects derived from statistical analyses without adjustments for measurement error are likely to be seriously misleading. If the prospect of positive or negative biases of 50 percent or more in our parameter estimates is not very worrisome, we should probably not be estimating the parameters in the first place. If that prospect *is* very worrisome, we should do whatever we can to incorporate adjustments for measurement error in our analyses.

Reasonable adjustments for measurement error do not necessarily require panel data. Analysts could, and should, make much more routine use of instrumental variables estimation strategies when data are sufficiently plentiful to allow for the detection of politically significant effects using the sorts of instruments typically available in opinion surveys (Bartels 1991). Moreover, estimates of measurement error variance from any source can be employed to produce consistent parameter estimates using either maximum likelihood or adjusted least squares approaches (Fuller 1987); measurement models employing redundant measures of key variables at a single point in time can serve as well as those employing panel data (Bollen 1989).

TABLE 2. Impact of Measurement Error on Estimates of Partisan Activation in the 1980 Presidential Campaign

	OLS June	EV June	OLS September	EV September
Carter thermometer rating	8.0	5.9	7.3	4.8
	(1.1)	(1.4)	(1.0)	(1.3)
Reagan thermometer rating	8.3	7.8	5.8	2.6
	(1.1)	(1.3)	(1.1)	(1.6)
Carter job approval (5 items)	6.9	4.5	11.3	6.5
	(1.8)	(2.2)	(1.6)	(2.1)
Carter character (3 items)	3.5	1.9	3.6	1.2
	(1.4)	(1.7)	(1.3)	(1.7)
Carter leadership (3 items)	7.6	5.6	6.6	1.1
	(1.3)	(1.7)	(1.3)	(1.8)
Carter competence (3 items)	5.4	2.4	7.5	2.9
	(1.3)	(1.8)	(1.2)	(1.8)
Reagan character (3 items)	3.9	2.3	7.6	5.4
	(1.2)	(1.5)	(1.2)	(1.6)
Reagan leadership (3 items)	6.0	4.9	7.0	3.3
	(1.2)	(1.5)	(1.3)	(1.7)
Reagan competence (3 items)	6.5	5.1	8.2	5.0
	(1.2)	(1.5)	(1.3)	(1.8)
Average	6.2	4.5	7.2	3.6
	(1.3)	(1.6)	(1.3)	(1.7)

Note: Average OLS and EV parameter estimates with average standard errors in parentheses, calculated from Bartels 1993. $N = 753$.

While panel data are by no means necessary to make allowances for measurement error in studies of opinion change, they remain the most common and best-tested source of measurement error estimates. These estimates need not come from the data set actually being analyzed; benchmark estimates of measurement error in a variety of frequently used explanatory variables could and should be calculated from available panel data and then routinely employed in settings where panel data are unavailable.[6] Nevertheless, for analyses employing explanatory variables whose measurement properties are not already familiar, panel data are likely to provide invaluable leverage for taking serious account of the substantial threats to statistical inference posed by measurement error in survey data.

Prior Measurement of Dependent Variables

The second primary virtue of panel data is that they allow for direct observation of individual-level change in attitudes and perceptions in response to campaign events. "Change scores" may be calculated from observed responses at two points in time and subjected directly to statistical analysis, or (more generally) new opinions may be analyzed as a function of old opinions and intervening characteristics or events.[7] This is in one sense a very familiar virtue of panel data, since an explicit focus on individual-level change is practically a defining feature of panel analysis. However, as with many familiar virtues, the very familiarity of this point may obscure our understanding of *why* direct measurement of prior attitudes and perceptions is so valuable.

My argument here is that direct measurement of prior opinion has two distinct but interrelated advantages, one essentially methodological and the other more substantive. On the one hand, given the relative stability of most political attitudes under most circumstances, including prior opinions among our explanatory variables will significantly increase the precision of our statistical analyses. Every student of regression analysis learns that the precision of regression parameter estimates is inversely proportional to the residual variance in the dependent variable, which reflects the impact of potential explanatory factors that are not included (either explicitly or by proxy) as explanatory variables. If there is any panel study of political campaigns in which prior opinions do not turn out to be strongly correlated with subsequent opinions, I have not met it. Conversely, if there is any cross-sectional study of political campaigns in which current opinions are so well accounted for by contemporaneous factors that adding lagged dependent variables would not significantly reduce the residual variance, I have not met it.[8] Thus, even if our real interest is in the causes of short-term opinion *change* rather than in opinion *stability*, panel data will greatly facilitate our ability to isolate the effects of specific campaign events or processes.

On the other hand, even if our real interest is in the causes of short-term opinion change, our substantive understanding of the specific events or processes that produce that change may be greatly enriched by juxtaposing change with stability. This point could also be expressed in methodological terms by reference to potential biases in parameter estimates stemming from the "omission" of prior opinions that "belong" in a "well-specified" regression model. However, it may be expressed more substantively by simply noting that, in situations where prior opinions *are* observed and their effects are sensibly estimated, the effects of even the most salient campaign events are likely to be modest by comparison.

It may seem odd to begin by arguing from "the relative stability of most political attitudes under most circumstances," when Converse (1964) and many others have emphasized the remarkable *in*stability of most survey responses in the political realm. The key to this apparent contradiction is the distinction between attitudes and survey responses, which brings us squarely back to the issue of measurement error. If we define a political attitude as the mean of a distribution of potential survey responses, and the variation around that mean as "measurement error," it may make perfect sense to say that underlying attitudes are quite stable while survey responses are quite unstable. Nothing in the formulation or estimation of the measurement error models described in the previous section ensures that underlying attitudes will, in fact, turn out to be quite stable once random measurement error in observed survey responses is taken into account. Nevertheless, that is the nearly invariable pattern in the empirical analyses carried out by Achen (1975), Feldman (1990), and many other scholars applying measurement models to panel data.

To illustrate this point without multiplying examples, table 3 provides a comparison of OLS and EV parameter estimates of opinion stability in the 1980 presidential campaign, again from Bartels 1993. This comparison parallels the comparisons of unadjusted and adjusted parameter estimates for media exposure and partisan effects presented in tables 1 and 2. As in tables 1 and 2, there is strong evidence in table 3 of biases in the ordinary regression parameter estimates due to measurement error in the various explanatory variables included in the analysis. As in the case of media exposure (but in contrast to the case of partisan predispositions), the consequence of measurement error is to greatly understate the effect of prior opinions on current opinions in each wave of the 1980 panel study. Significant biases are apparent in every one of the separate parameter estimates, and the average magnitude of these biases is even larger than for the media exposure effects in table 1.

What is more, since similar biases are apparent in both waves of the 1980 panel study, the cumulative stability of opinions over the course of the entire election year is even more distorted in the ordinary regression estimates. The stability coefficient for each political attitude from February through September is the product of its separate stability coefficients from February through June and from June through September. Since each component of this product is badly underestimated in the ordinary regression analysis, the product is even more seriously underestimated. This com-

TABLE 3. Impact of Measurement Error on Estimates of Opinion Stability in the 1980 Presidential Campaign

	OLS June	EV June	OLS September	EV September
Carter thermometer rating	.62	.81	.63	.78
	(.03)	(.06)	(.03)	(.04)
Reagan thermometer rating	.49	.67	.61	.89
	(.03)	(.05)	(.03)	(.07)
Carter job approval (5 items)	.39	.68	.52	.95
	(.03)	(.06)	(.03)	(.06)
Carter character (3 items)	.40	.77	.42	.79
	(.04)	(.12)	(.03)	(.10)
Carter leadership (3 items)	.42	.70	.46	.89
	(.03)	(.07)	(.03)	(.07)
Carter competence (3 items)	.42	.82	.40	.86
	(.03)	(.11)	(.03)	(.09)
Reagan character (3 items)	.38	.72	.43	.88
	(.03)	(.09)	(.03)	(.10)
Reagan leadership (3 items)	.37	.71	.43	.92
	(.03)	(.10)	(.04)	(.03)
Reagan competence (3 items)	.37	.70	.44	.84
	(.03)	(.10)	(.04)	(.10)
Average	.43	.73	.48	.87
	(.03)	(.08)	(.03)	(.07)

Note: Average OLS and EV parameter estimates with average standard errors in parentheses, calculated from Bartels 1993. $N = 753$.

pounded bias is evident in the first two columns of table 4, which compare estimates of the cumulative stability of campaign-related opinions between February and September derived from the OLS and EV estimates in table 3, respectively.

The OLS estimates in the first column of table 4 suggest that, on average, only a little more than 20 percent of respondents' opinions at the time of the first NES interview in February carried over to the third interview in September. Thus, the apparent stability of these opinions is quite low, even by comparison with the fairly arcane policy issues examined over a two-year interval by Converse (1964). The implication of these estimates is that impressions formed during the election year dominate electoral politics, at least at the presidential level. By contrast, the EV estimates in the second column of table 4 suggest that, on average, more than 60 percent of respondents' February attitudes and perceptions carried over to September—a threefold increase in apparent stability over the uncorrected estimates. By this somewhat less naive reckoning, most of what people believed about both Carter and Reagan in the midst of the general election campaign was already fixed months earlier, before the public phase of the campaign had even begun.

The difference between these two sets of estimates is of obvious significance for any general understanding of the electoral process. The apparent stability of candidate evaluations, once measurement error is taken into account, highlights the political significance of what Box-Steffensmeier and Franklin (1995) have referred to, in the context of Senate elections, as "the

TABLE 4. Impact of Measurement Error on Estimates of Cumulative Opinion Stability and "Distinctive Messages"

	OLS Stability	EV Stability	OLS Messages	EV Messages
Carter thermometer rating	.394	.628	4.8	1.0
Reagan thermometer rating	.296	.592	5.0	14.4
Carter job approval (5 items)	.205	.643	1.4	−8.0
Carter character (3 items)	.170	.617	3.4	7.5
Carter leadership (3 items)	.196	.626	3.0	−2.4
Carter competence (3 items)	.166	.695	4.7	−2.1
Reagan character (3 items)	.168	.634	4.9	1.8
Reagan leadership (3 items)	.172	.664	−4.3	−26.8
Reagan competence (3 items)	.163	.584	−3.9	−16.2
Average (absolute values)	.214	.631	3.9	8.9

Note: Averages based upon OLS and EV parameter estimates, calculated from Bartels 1993. $N = 753$.

long campaign." Their analysis suggests that job approval measured two years before the 1992 Senate elections had more impact on the 1992 election outcomes than changes in job approval between 1990 and 1992, and they concluded (1995, 314) that "the time of governing strongly affects public perceptions and evaluations, and so provides a key linkage between representatives and their constituents." By the same token, the results in table 4 suggest in the context of presidential elections that attitudes toward the candidates are more a product of long-term political assessments than of short-term reactions to campaign events. In an important sense, most of what is important in electoral politics happens before the election year even begins. If one of our aims is to gauge the broad political significance of campaigns, this is a crucial fact to keep in view.

In addition to being important in its own right, the stability of prior opinions in campaign settings has more subtle but equally important implications for our understanding of how prospective voters interpret and respond to campaign events. As I have argued elsewhere (Bartels 1993), reasoning from the logic of Bayesian opinion change, new information must compete with a relatively larger mass of prior beliefs than has generally been supposed and thus must itself be much more distinctive than has generally been supposed in order to produce the changes in opinion that we actually observe. Thus, somewhat counterintuitively, evidence that preexisting opinions are quite stable suggests, albeit indirectly, that the new information absorbed during campaigns must, at least occasionally, be quite distinctive.

This second-order implication of opinion stability is illustrated in the third and fourth columns of table 4, which presents estimates of the "distinctive messages" that would be necessary to account for observed changes in candidate evaluations and trait ratings among prospective voters exposed to television news reports during the 1980 presidential campaign. Again, the results are summarized from Bartels 1993 and are reported and interpreted in more detail there. For present purposes, it may be sufficient to explain that the "distinctive message" estimates summarized in table 4 represent differences (on the 100-point attitude scales) between the new information apparently absorbed over the eight months of the 1980 NES panel study by respondents maximally exposed to network television news and those completely unexposed to network television news. Thus, for example, the estimate of -16.2 for Reagan competence in the fourth column of the table suggests that the new information regarding

Reagan's competence absorbed by regular viewers of network television news between February and September was, on average, 16 points more negative (on the 100-point scales) than the corresponding new information absorbed by nonviewers.

The comparison of "distinctive message" estimates derived from ordinary regression analysis (in the third column of table 4) and EV analysis (in the fourth column of the table) indicates that here, too, adjustment for measurement error has substantial implications for the nature of our substantive conclusions about how campaigns matter. In the ordinary regression analysis, where the stability of prior opinions and the effects of television news exposure are both significantly underestimated, the apparent distinctiveness of the campaign messages received from television news never exceeds 5 points on the 100-point attitude scales. In the EV analysis, half of the estimates exceed 5 points and the *average* estimate is almost 9 points, suggesting that the campaign messages received by television news viewers were more than twice as distinctive as the uncorrected estimates suggest.

This analysis of "distinctive messages" provides an unusually clear example of the implications of opinion stability for our understanding and interpretation of campaign processes. The Bayesian model of opinion change on which the analysis is based highlights the interconnection of preexisting opinions and new information and also provides an explicit framework for using evidence of opinion stability to specify quantitatively the implications and significance of observed opinion change. However, even in the absence of a specific formal model of opinion change, it seems likely that the direct evidence of opinion stability provided by panel data will be of considerable value in informing and enriching our understanding of campaigns as dynamic phenomena.

Prior Measurement of Explanatory Variables

The third significant virtue of panel data is that they allow us to assess the effects of explanatory variables measured outside the immediate campaign period. Contemporaneous correlations among attitude variables are seldom subject to straightforward causal interpretation, since reciprocal causation and rationalization can seldom be ruled out. This general problem may be especially severe in campaign settings, since campaigners may actually strive to provide rationalizations and reinforcement for existing attitudes as much as they strive to create new, more favorable attitudes. If a prospective voter tells us that the candidate she intends to support is "moral," or has issue preferences similar to her own, or will keep the country out of war, are her perceptions causes or effects of her vote intention? In the absence of strong theoretical preconceptions about what causes what, we are likely to be left with a morass of intercorrelations, impossible to disentangle in any very convincing way, even using sophisticated simultaneous-equation techniques. What we need, and what panel data provide, are baseline measurements of preexisting opinions and attitudes, so that *temporal* priority can inform our conclusions about *causal* priority even in the absence of strong theory.

Thus, one familiar application of panel data is to estimate so-called *cross-lag* models, in which each of two interrelated variables is regressed on lagged values of both variables. Marked asymmetries in the apparent effects of the two variables are interpreted as evidence of causal priority: if changes in B can be well accounted for by previous values of A, *but not vice versa*, then A seems more likely to be a cause of B than an effect of B.[9]

Rahn, Krosnick, and Breuning (1994) used panel data in this way to assess the causal significance of responses to open-ended questions tapping prospective voters' "likes" and "dislikes" of the competing candidates in a gubernatorial campaign. They found that overall "thermometer" ratings of the candidates at the beginning of the campaign were strongly related to the balance of likes and dislikes at the end of the campaign, even after controlling for prior likes and dislikes, but that likes and dislikes at the beginning of the campaign had only modest effects on thermometer ratings at the end of the campaign after controlling for prior thermometer ratings. They concluded that the likes and dislikes were essentially rationalizations of evaluations formed earlier on other grounds rather than causes of those evaluations.

More generally, prior measurement of explanatory variables may shed significant light on issues of causality even when cross-lag analysis is impossible or uninteresting. The basic rationale in this case is similar: prior values of explanatory variables are less likely than current values to incorporate reciprocal effects of the presumed dependent variable arising from rationalization and the like. In the language of statistical analysis, they may more plausibly be considered "exogenous" rather than "endogenous," making interpretations of their apparent effects a good deal more straightforward and compelling.

Zaller and Hunt's (1995) analysis of support for Ross Perot in the 1992 presidential election provides a useful illustration of the significant differences that may appear in comparing exogenous and endogenous correlates of vote choices. Table 5 presents two distinct sets of parameter estimates for a logit model of support for Perot. The parameter estimates in the first column of the table are derived from an analysis using explanatory variables measured in the fall of 1992, at the same time as the vote choices they are used to explain. The parameter estimates in the second column of the table are derived from an analysis using the same explanatory variables measured two years earlier, when the same respondents were interviewed in the 1990 NES survey.

The parameter estimates in the first column of table 5 suggest that support for Perot in 1992 was strongly related to partisan independence, ideological centrism, worry about the federal budget deficit, and distrust of government—essentially the same set of issues stressed by Perot in his on-again, off-again presidential campaign and by political pundits attempting then and later to explain how Perot succeeded in attracting more popular support than any other challenger to the two-party system in eighty years.

TABLE 5. Correlates of Support for Ross Perot in 1992

	Explanatory Variables Measured in 1992	Explanatory Variables Measured in 1990
Intercept	−1.40	−.37
Strength of party attachment (0–3, pure independent to strong partisan)	−.51 (.11)	−.37 (.11)
Ideological centrism (centrist = 1; other = 0)	.52 (.22)	.18 (.23)
Distrust of government (1–5)	.36 (.14)	−.01 (.12)
Worry about budget deficit (0–1)	.38 (.21)	.19 (.22)
Disapproval of Congress (1–5)	.11 (.09)	.12 (.08)
White	1.78 (.61)	1.88 (.62)
Male	.36 (.21)	.33 (.21)
Age (in years, logged)	−1.97 (.63)	−1.73 (.62)
N of cases	901	903

Note: Logit parameter estimates with standard errors in parentheses, from Zaller and Hunt 1995.

By contrast, the parameter estimates in the second column of table 5 for these same explanatory variables measured in 1990 are much smaller—half as large in the case of the budget deficit, one-third as large in the case of ideological centrism, and nonexistent in the case of distrust of government. Only the coefficient for partisan independence remains statistically significant, and even it is almost 30 percent smaller when partisan independence is measured outside the immediate campaign context than when it is measured simultaneously with vote intentions. (By contrast, the coefficients for demographic variables remain essentially unchanged between the two columns, with whites, young people, and perhaps also men being especially likely to support Perot.)

The political implications of these differences should be obvious. The parameter estimates in the first column of table 5 suggest that Perot's independent campaign tapped a variety of strong currents of public dissatisfaction with the prevailing political system: distrust of government, dissatisfaction with the ideological extremism and rigidity of the major parties and their leadership cadres, and concern about the apparent inability or unwillingness of traditional politicians to put the government's fiscal house in order. However, most of these specific currents of public dissatisfaction evaporate in the second column of table 5, leaving lack of prior attachment to the party system (as measured by strength of party identification and less directly by age) as the sole apparent basis of Perot's support. Rather than mobilizing a preexisting complex of specific political discontents, Perot appears to have provided a convenient political rationale for rather free-floating alienation from the prevailing party system.

It seems likely that a good many vote equations would look significantly different if the relevant explanatory variables were measured outside of the immediate campaign setting—and that these differences would alter our interpretations of how and why the relevant explanatory variables seem to matter. Here I provide one more example, derived from Keith et al.'s (1992) analysis of the relationship between party identification and presidential votes. A key piece of evidence offered by Wattenberg (1990) and others in support of the hypothesis of declining partisanship in American electoral politics is that survey respondents are somewhat less likely than in the 1950s to say that they think of themselves as Republicans or Democrats and more likely to claim independence from the parties. However, Keith et al. (1992) pointed out that most of these "independents" acknowledge in response to the standard NES follow-up question that they are "closer" to one party or the other and that these "independent leaners" are, in fact, just as loyal in their voting behavior as self-acknowledged party identifiers.

Table 6 reports parameter estimates from simple probit analyses of three separate NES surveys with (major-party) presidential votes as the dependent variable and categories of party identification as the explanatory variables. The results are reproduced from Bartels 2000a, and more detailed discussions of the data and analysis are presented there. As in table 5, the

TABLE 6. Party Identification and Presidential Votes

	Current Party Identification	Lagged Party Identification	Instrumental Variables
1960 (N = 1,057)			
"Strong" identifiers	1.634	1.250	1.578
	(.103)	(.082)	(.155)
"Weak" identifiers	.866	.804	.669
	(.073)	(.070)	(.200)
Independent "leaners"	1.147	.546	1.185
	(.141)	(.119)	(.601)
Republican bias	.289	.251	.227
	(.054)	(.048)	(.052)
Log-likelihood, pseudo-R^2	−418.0, .43	−506.4, .31	−506.4, .31
1976 (N = 799)			
"Strong" identifiers	1.450	1.224	1.577
	(.117)	(.107)	(.188)
"Weak" identifiers	.684	.707	.491
	(.080)	(.081)	(.243)
Independent "leaners"	.781	.545	.848
	(.109)	(.104)	(.413)
Republican bias	.103	.141	.103
	(.053)	(.051)	(.052)
Log-likelihood, pseudo-R^2	−376.8, .32	−418.4, .24	−418.4, .24
1992 (N = 729)			
"Strong" identifiers	1.853	1.311	1.622
	(.146)	(.109)	(.176)
"Weak" identifiers	.948	.761	.745
	(.099)	(.088)	(.284)
Independent "leaners"	1.117	.530	1.092
	(.122)	(.105)	(.499)
Republican bias	−.073	−.072	−.045
	(.065)	(.057)	(.059)
Log-likelihood, pseudo-R^2	−236.9, .52	−343.1, .30	−343.1, .30

Note: Probit parameter estimates with standard errors in parentheses, from Bartels 2000a. Dependent variable is Republican presidential vote (major-party voters only); party identification variables scored +1 for Republican Party identifiers of indicated strength, −1 for Democratic Party identifiers of indicated strength, and 0 otherwise.

first column reports parameter estimates derived from analyses using party identification measured during the heat of each presidential campaign, and the second column reports comparable parameter estimates derived from analyses using party identification measured two years earlier.

The results in the first column of table 6 are strongly consistent with Keith et al.'s claim that independent leaners are closet partisans; while the leaners are notably less loyal in their presidential vote choices than strong party identifiers, they appear in each of the three election years to be somewhat *more* loyal than weak party identifiers. By comparison, the results in the second column are much less consistent with the notion that independent leaners are partisans at heart. Almost all of the estimated effects in the second column are weaker than those in the first column—not surprising, given the fact that partisan loyalties are here being measured two years before the vote choices they are used to explain. However, the decline from the first column to the second is especially steep in the case of independent leaners (a decline of about 45 percent, as against 23 percent for strong identifiers and 8 percent for weak identifiers).

The final column of table 6 provides comparable parameter estimates from analyses in which lagged party identifications are used as instruments for current party identifications in each election year. This instrumental variables analysis simultaneously addresses the problems of endogeneity and measurement error, which turn out in this instance to have largely offsetting effects—endogeneity biases all of the coefficients upward, whereas measurement error biases them all downward to a roughly similar extent. As a result, the instrumental variables parameter estimates are generally quite similar in magnitude to the simple probit parameter estimates in the first column of the table, except in the case of weak party identifiers. But that correspondence is a happy accident, not a reason to conclude that either problem can safely be ignored.

In general, the availability of panel data seems to provide significant leverage on questions of causal priority that could not be addressed convincingly with cross-sectional data, even from an unusually long and rich rolling cross-section. Similar questions of causal priority arise in every field of nonexperimental research, but they are likely to be especially prevalent in the field of campaign studies, where our aim is to understand complex psychological processes operating under the influence of strenuous efforts by campaigners to forge or dissolve links among a wide variety of potentially relevant political attitudes and perceptions.

Consequences of Panel Attrition and Conditioning

The preceding discussion emphasizes three attractive features of panel designs for the study of campaign effects but does not address the corresponding drawbacks of panel data. The most serious of these is that the sample surveyed in successive panel waves may become increasingly unrepresentative of the original population, either because some of the first-wave respondents cannot be relocated or refuse to be reinterviewed (panel attrition) or because the experience of being interviewed itself affects the subsequent behavior and responses of those who are reinterviewed (panel conditioning). In either case, observed opinion change in the surviving panel sample may provide a biased estimate of the corresponding opinion change in the relevant population.

Failure to reinterview some panel respondents may result in selection bias if the probability of being reinterviewed is correlated with substantively relevant characteristics of the respondents (Heckman 1976). However, selection bias due to panel attrition seems likely to be a relatively minor problem in practice, at least in cases where panel reinterview rates are not too low. In carefully conducted surveys they need not be low. For example, 75 percent of respondents were retained through three waves of the 1980 NES election-year panel, 78 percent over the two years of the 1990–92 NES panel, and about 90 percent over the six weeks or so between typical NES pre- and postelection interviews. Given these sorts of reinterview rates, the respondents who drop out of a panel would have to be quite different from the survivors in order for their absence to produce serious selection bias.

In any case, well-developed econometric techniques exist for analyzing data in the presence of selection bias (Heckman 1979; Achen 1986). Although these techniques have not, as far as I am aware, been applied to the specific problem of panel attrition, Brehm's (1993) analysis of selection bias due to nonresponse in cross-sectional surveys provides a useful (and, for the most part, reassuring) parallel. Brehm used data from the 1986 and 1988 NES surveys to estimate a variety of familiar regression models (of turnout, candidate evaluation, economic voting, issue preferences, and so on) with and without Heckman-style corrections for selection bias. He concluded (1993, 158) that most of the models "escaped with only small changes to the coefficients."[10]

Unfortunately, biases due to panel conditioning are less well understood and techniques to correct them are less well developed. The most straightforward way to investigate the potential effects of panel conditioning is to compare panel responses with responses from a parallel fresh cross-section unexposed to the conditioning process. I provided some comparisons of this sort in a study entitled "Panel Effects in the American National Election Studies" (Bartels 2000b), exploiting the combination of panel reinterviews and fresh cross-section interviews in the 1992 and 1996 NES surveys. As with Brehm's (1993) analysis of nonresponse bias, the results are mostly, though not uniformly, reassuring. Analyses of candidate trait ratings, ideological placements, economic perceptions, and vote choices were largely unaffected by panel conditioning. On the other hand, analyses of campaign interest and turnout produced rather different results among the panel respondents than among respondents in the parallel fresh cross-sections, suggesting that panel conditioning (or panel attrition or both) significantly diluted the value of the panel data for the purposes of those analyses.

Having assessed the magnitude of panel effects in NES surveys, I also proposed some methods for addressing those effects in contexts where they are large enough to be worrisome. Given appropriate auxiliary data, it may be possible to mitigate panel biases using a "semi-pooled" model, including a simple indicator for panel respondents (if the available data include both panel and fresh cross-section components), a proxy for selection bias à la Heckman (if data are available from panel dropouts), or some other fairly parsimonious representation of potential panel effects. If data from a parallel fresh cross-section are sufficiently plentiful, they may facilitate more elaborate "panel adjusted" analyses using a straightforward variant of Franklin's (1990) "auxiliary instrumental variables" estimator. Finally, if auxiliary data and firm prior beliefs about the specific nature of likely panel effects are both lacking, it may be sensible simply to discount the inferential weight of the panel data using "fractional pooling" (Bartels 1996). Examples derived from NES surveys suggest that discounts on the order of 10 to 15 percent may often be appropriate, except for analyses of campaign interest or turnout (Bartels 2000b, 13).

Combining Panel and Rolling Cross-Section Designs

Another potentially serious limitation of traditional panel designs is that they may provide less leverage than rolling cross-sections do on the impact of specific campaign events, if those events happen to occur between successive panel waves. In the 1980 NES panel, for example, observed opinion changes between June and September might in principle be attributable to any event that occurred in the intervening period, including both parties' nominating conventions, economic and foreign policy developments, Reagan's string of campaign gaffes, the emergence of John Anderson as an independent candidate, and media coverage of these and other events. Of course, some attention to *what* opinions changed (Reagan competence ratings? economic perceptions?) and *whose* opinions changed (committed partisans? television news viewers?) may go a long way toward compensating for a lack of precise information about *when* opinions changed. Nevertheless, the sort of simple and elegant interrupted time-series analysis of the impact of specific campaign events facilitated by rolling cross-section designs is likely to be much less feasible with typical panel data.

This limitation of panel data is exacerbated by the inclination of panel study designers to concentrate each wave of interviews in a relatively short and, if possible, relatively tranquil period, in order to minimize heterogeneity in political contexts within each panel wave. Thus, for example, the first two waves of the 1980 NES panel study were conducted in the relatively quiet periods just before and just after the spring primary season. The resulting data are simple to analyze in the traditional framework of panel analysis, since "t_1" and "t_2" may be treated for most purposes as constants rather than variables. However, the cost of this simplicity is that most of the real political action occurs between panel waves and is not amenable to detailed dynamic analysis.

An obvious and potentially attractive solution to this dilemma would be to combine panel and rolling cross-section elements in the same survey design, with each panel wave spanning a variety of potentially significant campaign events. In principle, a *rolling panel design* of this sort might span the entire campaign season, with second-wave interviews beginning as soon as (or even before) first-wave interviews end and so on.

When the separate waves of a panel survey are of short duration and widely separated in time, little is lost by treating all of the interviews in a single wave as though they were conducted at the same time. But the longer each panel wave is in the field—and the higher the proportion of potentially important campaign events that occurs within panel waves rather than between panel waves—the more important and potentially interesting it will be to exploit the date of interview as an explanatory variable within each wave, in essentially the same way that rolling cross-section analysis exploits the date of interview as an explanatory variable.

The unresolved problem is how to specify and estimate a model that melds the distinct approaches to dynamic analysis of traditional panel and rolling cross-section designs. Some of the difficulties may be illustrated by considering a general framework for temporal analysis:

$$Y_{it} = Y_{i0} + \sum_{w=0\ldots t-1} Y_{iw} \Gamma_w + \sum_{w=0\ldots t-1} X_i B_w + E_{it}, \qquad (1)$$

where Y_{it} is a $(1 \times M)$ vector of politically relevant attitudes and perceptions of respondent i on date t, Y_{i0} is the corresponding set of attitudes and perceptions on an arbitrary "date 0" representing the beginning of the campaign, X_i is a $(1 \times K)$ vector of fixed characteristics of respondent i, and E_{it} is a $(1 \times M)$ vector of respondent- and date-specific idiosyncratic components in the set of relevant attitudes and perceptions of respondent i measured on date t. The parameters to be estimated in this model include T distinct $(K \times M)$ matrices B_w relating the evolution of attitudes and perceptions to fixed characteristics of respondents—one for each day of the campaign—and T distinct $(M \times M)$ matrices Γ_w relating the evolution of attitudes and perceptions to previous attitudes and perceptions—again, one for each day of the campaign.

This model provides ample scope for potential campaign dynamics. Each relevant attitude or perception may evolve on each day of the campaign in a way that depends upon both exogenous characteristics of respondents and prevailing values of endogenous variables. Thus, in particular, reactions to specific campaign events may be conditioned by respondents' current attitudes (for example, candidate evaluations), fixed characteristics (for example, location in a specific media market), or both.

Unfortunately, this model is much *too* general as it stands. Even in a very simple system with five exogenous characteristics, five endogenous attitudes, and sixty campaign days, there would be three thousand distinct parameters to be estimated. Moreover, even if all these parameters could be estimated, they could not be estimated straightforwardly, because most of the previous values of endogenous variables represented in equation (1) by Y_{iw} (for $w = 0 \ldots t$) are unobserved.

In the present context, the only difference between rolling-cross section and panel data is that in a rolling cross-section *all* of the previous values of endogenous variables are unobserved, whereas with panel data at least *some* of these values are observed. In either case, the model must be simplified in a way that finesses the problem of missing data while doing as little violence as possible to the political processes at work in actual campaign settings.[11]

If Y_{it} represents attitudes measured in the second wave of a panel study, we do have one previous set of observations for each respondent, Y_{is}, with $s < t$. Applying the same model to Y_{is} as to Y_{it} and differencing produces

$$Y_{it} - Y_{is} = \sum_{v=s \ldots t-1} Y_{iv} \Gamma_v + \sum_{v=s \ldots t-1} X_i B_v + (E_{it} - E_{is}). \quad (2)$$

One thing to note about equation (2) is that the original disturbance term E_{it} in equation (1) now becomes $(E_{it} - E_{is})$. This change is likely to be a blessing, since the differencing eliminates any individual-specific fixed effects in the idiosyncratic components.[12] However, the second thing to note about equation (2) is that observed opinion change between the first and second waves still depends upon unobserved intervening values of the endogenous variables. We might deal with this complication in any of (at least) three ways.

(1) If the endogenous variables are believed to have only modest effects on reactions to campaign events, we might assume that $\Gamma_v = 0$ for all v. In that case, we are left with observed changes in the endogenous variables as time-varying functions of exogenous respondent characteristics. Even this simplest approach is likely to represent a considerable improvement over straightforward cross-sectional analysis, since only the incremental impact of endogenous variables, rather than their total impact, is omitted (or absorbed in the effects of the exogenous characteristics).

(2) If the endogenous variables evolve fairly slowly, we might be tempted to simply replace each intervening value Y_{iv} with the corresponding first-wave value Y_{is}. In that case, we are left with observed changes in the endogenous variables as time-varying functions of both exogenous respondent characteristics and first-wave values of endogenous variables. In exchange for the inelegance and added complexity of the resulting model, we at least allow for some possibility of investigating how attitudes at each point in the campaign condition responses to subsequent campaign events.

(3) If the endogenous variables do not evolve slowly and their

dynamic effects are non-negligible, it may be necessary to construct instruments for the intervening values of endogenous variables Y_{ip}, using the exogenous characteristics X_i or the observed first-wave values Y_{is} or both. Obviously, this is a much more daunting approach, since it requires both careful attention to identifying restrictions and a great deal of data. Whether the possibility is even worth pursuing seems to me to be an open question.[13]

Even if it is possible somehow to finesse the problem of missing data for intervening values of the endogenous variables, we are left with the problem of further simplifying the model to reduce the number of parameters to be estimated. A moment's reflection will confirm that distinct date-specific effects cannot be identified for any day on which there are no respondents. Thus, if all first-wave interviews occurred on a single day s and all second-wave interviews on a single day t, only a single ($K \times M$) matrix B and a single ($M \times M$) matrix Γ could be estimated for the intervening period $t - s$. Then we are back in the traditional panel framework, with no hope of distinguishing date-specific effects and with the problem of missing data for intervening values of endogenous variables suppressed but not eliminated.

Even if there are panel respondents on every day of the campaign, it will obviously not be feasible or desirable to estimate a separate ($K \times M$) matrix B_p and a separate ($M \times M$) matrix Γ_p for every day. This embarrassment of parameters might be reduced in a variety of ways, including

> grouping days into weeks or other potentially meaningful time periods,
> imposing linear or other constraints on the daily effects over part or all of the campaign period,[14] or
> setting daily effects to zero for days with no salient campaign events, such as major speeches, scandals, or debates.

Which of these simplifications (or others or combinations of these and others) will turn out to be most fruitful is a substantive—theoretical and empirical—question. Previous work with rolling cross-section models (e.g., Johnston et al. 1992; Blais and Boyer 1996) provides some relevant suggestions, but insight and experience will be required to adapt these suggestions in order to develop tractable models that fully exploit the distinctive virtues of panel data in complex dynamic settings.

NOTES

News about research design and data analysis have been significantly shaped by the precepts and examples provided over many years by Christopher Achen and Henry Brady. Achen, Kathryn Cirksena, Charles Franklin, Shanto Iyengar, Simon Jackman, John Jackson, Norman Nie, G. Bingham Powell, John Zaller, and anonymous referees provided helpful comments on three previous pieces (Bartels 1993, 2000a, 2000b) from which some of the arguments and data analysis presented here are adapted. Additional arguments and examples derive from discussions with Steven Rosenstone and John Zaller. All of my empirical analysis is based upon data from NES, originally collected by the Center for Political Studies, University of Michigan, and made available through the Inter-University Consortium for Political and Social Research. I am grateful to the Woodrow Wilson School of Public and International Affairs at Princeton University, the John Simon Guggenheim Memorial Foundation, and the Pew Charitable Trusts for generous financial support of the research reported here.

1. The job performance measures included a general approval item plus specific items on Carter's handling of the Iranian hostage crisis, inflation, unemployment, and the energy crisis. The specific trait measures for each candidate included three items each tapping character ("power-hungry," "moral," and "dishonest"), leadership ("inspiring," "provide strong leadership," and "weak"), and competence ("develop good relations with other countries," "solve our economic problems," and "knowledgeable"). Issue preferences and candidate issue placements were also analyzed by Bartels (1993) but are omitted here.

2. To guard against the possibility of estimating spurious partisan or media exposure effects, all of the analyses included age, education, and race as additional control variables.

3. The main assumptions underlying the Wiley and Wiley model are that the measurement process produces constant error variance in each wave of the panel and that measurement errors for the same respondent in different waves of the panel are uncorrelated. I augmented the standard Wiley and Wiley model to incorporate the effects of demographic characteristics—age, education, race, and party identification—on newspaper and television news exposure in each wave of the panel and to allow for possible correlations between unmeasured factors affecting newspaper exposure and television news exposure in each wave (though these correlations turned out to be small: .03 in June and −.13 in September). I also explored a variety of other generalizations of the standard Wiley and Wiley assumptions—for example, by allowing measurement error variances to differ across panel waves or by allowing measurement errors for different responses by the same respondent to be correlated; none produced more than marginal improvements in the statistical fit of the model, and none appreciably changed the substantive results. These results are consistent with those reported by Feldman (1990, 33, 38), who applied the Wiley and Wiley model to a variety of political survey items (party identification, issue positions, and candidate evaluations) using data from a five-wave panel, for which the model is, as here, overidentified. He concluded that "the simple measurement model fits very well."

4. For more on the interpretation and political significance of these media effects, see Bartels 1993; Zaller 1996.

5. A similar pattern appears in estimated newspaper exposure effects not reported here.

6. Green, Palmquist, and Schickler's (2002) work on the measurement properties of party identification provides a good example of benchmark analysis that could easily and fruitfully be drawn upon in subsequent analyses in which party identification appears as an explanatory variable. Of course, some experience will be required to gauge how much the measurement properties of different attitudes and perceptions vary across survey settings. Ironically, we know much more about the measurement properties of party identification than of many other common explanatory variables that are much less reliable.

7. Simply analyzing "change scores" as a function of intervening characteristics or events imposes the restrictive assumption that the magnitude and direction of change is uncorrelated with the original attitude or perception. This restrictive assumption is violated by many reasonable models of opinion change, including Bayesian models of the sort motivating the analysis of Bartels (1993) described here. Analyzing "change scores" with original attitudes as explanatory variables is equivalent to analyzing subsequent attitudes with original attitudes as explanatory variables, except for a one-unit shift in the coefficient attached to original attitudes.

8. I exclude from consideration here analyses in which current opinions are impressively "explained" by essentially redundant contemporaneous factors, as when vote intentions are "explained" by evaluations of the competing candidates.

9. The concept of "Granger causality" in time-series analysis is essentially identical. See, e.g., Freeman 1983; Freeman, Williams, and Lin 1989.

10. The two most notable exceptions to this generalization were a significant overestimate of the intercept in a model of turnout and a significant underestimate of the impact of political information (as measured by familiarity with the candidates) in a model of congressional voting. The latter bias is especially worrisome given the prominence of political information as a conditioning variable in recent campaign studies.

11. Brady and Johnston's (1996) discussion of rolling cross-section models is very much in this spirit. Specific comparisons between their models and the more general formulation offered here are left as an exercise for the reader.

12. In effect, this is another aspect of the increased efficiency of panel estimation referred to in the section "Prior Measurement of Dependent Variables."

13. I note in passing that, well before this point in their parallel discussion of cross-sectional models, Brady and Johnston (1996, 9–10) warn that "[i]f this kind of change occurs, then the estimation problem is very difficult, and the simple methods we are exploring in this paper may become problematic. We hope to explore this problem in detail in other papers, but for the moment we simply note that this poses some substantial difficulties."

14. Some guidance along these lines might be provided by the literature on time-varying parameter models in time-series analysis (Beck 1983; Newbold and Bos 1985).

REFERENCES

Achen, Christopher H. 1975. "Mass Political Attitudes and the Survey Response." *American Political Science Review* 69:1218–23.

———. 1983. "Toward Theories of Political Data." In *Political Science: The State of the Discipline*, ed. Ada W. Finifter. Washington, DC: American Political Science Association.

———. 1986. *The Statistical Analysis of Quasi-Experiments*. Berkeley: University of California Press.

Bartels, Larry M. 1988. *Presidential Primaries and the Dynamics of Public Choice*. Princeton: Princeton University Press.

———. 1991. "Instrumental and 'Quasi-Instrumental' Variables." *American Journal of Political Science* 35:777–800.

———. 1993. "Messages Received: The Political Impact of Media Exposure." *American Political Science Review* 87:267–85.

———. 1996. "Pooling Disparate Observations." *American Journal of Political Science* 40:905–42.

———. 2000a. "Partisanship and Voting Behavior, 1952–1996." *American Journal of Political Science* 44:35–50.

———. 2000b. "Panel Effects in the American National Election Studies." *Political Analysis* 8:1–20.

———. 2000c. "Campaign Quality: Standards for Evaluation, Benchmarks for Reform." In *Campaign Reform: Insights and Evidence*, ed. Larry M. Bartels and Lynn Vavreck. Ann Arbor: University of Michigan Press.

Beck, Nathaniel. 1983. "Time-Varying Parameter Regression Models." *American Journal of Political Science* 27:557–600.

Berelson, Bernard R., Paul F. Lazarsfeld, and William N. McPhee. 1954. *Voting: A Study of Opinion Formation in a Presidential Campaign*. Chicago: University of Chicago Press.

Blais, André, and Martin Boyer. 1996. "Assessing the Impact of Televised Debates: The Case of the 1988 Canadian Election." *British Journal of Political Science* 26:143–64.

Bollen, Kenneth A. 1989. *Structural Equations with Latent Variables*. New York: Wiley.

Box-Steffensmeier, Janet M., and Charles H. Franklin. 1995. "The Long Campaign: Senate Elections in 1992." In *Democracy's Feast: Elections in America*, ed. Herbert F. Weisberg. Chatham, NJ: Chatham House.

Brady, Henry E. 1993. "It's Not Just Measurement Error: Guessing and Interpersonal Incomparabilities in the Survey Response." Paper presented at the annual meeting of the Midwest Political Science Association, Chicago.

Brady, Henry E., and Richard Johnston. 1996. "Statistical Methods for Analyzing Rolling Cross-Sections with Examples from the 1988 and 1993 Canadian Election Studies." Paper presented at the annual meeting of the Midwest Political Science Association, Chicago.

Brehm, John. 1993. *The Phantom Respondents: Opinion Surveys and Political Representation*. Ann Arbor: University of Michigan Press.

Converse, Philip E. 1964. "The Nature of Belief Systems in Mass Publics." In *Ideology and Discontent*, ed. David E. Apter. New York: Free Press.

Cook, Thomas D., and Donald T. Campbell. 1979. *Quasi-Experimentation: Design and Analysis Issues for Field Settings.* Boston: Houghton Mifflin.

Feldman, Stanley. 1990. "Measuring Issue Preferences: The Problem of Response Instability." *Political Analysis* 1:25–60.

Finkel, Steven E. 1993. "Reexamining the 'Minimal Effects' Model in Recent Presidential Campaigns." *Journal of Politics* 55:1–21.

Franklin, Charles H. 1990. "Estimation across Data Sets: Two-Stage Auxiliary Instrumental Variables Estimation (2SAIV)." *Political Analysis* 1:1–24.

Freeman, John R. 1983. "Granger Causality and the Time Series Analysis of Political Relationships." *American Journal of Political Science* 27:327–58.

Freeman, John R., John T. Williams, and Tse-min Lin. 1989. "Vector Autoregression and the Study of Politics." *American Journal of Political Science* 33:842–77.

Fuller, Wayne A. 1987. *Measurement Error Models.* New York: Wiley.

Green, Donald P., Bradley Palmquist, and Eric Schickler. 2002. *Partisan Hearts and Minds: Political Parties and the Social Identities of Voters.* New Haven: Yale University Press.

Heckman, James J. 1976. "The Common Structure of Statistical Models of Truncation, Sample Selection, and Limited Dependent Variables and a Simple Estimator for Such Models." *Annals of Economic and Social Measurement* 5:475–92.

———. 1979. "Sample Selection Bias as a Specification Error." *Econometrica* 47:153–61.

Heise, David R. 1969. "Separating Reliability and Stability in Test-Retest Correlation." *American Sociological Review* 34:93–101.

Jennings, M. Kent, and Richard G. Niemi. 1981. *Generations and Politics: A Panel Study of Young Adults and Their Parents.* Princeton: Princeton University Press.

Johnston, Richard, André Blais, Henry E. Brady, and Jean Crête. 1992. *Letting the People Decide: Dynamics of a Canadian Election.* Montreal: McGill-Queen's University Press.

Johnston, Richard, and Henry E. Brady. 2002. "The Rolling Cross-Section Design." *Electoral Studies* 21:283–95.

Jöreskog, Karl G. 1979. "Statistical Models and Methods for Analysis of Longitudinal Data." In *Advances in Factor Analysis and Structural Equation Models,* ed. Karl G. Jöreskog and Dag Sörbom. Cambridge, MA: ABT Books.

Just, Marion R., Ann N. Crigler, Dean E. Alger, Timothy E. Cook, Mantague Kern, and Darrell M. West. 1996. *Crosstalk: Citizens, Candidates, and the Media in a Presidential Campaign.* Chicago: University of Chicago Press.

Keith, Bruce E., David B. Magleby, Candice J. Nelson, Elizabeth Orr, Mark C. Westlye, and Raymond E. Wolfinger. 1992. *The Myth of the Independent Voter.* Berkeley: University of California Press.

Lazarsfeld, Paul F., Bernard Berelson, and Hazel Gaudet. 1948. *The People's Choice.* New York: Columbia University Press.

Markus, Gregory B. 1982. "Political Attitudes during an Election Year: A Report on the 1980 NES Panel Study." *American Political Science Review* 76:538–60.

Newbold, Paul, and Theodore Bos. 1985. *Stochastic Parameter Regression Models.* Newbury Park, CA: Sage.

Patterson, Thomas E. 1980. *The Mass Media Election: How Americans Choose Their President.* New York: Praeger.

Patterson, Thomas E., and Robert D. McClure. 1976. *The Unseeing Eye: The Myth of Television Power in National Elections.* New York: Putnam.

Rahn, Wendy M., Jon A. Krosnick, and Marijke Breuning. 1994. "Rationalization and Derivation Processes in Survey Studies of Political Candidate Evaluation." *American Journal of Political Science* 38:582–600.

Sanders, Mitch S. 1996. "Beneath Stormy Waters: The Evolution of Individual Decision Making in the 1984 and 1988 Presidential Elections." PhD diss., Department of Political Science, University of Rochester.

Vavreck, Lynn. 1997. "More than Minimal Effects: Explaining Differences between Clarifying and Insurgent Campaigns in Strategy and Effect." PhD diss., Department of Political Science, University of Rochester.

Wattenberg, Martin P. 1990. *The Decline of American Political Parties, 1952–1988.* Cambridge, MA: Harvard University Press.

Wiley, David E., and James A. Wiley. 1970. "The Estimation of Measurement Error in Panel Data." *American Sociological Review* 35:112–17.

Wright, Gerald C. 1990. "Misreports of Vote Choice in the 1988 NES Senate Election Study." *Legislative Studies Quarterly* 15:543–63.

———. 1993. "Errors in Measuring Vote Choice in the National Election Studies, 1952–1988." *American Journal of Political Science* 37:291–316.

Zaller, John R. 1992. *The Nature and Origins of Mass Opinion.* New York: Cambridge University Press.

———. 1996. "The Myth of Massive Media Impact Revived: New Support for a Discredited Idea." In *Political Persuasion and Attitude Change,* ed. Diana C. Mutz, Paul M. Sniderman, and Richard A. Brody. Ann Arbor: University of Michigan Press.

Zaller, John, and Stanley Feldman. 1992. "A Simple Theory of the Survey Response: Answering Questions vs. Revealing Preferences." *American Journal of Political Science* 36:579–616.

Zaller, John, and Mark Hunt. 1995. "The Rise and Fall of Candidate Perot: The Outsider versus the Political System—Part II." *Political Communication* 12:97–123.

The Rolling Cross-Section and Causal Attribution

Henry E. Brady and Richard Johnston

FOR CAPTURING CAMPAIGN EFFECTS, the main alternative to the panel design is controlled daily release of sample, the "rolling cross-section." Unlike the panel, the rolling cross-section cannot by itself capture individual change, but it is a more practical and cost-effective alternative for capturing aggregate shifts. It can, moreover, be combined with a panel, such that each design adds power and precision to the other. By some substantive criteria, the rolling cross-section dominates all alternatives. All respondents are "new to the survey" so conditioning effects are minimized. The potential fine "granularity" of sample release facilitates causal attribution by making it possible to link campaign events directly with subsequent opinion change. After fieldwork is completed, at the analysis stage, the design is supremely flexible because the sample can be cut apart at any time point, whereas panels require ex ante decisions about the choice of interview dates. As a result, the design can muster far more statistical power than might first appear from the inevitably small sample collected for any given day. The unifying fact behind these advantages is that the probability a respondent will be interviewed on any given day is as much a product of random selection as is that respondent's initial presence in the sample. But the smallness of daily samples is a serious issue. The granularity made possible by continuous, unbroken, but low-intensity fieldwork comes at a price: the limited statistical power to distinguish individual days.

This essay addresses these issues. It opens with a paradigmatic illustration of causal attribution from the closely fought 2000 presidential campaign. The illustration shows the limitation of a panel design in causal attribution, but it also shows the limits of the rolling cross-section. This forces us to ask just what the rolling cross-section is and how it might be deployed, the topic of the second section. Then follows an exposition of the logic of the primary method of compensating for the potential lack of statistical power: graphical smoothing. Part of the argument is for graphs as such: the rolling cross-section makes their use both desirable and relatively unproblematic. They are desirable in that they greatly facilitate primary research—not to mention exposition—where a major element in analysis is real time. They are relatively unproblematic because of the random assignment of each respondent to an interview date; controls for respondents' accessibility are just not required. But the smallness of daily samples forces graphical data to be smoothed, and choices among smoothing alternatives are not simple. We end with the discussion of a mixed design and a quick overview of other literature about analyzing the rolling cross-section design.

An Example

Johnston, Hagen, and Jamieson 2004 argue that a pivotal feature of the 2000 campaign was a shift in perceptions of Al Gore's character, in particular of his honesty. It would be natural for a researcher to assume beforehand that one of the major campaign events causing opinion shifts would be the presidential debates and to design a panel to capture possible shifts. Figure 1 certainly points in this direction. Figure 1a sets up data from the 2000 National Annenberg Elections Study (NAES)[1] as if resources had been committed to a simple three-wave panel with interviews before the debates (September and the first two days of October), between the first and last debate (October 3 to 16), and after the last debate (October 17 to the end). Mean values for Gore's honesty rating are indicated by solid horizontal bars, with 95 percent confidence intervals around them, for each of the three periods. For interpretive ease, ratings have been rescaled to the -1 to $+1$ interval, with values below zero conveying negative judgment.[2] The narrow confidence intervals reflect the massive accumulation of sample in the NAES.

Unquestionably, Al Gore was better regarded before the first debate than after it. The predebate mean is positive while the postdebate mean is negative. The confidence intervals suggest that there is no possibility that

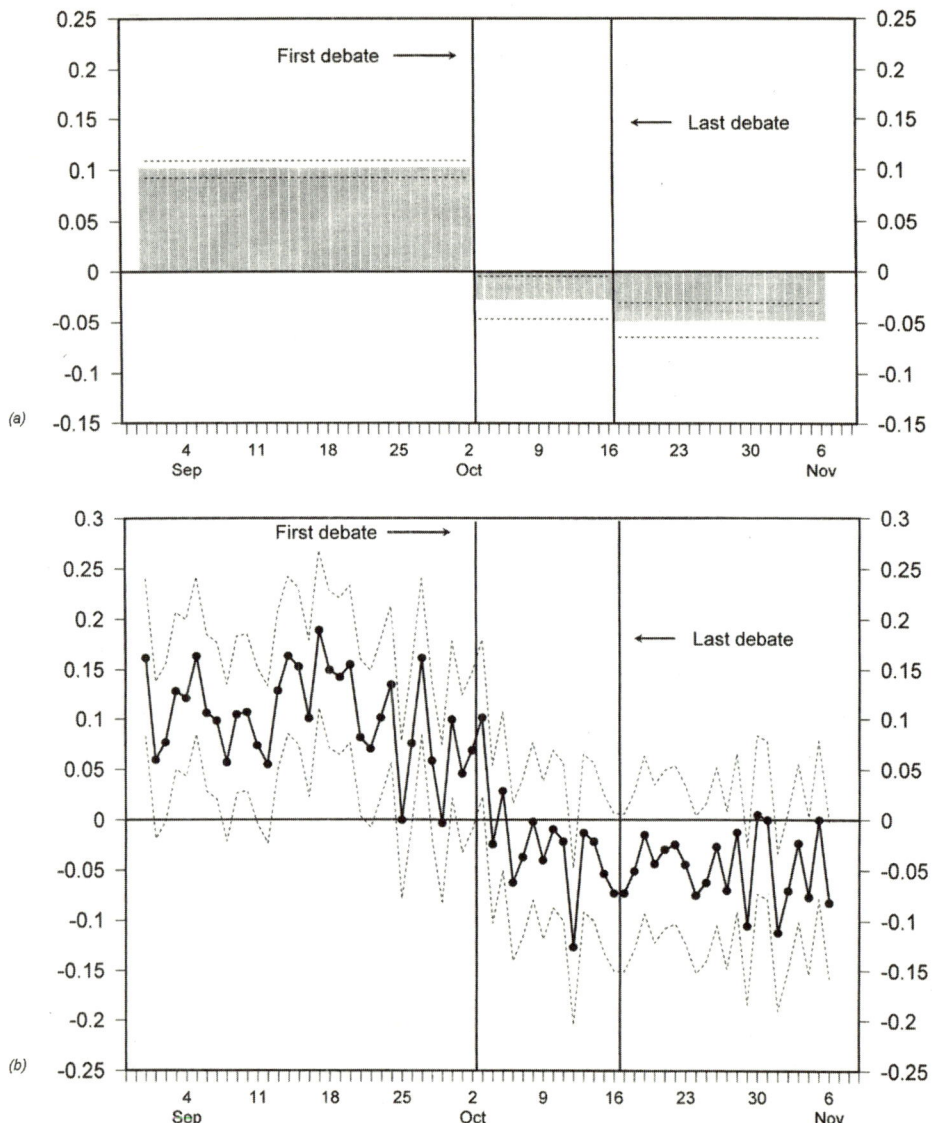

Fig. 1. Debates and perceptions of Al Gore's honesty. (*a*) Pre-post means; whole-period estimates; dashed lines are approximate 95 percent confidence interval. (*b*) Daily means; daily estimates; dashed lines are approximate 95 percent confidence interval. (Data from 2000 Annenberg Election Survey.)

these results were generated from the same underlying distribution. If any debate mattered, it must have been the first one, as the first shift is both larger and statistically less ambiguous than the second one. There is a suggestion that opinion on Gore deteriorated further after the second debate, but even the large sample sizes in the period do not allow us to reject the null hypothesis of no difference between the days before and the days after the last debate.

But how do we know that any debate was critical? The data were cut arbitrarily at the dates of the public events to simulate the results from a panel designed on the premise that debates are crucial moments in the history of a campaign. It is, of course, a reasonable supposition that if anything has dynamic impact, debates will. But the analysis is based on that supposition, not on any consideration of actual dynamics. Certainly, if one is precommitted to a panel design, it would not make sense to mark the boundary between interview and reinterview at anything other than a major public event. The campaign is about more than public events, however.

Figure 1b suggests that using only a crude pre-/postevent design might lead to an inappropriate causal attribution. In this panel the NAES data are fully rolled out as a daily tracking. The data are noisy, of course, as indicated both by the amount of surplus day-to-day vertical movement in the data and by the 95 percent confidence interval, which is an order of magnitude larger than those in figure 1a. Notwithstanding the noise, the first debate does not seem to be the whole of it. Values in the week or so before the first debate are lower than those that typify early September. There is a strong hint, then, that downward movement started even before the debates. But there is also a suggestion that emphasis on the first debate is not entirely misplaced. The day after the first debate witnessed a sharp drop in Gore's rating. The drop was not the largest of the series, but it is one of the few that were not corrected by immediately following observations. Could it be that the debate accelerated the decay? The picture also suggests that other debates did *not* affect Gore's ratings. The entire drop after the first debate occurred in the first few post–first debate days.

The picture so far is unclear. The temporally crude but statistically powerful periodization in panel a confirms that Gore's ratings dropped. There is no question that a sharp contrast exists between the period before and after the first debate. But figure 1b indicates that focus on the first debate does not do justice to the data. Movement probably predated the debate and may not have been affected by it. Then again, it might have, and identification of the real predebate turning point is next to impossible. As the rolling cross-section data are presented in panel b, they are powerful enough to undermine an exclusive emphasis on the debate but not powerful enough to underpin a conclusive alternative interpretation.

The Design

What is the design that gets us to this point? In essence, a "rolling" cross-section is just a cross-section of respondents, but with a twist. In any survey, when the list of potential respondents is released to interviewers to begin the process of contacting them for an interview, the interviewers are asked to follow a careful mix of calling at different times of the day and on different days of the week in order to maximize the chance of eventually finding the respondent at home. The process of completing interviews in this way is called "clearing the sample." Aggressive and systematic clearance compensates for the accidents of daily life that cause people to be away from their telephone at different times. Much of the variation in the quality of surveys and of survey houses lies in the willingness to spend money on clearance. As a result, any self-respecting survey will have several days for clearance built into it.

At the same time, the more such days, the more vulnerable the survey will be to changes in responses because of real events. People called by pollsters after September 11, 2001, for example, had much different attitudes on terrorism and defense than people called just before the tragic events of that day. But to complicate things, some of the apparent effect of time will not be from events in real time but from differences in the respondents: from any sampling frame, respondents interviewed later in the clearance period are likely to differ systematically from those easier to reach and thus interviewed earlier (Dunkelberg and Day 1973; Hawkins 1975; Groves 1989). Disentangling impact from factors evolving in real time from impact due to mere accessibility of respondents is a formidable task. But failure to take the task on may lead an analyst to misrepresent the data.

The rolling cross-section design converts the "bug" of temporal heterogeneity into a "feature." The steps in executing the design for a telephone survey are as follows.

1. Generate enough random four-digit numbers (married to known live exchanges and area codes, obviously) to achieve a target number of completed interviews over a specified period.
2. Divide the total body of telephone numbers into "replicates," each large enough to generate a given target of completions, where the target is the minimum number of completions for a subperiod, say, a day. The division of the total into replicates is essentially a random subsampling process.
3. Release replicates to the interviewers in a controlled fashion. This can be an equal number per day, or the number of replicates released on any given day can reflect priors on the importance of events in a period or on the "frequency domain" of political time.
4. Whatever the schedule for release, treat each replicate the same as every other. This means holding the numbers open for a specified number of days and applying a callback schedule that yields a constant clearance profile over the days that follow release to field. The callback schedule may vary over days of the week and over weeks of the year, reflecting known facts about the general accessibility of persons and households. Samples have to be worked harder on weekends and in holiday seasons, for example, to ensure equal probabilities of contact between normal weekdays and weekends or holidays.[3]

Figure 2 illustrates this for a representative day in the 2000 NAES. On July 5, 2000, enough numbers were released to complete 300 interviews, the target that was used for every day for the rest of the campaign. This represents six NAES replicates, where each replicate had a completion target of 50. The number of NAES replicates released per day reflected the intensity of campaigning: quite high during the presidential primaries, low in the fallow period of late spring, and higher than ever from July 5 to Election Day. Figure 2 shows the time path by which the 275 ultimate completions from the July 5 replicates were accomplished. Of all such completions, just over 40 percent (115 to 120 interviews) were recorded on July 5 itself. Over half of these interviews stemmed from the first call, and most of the rest took place on the second call. One number received four calls. Just under 20 percent of all completions (about 50 interviews) came the next

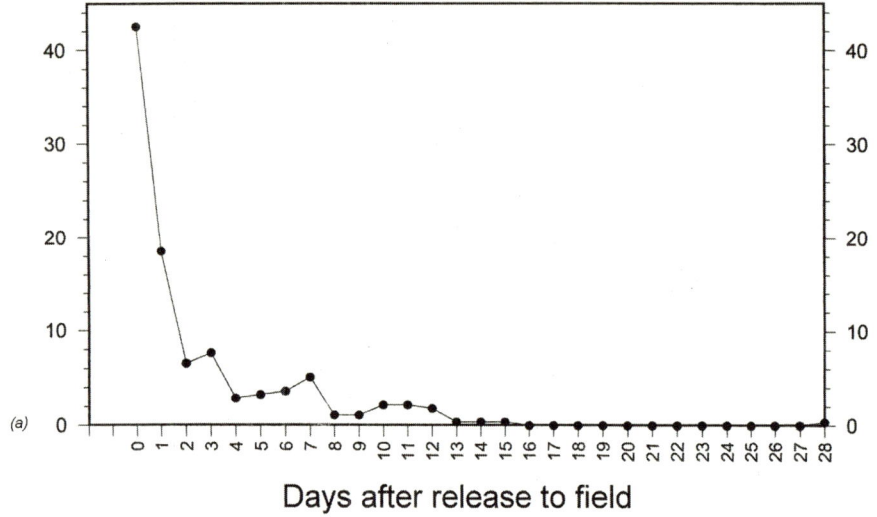

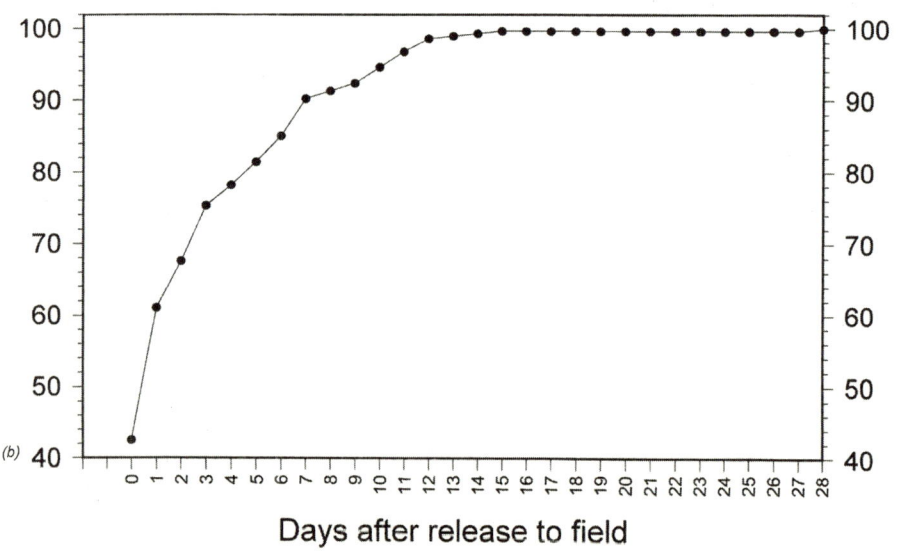

Fig. 2. Calls to completion, replicates released on July 5. (a) Percentage by day. (b) Cumulative percentage. (Data from 2000 Annenberg Election Survey.)

day, such that by the end of this day over 60 percent of interviews that would ultimately be completed were in the bank. Thereafter, increments were small: under 10 percent of ultimate completions for days 3 and 4 and under 5 percent for all succeeding days. By one week out, over 90 percent of ultimate completions had been recorded, and by two weeks (the nominal end of the interviewing window for any replicate) over 99 percent of interviews were in the bank. As it happens, one interview from the July 5 sample was conducted four weeks after release.

Now imagine the transposition of this sequence into the completion pattern for replicates released on later days. If the second day's replicates have exactly the same distribution as the first, then about 115 to 120 interviews on day 2 will be from that day's replicates, and about 50 interviews completed that day will be from replicates released the day before. The total number of interviews on day 2 should be about 165. On the third day, another 115 to 120 interviews will accrue from that day's release, along with about 50 from day 2 and 20 from day 1, for a total of about 210. The daily total will build for about two weeks, at which point earlier replicates will have been exhausted and dropped. From this point on, we can say that the day on which a respondent is interviewed is the product of a random draw.[4] Practically speaking, this is effectively true after about a week of interviewing so that from that time on the group of people interviewed on each day can be treated as a representative cross-section of the population.

Reality is slightly messier, but only slightly, according to figure 3. This figure tracks actual completions from July 5 to Election Day. The actual number of completions on July 5 is larger than the number implied in figure 2, as the NAES was already in the field. Before the Independence Day holiday, only one replicate was released per day, with an average daily completion rate of 50 interviews. The ramping up of fieldwork required close to two weeks, although the presence of open numbers from before July 5 accelerated the uptake modestly. In any case, from mid-July on, completions oscillated around the 300-person target.[5]

Advantages

For all the apparent complication of sample release and clearance, what results is just a set of daily cross-sections that can be combined into a large cross-section. And almost any temporal subsample can be combined into a

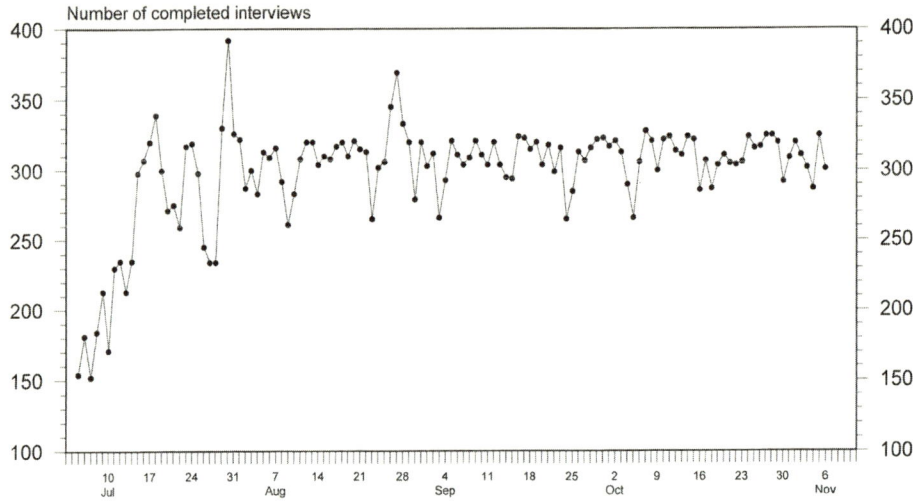

Fig. 3. Completed interviews by day, July 5 to Election Day. (Data from 2000 Annenberg Election Survey.)

representative cross-section, for example, the predebate, between-debate, and postdebate samples used in figure 1.[6] From this flow several benefits: low cost, uncontaminated respondents, and flexibility in choice of subperiods, with potentially high "granularity." Some of these advantages also carry corresponding disadvantages.

Low Cost

The cost of a rolling cross-section is only marginally more than of any other telephone cross-section with correspondingly aggressive clearance. Somewhat more management overhead is dictated by the need to monitor the process every day. A nonmonetary cost is paid in response rate, for two reasons. Assignment of the house's best interviewers to reluctant cases takes place earlier in a schedule that keeps cases open for only two weeks. This probably yields fewer conversions.[7] Most critical, however, is the arithmetic of the late campaign. Note in figure 3 that the rate of completion remained quite steady right to the end. Consider what this implies from the logic of figure 2. The replicates released on the last day of interviewing had one day only, that last day of interviewing, to be cleared. Replicates released the day before had only two days and so on. Inescapably, the NAES response rate started to drop two weeks before the end, and the same will be true, mutatis mutandis, for any rolling cross-section.[8] Initial response-rate decline is tiny, but it accelerates, essentially, on the temporal inverse of the pattern in figure 2b. The crucial point, however, is that each daily cross-section is representative of the population.

Fresh Respondents

Merely by virtue of their selection for a conversation that represents a more pointed focus on politics than most persons would ever experience in ordinary life, respondents are transformed by their encounter with a survey. But it seems likely that this conditioning is the result of the interview process, not just the fact of being contacted to do an interview. Consequently, compared to respondents at second and subsequent waves of panels, rolling cross-section respondents are only minimally conditioned. This seems like a major advantage even for events around which panels are commonly constructed. If one observes a pre–post effect from a debate, how much does that effect reflect conditioning from the initial interview?[9]

The price, of course, is that individual-level change cannot be captured. Analysis can close in on archetypal subgroups or profiles, to the extent that the variables defining group or profile membership are exogenous and thus insensitive to the passage of time. Demographic characteristics fit this criterion. Certain political "fundamentals" (Zaller 1998), such as party identification and ideological self-designation, come close but do not absolutely qualify.[10] Variables that respond to the campaign, such as exposure to and interest in media coverage, are clearly inappropriate as controls. And even the most stable of attribute distributions—race and religion, for example—still leave us short of capturing individual response.

Flexible Subperiods and "Granularity"

Figure 1 illustrates the flexibility of the design, as subperiods were adjusted after the fact to the dates of debates. In this case, we *chose* to divide the sample at the debates; we were not forced to do so by the logic of ex ante anticipation. At the same time, we achieve an efficient record of the time path of debate (or any event) effects, in that the first day after the event—as is also true of all further days—is just as much a cross-section as any single day or any number of days before the event. If the researcher is interested in, say, the immediacy with which impact unfolds and or in differences in time path between critical partitions of the sample (for example, whether or not the respondent saw any of the debate or the respondent's general exposure and attention to the mass media), relevant data not compromised by accessibility bias appear immediately after the event.[11] Meanwhile, joining up any combination of consecutive days is unproblematic. From the sampling perspective, all that adding or subtracting a day does is reduce or expand standard error. No other aspect of sample selection is being tweaked in the slightest. So the design combines flexibility in periodization with power in combination of days.

If this approach to seeking campaign effects seems ad hoc, the accusation is not troubling given the lack of theory about what drives the twists and turns of campaigns. Theory leaves us short of expectations for the identification of important campaign events, much less their timing and temporal shape. Holbrook (1996, chap. 6) very usefully and imaginatively goes beyond conventions and debates by considering other kinds of campaign events, but his criteria for selection events is "admittedly vague" (127), and he does not consider their temporal shape. Shaw's 1999 work catalogs alternative time paths suggested by control theory, and he tries to see what kinds of events follow which paths. But even he does not supply more than a typology of dependent-variable distributions. There is, so far, no body of propositions that might distinguish debates from conventions, for example, or a news impact from an advertising one. At the very least, the rolling cross-section allows us to maximize the variance to be explained. Down the road, it should allow us to build an inventory of dynamic patterns.

What makes this possible, of course, is daily management of data collection, such that any single day yields a random subsample of the total sample. Apart from the flexibility this affords us, the natural temptation is to focus on individual days, but the idea, just fronted, of identifying dynamic patterns involves more than juxtaposing consecutive days. It requires examining the pattern *within* that body of days or consecutive groups of small numbers of days, ideally by day-by-day comparison. The problem is illustrated by the example this essay opened with. We noted that there *did* seem to be some effect of the first debate, in that the immediately following days seemed to yield low readings, relative to the days before. But the days before also seemed to exhibit a drop in Gore's rating. This cast some doubt on the independent effect of the debate. But identifying an earlier point of discontinuity defied the naked eye. Realizing the full value of the design requires some mode of induction that captures the signal of true turning points from the noise of sampling error.

Graphical Smoothing

The Smoothing Problem

Smoothing methods for rolling cross-sections make it easier to identify the shape of true responses when they may be obscured by noise from sampling error, but smoothing methods must deal with two fundamental problems in separating "signal" from "noise." First, the shape of the signal poses analytical difficulties because different methods are needed to identify smooth versus abrupt changes in true responses. Yet, even for presidential debates, which have been studied for over forty years, we do not know whether poor performances have immediate impacts on public opinion like falling off a cliff or slower impacts like descending in an airplane. Second, sampling error presents problems because it creates noise that can be mistaken for real effects. Sampling error results from the variation in responses from observation to observation, and it is reduced by increasing the number of observations to allow the law of large numbers to smooth things out.

In election surveys, the variation in responses from subject to subject consists of two things: true differences in opinions across respondents and temporary differences within a respondent due to the vagaries of each person's response to questions. The former reflects heterogeneity in the population, and the later reflects measurement error due to imperfect questions and imperfect interviewing methods. If the population were homogeneous and every subject had the same opinion, then just one subject could be chosen to represent the population, but there is typically substantial heterogeneity in the population, and different people have different true opinions leading to variation from subject to subject. If we had a panel design in which the same person was observed again and again over time, then, putting aside the problems of conditioning and measurement error, any changes in the person's opinions could be ascribed to campaign events. But with heterogeneity and new cross-sections in every time period, variation in responses from one time period to the next could be due to differences in the people who are chosen and not the impacts of the campaign. The solution to this problem is to observe enough people in each time period—to have a large enough sample size—so that variation from one time period to the next due to sampling error is small compared to variation from campaign events.

Even if the population were homogenous or even if we had a panel, the variation from period to period might be due to measurement error—the different ways that people can answer questions when they have the same opinions. People with the same opinions may interpret the question in different ways because of interviewer effects or simply the imprecision of the question. Once again, with rolling cross-sections, the solution to this problem is to have a large enough sample size so that average measurement error is small compared to variation due to campaign events.

The Mean-Squared Error Criterion for Smoothing

A large sample size is the best way to smooth the data because it improves the signal to noise ratio by diminishing sampling error, but large samples are costly and constrained by limited budgets. Given the limits on daily sample sizes, the problem is to find the best way to extract signal from noise given the data at hand. For the Annenberg study this means finding the best way to analyze data on about three hundred respondents per day as shown in figure 3. The goal is to get the best rendition of the course of public opinion—the shape of the curve u_t where t is time and u_t is the true daily mean of opinion.

To do this, we need some criterion by which we can judge whether we have done a good or a bad job of smoothing the data. One criterion is unbiasedness. By this standard, if we want to know the population's average estimate of Gore's honesty (denoted by u_1, u_2, and u_3) for the three periods 1, 2, and 3, then the best estimate for each mean is the sample average of Gore's honesty ratings in each period from the three hundred respondents who were interviewed during that period. We denote these sample averages by u_1^*, u_2^*, and u_3^*. It is a standard result that with random sampling the expected value of each of these is equal to the true mean for that particular day; that is, u_1^*, u_2^*, and u_3^* are unbiased estimates of u_1, u_2, and u_3, respectively. For period 1, for example, this means that if we were to repeatedly sample from the population and get many estimates of u_1^* (say, from different polling firms operating on that same day), then the average of these many estimates would equal the true population value u_1. Unbiasedness of this sort is an especially useful property if we are looking for turning points because we want to make sure that each daily estimate is an unbiased estimate of the true signal for that day.

But another criterion is minimizing variance so that the standard errors of estimates of views about Gore's honesty are as small as possible. Since standard errors are a measurement of the amount by which our estimates vary from sample to sample, minimizing them means that we have reduced noise to a minimum. If we assume that the total variance due to heterogeneity and measurement error is s^2, then the sampling variance for each of u_1^*, u_2^*, and u_3^* is s^2/n, where $n = 300$, the number of observations in each period. For small n the quantity s^2/n can still be quite large. We could get an even smaller sampling variance if we assumed that Gore's honesty did not change over periods 1, 2, and 3 so that we could average u_1^*, u_2^*, and u_3^* to get $u^\# = (u_1^* + u_2^* + u_3^*)/3$ with a variance of $s^2/3n$—one-third the size of the previous sampling variance.

The quantity $u^\#$ is a three-period average, and if for any time-series with observations $t-1$, t, and $t+1$ we define $u_t^\# = (u_{t-1}^* + u_t^* + u_{t+1}^*)/3$, then we have a *three-period moving average*. The equal weights of (1/3, 1/3, 1/3) that define this estimator $u_t^\#$ are called the kernel weights in the statistical literature or just the kernel. Note that the weights always sum to one, but different patterns of weights define different estimators. The kernel for the estimator that takes just the *current period's mean* u_t^* from among $(u_{t-1}^*, u_t^*, u_{t+1}^*)$ is (0,1,0). Hence, the kernel defines different ways to combine the daily sample means to produce an estimator, and kernels have different shapes ranging from the flat or "uniform" distribution with equal weights for the three-period moving average to the sharply peaked (at the middle value) shape for the current period's mean.

Unfortunately, $u^\#$ might be a biased estimate of even u_2, the middle period's value for Gore's honesty if Gore's honesty varies by period.[12] Thus, there is a tradeoff between bias and sampling variance, but we might be willing to trade a little bit of bias for a lot smaller sampling variance. There are, of course, limits to this, and we would not be willing to trade a lot of bias for a slightly reduced sampling variance. Statisticians formalize this tradeoff by considering mean squared error as a summary criterion for any estimator. Mean squared error is equal to the bias squared plus the sampling variance. To simplify the computation of mean squared error in this case, we set the zero point of the honesty scale by assuming that the middle value u_2 for honesty is equal to zero. There is no loss in generality in doing this because the scale is arbitrary to begin with. With this costless simplification, we can easily compute the mean squared error for $u^\#$ as an estimator of u_2:[13]

$$\text{MSE}(u^\#) = [u_1 + u_3]^2/9 + s^2/3n.$$

The formula for the bias term $[u_1 + u_3]^2/9$ may not seem intuitively obvious so we explore its properties in more detail later. We can also compute the mean squared error from using u_2^* as the estimator for u_2, which will be just equal to the variance of u_2^* since u_2^* is an unbiased estimator of u_2:

$$\text{MSE}(u_2^*) = s^2/n.$$

Under what conditions should we use $u^\#$ versus u_2^*? That is, under what conditions should we use the three-period moving average versus the one period estimate? As the variance s^2 gets bigger, there is more noise in the data. It makes sense in this situation to use $u^\#$ instead of u_2^* because the bias term in $\text{MSE}(u^\#)$, that is, $[u_1 + u_3]^2/9$, will be dominated by the variance term, $s^2/3n$, so it is worth accepting some bias from averaging all three periods to get the much smaller variance term ($s^2/3n$) in $u^\#$ compared to that (s^2/n) in u_2^*. As n gets bigger and bigger, the bias term in $\text{MSE}(u^\#)$ will dominate the variance term so it will make sense to use u_2^*, which does not have any bias term. With more observations, there is no need to average over adjoining periods in order to reduce noise—the number of observations in a single period does that nicely. Similarly, as the bias term gets bigger and bigger, it makes sense to use u_2^* instead of $u^\#$ because u_2^* is unbiased. That is, if the twists and turns of the campaign cause the variable of interest to change a lot, then we should refrain from averaging over adjacent periods.[14] In summary, for large variance, small n, and small bias, it makes sense to use $u^\#$. For small variance, large n, and large bias, we should use u_2^*.

The Shape of the Response Curve as a Crucial Factor

The bias term, $(u_1 + u_3)^2$, deserves some additional discussion because it summarizes the shape of the response curve—the way that ratings of Gore's honesty can be expected to go up and down. Because we have set $u_2 = 0$, this quantity attains its smallest possible value of zero when u_1 and u_3 are also zero. In this case, it clearly makes sense to combine the three periods to estimate Gore's honesty because the true value is the same for all three periods. But the bias term also attains its smallest possible value when $u_1 = -u_3$ and the three points lie along a straight line u_t with a constant slope. Thus, the bias term is only nonzero when the three points u_1, u_2, and u_3 depart from lying along a straight line—only when the slope of the curve u_t is changing. The classic measure of the change in a slope is the second derivative of the curve. Consider the standard difference-in-differences approximation of a second derivative:

$$u_t'' = \partial^2 u(t)/\partial t^2 \approx \{[(u_3 - u_2)/h] - [(u_2 - u_1)/h]\}/h,$$

where h is some small unit of time. Since we have assumed that $u_2 = 0$, this amounts to $u_t'' \approx [u_3 + u_1]/h^2$ so that by a little algebra, $h^2 u_t'' \approx [u_3 + u_1]$, which is the square root of the bias term. This result will come in handy later because $[u_t'']^2$ is a convenient measure of the shape of the response that we want to detect.

Choosing the Bandwidth

So far, we have been thinking about the problem of smoothing as one in which we want to choose the optimal weights (or kernel) for an estimator that uses data from three time periods. In some cases, as discussed previously, this might mean that very little smoothing takes place, and in others it might mean that a great deal of smoothing occurs. There is, however, another way to think of the problem. Instead of choosing the optimal kernel for three periods, we might choose a particular kernel shape (uniform, peaked, or some other shape) and then ask how many periods should be smoothed with this kernel. If the number of periods is very small (for example, a few hours instead of weeks or months, which consist of many hours), then the kernel will smooth over a very short period of time. If the number of periods is very large, then the kernel will smooth over a longer period of time. One reason for reformulating the problem in this way is that it turns out that the shape of the kernel typically matters less than the period of time over which the smoothing takes place, and there appears to be good arguments for always choosing particular shapes such as the parabolic Epanechnikov kernel (Hardle 1990, 24–26, 133–37).

To reformulate the problem in this way, suppose that observations are spread evenly over the total campaign that is being studied so that we can slice the time periods smaller and smaller and still get some observations. Thus months can be split into weeks and weeks into days. Of course, there is a limit to how far we can do this with the rolling cross-section design because our smallest unit is a day, but this thought experiment is nevertheless useful. Assume that the total length of the time period on the horizontal axis is one unit and that there are N observations spread evenly over this entire time period. We break the horizontal axis into a number of evenly spaced time periods, each of which is h units apart, where h is some fraction of one. These time units might be months, weeks, or days. Then for any given time period, there are $n = hN$ observations. Our goal will be to see what happens as we change h, which is called the bandwidth in smoothing language. Intuitively, we would expect that as the bandwidth h gets smaller, the amount of bias in the estimator will decrease, but the number of observations $n = hN$ will also get smaller, causing the variance in the estimator to increase. Thus the choice of bandwidth is an essential aspect of choosing a smoother because a good choice will minimize the mean squared error.

We choose the equal weighting kernel (moving average) so that the mean squared error is as stated earlier:

$$\mathrm{MSE}(u^\#) = [u_1 + u_3]^2/9 + s^2/3n.$$

Using the previous result for the bias $[h^2 u_t''] \approx [u_3 + u_1]$ and the fact that $n = hN$, we can rewrite this as[15]

$$\mathrm{MSE}(u^\#) \approx h^4[u_t'']^2/9 + s^2/3hN.$$

In words, we can write the MSE as follows:[16]

$$\mathrm{MSE}(u^\#) \approx (\text{Bandwidth})^4 (\text{Deviation from linearity of curve})^2/9$$

$$+ [\text{Variance of Error}]/[3 \times \text{Bandwidth} \times \text{Total Sample Size}]$$

Just as we expected, as the bandwidth h gets bigger, the bias term increases but the variance term gets smaller. Furthermore, the amount of bias depends upon the size of the second derivative and the curve's deviation from linearity. The more "wiggly" the curve, the more bias there is in the estimator.

To minimize mean squared error, we can choose the optimal bandwidth by taking the derivative of MSE($u^\#$) with respect to h, setting the resulting derivative to zero, and solving for h. We obtain

$$h^5 = 3s^2/[4N(u_t'')^2].$$

The optimal bandwidth gets wider with greater population variance s^2 and narrower with increasing N and increasingly wiggly curves.

Analyzing the Annenberg Data on Gore's Honesty

We can use this formula to determine the optimal smoothing for the Annenberg data on Gore's honesty. From the daily data, we can estimate s^2 as the average of the daily variances.[17] The result is a value of about .48. The value of N for the sixty-eight days of interviewing is 20,892. The value of u_t'' depends upon the kinds of responses we expect to find in the general population. One natural measure of a unit of response is the cross-sectional standard deviation in the variable of interest, such as perceptions of Gore's honesty. Changes in the mean equivalent to about 5 percent of the standard deviation might be considered significant, although they might also be hard to detect. Changes in the mean equivalent to about 25 percent of the standard deviation would certainly be substantial, and we would want to be able to detect them. Consider each of these possibilities.

Assume that we expect changes in the mean value of Gore's honesty of one-quarter of the cross-sectional standard deviation, and assume that we expect that these changes might happen within three days. Then we can calculate an approximate value for u_t'' as follows. Suppose that the trend line is flat and that it changes upward (or downward) by one-quarter of a standard deviation (.25 units on the honesty scale) in three days, which is about one-twentieth (.05) of the total sixty-eight days on figures 1a and 1b. Then u_t'' will be $.25/.05 = 5$ over this period. Putting this number along with the variance s^2 (.48) and the total number of interviews (20,892) in the previous formula yields $h = .058$ so that $n = hN$ will be about 1,200, or four days of interviewing at three hundred respondents per day. Similarly, if we are expecting changes of 5 percent of a standard deviation, then $u_t'' = .05/.05 = 1$ and $h = .111$ so that n will be about 2,400, or eight days of interviewing. These results suggest that the ideal amount of smoothing will be something like four to eight days.

Figure 4 presents three-, five-, and seven-day moving averages of the data on perceptions of Gore's honesty presented in figure 1.[18] The most remarkable feature of these graphs is the strong impression that Gore's decline started well before the first debate—perhaps as much as two weeks before and certainly ten days before. The debate may have accelerated the decay in judgment on Gore. Certainly the downward slope seems to increase its pitch right after the debate. Then again, the total drop after the debate is no greater than what occurred before. But the basic point stands: the turning point that is the pivot for the whole campaign came two weeks *before* the debates. This fact would almost certainly have been missed by any other design for fieldwork. Johnston, Hagen, and Jamieson (2004, chap. 6) interpret that turning point in terms of media attacks on Gore's credibility, starting with stories about factual errors in claims made in high-profile speeches and ending with the controversy over his request to President Clinton to release oil from the nation's strategic reserve. They would not have been led to any such interpretation but for the rolling cross-section design.

This discussion has just scratched the surface of what can be done with smoothing methods, and it has used one of the very simplest methods. A several day moving average is a very simple form of the more general technique of polynomial smoothing where the data at each point are approximated by a weighted polynomial regression. In the case of moving averages, this "regression" is just a constant produced by the weighted average of nearby observations where the kernel defines the weights and the bandwidth defines what is considered nearby. More sophisticated polynomial smoothing methods fit local linear regressions (with a constant and a linear time term) or higher order polynomials to each point by estimating a polynomial regression around that point with weights equal to the kernel weights.

Since the publication of William Cleveland's "Robust Locally Weighted Regression and Smoothing Scatterplots" (1979), most researchers favor polynomial methods that at least use linear regressions and that employ robust methods that reduce the impacts of local outliers. Cleveland's LOWESS (Locally weighted scatterplot smoothing) or LOESS is applied to the data on Gore's honesty in figure 5 with different bandwidths ranging from .07 to .125. The results are similar to the moving averages in figure 4.

There are also many smoothing methods other than polynomial smoothing, of which the most popular is various forms of splines (see

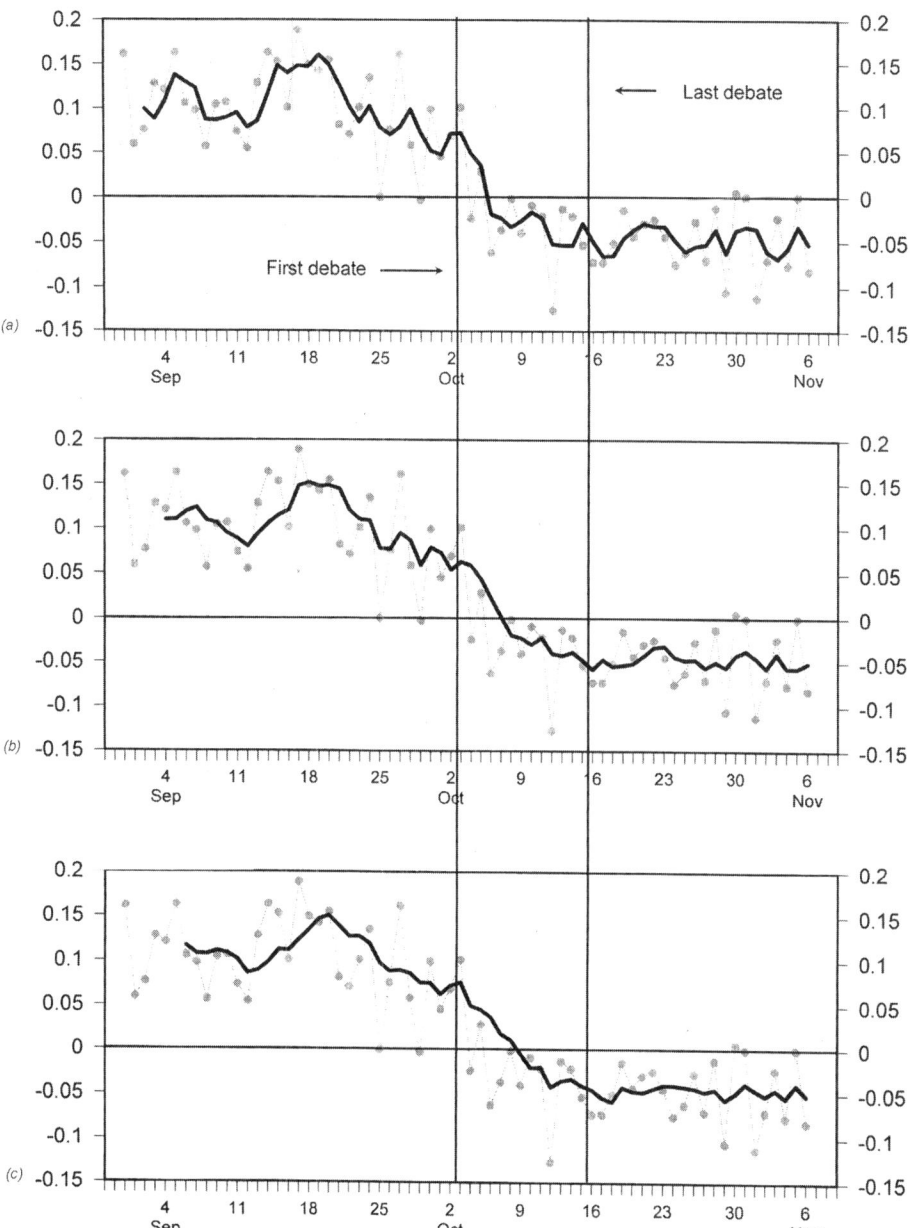

Fig. 4. Smoothing by prior moving average. (*a*) Three-day. (*b*) Five-day. (*c*) Seven-day.

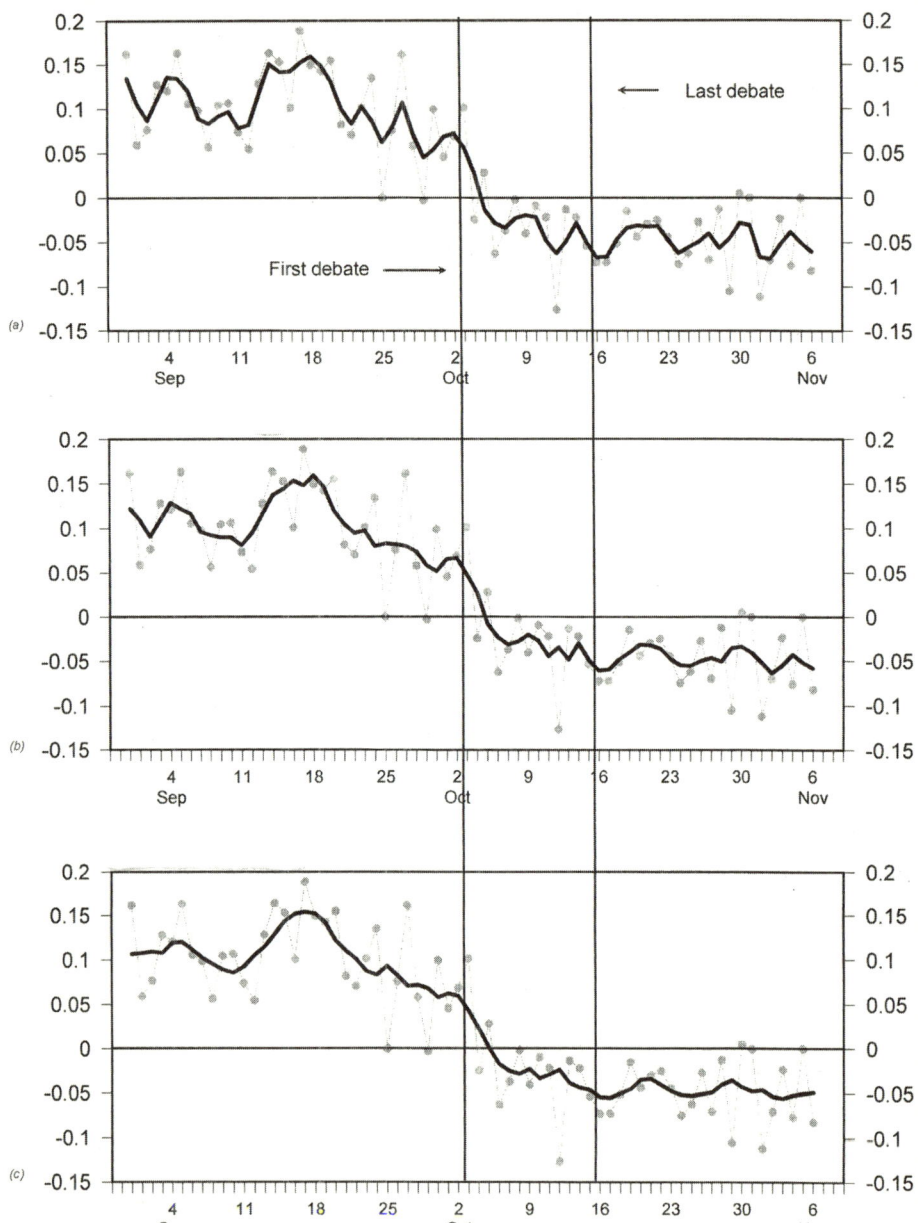

Fig. 5. Smoothing by LOESS. (a) bandwidth = 0.075. (b) bandwidth = 0.100. (c) bandwidth = 0.125.

Green and Silverman 1994; Ruppert, Wand, and Carroll 2003) that smooth data by fitting them to piecewise polynomial (often linear) functions that are spliced together at knots. There are close relationships among these methods. Silverman (1985, 3–4), for example, shows that spline smoothing can be considered a form of weighted moving average smoothing with a particular kernel and varying bandwidth (see also Hardle 1990, 56–64).

Although we have focused on the optimal smoothing problem, statisticians have also given considerable attention to the problems of inference from smoothed data, and they have developed methods for describing confidence intervals for the curves produced by smoothing. These methods provide ways to address the statistical power issues highlighted by John Zaller (2002) in his studies of the inferences that can be made from election studies. Some representative references are Hardle 1990, chapter 4; and Ruppert, Wand, and Carroll 2003, chapter 6.

A Mixed Design

Although this essay began by treating the rolling cross-section and the panel design as substitutes, in fact they are better seen as complements. That is, a properly constructed election survey can be both a rolling-cross section and a panel; all that is required is for one wave of interviewing to have controlled release of sample. It might be tempting to deploy a precampaign cross-section as a baseline and then meter the next wave over the campaign. But if the point of the initial wave is to establish a baseline, this can be achieved by examination of distributions and parameters in the early days of the campaign. As most comparisons to baseline that truly matter are aggregate ones, reinterviewing adds little value. Meanwhile, panel conditioning might distort estimates of aggregate change. It might be best to compare fresh cross-section with fresh cross-section.

The obvious way to connect the designs is with a simple pre–post setup, where the preelection, or campaign, wave is the temporally metered rolling cross-section. Temporal metering of the postelection wave might also be undertaken but on a different basis: release of numbers at the postelection wave should be as uncorrelated as possible to the timing of first-wave completions.[19] This makes it possible to do two things. First, the postelection rolling cross-sections can be used to monitor aggregate changes that occur in the postelection period in the same way as the preelection rolling cross-sections are used. Second, over-time changes in individuals can be more reliably ascribed to events if there is no correlation between the interview date on the postelection wave and the preelection rolling cross-sections.

Suppose, for example, that we wanted to know whether a debate had a negative impact on the rating of a candidate. The obvious approach would be to take people interviewed before the debate and those interviewed after the debate and to calculate the difference in their preelection rating and their postelection rating of the candidate. If this difference is smaller for the postdebate group than for the predebate group, then we might claim that the debate did reduce the candidate's rating. But this claim would be at risk if there was a correlation between the preelection interview date and the postelection interview date. In the worst scenario, all those interviewed before the debate might have been reinterviewed within two weeks of the election while those initially interviewed after the debate might have been reinterviewed several weeks after the election. Then some negative event two weeks into the *post*election period might explain the difference-in-differences that was found. This possibility can be ruled out by making sure that the date of reinterview is uncorrelated with the initial interview date.[20]

When done in this way, combining designs increases the power of each. The panel element benefits from the fine granularity of intervals between the pre- and the postelection interview, which makes it possible to determine how time and events affect opinion change. Moreover, the panel design is greatly strengthened by paying attention to this granularity and making sure that the date of the initial interview and the reinterview are uncorrelated. Indeed, it is quite possible that panels have sometimes suffered from correlations between the two dates that may have confounded inferences made from them.

At the same time, there is no penalty in the more prosaic, but no less useful, features of the pre–post design. For example, questions where postelection rationalization is a problem because voters might try to make their opinions fit their electoral choices (or might try to make their opinions fit the electoral choices of the majority of voters) are best asked before the election when final choices have not yet been made, even if they are subsequently used in analysis of questions such as vote choice best asked after the event. There will, of course, be temporal heterogeneity in the preelection response, with potentially adverse impact on the stability of estimates. But this takes us right back to where we started. *Any* fieldwork that stretches over more than a few days is likely to have temporal heterogeneity, as several essays in this volume show. It is best that that heterogeneity be recognized explicitly, guarded against if possible by making sure that the dates of interviews are uncorrelated with one another, and ultimately modeled directly if it still remains a problem. And, of course, the heterogeneity produced by events ought not to be confused with heterogeneity produced by differences in respondent accessibility.

The rolling cross-section component benefits from the merger of the two designs by clearer separation of cross-sectional and longitudinal variance. A simple example of such leverage is portrayed in figure 6, for analysis of a debate effect. If one observes after a debate a difference between those who saw the debate and those who did not, is the difference the result of actual exposure to the debate, or is it merely symptomatic of an abiding difference that also correlates with the likelihood of viewing the debate in the first place? By itself, a rolling cross-section data file cannot address this question. But one linked to a postelection wave can. A critical fact about the postelection wave is that debate exposure information can be gleaned from *all* respondents, including those first interviewed before the debate. The postelection data allow us to read back through the event and to distinguish its endogenous and exogenous components.

The example in figure 6 is from the 1988 Canadian Election Study. In that year's debate among the party leaders, John Turner of the Liberal Party apparently scored a clear victory. This both primed and moved opinion on the main issue, Canadian–U.S. free trade, and it rehabilitated Turner's reputation as a leader. Figure 6 shows the extent to which this rehabilitation was conditional on exposure to the event itself. Exposure is indicated by response to a postelection question, and so the comparison extends back virtually to the start of the campaign. Smoothing is by prior moving averages (the technique exemplified in fig. 4 and in Johnston, Hagen, and Jamieson 2004), and so any turning points should be correctly located. There is the merest hint that respondents who would watch the debate began to reevaluate Turner just before the event.[21] In general, however, it appears that debate watchers did not bring any different beliefs to the moment than did nonwatchers. So the difference right after the event is mostly real, in the sense that it truly reflects impact from the moment, not from selection bias.

Impact from the moment is not entirely the same as impact from the debate, however. This potential indeterminacy shows how leverage can work the other way.

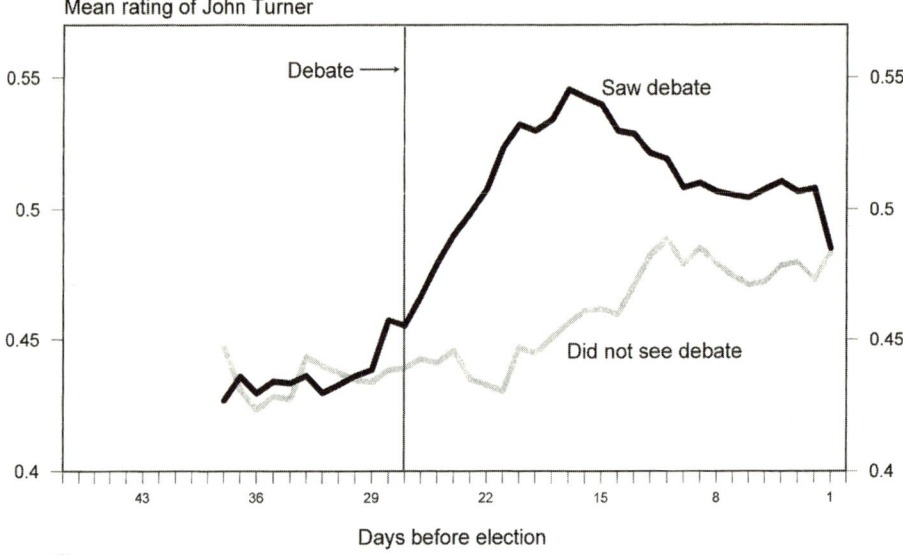

Fig. 6. Impact of debates (English-speaking respondents only), smoothed by nine-day prior moving average. (Data from 1988 Canadian Election Study.)

Even if watchers and nonwatchers bring identical priors to the moment, the difference that subsequently emerges between the groups may not be from direct exposure to the event as opposed to coverage of it. Inspection of daily values suggests that most of the postdebate gap appeared the day after the debate, and so it is probably the result of debate viewing itself, not of general media exposure. But the gap continued to grow for a few days, and this is unlikely to be just the product of unassisted reflection. Johnston et al. 1992 show that the same media orientation that delivered an audience for the debate itself also produced exposure to the generally positive coverage of Turner that followed the debate.[22] A simple pre–post design, even if the second wave follows immediately on the event, would struggle to separate these components.

Late in the campaign, coverage of Turner turned negative, and that fact is also reflected in the data. Respondents who saw the debate were also sensitive to this shift and turned against the Liberal leader, such that the net effect of the whole campaign on evaluation of Turner was very modest. Nonwatchers, meanwhile, absorbed campaign stimuli, only with some lag. By the end, watcher/nonwatcher differences were completely washed away. This shows that conditioning on a debate exposure question asked more than a few days after the event is likely to yield to a false negative for the event.[23]

Multivariate Analysis of the Rolling Cross-Section Design

The simple bivariate example in figure 6 belongs to a more general class of cases. Many relationships in a rolling cross-section data set embody both cross-sectional and longitudinal covariance—cross-sectional because people have different reactions to the same events and longitudinal because people are exposed to different events over time (Johnston and Brady 2002; Zaller 2002). Ignoring time when estimating a cross-sectional relationship or ignoring cross-sectional variation when estimating a time-series risks conflating the two components. The most obvious problem is the failure to specify the right relationship when either time or individual variation is ignored. But attitudinal data present special problems that can confound even sensible specifications. Many variables that shift over a campaign and so have potential dynamic significance also carry "projective" cross-sectional variance from, for example, respondents' party identifications. Perceptions of honesty, for example, not only change with events, but they are also the result of party identification, which colors people's perceptions about the candidates. To an extent, this projective component can be mitigated by controlling for the variable that is its source—by, for example, analyzing people with different party identifications separately or including party identification in a regression equation. But measurement error in party identification and other individual characteristics may mean that control is incomplete so that covariance is, as it were, left on the table for the target variable of interest (such as honesty) to pick up—leading to false inferences about the impact of the target variable.

In the ideal case, we should isolate the target variable's longitudinal component, the element least likely to carry extraneous impact, from cross-sectional variation, but this is not always easy to do. Johnston and Brady (2002) include an extensive discussion of how to approach the problem. They make a case that the ideal way to proceed is to exploit the study's panel property, if one exists. This requires a pre–post design with repetition (where possible) of questions asked in the campaign wave. In a properly conducted postelection wave, variance on the key indicators should be only cross-sectional. To this end, postelection fieldwork should be conducted with deliberate speed. To the extent that fieldwork is stretched out, rerelease of sample should be, as described previously, uncorrelated with the campaign-period release schedule. Thus, even if time lurks in the postelection data, it is essentially irrelevant to impact from true "campaign time." With such data in hand, the postelection wave captures the cross-sectional component in any relationship. By including these postelection indicators in the estimation, impact from the preelection indicators is rendered longitudinal.

What can be done, however, when only repeated cross-sections are available? Johnston and Brady (2002) also considered multivariate methods for analyzing rolling cross-sections when there is no panel information, but their method works best with large cross-sections. Deaton (1985) considers a related problem with a time-series of repeated cross-sections, and he shows how cohorts, defined as groups with fixed membership and exogenously defined characteristics, can be tracked through these data and corrections can be made for cohort-based fixed effects using errors-in-variables methods. Moffitt (1993) extends this analysis in several ways, such as the consideration of autoregressive linear models and discrete dependent variables. Verbeek and Nijman (1992a) consider the general question of whether cohort data can be considered as genuine panel data, and they summarize the state of knowledge about "Pseudo-Panels" in Verbeek and Nijman 1992b. Much more work needs to be done to adapt these methods to the circumstances of election studies where measurements contain substantial error and where the cross-sections are very small and there are many temporal observations.

Conclusions

The rolling cross-section design is a powerful one for detecting the impact of events over time, and it has strengths that are lacking in the standard panel design. Indeed, we show that panels can miss important turning points and events. Moreover, designers of panels have probably underestimated the problems that can arise in making inferences from panels when fieldwork for each wave is spread out, as it almost inevitably has to be, over a period of time. Because of its focus on temporal change, the rolling cross-section design suggests ways that panels themselves could be improved by incorporating rolling cross-sections in each wave.

Despite its advantages, the rolling cross-section design also presents substantial analytical challenges due to the small size of each period's sample and the problem of separating out individual cross-sectional variability from temporal change. Panels provide some advantages with respect to this problem, but new statistical techniques have made it possible to attack these difficulties in fruitful ways for rolling cross-sections. Moreover, both practical experience and theoretical advances with the design suggest that a hybrid of the rolling cross-section with a culminating panel can provide substantial inferential power.

NOTES

1. For details on the NAES, see Romer et al. 2003.
2. The question is, "Does the word 'honest' describe Al Gore extremely well, quite well, not too well, or not well at all?"
3. The rigidity of the callback sequence is modified when interviewers pursue opportunities presented by the field. For example, if a contact expresses willingness to make an appointment outside the normal two-week clearance window, interviewers are commonly instructed to make the appointment, as maximizing response rate is always a serious priority. Similarly, if a call attempt indicates that the respondent is at home but already engaged with a call, the interviewer will phone back promptly.
4. Thus, although the completions on a given day come from different replicates—from today's, the preceding day's, the replicate from the day before that, and so forth—they should still amount to a random sample of the population if the samples have all been worked with the same intensity. By working the samples with the same intensity, we ensure that today's interviews from the replicate of five days ago are statistically valid substitutes for the group of people from today's replicate who will be ultimately interviewed five days from now. The "same intensity" assumption, therefore, allows us to make the jump from random replicates to the assumption that those interviewed on a given day represent a representative sample of the population.
5. The data show that the fieldwork house, Shulman, Ronca, and Bucuvalas, Inc. (SRBI), struggled early on to find the target but was on top of the task by early August.
6. The only exceptions to this rule are samples from transitional subperiods, such as the days following July 5. Relatively inaccessible respondents will be underrepresented, relative to other periods, at transitions that involve increasing sample size and overrepresented at transitions involving reductions in sample size. Analysis for transitional days should, strictly speaking, employ weights for accessibility.
7. We are grateful to David Northrup, project director on the Canadian Election Studies, for this insight.
8. Well, maybe not in Canada. In the 1993, 1997, and 2000 Canadian Election Surveys, completion numbers climb in the last week, quite without any change in fieldwork intensity. The heart of the matter seems to be that respondents who

earlier would schedule a later interview now agree on the spot or agree to be interviewed promptly, under the shadow of the deadline.

9. Some leverage on this question could be gained by drawing a fresh postdebate cross-section and using this for calibration. This starts to inflate costs, however, and it presents its own comparison problems, as the second wave of the panel is not itself a cross-section.

10. Johnston, Hagen, and Jamieson (2004), for example, find that both party identification and liberal/conservative ideology drift toward the temporarily advantaged party and then away as the advantage shifts. Such endogenous movement in party identification can be minimized by using response to the root question. This means that the seven-point scale, where "leaners" are assigned to parties and partisans assigned intensity scores, is inappropriate for rolling cross-section analysis.

11. Postevent surveys started right after the event and completed within a day or two overrepresent those respondents who are easily accessible by the interview method. The rolling cross-section overcomes this problem. Consider, for example, a population in which "stay-at-homes" almost always answer on the first day of interviewing whereas those who "get-out-of-the-house" typically require several days of calls. Further assume that after a week's effort, both groups are just about as likely to be interviewed. A postevent survey conducted for one or two days would have very high response rates for "stay-at-homes" and consist mostly of such people. A rolling cross-section would interview the correct proportions of each group because it would pick-up those who "get-out-of-the-house" and were not interviewed before the event from replicates released before the event. If "stay-at-homes" are different from those who "get-out-of-the-house" (and there is abundant evidence that they are), then the postevent survey will provide a biased picture of the impact of the event. Brady and Orren (1992) provide an example with respect to the Canadian debates.

12. The bias in using $u^{\#}$ to estimate u_2 comes from using information that is one period away from period 2 (namely, information from periods 1 and 3) as well as contemporaneous information. It seems likely that there will be even more bias in using $u^{\#}$ to estimate u_1 or u_3 because $u^{\#}$ uses some information from two periods away.

13. We can generalize the result a bit by assuming that $u^{\#} = a_1 u_1^* + a_2 u_2^* + a_3 u_3^*$ with the weights adding up to one ($a_1 + a_2 + a_3 = 1$). Since $u^{\#}$ is an estimator for u_2, it makes sense to assume a symmetrical treatment of period 1 and period 3 observations so that $a_1 = a_3$. Then we can write $u^{\#} = a u_1^* + (1 - 2a) u_2^* + a u_3^*$. The expected value of this is $E(u^{\#}) = a u_1 + (1 - 2a) u_2 + a u_3$, and the true value of the period 2 average is u_2 so that the expected bias is $\text{Bias}(u^{\#}) = E(u^{\#}) - u_2 = a u_1 + (-2a u_2) + a u_3$. Since we have set $u_2 = 0$, this simplifies to $\text{Bias}(u^{\#}) = a(u_1 + u_3)$. The variance of $u^{\#}$ can also be easily calculated as $\text{Var}(u^{\#}) = (6a^2 - 4a + 1)s^2/n$. Hence, the mean squared error is

$$\text{MSE}(u^{\#}) = a^2(u_1 + u_3)^2 + (6a^2 - 4a + 1)s^2/n.$$

If $a = 1/3$, then this becomes the expression in the text for the three-period moving average.

14. This analysis can be done more formally with the results from the preced-

ing footnote by minimizing the mean squared error in that footnote with respect to the parameter a, which produces $u^\#$ when $a = 1/3$ and u_2^* when $a = 0$. We can find the value of a by taking the derivative of the MSE in the preceding footnote with respect to a, setting the derivative equal to zero, and solving for a. The result, after some algebra, is

$$a = 2/\{6 + n[(u_1 + u_3)^2/s^2]\}.$$

Clearly this has the two limits 1/3 (producing $u^\#$) and zero (producing u_2^*). Furthermore, for small n or small $(u_1 + u_3)^2$, we obtain something close to $u^\#$, whereas for large n or large $(u_1 + u_3)^2$ we get u_2^*. For large s^2 we get $u^\#$, and for small s^2 we get u_2^*.

15. Note that we conveniently choose the interval b for computing the approximation to the derivative to be the same as the bandwidth. This means that the expression for MSE($u^\#$) is only approximate.

16. If we carry through with the more general case in the preceding footnotes, we get that

$$\text{MSE}(u^\#) \approx a^2 b^4 [u''(t)]^2 + [6a^2 - 4a + 1] s^2/bN.$$

And if we think of a kernel as a function $K(t)$ that defines weights for each value of t, then we can define

$$c = \sum_t [K(t)]^2 = \text{Sum of Square of Kernel Weights} = 6a^2 - 4a + 1$$

$$d = \sum_t u^2 K(u) = \text{Variance of Kernel weights} = 2a,$$

so that we can write MSE($u^\#$) $\approx b^4(d^2/4)[u''(t)]^2 + cs^2/bN$. This result is identical to the general result of Gasser and Muller reported in Hardle as Theorem 3.1.1 (Hardle 1990, 29–30).

17. We are eliding a potential complication here by assuming that s^2 is constant across the campaign. Brady and Johnston (1987, 170–73) show how standard deviations for trait batteries become greater over the course of a primary campaign (see also Campbell 2000; Wlezien and Erickson 2002). In this case, the variation in s^2 is probably a second-order problem, but it will not be in every case.

18. We use "prior" moving averages in which the smoothed point on day t from a p-period moving average is calculated from average of day $t, t - 1, t - 2, \ldots, t - p - 1$. Prior moving averages have the virtue that, if a turning point occurs in the underlying true series u_t, then the prior moving average will only start to turn at the point where the true series begins to turn. They have the defect that the prior moving average may underestimate the size of the turn.

19. It is impossible to ensure that the actual gap between first- and second-wave interviews is uncorrelated to first-wave timing. The closest we can come is to make rerelease of the number to field uncorrelated to the initial completion date.

20. Note that this analysis is symmetrical and that it would also allow inferences about the impacts of postelection events by comparing groups interviewed before and after some postelection occurrence.

21. The predebate uptick among eventual debate watchers reflects one outlier. All other observations for this group in the period indicate no predebate shift.

22. Indeed, much of this coverage was simple repetition of the key moment in the debate.

23. This observation applies to any postevent retrospective question, not just one posed in the second wave of a panel.

REFERENCES

Brady, Henry E., and Richard Johnston. 1987. "What's the Primary Message: Horse Race or Issue Journalism?" In *Media and Momentum*, ed. Gary Orren and Nelson Polsby. Chatham, NJ: Chatham House.

Brady, Henry E., and Gary Orren. 1992. "Polling Pitfalls: Sources of Error in Public Opinion Surveys." In *Media Polls in American Politics*, ed. Thomas Mann and Gary Orren. Washington, DC: Brookings Institution.

Campbell, James E. 2000. *The American Campaign: U.S. Presidential Campaigns and the National Vote*. College Station: Texas A&M Press.

Cleveland, William. 1979. "Robust Locally Weighted Regression and Smoothing Scatterplots." *Journal of the American Statistical Association* 74:829–36.

Deaton, Angus. 1985. "Panel Data from Time Series of Cross-Sections." *Journal of Econometrics* 30:109–26.

Dunkelberg, William C., and George S. Day. 1973. "Nonresponse Bias and Callbacks in Sample Surveys." *Journal of Marketing Research* 10:160–68.

Green, P. J., and B. W. Silverman. 1994. *Nonparametric Regression and Generalized Linear Models*. London: Chapman and Hall.

Groves, Robert M. 1989. *Survey Errors and Survey Costs*. New York: Wiley.

Hardle, Wolfgang. 1990. *Applied Nonparametric Regression*. Cambridge: Cambridge University Press.

Hawkins, Thomas M. 1975. "Estimation of Nonresponse Bias." *Sociological Methods and Research* 3:461–88.

Holbrook, Thomas M. 1996. *Do Campaigns Matter?* Thousand Oaks, CA: Sage.

Johnston, Richard, André Blais, Henry E. Brady, and Jean Crête. 1992. *Letting the People Decide: Dynamics of a Canadian Election*. Stanford: Stanford University Press.

Johnston, Richard, and Henry E. Brady. 2002. "The Rolling Cross-Section Design." *Electoral Studies* 21:283–95.

Johnston, Richard, Michael G. Hagen, and Kathleen Hall Jamieson. 2004. *The 2000 Presidential Election and the Foundations of Party Politics*. Cambridge: Cambridge University Press.

Moffitt, Robert. 1993. "Identification and Estimation of Dynamic Models with a Time-Series of Repeated Cross-Sections." *Journal of Econometrics* 59:99–123.

Romer, Daniel, Kate Kenski, Paul Waldman, Christopher Adasiewicz, and Kathleen Hall Jamieson. 2004. *Capturing Campaign Dynamics: The Annenberg National Election Survey*. New York: Oxford University Press.

Ruppert, David, M. P. Wand, and R. J. Carroll. 2003. *Semiparametric Regression*. Cambridge: Cambridge University Press.

Shaw, Daron R. 1999. "A Study of Presidential Campaign Effects from 1952 to 1992." *Journal of Politics* 61:387–422.

Silverman, B. W. 1985. "Some Aspects of the Spline Smoothing Approach to Non-

Parametric Regression Curve Fitting." *Journal of the Royal Statistical Society, Series B (Methodological)*, 47:1–52.
Verbeek, M., and T. Nijman. 1992a. "Can Cohort Data Be Treated as Genuine Panel Data?" *Empirical Economics* 17:9–23.
———. 1992b. "Pseudo Panel Data." In *The Econometrics of Panel Data: Handbook of Theory and Applications*, ed. Laszlo Matyas and Patrick Sevestre. Dordrecht, the Netherlands: Kluwer Academic Publishers.
Wlezien, Christopher, and Robert S. Erikson. 2002. "The Timeline of Presidential Election Campaigns." *Journal of Politics* 64:969–93.
Zaller, John. 1998. "Monica Lewinsky's Contribution to Political Science." *PS: Political Science and Politics* 31:182–89.
———. 2002. "The Statistical Power of Election Studies to Detect Media Exposure Effects in Political Campaigns." *Electoral Studies* 21: 297–329.

III Campaign Effects in Congressional and Senatorial Races: Information and Issues

Measuring Campaign Spending Effects in U.S. House Elections

Gary C. Jacobson

IT WOULD SCARCELY OCCUR TO anyone who studies modern-day congressional elections in the United States to ask, "Do campaigns matter?" Virtually everything we have learned from forty years of survey research on voting behavior in congressional elections tells us that campaigns *should* matter, and virtually everything we have learned by examining the effects of campaign-specific variables on election results tells us that, in one way or another, campaigns *do* matter. What remains in question is *how* campaigns matter. Here the consensus dissolves, and it has become increasingly clear that progress on the question requires new research strategies.

Campaigns *should* matter if only because congressional election voting decisions are strongly affected by knowledge and evaluations of individual candidates, both of which are highly variable and susceptible to the kind of information supplied by campaigns. Every National Election Study (NES) of congressional election voting since the first in 1958 has confirmed that simple knowledge of the candidates' names is both far from universal among voters and strongly associated with the vote choice. Other things equal, voters tend strongly to prefer candidates whose names they remember, or at least recognize, over unknown candidates (Stokes and Miller 1966; Jacobson 2004). If campaigns do nothing but alter the relative level of public awareness of candidates, they can influence election results. And no one, I think, doubts that campaign advertising can affect the public awareness of candidates. Beyond simple awareness, voting decisions are shaped by evaluations of candidates, and evaluations of candidates are also subject to the kind of information, priming, and framing that campaigns can provide (cf. Lodge, Steenbergen, and Brau 1995).

That campaigns *do* matter is equally beyond dispute. The strongest evidence comes from studies of the effects of campaign spending on election results. Although scholars disagree vehemently about just how (or whose) campaign spending influences elections, almost no one claims that election results are *not* affected in some important way by how much the candidates spend on their campaigns. The unresolved questions concern how spending matters, how much it matters, and for whom, and these are the questions I propose we attack through an innovative survey design.

Campaign Spending and Campaigns

Questions about how campaign spending matters are really questions about how campaigns matter, for although the point is often left implicit in the literature, the amount of money spent is just a handy surrogate for what is really expected to influence voters, the total campaign effort, its quality as well as its quantity. To be sure, spending measures campaigning with considerable error, but there is no evidence that the error is systematic, and as long as we do not pretend to estimate effects with greater precision than warranted ("spend another seventy-five thousand dollars and you'll get 1,572 more votes"), we are not likely to be led too far astray.[1] Because arguments about the effects of campaign spending are really arguments about the effects of campaigning, any credible claims regarding campaign spending effects must be fully consistent with our understanding of campaign effects. The more we learn about the effects of campaigning, the more we should know about the effects of campaign spending, and vice versa. Despite more than twenty years of research, we still have plenty to learn about both.

Whose Campaign Spending Matters?

The most enduring controversy in the literature on campaign money concerns the relative impact of spending by incumbents and challengers. The issue arose almost as soon as the first reliable campaign spending data began to appear in the early 1970s (as a consequence of the disclosure provisions of the Federal Election Campaign Act of 1971). The data showed that campaign spending was strongly related to congressional election results, but in

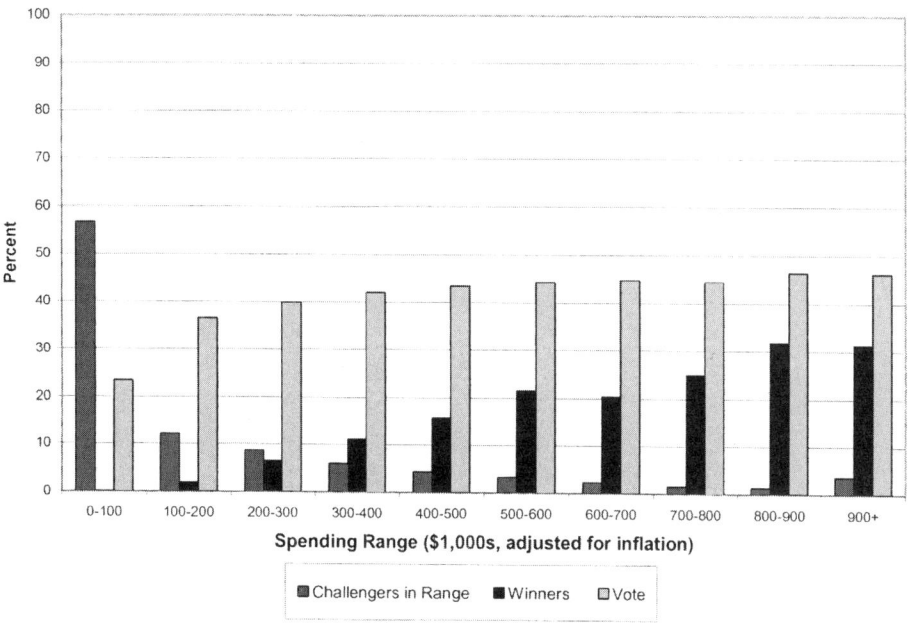

Fig. 1. Challenger campaign spending and House election results, 1972–2002

a peculiar way. The relationship between spending and votes looked very different depending on the candidate's incumbency status. The more candidates who challenged incumbent officeholders spent, the better they did on Election Day; the more incumbents spent, the worse they did. These relationships, which have reappeared in every election since 1972, are displayed graphically for House candidates in figures 1 and 2. For challengers, both the average vote and frequency of victories grow with the level of campaign spending, at least until the total exceeds eight hundred thousand dollars in inflation-adjusted dollars (2002 = $1.00). For incumbents, votes and victories decline as the level of spending rises.[2]

No one has ever been so naive as to take this pattern to mean that incumbents actually lose votes and elections by spending too much money. The consensus explanation is that campaign spending by incumbents rises with the magnitude of the electoral threat they face; the more trouble they are in, the more they spend. Figure 1 suggests that the magnitude of the threat is measured tolerably well by the challenger's level of spending. When this is taken into account (typically by estimating a multivariate model that includes measures of spending by both candidates plus other

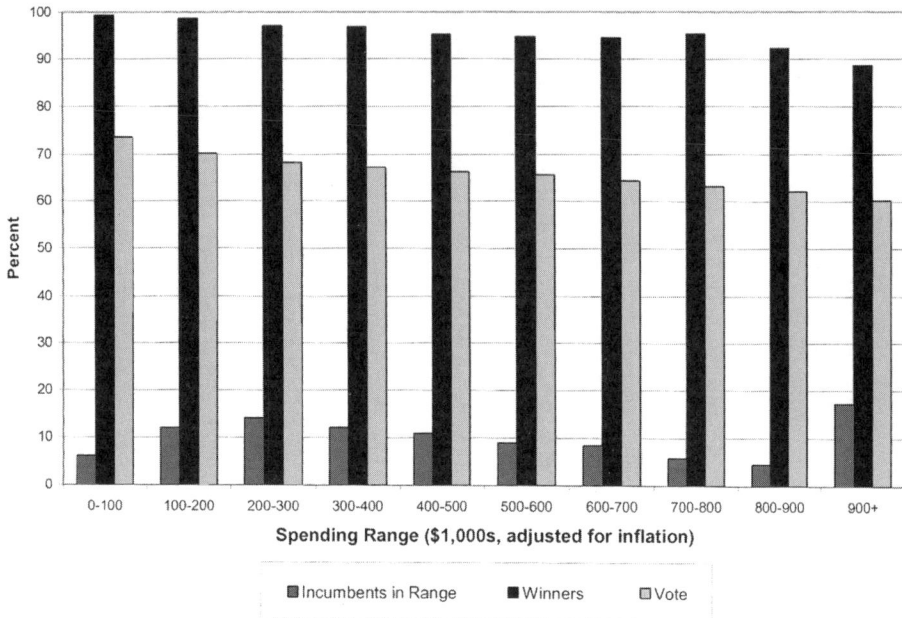

Fig. 2. Incumbent campaign spending and House election results, 1972–2002

variables thought to influence congressional election results), the incumbent's spending no longer (in most models) appears to cost votes; but, almost as disconcertingly, it appears to have little or no effect on the results. Spending by challengers, in contrast, is strongly related to the outcome; under every set of controls examined, the more challengers spend, the better they do in the election.[3] Table 1 presents a pair of simple illustrative models, with votes and victories as alternative dependent variables. Controlling for the previous district vote and the national swing, the incumbent's spending appears unrelated to the vote. The incumbent's spending does, however, appear to have a significant positive effect on the likelihood of winning, though the estimated payoff for a given level of spending continues to be much greater for challengers.

These results are not credible either, for there are compelling reasons to believe that they overstate the effect of the challenger's spending and understate the effect of the incumbent's spending. The problem is that candidates and campaign contributors act strategically. Donors resist wasting money on hopeless causes. The better a challenger's prospects, the more contributors are willing to invest in their campaigns. High-quality challengers have better prospects and are more likely to run when conditions point to success, so they attract the most money. The connection between spending and votes or victories is thus at least potentially reciprocal; money may help win votes, but the expectation that a candidate can win votes also brings in money. To the degree that (expected) votes influence spending, ordinary least squares (OLS) estimates of the effects of challengers' spending on votes will be exaggerated.[4]

Spending by incumbents is also related to the expected outcome, but in the opposite way: the higher the incumbent's expected vote and the greater the likelihood of victory, the *less* money flows into the campaign. Not that secure incumbents have trouble raising money. Quite the contrary; many access-seeking contributors are happy to back sure winners. But raising funds is a time-consuming and, for most incumbents, unpleasant chore that they undertake only to the extent that they think they need the money. Again, the anticipated vote affects spending, but for incumbents, the relationship is negative: the larger their expected vote, the less they raise and spend. To the degree that (expected) votes influence spending, OLS analyses underestimate the effects of incumbent spending on votes.

TABLE 1. Single-Equation Models of House Campaign Spending Effects, 1972–2002

	Vote Share (OLS regression)	Probability of Victory (logistic regression)
Constant	71.20***	11.41***
	(1.75)	(1.77)
Incumbent's vote in previous election	.40***	.06***
	(.01)	(.01)
National swing to or from incumbent's party	.74***	.30***
	(.03)	(.03)
Incumbent's spending (log)	−.06	.61***
	(.10)	(.11)
Challenger's spending (log)	−2.75***	−1.58***
	(.06)	(.12)
Adjusted R^2	.66	
Log-likelihood		−621.28
Percentage correctly predicted		94.7
Null		94.2
Number of cases	4,713	4,713

Note: The dependent variables are (1) the incumbent's share of the two-party vote and (2) 1 if the incumbent won, 0 otherwise; the national swing to the incumbent's party is the difference in the average vote won by all of the incumbent's party's House candidates in the current and previous election; all candidates are assumed to have spent at least $5,000, the Federal Election Commission's reporting threshold; spending is adjusted for inflation (2002 = 1.00); standard errors are in parentheses.
***$p < .001$

In short, heavy spending by incumbents is a sign of electoral weakness, while heavy spending by challengers is a sign of electoral strength. Campaign spending is endogenously determined by expectations about election results, so unless we can model expectations perfectly in the equation (which we cannot), the estimated coefficients on spending will be biased and inconsistent.[5] Specifically, the coefficient on challenger spending will be biased upward, the coefficient on incumbent spending, downward.

The problem was recognized early on (Jacobson 1978; Welch 1981), but after more than two decades of work there is no agreed-upon solution. The standard technical fix-up is to use a two-stage procedure, in which instrumental variables "purged" of the effects of the reciprocally related variables or of the component correlated with biasing omitted variables. The success of this exercise in the present case depends on finding exogenous variables that affect spending but not, directly, the vote (Johnston 1972). This has proven difficult, and the results remain inconclusive. Different choices of exogenous variables to identify the equations and compute the instruments produce a bewildering variety of estimates of the relative effects of campaign spending by challengers and incumbents.

Reported results from various two-stage (sometimes three-stage) models of campaign spending effects range from repetition of the OLS findings in which challenger spending has a large effect while incumbent spending has no effect at all on the vote (Jacobson 1978, 1980, 1985) to estimates suggesting that spending by incumbents is as least as productive as spending by challengers (Green and Krasno 1988, 1990; Grier 1991; Ansolabehere and Snyder 1996), with others falling in between (Bartels 1991; Goidel and Gross 1994). Alternative approaches produce an even broader range of results, from evidence that neither candidate's spending matters much (Levitt 1994) to evidence that the incumbent's spending may be much more productive than the challenger's spending (Erikson and Palfrey 1998), with others again taking the middle ground that incumbents do help themselves by spending money on campaigns but with a lower marginal rate of return on their investment than challengers (Box-Steffensmeier 1992; Kenny and McBurnett 1997; Coates 1994). To have matters so uncertain after so much research is disconcerting to anyone hoping for a modicum of scientific progress. Moreover, the issue is far from merely academic, for different results bear profoundly different implications for evaluating the campaign finance reform proposals that spring up like hardy perennials after every election.

Back to Basics

The profusion of disparate models and conflicting results suggests that we need to go back to basics and that we need to consider alternative ways of measuring campaign spending effects. The basic reason for expecting that campaign spending would be more productive for challengers than for incumbents is that there are compelling reasons for thinking that *campaigns* are more important to challengers than to incumbents. Incumbents usually begin the election much better known than their opponents, and, if they retain that advantage, they win handily. Moreover, if they have been properly attentive to constituents, as the overwhelming majority are, they normally go into the campaign period with a cushion of public regard as well. Voters rarely turn on them without a good reason and an acceptable replacement. It is almost always up to the challenger's campaign to acquaint voters with both reason and the replacement. There may be a few instances where voters know the challenger and the reasons for dumping the incumbent before the campaign begins, but they are certainly rare. Even the most attractive challenger with the most compelling case for replacing the incumbent will not get far if voters remain ignorant of the challenger and the case. It matters how much challengers spend because it matters how much they campaign.

Incumbents, in contrast, typically enjoy a wide head start with the electorate and can coast to victory with minimal campaigning if spared a serious opponent, as they frequently are (observe figure 1). Whatever campaigning they do undertake comes on top of continuous, long-term work to cultivate voters, including previous campaigns. Because diminishing returns apply to campaigning, it stands to reason that the marginal returns on their campaign efforts should be smaller than they are for challengers.

This does not, however, imply that incumbents' campaigns should have no effect at all. Although incumbents are, on average, much more familiar to voters than are challengers, no more than about half of the voters surveyed can remember the incumbent's name, though more than 90 percent will recognize it from a list (Jacobson 2004, 124). More important, an incumbent who did not respond to a vigorous challenge would concede the framing of the vote choice to the opposition, a concession likely to be fatal, which is why we so rarely observe an incumbent *not* responding to a vigorous challenge.[6] Campaigning should also matter whenever incumbents have to get out a *new* message, when, that is, an incumbent is in trouble for some reason—personal, such as involvement in the House banking scandal in 1992, or political, as with Democrats facing the Republican tide in 1994—and needs to counter with a new pitch. Unless one is willing to argue that the *content* of campaigns is irrelevant, then it is impossible to believe that incumbents' campaigns have no effect.

It is also difficult, as many scholars have pointed out, to understand why incumbents would raise and spend so much money if spending had no benefit. It is not at all difficult, however, to understand why they would spend very large amounts of money in response to a serious challenge even if the marginal returns on spending are small, partly because the marginal returns *are* small and partly because in the tight contests produced by serious challenges even a small proportion of the vote can spell the difference between victory and defeat.

It is no mystery, then, why scholars have never been comfortable with any of the analytical results suggesting that incumbent campaign spending (that is, campaigning) has no effect on election results. But there are equally compelling reasons for doubting recent results suggesting that the returns on spending are equal for challengers and incumbents, let alone that incumbents may get more bang for the buck than challengers. If incumbents get as much out of their campaign spending as do challengers, then it is difficult to understand how any of them ever loses. More than two-thirds of the losing incumbents in elections from 1980 through 2002 outspent the winning challenger; on average, losers outspent their opponents by $133,000 ($862,000 to 729,000).[7] If we accept equal marginal returns, we have to conclude that these successful challengers would have done even better had both candidates limited their spending to, say, $100,000. But when we observe that *none* of the 2,196 challengers who did not spend more than $100,000 won during this period, this conclusion seems, to put it mildly, implausible. Taken further, the results suggest that, because incumbents almost always outspend challengers (by an average of more than $436,000 in elections from 1980 through 2002), elections would be more competitive and more challengers would win if neither candidate spent anything on the campaign and the campaigns were therefore virtually invisible. Knowing what we do about the incumbent's usual head start in voter familiarity and regard, a product of the perpetual, taxpayer-financed effort to cultivate constituents undertaken between elections, this conclusion also seems wildly implausible. When the most sophisticated and thorough econometric work in the literature (Ansolabehere and Snyder 1996) carries such an implication, it is time to consider some alternative way of getting at the problem.

A Focus on Change

One solution to at least some of the difficulties in measuring campaign spending effects is to focus on *changes* over the course of the campaign in support for the candidates. To the degree that challengers win votes by campaigning, the more they spend, the more votes they should gain over the course of the campaign. To the degree that the strong, positive relationship between spending and support for challengers simply reflects the reality that challengers with the most initial support raise the most money, spending levels should be strongly related to initial support but unrelated to subsequent changes in support. Similarly, if incumbents in trouble spend more money and their more extensive campaigns shore up support, we should find that high-spending incumbents begin with lower levels of popular support and that, other things equal, the extent to which they gain or lose votes will depend on their level of campaign spending. In short, knowing where candidates stand with voters before the campaign begins and observing how their standing changes during the course of the campaign should help us to distinguish the effect campaign spending has on voter support from the effect voter support has on campaign spending.[8]

There are two basic ways to measure changes in voters' views of candidates over time: panel surveys, in which the same respondents are interviewed at two or more junctures in the campaign, and a series of separate cross-sectional surveys taken at intervals before, during, and after the campaign (or, equivalently, a rolling cross-section). Fortunately, we already have some evidence of the possibilities and pitfalls of both methods. The evidence suggests that they have complementary advantages and disadvantages and that the ideal study would use them in combination. The evidence also suggests that the intuitions about campaign spending effects derived from considering the different campaign circumstances faced by incumbents and challengers are on target.

The 1996 American NES

The American NES for 1996 (Rosenstone 1997) incorporated both sequential cross-section and panel elements that can be used to investigate congressional campaign spending effects. For the first time, the NES's preelection wave included some content on the congressional races, including a vote preference question and the usual questions testing the ability of respondents to recall or recognize the candidates' names.[9] The preelection sample was divided into four subsample replicates that were released approximately two weeks apart beginning nine weeks before the election.[10] Postelection interviews were conducted in November and December, with most (86 percent) completed within three weeks of Election Day. The postelection interviews repeated the name recall and recognition questions as well as asking how respondents had voted. Interviews were completed with 1,714 respondents, of whom 888 reported voting in a race pitting an incumbent against a major party challenger, and this subset is the focus of my analysis.[11]

The preelection wave is less than ideal for examining the effects of campaigning (campaign spending) on changes in voters' knowledge and evaluation of candidates because the interviews were taken after most campaigns had been under way for some time, with nearly half of them coming within thirty days of the election. And the postelection responses are, as we shall see, contaminated by the preelection questions. Yet the substantive results make intuitive sense in light of our understanding of how campaign spending should matter in House elections, adding to our confidence that, in combination, these are productive approaches to studying campaign spending effects.

Consider, to begin, the relationships between campaign spending and changes in the knowledge of House candidates over the course of the period covered by the NES surveys. Some elementary patterns are displayed in figures 3 and 4. Figure 3 shows how levels of name recall vary by the date of the interview and whether the candidate spent more than four hundred thousand dollars on the campaign (a threshold chosen to approximate what it costs to run a minimally competitive campaign in 1996). Figure 4 does the same for name recognition.

Figures 3 and 4 illustrate several points:

> High-spending challengers and incumbents are more familiar to voters than their low-spending counterparts in every time period, but the difference is much greater for challengers than for incumbents.[12]
> Knowledge of all types of candidates—challengers and incumbents, high and low spenders—rises during the campaign period.

Among challengers, the increase in familiarity is greater for high-spending challengers than for low-spending challengers. For example, high-spending challengers raise their recall rate by 19 percentage points from the earliest to the latest preelection period, compared to only 9 percentage points for low-spending challengers. Similarly, recognition rates rise 31 percentage points for high-spending challengers, compared to 18 percentage points for low-spending challengers.

The knowledge gap between high- and low-spending incumbents is modest to begin with and narrows over the course of the campaign.

By the end of the campaign period, high-spending challengers have sharply reduced the incumbent's familiarity advantage, while low-spending challengers remain far behind.

Familiarity increases sharply between the pre- and postelection waves as well (except for recognition of incumbents, which is already so high as to leave little room for improvement). This cannot, however, be taken as an accurate measure of the campaigns' additional effects on information about the candidates, because the postelection respondents had undergone an intensive civics lesson in the form of a lengthy (seventy minutes on average) preelection interview. There is no question that this experience enhanced their subsequent awareness of the candidates. For example, recall rates of both incumbents (64 percent) and challengers (39 percent) exceed their 1978–94 means (46 percent and 22 percent, respectively) by more than four standard deviations. Clearly, changes in candidate familiarity during the campaign are measured more accurately by sequential cross-sections than by panels.

To develop a fuller picture of how time and campaign money combined to affect voters' knowledge of the candidates, I computed logit estimates of recall and recognition of challengers' and incumbents' names in the preelection poll as a function of how much the candidate spent (in logarithmic form[13]) and how many days before the election the interview was conducted. The results are reported in table 2. They show that spending by both incumbents and challengers has a substantial positive effect on the probability that a voter will recall the candidate's name when asked or will recognize it on a list prior to the election. They also show that, controlling for campaign spending, familiarity with the candidates increases significantly as

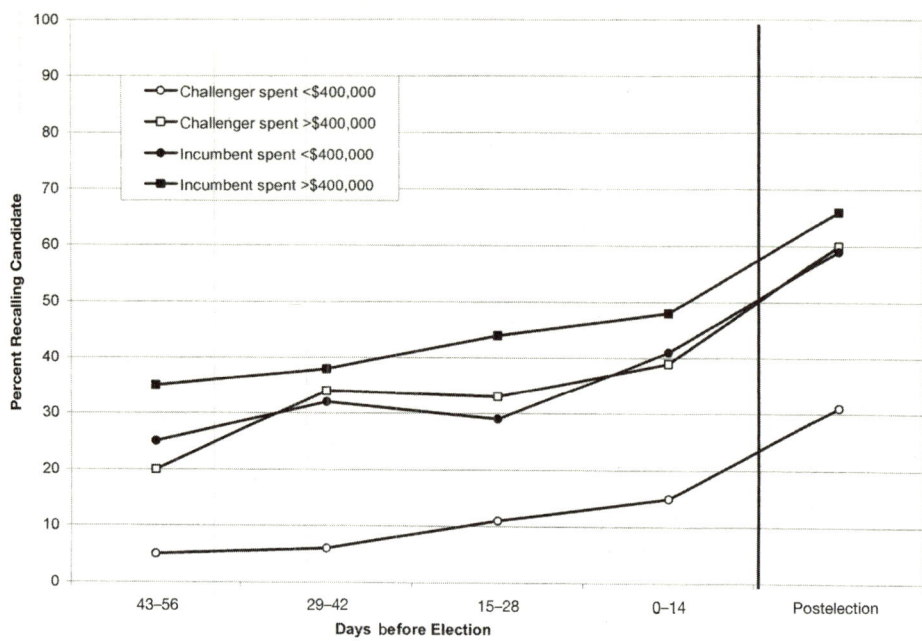

Fig. 3. Time, campaign spending, and recall of House candidates

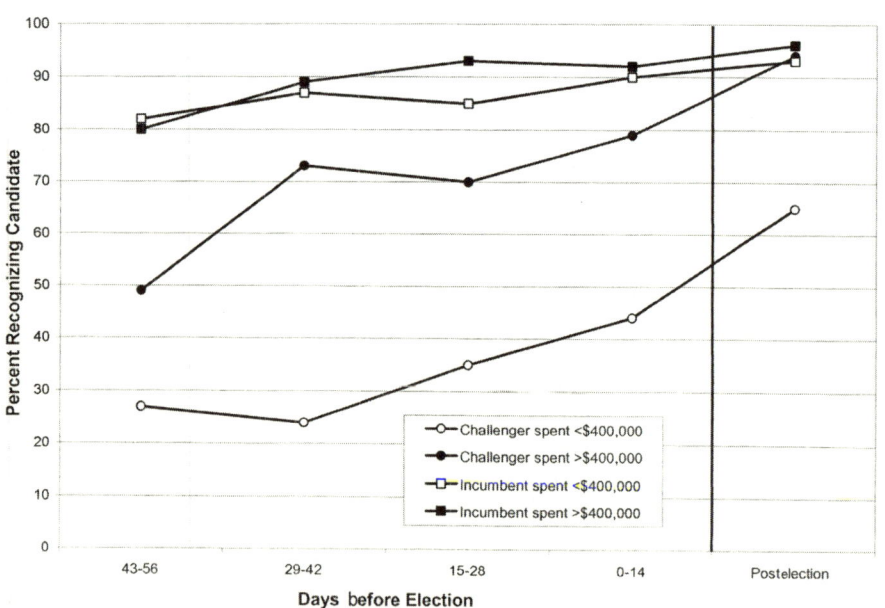

Fig. 4. Time, campaign spending, and recognition of House candidates

Election Day approaches. The coefficient on time is twice as large for challengers as it is for incumbents, consistent with the idea that the campaign period is more crucial to challengers for reaching voters. The magnitudes of the spending effects appear to be similar for both kinds of candidates, but challengers actually get considerably more for their marginal dollar because incumbents are so much more familiar to voters initially.

The greater benefit of spending to challengers is apparent from the data in table 3, which displays the estimated effects of several levels of spending on knowledge of candidates at two points in the campaign, on September 3 (when the first surveys were taken) and on Election Day (that is, with "days before the election" set at zero). The minimum assumed for any candidate ($5,000) applies only to challengers. The least the incumbent in any district in the data set spent was $110,500, hence that is the level at which their estimates begin. Comparisons are also made for spending at the $400,000 and $800,000 levels. The data confirm that higher-spending

TABLE 2. Campaign Spending and Knowledge of House Candidates—Preelection (logit estimates)

Dependent Variable	Incumbents	Challengers
Recalled candidate's name		
Constant	−6.408***	−9.092***
	(1.544)	(1.052)
Campaign spending (log)	.477***	.669***
	(.115)	(.084)
Days before the election	−.013**	−.024***
	(.004)	(.006)
Log-likelihood	−571.69	−308.43
Percentage correctly predicted	63.7	85.8
Null	62.6	85.9
Number of observations	888	888
Recognized candidate's name		
Constant	−3.877	−4.733***
	(2.172)	(.055)
Campaign spending (log)	.478**	.436***
	(.164)	(.047)
Days before the election	−.014*	−.023***
	(.006)	(.004)
Log-likelihood	−327.10	−533.37
Percentage correctly predicted	87.5	70.3
Null	87.5	60.8
Number of observations	888	888

Note: The dependent variable takes the value of 1 if the candidate's name is recalled (recognized), 0 otherwise; standard errors are in parentheses.
*$p < .05$, two-tailed test   **$p < .01$, two-tailed test   ***$p < .001$, two-tailed test

candidates of both kinds are better known to begin with, but they also show that the bigger spenders make bigger gains in familiarity over the course of the campaign (unless they have already reached very high levels of familiarity, as with recognition of incumbents). The gain in familiarity over time associated with a given level of campaign spending is notably larger for challengers than for incumbents; the higher the level of spending by both candidates, the narrower the incumbent's information advantage at the end of the campaign.

From what we can tell from the sequential cross-sections in the preelection wave, it appears that spending increases voter familiarity with both incumbents and challengers, but with challengers getting a larger payoff for each marginal dollar. The panel component of the survey offers another perspective on these relationships, for it allows us to measure the relationship between spending and changes in individuals' knowledge of the candidates between the pre- and postelection waves of the study. The fact that the interview itself sharply increased the respondents' awareness of House candidates is not a problem if the interview effect is uncorrelated with other variables (only the intercept would be affected), but this may not be the case. The preelection interview and campaign advertising may interact positively: respondents primed by the preelection questions may be more responsive to campaign advertising than respondents who are not primed, exaggerating the estimated effect of spending. Priming could also lead to underestimates of campaign spending effects by reducing the proportion of voters whose knowledge of the candidates depends on the level of cam-

TABLE 3. Estimated Effects of Campaign Spending on Preelection Knowledge of House Candidates (probabilities)

	Incumbents			Challengers		
	September 3	Election Day	Change	September 3	Election Day	Change
Recall candidate						
$5,000				.01	.03	.02
$110,500	.15	.29	.14	.06	.21	.15
$400,000	.25	.43	.18	.12	.38	.26
$800,000	.32	.52	.20	.18	.49	.33
Recognize candidate						
$5,000				.00	.02	.02
$110,500	.69	.84	.15	.25	.58	.33
$400,000	.80	.91	.11	.36	.70	.34
$800,000	.85	.93	.07	.44	.76	.32

Source: Equations in table 3 are based on estimations in table 2.

paign advertising (as opposed to having been interviewed). Thus these data should be viewed with some caution.

Table 4 reports the results of logit estimates of postelection recall and recognition as a function of the candidate's spending for those respondents who were unfamiliar with the candidate in the preelection wave. Here, the effects of spending are clearly different for incumbents and challengers. The amount spent by incumbents had no significant effect on postelection recall or recognition among these respondents, while the challenger's spending had a significant and substantial effect on the likelihood that initially uninformed respondents would learn their names. Again, it is evident that the challenger's ability to grab the attention of voters is more sensitive than the incumbent's to the level of campaign spending.

Spending and Candidate Preference

The electoral bottom line is, of course, the vote decision. Table 5 reports three bare-bones logit models of the 1996 House preference (preelection

TABLE 4. Campaign Spending and Knowledge of House Candidates among Initially Uninformed Voters (logit estimates)

Dependent Variable	Incumbents	Challengers
Recalled candidate's name		
Constant	−1.697	−4.731***
	(1.781)	(.585)
Campaign spending (log)	.123	.348***
	(.135)	(.050)
Log-likelihood	−384.54	−448.73
Percentage correctly predicted	51.3	67.4
Null	52.0	68.5
Number of observations	556	763
Recognized candidate's name		
Constant	−2.438	−3.466***
	(4.669)	(.615)
Campaign spending (log)	.270	.356***
	(.358)	(.057)
Log-likelihood	−62.40	−342.51
Percentage correctly predicted	74.8	64.6
Null	74.8	59.8
Number of observations	111	540

Note: The dependent variable takes the value of 1 if the candidate's name is recalled (recognized), 0 otherwise; standard errors are in parentheses; data include only voters who did not recall (recognize) the candidate in the preelection wave.

*$p < .05$, two-tailed test   **$p < .01$, two-tailed test   ***$p < .001$, two-tailed test

wave) and vote choice (postelection report). The first two equations treat the respondent's support for the incumbent as a function of party identification, campaign spending, the party of the incumbent, and the respondent's presidential preference. The third measures the effects of these variables on changes in respondents' preferences by including the preelection candidate preference (if any) on the right-hand side. Together, the three equations tell an interesting story.

The first two equations suggest that challengers helped themselves by spending money while incumbents did not. These models are, of course, subject to the biases thought to afflict all such single-equation cross-sectional models of campaign spending effects. The preelection equation illustrates the problem nicely, as the coefficient on incumbent spending is large (although its t-ratio of -1.44 leaves it a bit below conventional levels of statistical significance) and displays the wrong sign, un-

TABLE 5. Campaign Spending and the House Vote (logit estimates)

	Initial Preference (preelection wave)	Vote (postelection wave)	
Constant	9.099**	3.446	1.680
	(3.119)	(2.562)	(2.967)
Incumbent's spending (log)	−.387	.050	.093
	(.268)	(.221)	(.258)
Challenger's spending (log)	−.177+	−.188**	−.158+
	(.097)	(.077)	(.089)
Democratic incumbent	.111	−.784***	−1.153***
	(.271)	(.232)	(.250)
Party identification	1.121***	1.109***	.903***
	(.198)	(.152)	(.174)
Favored incumbent's presidential candidate	.962	2.026***	1.807***
	(.530)	(.403)	(.438)
Favored challenger's presidential candidate	−1.494***	−.795**	−.967**
	(.433)	(.311)	(.351)
Preferred incumbent—preelection			2.191***
			(.303)
Preferred challenger—preelection			−.895**
			(.300)
Log-likelihood	−218.07	−331.61	−263.45
Percentage correctly predicted	84.3	85.4	88.5
Null	74.8	72.5	72.5
Number of observations	624	888	888

Note: The dependent variable is 1 if the respondent reported preferring or voting for the incumbent, 0 if for the challenger; "party identification" is 1 if respondent identified with incumbent's party, −1 if with the challenger's party, 0 if independent (leaners are classified as partisans); standard errors are in parentheses.

+$p < .10$, two-tailed test   *$p < .05$, two-tailed test   **$p < .01$, two-tailed test   ***$p < .001$, two-tailed test

derlining the reality that incumbents in trouble spend more money. The postelection equation reiterates the customary OLS finding that spending by challengers matters while spending by incumbent does not. It also indicates an electoral bias against Democrats that was not evident during the preelection period.

The third equation examines the effects of these variables on the vote choice conditional on the respondent's initial vote preference. The negative effects of the challenger's spending on the likelihood of voting for the incumbent is reduced slightly but remains marginally significant ($t = -1.78$). The coefficient on the incumbents' spending increases a bit and displays the correct sign, but it continues to be measured with so much error that it cannot reliably be distinguished from zero. Substantively, the coefficient on the challenger's spending indicates that, for example, if the other variables made the estimated probability of voting for the incumbent .75 with the challenger spending $5,000, it would fall to .65 if the challenger spent $100,000, to .60 if the challenger spent $400,000, and to .57 if the challenger spent $800,000. Money spent by the incumbent would be projected to have a smaller effect; for example, if the other variables made the estimated probability of voting for the incumbent .50 if the incumbent spent $100,000, it would increase to .53 at $400,000 and to .55 at $1 million. Unfortunately, we have little reason to believe that this coefficient is accurate. This seems to be the appropriate point to plead for more research.

The equations in table 5 tell us one more thing about campaign effects: national campaigns may matter too. Democrats suffered a significant loss of support between the pre- and postelection waves of the survey across the board. In preelection preferences, Democrats were the choice of 51.9 percent of respondents who preferred either a Republican or a Democrat, but only 48.1 percent reported voting for a Democrat in the postelection wave. This swing to Republicans was not simply the result of the comparable decline in support for Bill Clinton between the pre- and postelection waves,[14] for this is already registered in the equation (through the presidential support variables). It may have had something to do with the desire among some voters to keep the House in Republican hands once Clinton's victory was no longer in doubt—another campaign effect, because strategic voting of this sort depends on news coverage of the "horse race" aspect of presidential contests. Whatever its source, the swing almost certainly preserved the Republican House majority.

What Next?

Despite the fact that neither of these surveys was designed to study the effects of campaign spending in House elections, they demonstrate that examining the relationship between spending and changes in voters' information and preferences over the course of the campaign is a promising research strategy. They also suggest that an ideal study of campaign effects would combine serial cross-section and panel components. The serial cross-section component would have to carry most of the analytical burden, for panel respondents, having endured an intense civics lesson by lengthy interview earlier in the campaign, are no longer representative of ordinary citizens. We do not know if or how this experience affects their vote choice, but it certainly heightens their awareness of the candidates. A fresh postelection cross-section is thus essential.

Interviews for the cross-sectional component should begin well before September. Just how much earlier is difficult to say, for the primary election calendar extends from March through early October. Assuming we are using national samples, the ideal strategy would be to do the first cross-section before any primary (say, in January) to gauge the incumbent's electoral standing, then take repeated cross-sections at fixed intervals until after the election, picking up nominees as they are added when states hold their primaries, with the primary election date entering analyses as a control variable.

Regardless of when the first cross-section is taken, the last cross-section (an extra large one) should come after the election. This would be matched by a panel (a sample or all of the respondents interviewed in the earlier cross-section) so that we could get the fullest possible picture of how the volume of campaigning, as measured by campaign spending, is related to changes in individuals' views of candidates. To the extent that the same effects show up in repeated cross-sections and in repeated interviews with the same respondents, we can have much greater confidence that they are real. The panel component would also give us a better fix on how susceptibility to campaigns varies with the individual characteristics of voters (Jacobson 1990).

The content of the surveys could be built on the familiar NES questions: name recall and recognition, vote preference, perhaps likes and dislikes, along with the usual political and demographic controls. A special effort should also be made to learn if active campaigns can change how voters think about the vote decision, what they think the House vote is *about*. We know that campaigns compete to frame the choice in terms that favor their side. To what degree does success depend on how much they can spend trying to impose their frame? To do this, of course, we would have to have at least rudimentary information about the major themes used by the candidates. This is probably easier now than it has been for decades, because House candidates of both parties have been drawing on common sets of partisan themes (developed by the national party organizations) in recent campaigns. The survey instrument should also be designed to pick up on national themes and issues that may emerge or evolve during the course of the campaign.

It would also be useful to get as detailed as possible a breakdown on the timing of campaign spending. We would also want to include measures of campaign activities beyond the candidates' own campaigns—the "independent" and "voter education" campaigns conducted by parties and interest groups that have become prominent in recent elections (Magleby and Monson 2004). The more fully we can measure campaign components the better. But for the central task of figuring out how campaign spending is related to election results, we would still learn a great deal if our only measure of campaigning was the total amount of money spent on the campaign.

The research strategy I propose, then, is to use evidence on changes over time in knowledge and evaluations of House candidates as leverage on the question of how campaign spending—which is to say, campaigning—affects election results. Knowing where the candidates stand with voters before they begin campaigning and observing how their relative standings change as they spend money on campaign activities will help us to distinguish the effect that campaign spending has on voter support from the effect that voter support has on campaign spending. This is, to my mind, the most promising way to resolve some of the enduring scientific and policy controversies surrounding the relative effects of campaign spending by challengers and incumbents.

NOTES

1. For a more detailed discussion, see the longer version of this essay, delivered as a paper at the colloquium upon which this volume is based (available from the author).

2. Among candidates for open seats, votes and victories rise with campaign spending, although more steeply for Republicans than for Democrats.

3. See, e.g., the OLS models in Glantz, Abramowitz, and Burkhart 1976; Jacobson 1978, 1980, 1985; Green and Krasno 1988; Bartels 1991; Erikson and Palfrey 1998; and Ansolabehere and Gerber 1994. The results also hold for U.S. Senate races; see Jacobson 1978, 1980; Abramowitz and Segal 1992.

4. At least if the OLS equation fails to include a complete set of variables covering every measure of the candidate's prospects, which all of them almost certainly do.

5. As Ansolabehere and Snyder (1996) point out, the bias stems from omitted variables, not classic simultaneity bias, but the problem and solution are essentially the same.

6. In House elections from 1980 through 2002, 726 of 762 incumbents (95.3 percent) facing challengers who spent more than $400,000 themselves spent more than $400,000 (in inflation-adjusted dollars, 2002 = $1.00).

7. In inflation-adjusted dollars (2002 = $1.00); the respective medians are $712,000 and $607,000, a difference of $105,000.

8. For a discussion of some issues this approach does not resolve, see the longer version of this essay, delivered as a paper at the colloquium upon which this volume is based (available from the author).

9. As usual, the feeling thermometers were used as an unobtrusive way of ascertaining name recognition.

10. The distribution of preelection interviews by the date they were actually taken for the subset of respondents analyzed here is as follows:

Weeks before the Election	Number of Respondents
0–2	127
3–4	251
5–6	176
7–8	228
9	106

11. Approximately 79 percent of these respondents were part of a panel surveyed in 1994; the rest were from a fresh cross-section drawn for 1996. I found no difference in the behavior of the two groups in any of the analyses I performed. I excluded respondents who moved between the pre- and postelection waves of the survey.

12. For challengers, the difference is significant at $p < .002$ or greater for every comparison and time period; for incumbents, none is significant for any time period.

13. Candidates who spend less than five thousand dollars are not required to report their spending to the Federal Election Commission; for purposes of this analysis, all candidates are assumed to have spent at least five thousand dollars.

14. Clinton's support fell from 55.0 percent to 50.7 percent between the pre- and postelection waves; Dole's support increased slightly from 40.3 percent to 41.0 percent, and support for Perot and other minor party candidates increased from 4.7 percent to 7.1 percent among respondents included in this analysis.

REFERENCES

Abramowitz, Alan I., and Jeffrey A. Segal. 1992. *Senate Elections*. Ann Arbor: University of Michigan Press.

Ansolabehere, Stephen, and Alan Gerber. 1994. "The Mismeasure of Campaign Spending: Evidence from the 1990 House Elections." *Journal of Politics* 56: 1106–18.

Ansolabehere, Stephen, and James M. Snyder Jr. 1996. "Money, Elections, and Candidate Quality." Typescript, Massachusetts Institute of Technology.

Bartels, Larry M. 1991. "Instrumental and 'Quasi-Instrumental' Variables." *American Journal of Political Science* 35:777–800.

Box-Steffensmeier, Janet M. 1992. "Analyzing the Effect of the Timing of Campaign Expenditures on Electoral Outcomes." Paper presented at the annual meeting of the Midwest Political Science Association, Chicago, April 9–11.

Coates, Dennis. 1994. "Interaction Effects in Campaign Spending—Vote Share Relations." Typescript, University of North Carolina.

Erikson, Robert S., and Thomas Palfrey. 1998. "Campaign Spending and Incumbency: An Alternative Simultaneous Equations Approach." *Journal of Politics* 60:355–73.

Glantz, Stanton A., Alan I. Abramowitz, and Michael P. Burkart. 1976. "Election Outcomes: Whose Money Matters?" *Journal of Politics* 38:1033–38.

Goidel, Robert K., and Donald A. Gross. 1994. "A Systems Approach to Campaign Finance in U.S. House Elections." *American Politics Quarterly* 22:125–53.

Green, Donald P., and Jonathan S. Krasno. 1988. "Salvation for the Spendthrift Incumbent." *American Journal of Political Science* 32:884–907.

———. 1990. "Rebuttal to Jacobson's New Evidence for Old Arguments.'" *American Journal of Political Science* 34:363–72.

Grier, Kevin B. 1991. "Campaign Spending and Senate Elections: Identification and Impact." Typescript, George Mason University.

Jacobson, Gary C. 1978. "The Effects of Campaign Spending in Congressional Elections." *American Political Science Review* 72:469–91.

———. 1980. *Money in Congressional Elections*. New Haven: Yale University Press.

———. 1985. "Money and Votes Reconsidered: Congressional Elections, 1972–1982." *Public Choice* 47:7–62.

———. 1990. "The Effects of Campaign Spending in House Elections: New Evidence for Old Arguments." *American Journal of Political Science* 34:334–62.

———. 2004. *The Politics of Congressional Elections*. 6th ed. New York: Longman.

Johnston. J. 1972. *Econometrics*. 2d ed. New York: McGraw-Hill.

Kenny, Christopher, and Michael McBurnett. 1997. "Up Close and Personal: Campaign Contact and Candidate Spending in U.S. House Elections." *Political Research Quarterly* 50:75–96.

Levitt, Steven. 1994. "Using Repeat Challengers to Estimate the Effect of Campaign Spending on Election Outcomes in the U.S. House." *Journal of Political Economy* 102:777–98.

Lodge, Milton, and Marco R. Steenbergen, with Shawn Brau. 1995. "The Responsive Voter: Campaign Information and the Dynamics of Candidate Evaluation." *American Political Science Review* 89:309–26.

Magleby, David B., and J. Quin Monson, eds. 2004. *The Last Hurrah? Soft Money and Issue Advocacy in the 2002 Congressional Elections.* Washington, DC: Brookings Institution.

Rosenstone, Steven J., Donald R. Kinder, Warren E. Miller, and the National Election Studies. 1997. *American National Election Study, 1996: Pre-and Post-Election Survey.* Computer File. Ann Arbor: University of Michigan, Center for Political Studies (producer), Inter-university Consortium for Political and Social Research (distributor), 1997.

Stokes, Donald E., and Warren E. Miller. 1966. "Party Government and the Saliency of Congress." In *Elections and the Political Order,* ed. Angus Campbell, Philip E. Converse, Warren E. Miller, and Donald E. Stokes. New York: Wiley.

Welch, William P. 1981. "Money and Votes: A Simultaneous Equation Model." *Public Choice* 36:209–34.

Informational Rhythms of Incumbent-Dominated Congressional Elections

Laurel Elms and Paul M. Sniderman

INCUMBENCY ADVANTAGE AND informational asymmetries go together in campaigns for the U.S. House of Representatives. It is an uncontroversial proposition that challengers do less well on Election Day in large measure because fewer citizens know who they are and because those citizens that do so know less about the challenger than the incumbent (Mann and Wolfinger 1980; Jacobson 1997b). The information voters have about candidates obviously matters. But when must the information, if it is to matter, be acquired? And how is what is learned about the challenger and the incumbent, and, not least, when it is learned in the course of a campaign, tied to what candidates actually do?

By way of an analytic strategy we shall parse a question profitably posed in quite a different context—who knew what and when? In particular, we want to explore the notion of knowledge and the rhythms of its acquisition. We will examine candidate knowledge including and beyond simple name recognition and recall. More fundamentally, we shall argue that the significance of knowledge in congressional elections hinges on when it was acquired. By applying the first rolling cross-sectional survey design to House elections, we will explore the informational dynamics of congressional campaigns.

Informational Rhythms: Arguments and Hypotheses

Our primary objective is to take seriously the dynamics of congressional campaigns. This requires exploring not only the consequences of an election campaign but also the timing of those consequences in the course of the campaign. Consider the classic studies of congressional elections. With few exceptions (Mann 1978; Abramowitz 1975), they assess what citizens know at a single point in time, usually after the campaign is over. But it is indispensable to establish when in the course of the campaign citizens learned whatever they wound up learning about the candidates.

It is indispensable because when voters learn about candidates and how much they learn about them are connected. Consider the quite different situations of two citizens who are attempting to decide whether to support the incumbent or the challenger. One of them has followed both candidates throughout the campaign; the other stumbled across the name of the challenger while preparing a practice ballot. When interviewed after the election, both voters may recall the challenger's name and appear equally informed. But the challenger had a month to make a case to the first voter and no more than a week to the second voter. The second voter ends up with the same information as the first voter but experienced the campaign quite differently. Because how much voters know about candidates tends to be tied to how long they have known about them, it is necessary to establish not only what voters know about the candidates but also when they learned what they know.

The public opinion survey we analyzed, focusing on the congressional elections in Missouri in 1994, is the first to have utilized a daily rolling cross-sectional design to study House elections. Until 1996, almost all measures of candidate knowledge in congressional elections were obtained only after the election. The 1996 National Election Study (NES) was the first to include a limited number of questions about the congressional candidates in the preelection wave. The 1996 NES has four random quarter samples, while the Missouri Election Study consists of daily random samples. Although restricted to a single state, the 1994 Missouri Election Study included respondents from all nine congressional districts, exposed to campaigns conducted at a variety of levels of intensity. Although no challenger won, a restriction that should be kept in mind in evaluating the generality of our results, a number of them put up good fights. The fine granulation of the daily random samples, taken together with the variation in campaign intensity, offers a unique opportunity to observe how congressional campaigns, when they are actively contested, can change the informational landscape.

Informational gains, if any are realized, are our principal concern. But, supposing for argument's sake that citizens do learn about candidates in the course of a campaign, what do they learn?

Awareness of the candidates, initially, was equated with an ability to recall who was running. But it became clear quickly that knowledge comes in more than one form. As Mann and Wolfinger demonstrated (1980), many people unable to recall the names of congressional candidates can still recognize them. A gradient was apparent: recall is a more demanding test than recognition, though both are tests of knowledge.

The distinction between voters' recognition and recall of candidates' names is well established, as are the minimal levels of knowledge characteristic of ordinary citizens. However, it is worth examining an even broader range of what it means to say that voters know about congressional candidates. Merely being able to come up with the name of someone running for Congress is not a guarantee of support for that candidate. Certainly it is not a guarantee of being cognizant of the candidate's potential credentials for office.

The part that knowledge about candidates plays in the voting process and the role that campaigns play in promoting knowledge of candidates requires using more than just name recognition to measure citizens' information about the choices before them. We use an expansive conception of candidate knowledge and examine a range of measures of voters' level of candidate information. In addition to name recall and recognition of political candidates, we consider other types of candidate familiarity and the differences in the levels of these types of awareness during the campaign.

Our study aims to be distinctive by plotting, for the first time, changes in citizens' levels of knowledge about, and evaluations of, incumbents and challengers through the course of congressional campaigns. By measuring various types of knowledge about congressional candidates during the campaign, we test how much of an educational role campaigns play and how this role varies by the effort and ability of the candidates to inform citizens about their electoral choices.

Study Design

The 1994 Missouri Election Study was a daily rolling cross-sectional survey of voting-age adults in the state's nine congressional districts. The survey began sixty-three days before Election Day, from the beginning of September through the day before the election, with interviews completed every day of the week.[1] As the primary elections in Missouri were held on August 4, the timing of the study overlaps with the most intense part of the congressional campaign. An average of fourteen respondents were interviewed each day, with a total of 863 interviews completed in the eight districts with incumbent candidates. Although this number is quite low in comparison to the seventy daily interviews conducted for the 1988 Canadian Election Study (Johnston et al. 1992), general trends can be clearly observed in the data. Crucially, the daily random samples allow us to chart the dynamics of House campaigns in a far more detailed way than was possible with more limited panel data previously analyzed (Mann 1978; Jacobson 1990; Kenny and McBurnett 1992).

The Campaign Context: Strong and Weak Challengers in Missouri

Since Jacobson and Kernell's study (1983), it has been recognized that a theory of congressional voting requires a theory of campaigns. A starting point of an account of congressional elections is the quality of the challenger. How voters choose is a function of how effectively candidates campaign in order to win support. If the challenger fails to mount an effective campaign, whether due to a lack of competence or resources, then however much voters might be in favor of change, they will not rally around the challenger's standard.

Westlye (1991) has driven home the fundamental contrast in the dynamics of Senate elections depending on whether they are low or high intensity. Variations in campaign intensity matter because incumbents follow satisficing rather than optimizing strategies: how much of an effort they make in a campaign is in part a function of how much of a challenge their opponent mounts.

If incumbents rise to meet the challenge, it follows that a key parameter is the variation in the intensity of the campaigns that challengers mount. The eight incumbent members of Congress up for reelection in the state of Missouri in 1994 faced a range of challengers, from several very weak, barely visible candidates to a few relatively well-financed, serious opponents. Although all eight of the Missouri incumbents won decisively, the range of talent they faced allows us to demonstrate some of the over-time differences in campaigning between moderately intense and barely contested races. Two of the eight incumbent-contested 1994 races in Missouri qualify as "hard-fought" according to either of Westlye's (1991, 23) coding schemes, based on the October previews in *Congressional Quarterly Weekly Report* or the amount of money spent by the challenger relative to the incumbent. In addition, Richard Gephardt's campaign against Gary Gill, who posed "a serious challenge" (Barone and Ujifusa 1995, 777) to the then House majority leader, also exhibited aspects of a high-intensity contest; in terms of challenger spending and voters' levels of information about both candidates, it resembled a hard-fought race far more than it resembled any of the five clearly low-key races. These three moderately contested districts provide a sufficient number of cases for over-time analysis ($N = 314$) and comparisons with the five completely incumbent-dominated races ($N = 549$). Although all eight incumbents won by margins of at least 6 percent and only one was ever in danger of losing his seat in Congress, the varying quality of their opponents had a significant impact on what voters in their district knew about each candidate and apparently on the fierceness of the incumbents' campaigning. By examining differences between the effects of campaigns on various measures of candidate knowledge of these two distinct levels of intensity, we can determine when citizens become aware of the challengers, learn even more about the incumbents, and learn how this varies by the strength of the challenger.

Informational Campaign Rhythms: Findings

Campaigns can have a quite different character depending on whether they are viewed from the perspective of challenger or incumbent. We shall, accordingly, start with the challenger, beginning with issues of information and then considering the relation between familiarity and favorability.

Challengers

One of the easiest tests of candidate awareness is name recognition. Accordingly, the question we want to take as our starting point is this: How effectively do challengers use campaigns as a way of becoming known to voters?

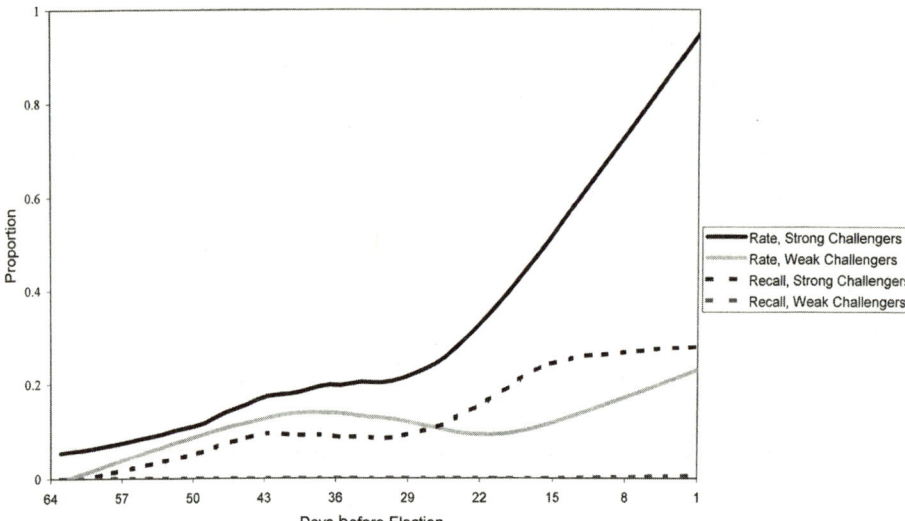

Fig. 1. Daily proportion rating (recognizing) and recalling the names of strong and weak challengers: $N = 314$ (strong challengers); $N = 548$ (weak challengers). Data smoothed using LOWESS; bandwidth = 0.5.

Since campaign effectiveness is in part a function of campaign intensity, the black lines in figure 1 represent the daily proportion[2] of respondents recognizing the challenger through the course of the election campaign, taking readiness to rate them on a feeling thermometer–type measure as a form of recognition.

Two points stand out. First, the campaigns of strong and weak challengers differ dramatically. It is true that weak, poorly funded candidates became somewhat more familiar to the electorate during the campaign. But what is conspicuous is the modesty of their accomplishments: even at the very end of the campaign, and even using the least strong of tests, only about one in every five respondents recognize them. Consider, by contrast, the gains that strong challengers reap in the course of a campaign. By the end of the campaign these candidates have made their presence felt. They are, by the time of the election, not universally known but very nearly so, recognized by over eight out of every ten respondents.

Campaigns, by the standard of increasing the challenger's name recognition, matter. They are the means—indeed, very likely the only means—by which a new candidate for public office can get himself or herself introduced to the public at large. Campaigns obviously do not guarantee that voters will learn anything about such candidates. Being known is not an automatic by-product of taking part in a campaign. The effects of a campaign hinge, as figure 1 drives home, on how aggressively it was undertaken. Weak challengers may take part in campaigns, but they do not apparently benefit much from them. Strong challengers make use of campaigns; they are, by the end, recognized by nearly as many citizens as are incumbents.

But, and this is the second point revealed in figure 1, strong challengers make their recognition gains only in the last month of the campaign. Indeed, if the curve plotting their recognition level is scrutinized, it is only with two weeks to go that a majority of respondents recognize the challenger's name, and with only a week to go nearly a third still do not. By this standard, for roughly half of the electorate, the campaigns of even these determined challengers really only began in the penultimate week of the campaign.

And this standard of candidate knowledge is one of the most lenient possible. On more demanding measures of awareness and knowledge, voters became more familiar with the strongest challengers, but still only a minority had any familiarity beyond their ability to assign the challengers a rating. Voters continued to know practically nothing at all about the weak challengers, even by Election Day. To get a clearer picture of what citizens knew about candidates, we created a direct measure of recognition, one more difficult than the ability to assign a rating score. Respondents were asked to recognize the name of each candidate by answering what the person named was "doing that puts him/her in the news now." Only respondents knowing specifically that the individuals were candidates for the U.S. Congress were scored as recognizing their names. In contrast to the high levels of voter awareness as measured by the ability to rate candidates, on the direct measure of name recognition the three strongest challengers rose from a negligible level to only about 40 percent. The increase in this strict form of recognition is quite large, but it indicates that by the last week before the election only four out of ten people in the most contested districts could identify the challengers as House candidates when read their names. (Twice as many respondents could identify the incumbents as candidates or as their representatives.)

Name recall, the ability to remember the challenger's name when asked who was running for the U.S. House of Representatives, follows a very similar pattern to strict name recognition. The stronger challengers make considerable gains in the last month. Even so, less than 25 percent of respondents could recall the challengers' names during the final two weeks before Election Day (see the gray lines toward the bottom of fig. 1). Since name recall is a more difficult task than either rating candidates or recognizing their names when given them (Mann and Wolfinger 1980), it is not surprising that the proportion recalling the challengers is so much lower. However, that only a quarter of all respondents could recall the names of even the most well-financed challengers in the final moments of the election suggests that these challengers were successful in getting their names at least vaguely recognized but that few potential voters were thinking very actively about them.

Another indication that information about the stronger challengers was quite limited even by the close of the campaign is the small number of people who could name either something they liked or something they disliked about these candidates. The ability of respondents to name either a like or dislike was very low throughout most of the election. The general election campaign did increase the proportion of respondents able to mention a liked or disliked quality about the candidates to about a third of the sample, but even on this combined measure it is clear that respondents had little to say, positive or negative, about even the strongest challengers.

Candidate Evaluations: The Exposure Slide

Our findings make plain that challengers, at least when they make a relatively strong effort, can become widely known, but being widely known does not translate into being well known, at least at the level of challengers we observe. The core issue, though, is whether it translates into being well regarded. Initially, it was supposed that the connection between the two is straightforward: familiarity breeds not contempt but support (Stokes and Miller 1966). Subsequently, it became evident that the connection between recognition and approval is by no means straightforward (Abramowitz 1975). But recognizing that the connection between the two is complex is not the same thing as specifying the complexities of how the two are connected. We want to take a step in this direction, by exploring how the relation between recognition and approval can be conditional on the phases of the campaign.

As we have seen, challengers are recognized by only a relative handful of citizens at the beginning of the campaign. Their necessary task is thus

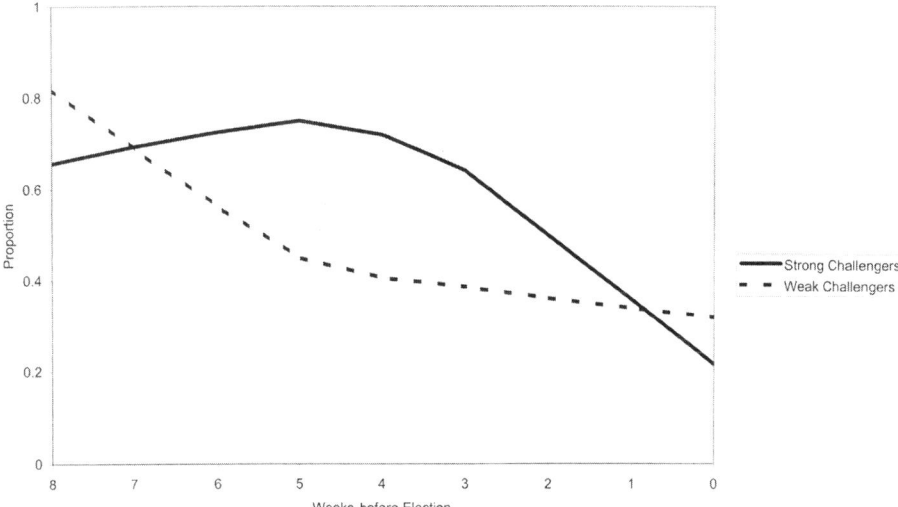

Fig. 2. Weekly proportion of favorable (6–10) ratings of strong and weak challengers: $N = 99$ (strong challengers); $N = 63$ (weak challengers). Data smoothed using LOWESS; bandwidth = 0.8.

to become known by more. But figure 2 describes the characteristic price they pay for their growing familiarity. It records the path of favorable ratings for weak and strong challengers over the course of the campaign, showing the proportion of respondents rating challengers who gave them a favorable score, plotted by week due to the small number of respondents able to rate the challengers. Both strong and weak challengers slide in popularity almost continuously during the last two months before the election. Strong challengers are able to maintain their proportionate level of support in the first month of the campaign, sliding in the second. Figure 2 thus exposes the strategic problem of challengers. They start off well regarded within their small circle—they have, after all, just won the nomination of their party. They must then make themselves known to a wider audience. But as they reach out and make their name more widely known, the proportion of those disposed to think well of them under most circumstances is fated to shrink. Hence the exposure slide—the more people recognizing the challenger, the fewer proportionately favoring him or her—recorded in figure 2.

It is obviously wrong to treat this exposure slide as though it is an inexorable dynamic. Upsetting an incumbent is an uphill fight, but challengers can win. Moreover, though they are proportionately losing support, the challengers are not necessarily losing supporters. No doubt, particularly disastrous challengers can find their support undercut in the course of a campaign, but looking at the reported vote of respondents who gave a higher rating to the challenger than to the incumbent, we see no sign that early supporters of the challenger defected to the incumbent.

The problem that challengers face is thus not the risk of losing the supporters they have garnered but the difficulty of winning over those not initially predisposed to support them. Certainly absent special circumstances, challengers will find attracting support at an increasing rate increasingly difficult, since to keep adding to their following they increasingly are faced with converting citizens who have a reason in place to favor the incumbent. These precommitment effects do show up in our analyses but are not in truth as strong as we had initially supposed, certainly not strong enough to account for the precipitous slide of determined challengers in the second month of the campaign. Indeed, the challengers' own partisans, and not only those of the incumbents, are less favorable to the challengers as Election Day approaches.

In order to see more clearly why even determined challengers tend to run into trouble, it is helpful to remember that elections are indeed competitive contests. What happens to one candidate is almost certainly connected in some way to the actions of the other candidate. We accordingly now shall shift sides and examine the campaign from the perspective of the incumbent.

Incumbents' Campaign Effectiveness: Rising to Meet the Challenge

The strategic informational advantage of incumbents is being widely known. Incumbents, preelection polls have demonstrated, start the campaign very nearly universally recognized (Mann 1978; Jacobson 1997b). The black lines at the top of figure 3 plot, for the Missouri study, an easy form of incumbent recognition, as measured by willingness to assign a rating for incumbents through the course of the congressional campaign. Whether they are facing a strong or a weak challenger, incumbents start off the campaign known to the overwhelming majority of the public. There is a marginal increase in this type of name recognition through the course of the campaign, but given the levels of recognition at the beginning of the campaign there is clearly a ceiling effect in operation.

Incumbents' already overwhelmingly high levels of name recogni-

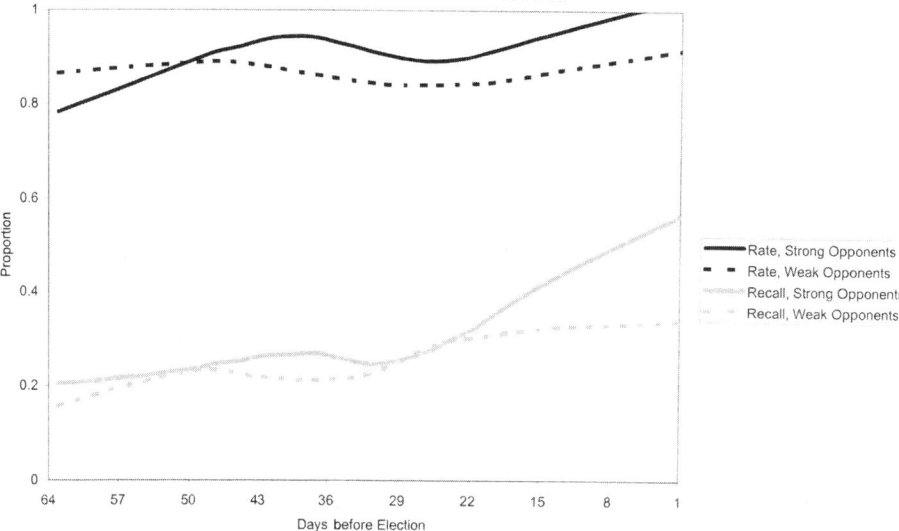

Fig. 3. Daily proportion rating and recalling the names of incumbents with strong and weak opponents: $N = 314$ (strong opponents); $N = 548$ (weak opponents). Data smoothed using LOWESS; bandwidth = 0.5.

tion at the beginning of the general election campaign naturally led some analysts to the hypothesis that, whatever advantages incumbents obtain from campaigns, informational gains were not among them (e.g., Jacobson 1981). More recent studies have clearly demonstrated that House campaigns do affect what voters know about the incumbents (Jacobson 1997a). We want, accordingly, to examine more closely this "ceiling effect" hypothesis. The impression that incumbents do not obtain informational gains from short election-year campaigns followed in part from a focus on name recognition and recall. High levels of such awareness are an important incumbent strength; they provide a necessary base to build appeals during the campaign. But the distinctive advantage of being known, we want to suggest, is that it facilitates becoming better known. Incumbents may, by taking advantage of the campaign, make their credentials better known to the public. But of course nothing is free. It requires effort and resources to become better known. It follows, on this reasoning, that incumbents are likely to make more of an effort to increase voters' knowledge about them if they have a good reason for doing so—that is, if they find themselves faced with a determined challenger.

We next examine the results of two more demanding tests of voters' awareness of their congressional representatives. First, consider the level of strict name recognition for incumbents, measured not merely by a readiness to rate the incumbent but by the ability to identify the incumbent's name as a candidate for Congress or as the current representative. The results strongly support the hypothesis that incumbents rise to the challenge. For incumbents with stronger opponents, strict name recognition rises from about 50 percent to around 80 percent of the electorate, while staying very steady for incumbents with weak challengers (data not shown). Second, consider an even more difficult task, recalling the name of the current House member (a question asked before the candidates' names were mentioned in the survey interview). Name recall of incumbents in the three most contested rraces increases from about 20 percent of respondents to over 50 percent by the end of the campaign (see the solid gray line in fig. 3). These significant increases in voters' awareness of incumbents suggest that even candidates with already high levels of name recognition (as shown by the black lines in fig. 3) have much to gain from campaigning, and will do so when they feel threatened by moderately serious challengers. The incumbents facing much weaker opponents did not by any means refrain from campaigning, but their levels of familiarity did not increase by anywhere near the same degree as those of the more seriously challenged officeholders. Lower levels of media coverage for these less intense campaigns might account for part of this difference.

Still more important, the over-time data demonstrates clearly that incumbents took advantage of the campaign to get across their credentials when they faced a moderately serious challenger. As one facet of the over-time record of the campaign, we explored whether the electorate could remember "anything special" the incumbent had done for the district while in office. Figure 4 plots the proportion naming such a deed through the course of the campaign, contrasting incumbents facing strong and weak opposition. The findings support the hypothesis that incumbents, when they feel the need, can use the campaign to put their credentials across. At the beginning of the most competitive campaigns, less than 30 percent of the public could identify something special the incumbent had done for the district; by the end, nearly 60 percent could do so. By contrast, incumbents facing weak challengers, though starting from the same level, had increased awareness of their service to a much smaller degree by the end of the campaign. The results in figure 4 are thus quite consistent with the hypothesis that

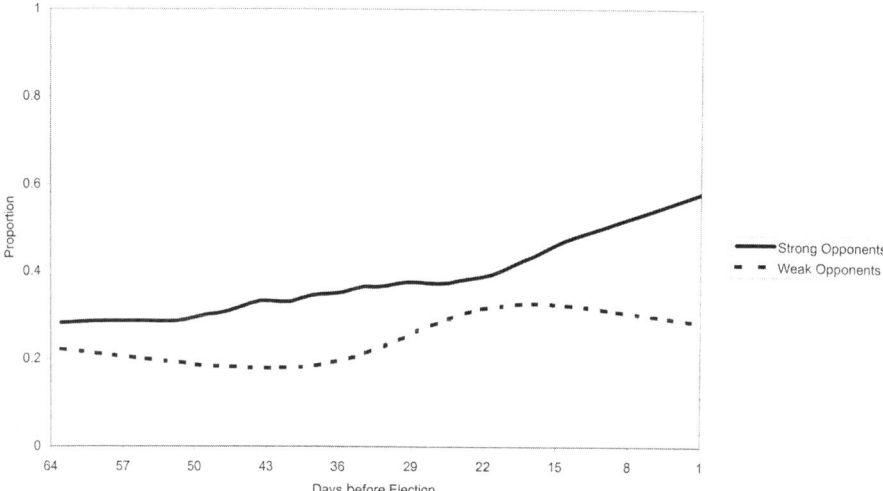

Fig. 4. Daily proportion mentioning something special the incumbent has done for district: $N = 310$ (strong opponents); $N = 525$ (weak opponents). Data smoothed using LOWESS; bandwidth = 0.5.

campaigns offer incumbents the means, if they wish to make use of it, to put their credentials across, and they are likely to exploit it precisely when they are faced with credible and well-funded opponents.

Not only were incumbents faced with moderately strong challengers able to increase the extent to which they were known, but they were also apparently able to improve the public's view of themselves and their job performance. In sharp contrast to the challengers, incumbents received a greater proportion of favorable ratings as the campaign progressed, at least those incumbents in the most intense races (see fig. 5). In addition, the average daily job approval rating for incumbents in relatively hard-fought contests increased over the last two months of the campaign. Although incumbents facing only weak challengers had higher performance ratings throughout the campaign, as we would expect, their level of job approval remained relatively consistent over time, in contrast to the gradual improvement of the incumbents in more intensely contested races. Respondents' evaluations of incumbents in the more intense races not only improved over the course of the campaign, but they also ended up at roughly the same level as the incumbents who did not attract such strong opponents.

The ability of incumbents to increase both their constituents'

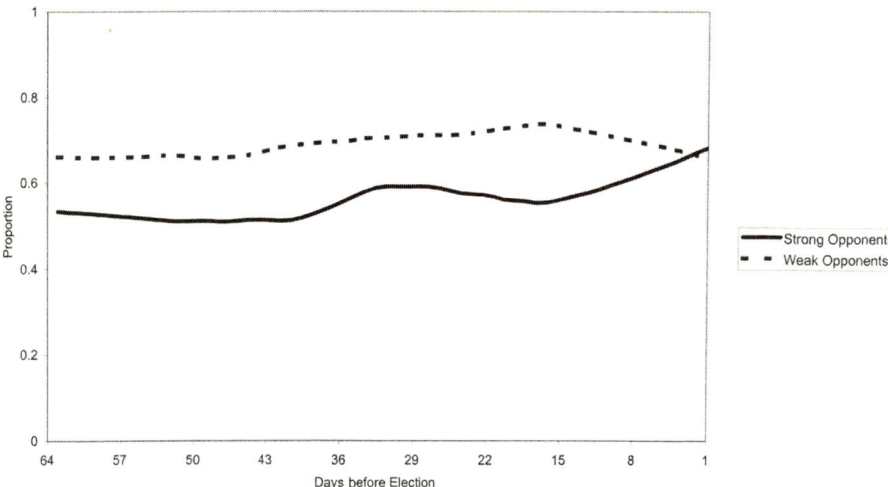

Fig. 5. Daily proportion of favorable (6–10) ratings of incumbents with strong and weak opponents: $N = 281$ (strong opponents); $N = 469$ (weak opponents). Data smoothed using LOWESS; bandwidth = 0.5.

awareness of their names and district service as well as to improve their evaluations during the final two months of the campaign demonstrates that, when they feel it is necessary, incumbents can make relatively rapid changes in how much voters know and what they think. When it may not be worth the effort, incumbents may not exert themselves enough to produce noticeable shifts so quickly or they may not receive sufficient media attention to increase their level of familiarity. Although it seems likely that varying amounts of media coverage also contribute to this trend, the fact that voters became more positive toward incumbents facing relatively strong opposition strongly suggests that the incumbents' campaign activities played a central role in these campaign shifts.

Campaign Spending

Our findings thus highlight intertwined sets of results, one set applying to challengers, the other to incumbents. Challengers, even determined challengers, slide in the standings as a wider circle of the electorate comes to know them, while incumbents, if they are facing a determined challenger, put their credentials across as Election Day approaches and become both better known and better liked. These results are intertwined because both are products of the readiness and capacity of incumbents, when faced with determined opponents, to rise to the challenge.

Consider patterns of campaign spending. Individual districts displayed quite different patterns of incumbent and challenger spending (see table 1). For the three races with strong challengers, the incumbent-challenger spending ratio varied widely. Richard Gephardt spent just over $2.6 million, the second highest amount in the country and over ten times what his opponent spent. In contrast, Mel Hancock was slightly outspent by his opponent, with Democratic challenger James Fossard spending nearly $240,000 to Hancock's $218,000.[3] In the most competitive race, ninth district incumbent Harold Volkmer spent more than twice as much as his Republican opponent, Kenny Hulshof.[4] Such considerable variations in spending patterns demonstrate the importance of the context of individual campaigns. The variations between districts also underline some of the limitations of combining candidates into general categories for analysis. We will look at campaign spending separately for each district since

TABLE 1. 1994 Missouri U.S. House Election Results and Campaign Spending

House District	Party	Candidate	1994 Vote Total (%)	Total Campaign Spending ($)	Challenger's Spending as % of Incumbent's	Total Spending on Communications ($)	Challenger's Spending on Communications as % of Incumbent's
Strong Challengers							
3	D (Inc)	Richard Gephardt	58	2,621,479		903,793	
	R	Gary Gill	40	196,461	7	81,003	9
7	D	James Fossard	40	239,681	110	97,782	84
	R (Inc)	Mel Hancock	57	218,098		116,108	
9	D (Inc)	Harold Volkmer	51	473,716		231,515	
	R	Kenny Hulshof	45	185,418	39	44,672	19
Weak Challengers							
1	D (Inc)	William Clay, Sr.	63	305,029		18,899	
	R	Donald Counts	33	9,461	3	2,238	12
2	D	Pat Kelly	31	135,867	18	21,294	5
	R (Inc)	James M. Talent	67	773,953		388,100	
4	D (Inc)	Ike Skelton	68	427,184		18,910	
	R	James Noland, Jr.	32	15,666	4	5,227	28
6	D (Inc)	Pat Danner	66	474,038		250,023	
	R	Tina Tucker	34	42,378	9	21,154	8
8	D	James Thomson	27	3,752	1	342	0.2
	R (Inc)	Bill Emerson	70	396,967		170,039	

Source: Barone and Ujifusa 1995; Federal Election Commission's candidate index reports and itemized candidate disbursement reports.

district-level variations were much more pronounced for campaign spending than for informational changes during the campaign.

We examined patterns of candidate spending during the final five weeks of the campaign, the period of greatest change in levels of candidate awareness. By definition, the stronger challengers had more money to spend throughout the campaign than did the weak challengers, but only one of the three strongest challengers could match the spending of the incumbent during the last five weeks of the campaign. The other two "strong" challengers were outspent many times over. However, these challengers each spent as much as all five of the weak challengers combined during the final month of the campaign. Two Democratic incumbents facing very weak challengers in heavily Democratic districts spent very little during the final weeks. In contrast, the three incumbents facing weak challengers who occupied seats in far less safe districts spent considerable sums in this period, completely burying their already underfunded opponents.[5]

But what were these candidates buying with their money in the final stretch of the campaign? Both the timing and the object of campaign spending can determine whether candidates reach voters. As Ansolabehere and Gerber have argued (1994), simply examining total campaign expenditures obscures important differences in what candidates actually spent the money on, whether on overhead costs such as office rent and staff salaries or on activities likely to increase their name recognition and support (or decrease support for their opponents) such as advertising in the mass media and other forms of voter contact. To compare the spending patterns of incumbents and challengers, we determined each candidate's expenditures on anything likely to communicate with voters, based on the itemized campaign disbursement reports they filed with the Federal Election Commission.[6] We used a coding scheme similar to Ansolabehere and Gerber's "campaign communication spending," a combination of Fritz and Morris's "advertising" and "other campaign activity" categories, except that we included mailing expenses as part of "campaign communications" expenditures rather than keeping mailings that might have been part of fund-raising attempts separate (Fritz and Morris 1992). As can be seen from table 1, the advantages of the incumbents in total spending is matched by their spending on voter contacts. Nearly all incumbents, regardless of the strength of their opponents, dedicated much higher amounts in the final month to media, whether television, radio, or newspaper advertisements, as well as to mailings, campaign signs, and other types of self-promotion. Only the two incumbents facing very weak challengers in safe districts did not spend over half of their total general election budget on such campaigning costs during the final five weeks. All but one of the challengers were significantly outspent overall and on campaign communications by the incumbents. Several of the challengers had very little money to spend in the first place and had little left after paying for basic overhead necessities such as office rent and telephone service. Even those with relatively large sums of money were outspent by the incumbents. Although the stronger challengers were spending the majority of their general election campaign funds during the period of time when they were becoming more widely known, so were the better-funded incumbents. All but one of the challengers were unable to spend even a third of what the incumbent was spending on reaching out to voters during the crucial final month of the campaign.

Conclusions

Congressional elections usually pit an almost universally known incumbent against a challenger, often poorly prepared and typically unfamiliar to the public as a whole. The result is foreordained or appears ominously so. Incumbents prevail and elections appear more a mechanism of coronation than of deliberation. For if elections really were a matter of deliberation, then surely their outcome should not be so predictable before the campaign even gets under way. Incumbents win the vast majority of the time, and the only question genuinely open to debate is whether the predictability of the final vote is to be understood as a consequence of the special resources that incumbency vouchsafes or as a result of characteristics of minimally informed voters that commit them to the incumbent's camp before the campaign begins or as the interaction of the two.

This notion that elections register decisions made before election campaigns even begin and that campaigns are essentially an institutionalized interlude between establishment of a candidate preference and its official expression has gained ground in recent years (Gelman and King 1993). If the outcome can be predicted before the campaign even begins, then whatever happens during the campaign hardly appears important. But this argument from predictability owes its plausibility, we think, to a confusion of contingency and agency. It is not necessary to argue that an election's outcome must in a substantial sense be a matter of chance to believe that what happened happened because the candidates—and, in the case of congressional elections, the incumbent in particular—acted as they acted, doing what they did.

The expression of agency, obviously enough, is obscured by the standard postelection design of most previous studies of congressional elections. It is not possible to catch sight of when people pick up information in the course of a campaign, let alone what the sources of this information might be, if what they know is assessed only after it is all over. And when they learn what they learn can matter as much as what they learn—hence our concern with the informational rhythms of congressional campaigns. Determined challengers can make themselves known. Assessed by standard measures, by Election Day an overwhelming number of the electorate recognize them, as we have seen. But time defines their strategic problem. To make their case they must make their credentials known, but to manage this they must first make themselves known, and this characteristically takes them the better part of the campaign. Incumbents, because they are in the public eye from the start, have a campaign that lasts two months or more. Challengers, because they are not, characteristically are in the public eye for only the last several weeks. They have, unless they can mount an exceptional effort, enough time to become widely known but not enough to become well known. Incumbents, conversely, are both well known enough and well funded enough to make their case to voters.

There is nothing foreordained about any of these outcomes. Candidates, to be sure, must have the resources necessary to wage a competitive campaign. But they also must make the effort. Determined challengers do; weak challengers don't; and incumbents do, but much more so when faced with determined challengers. This is a story about agency, not inevitability. Incumbents characteristically start ahead and finish ahead. But it does not follow that their campaigns do not matter. On the contrary, if our findings apply generally to congressional elections, the point is precisely that incumbents do well on Election Day because they have done well during the election campaign.

APPENDIX: Wording of Items from the Missouri Election Study

Ability to Place Candidate on Scale/Candidate Rating
"Now I'll ask you about some people and ask you to rate each on a scale that runs from 1 to 10. Ratings between 1 and 5 mean that you rate that person UNFAVORABLY. Ratings between 5 and 10 mean that you rate that person FAVORABLY. You may use any number from 1 to 10. If you come

to a person whose name you don't recognize, just tell me and we'll move on to the next person."

"What about [candidate's name]? How would you rate him/her from 1 to 10?"

Strict Recognition
"Now I'm going to read you some names of people who have been in the news. Very few people know all the names, so if you don't know some, just say so. When I ask you about a person, please tell me if you recognize him or her, and if you do, why they have been in the news recently."

"What about [candidate's name]? What is [candidate's name] doing that puts him/her in the news now?"

Respondents were coded as recognizing the candidate if they knew he/she was the incumbent or a candidate for U.S. Congress.

Name Recall
"And how about the candidates who are running for Congress in your congressional district? Do you happen to remember what their names are?"

Likes and Dislikes
"Is there anything in particular that you like [DON'T like] about [candidate's name], the Democratic candidate for the U.S. House of Representatives?"

Remember Something Special Incumbent Has Done
"Do you happen to remember anything special that [incumbent's name] has done for the people of this district while he/she has been in office?"

Incumbent Job Approval
"In general, do you approve or disapprove of the way [incumbent's name] is handling his/her job? Do you approve/disapprove strongly, or not strongly?"

NOTES

1. Telephone interviews were conducted every day from September 6, 1994, through November 7, 1994, with the exception of November 4, when no interviews were completed. The interviews were conducted by the Center for Advanced Social Research at the University of Missouri at Columbia.

2. All figures present LOWESS curves. LOWESS (locally weighted scatterplot smoothing) is a data smoothing procedure that reduces the distorting effect of outliers (Cleveland 1979, 1985).

3. Hancock and Fossard both probably benefited in terms of exposure from the campaign for and against Hancock II, a controversial, and ultimately unsuccessful, ballot proposition named for the incumbent.

4. In 1996 a better-funded Hulshof outspent his incumbent opponent and was able to knock Volkmer out of the seat he had held for twenty years.

5. Two of these candidates were running their first reelection campaigns after beating incumbents two years earlier (Barone and Ujifusa 1995).

6. All spending and contribution data were obtained from Federal Election Commission reports filed by the candidates. The accuracy and clarity of these reports vary by candidate.

REFERENCES

Abramowitz, Alan I. 1975. "Name Familiarity, Reputation, and the Incumbency Effect in a Congressional Election." *Western Political Quarterly* 28:668–84.

Ansolabehere, Stephen, and Alan Gerber. 1994. "The Mismeasure of Campaign Spending: Evidence from the 1990 U.S. House Elections." *Journal of Politics* 56:1106–18.

Barone, Michael, and Grant Ujifusa. 1995. *The Almanac of American Politics 1996.* Washington, DC: National Journal.

Cleveland, William S. 1979. "Robust Locally Weighted Regression and Smoothing Scatterplots." *Journal of the American Statistical Association* 74:829–36.

———. 1985. *The Elements of Graphing Data.* Monterey, CA: Wadsworth.

Fritz, Sara, and Dwight Morris. 1992. *Handbook of Campaign Spending: Money in the 1990 Congressional Races.* Washington, DC: Congressional Quarterly Press.

Gelman, Andrew, and Gary King. 1993. "Why Are American Presidential Election Polls So Variable When Votes Are So Predictable?" *British Journal of Political Science* 23:409–51.

Jacobson, Gary C. 1981. "Incumbents' Advantages in the 1978 U.S. House Congressional Elections." *Legislative Studies Quarterly* 6:183–200.

———. 1990. "The Effects of Campaign Spending in House Elections: New Evidence for Old Arguments." *American Journal of Political Science* 34:334–62.

———. 1997a. "Measuring Campaign Spending Effects in U.S. House Elections." Paper presented at the Conference on Capturing Campaign Effects, Vancouver, British Columbia.

———. 1997b. *The Politics of Congressional Elections.* 4th ed. New York: Longman.

Jacobson, Gary C., and Samuel Kernell. 1983. *Strategy and Choice in Congressional Elections.* 2d ed. New Haven: Yale University Press.

Johnston, Richard, André Blais, Henry E. Brady, and Jean Crête. 1992. *Letting the People Decide: Dynamics of a Canadian Election.* Montreal: McGill-Queen's University Press.

Kenny, Christopher, and Michael McBurnett. 1992. "A Dynamic Model of the Effect of Campaign Spending on Congressional Vote Choice." *American Journal of Political Science* 36:923–37.

Mann, Thomas E. 1978. *Unsafe at Any Margin: Interpreting Congressional Elections.* Washington, DC: American Enterprise Institute for Public Policy Research.

Mann, Thomas E., and Raymond E. Wolfinger. 1980. "Candidates and Parties in Congressional Elections." *American Political Science Review* 74:617–23.

Stokes, Donald E., and Warren E. Miller. 1966. "Party Government and the Saliency of Congress." In *Elections and the Political Order,* ed. Angus Campbell, Philip E. Converse, Warren E. Miller, and Donald E. Stokes, 194–211. New York: Wiley.

Westlye, Mark C. 1991. *Senate Elections and Campaign Intensity.* Baltimore: Johns Hopkins University Press.

Alternative Tests for the Effects of Campaigns and Candidates on Voting Behavior

Benjamin Highton

Do CANDIDATES AND CAMPAIGNS influence voting behavior? In order to answer this question, scholars often associate the former with the latter. For example, in their analysis of the 1992 U.S. presidential election, Alvarez and Nagler (1995) find a significant effect of voters' preferences regarding abortion policy and link it to the candidates' positions: "Some issues raised during the campaign did matter.... [G]iven the powerful influence of abortion in determining respondents' vote choices it appears that Bush's pro-life stance was quite costly. The family values night at the Republican convention may have imposed substantial political costs on Bush" (738–39).

The validity of an inference that links a campaign factor to a variable that influences voting behavior depends on what one would observe in the counterfactual condition. If the candidates and their campaigns matter, then one would find a smaller, and perhaps nonexistent, effect in the counterfactual condition. In the context of the example just given, if voters responded to Bush's pro-life position and the emphasis on family values at the Republican convention (which contrasted with the pro-choice position espoused by Bill Clinton), then had Bush been pro-choice, voters' abortion policy preferences would not have influenced their ballot choices.

Of course, counterfactual conditions cannot be observed, and analysts are consequently faced with what Holland (1986, 947) has called "the Fundamental Problem of Causal Inference." This essay describes and demonstrates several research designs that address this problem. The key to all of the approaches are comparisons that attempt to approximate the counterfactual condition. To the extent that they are successful, the persuasiveness of causal claims (one way or the other) regarding the influence of campaigns and candidates is enhanced.

Scope of the Analysis

U.S. Senate elections are the focus of the empirical investigation in this essay. Two considerations make this an attractive choice. First, because there are over thirty Senate elections in any election year, one can observe and measure variation in election-level variables. Second, because of a relatively recent data collection effort (Miller et al. 1993), there now exists a valuable source of individual-level survey data, the Senate Election Studies, that may be used to study voting behavior in Senate elections.[1] All the research designs employed in this essay depend on the interaction between variables at individual and election levels. Obtaining data at both levels is therefore crucial.[2]

Abortion policy is the substantive focus of the analysis. Several factors make it an appealing issue to analyze. In the wake of the Supreme Court's 1989 ruling in *Webster v. Reproductive Health Services* that granted states more freedom to restrict abortions, abortion policy gained greater national prominence. Congress passed two appropriation bills that President Bush vetoed because of what he said were inadequate abortion restrictions. Later in the year, supporters of abortion rights introduced the Freedom of Choice Act, a bill intended to codify the principles of *Roe v. Wade*. Equally important, from an analytical perspective, Senate candidates, sometimes, but not always, adopt different positions regarding abortion policy.[3] Although the national party platforms have contrasted greatly since 1980,[4] pro-life Democrats and pro-choice Republicans are not uncommon among Senate candidates. At the individual level, the possibility of abortion policy voting exists because most voters have opinions regarding abortion. In addition, whereas voters are susceptible to persuasion by the candidates on some issues about which they care less deeply, individuals' abortion views are unlikely to be changed by Senate candidates and their campaigns.[5] Therefore one can be confident that, for an observed relationship between abortion policy preferences and candidate choice, causality runs from the former to the latter, not vice versa.

The primary hypothesis to be investigated specifies that voters respond to abortion policy positions of the Senate candidates. If the candidates hold opposing views, then voters' abortion positions will influence their ballot choices. If the candidates share similar views, then voters' abortion positions will not be of consequence for whom they vote. In other words, the hypothesis specifies that candidates' positions are a cause of the level of policy voting.[6]

Data and Measurement

The sixty-six contested U.S. Senate races in 1990 and 1992 constitute the sample of Senate elections considered.[7] A dichotomous variable that indicates whether the Senate candidates held similar or opposing abortion positions is the primary election-level variable.[8] To classify each of the races, I conducted an extensive search of the LEXIS/NEXIS on-line campaign library. The campaign library is an especially useful data source because it contains numerous national campaign periodicals such as *The Cook Political Report*, *The Hotline*, and *The Abortion Report* in addition to a large number of local newspapers. A preliminary search using the keywords "Senate" and "abortion" made possible the classification of many of the races. Follow-up searches that focused on specific campaigns enabled me to complete the codings. Overall, thirty-five of the sixty-six races involved candidates who held different positions regarding abortion policy.[9] Of the remaining thirty-one, twenty races had candidates who were both pro-choice, and in eleven, both candidates were pro-life.

Of obvious importance for distinguishing abortion policy voting is a measure of voters' abortion policy preferences.[10] The 1990 and 1992 Senate Election Studies provide the data. Answers to three questions combined into a single trichotomous measure serve as the indicator of abortion policy preferences, which measures the level of opposition to abortion restrictions.[11]

Isolating the effects, if any, of abortion policy preferences on voting behavior requires a model that takes into account other political attitudes. In general, those more supportive of restrictive abortion policies tend to have more conservative policy preferences and identify as "conservatives" and "Republicans." In a model that only included voters' abortion policy preferences, the parameter estimate might merely pick up effects that theoretically should be captured by variables that measure general policy liberalism, ideological and partisan identification.[12]

Three variables tapping voters' general political orientations are used in order to distinguish the independent effects of voters' abortion policy preferences. The first is the traditional National Election Studies (NES) measure of party identification.[13] The second is a measure of general policy liberalism, which is made up of answers to ten policy questions. The third is ideological self-identification. Voters were categorized as "conservative," "liberal," or "moderate."[14]

Designs and Results

Basic Design

With the preliminaries out of the way, recall that the primary hypothesis of interest specifies that voters respond to the policy positions of Senate candidates. Specifically, if the candidates hold opposing abortion positions, voters' preferences regarding abortion policy exert a greater effect on their ballot choices than if the candidates hold similar abortion policy positions. I will refer to this as the responsiveness hypothesis.

Before directly addressing the issue of causality, the first step of the analysis will be to ascertain whether there exists a connection between individuals' abortion policy preferences and their votes in the Senate races, where one candidate was pro-choice and the other was pro-life. If the responsiveness hypothesis is correct, then this relationship should be apparent.

The results reported in table 1 clearly suggest that voters' opinions regarding abortion policy influenced their ballot choices in races where the

TABLE 1. Logit Parameter Estimates of Voting for the Democratic Senate Candidate (races in which the candidates held different abortion policy positions)

Variable	Parameter Estimate	Standard Error
Abortion views	.88	.19
Party identification	1.84	.17
Ideological self-identification	.81	.20
Policy liberalism	.54	.19
Incumbency	.82	.08
Number of observations: 1,262		
Log-likelihood: −626.5		

Source: Pooled Senate Election Studies and data collected by author.

Note: Each of the independent variables listed in the table was coded as a trichotomy ranging from 0 (least liberal/Democratic) to 1 (most liberal/Democratic). See essay and appendix for details. Although they are not reported, the model includes an intercept and variables indicating age, education, family income, gender, race, and religion.

Senate candidates held different abortion positions. In the elections where the Democratic candidate was pro-choice and the Republican candidate was pro-life, the multivariate model estimates indicate that voters who supported less restrictive abortion laws were more likely to vote for the Democratic Senate candidate. In these races, with the exception of party identification, voters' opinions regarding abortion exerted the largest effect on their ballot choices. For an otherwise indifferent voter, the logit estimate of .88 suggests that favoring less, rather than more, restrictive abortion laws increased the probability of voting for the Democratic candidate by .22.[15]

Although finding an effect of abortion views in elections where the candidates held opposing positions is necessary for the responsiveness hypothesis to be true, it is far from sufficient. There are a variety of competing hypotheses that predict the same relationship. Thus the statistical results have yet to provide any strong evidence regarding the cause of the relationship between abortion policy preferences and voting behavior. For example, Jacobson and Wolfinger (1989) analyzed a California Senate race in which the candidates held different positions on the Equal Rights Amendment (ERA) and showed a connection between individuals' opinions of the ERA and their votes. They hesitated, however, to conclude that voters were responding to the candidates.

> An issue question may simply identify a subset of voters with a particular political bias; for example, other things being equal, people who favor the ERA may also favor liberal Democrats like Alan Cranston and might have supported him just as consistently had Gann [the Republican] endorsed the ERA, killing it as a campaign issue. Just because an issue position is related to the vote does not mean that the issue itself influenced the vote. (526)

Jacobson and Wolfinger cite one plausible alternative. Voters with particular policy preferences may simply habitually vote for candidates of one of the parties. There are other plausible explanations too. These alternative hypotheses will be assessed in the ensuing sections as more elaborate research designs are introduced.

The more general point is an important one. Hypotheses about campaign effects, be they the responsiveness one investigated here or others, specify that voting behavior is influenced by election and campaign characteristics. To test these hypotheses, it is therefore important to demonstrate that variation in election characteristics is associated with variation in voting behavior.[16] The "basic" design provides no variation in the campaign variable of interest and therefore can provide no information about how voting behavior might be different if the election context were different.[17] This is a limitation that analysts of presidential elections often face. For instance, was the abortion policy voting that Alvarez and Nagler (1995) identified in the 1992 presidential election caused by the candidates' opposing positions? With only a single election, it is impossible to tell.

Multiple Races Design

Ideally, one would compare the effect of voters' views regarding abortion policy in races where the candidates held different positions to the effect of abortion opinions in the counterfactual condition of the candidates sharing similar abortion positions. But the fundamental problem of causal inference prevents conducting this test. However, there are a number of comparisons that can be made that will help explain why abortion policy opinions affect voting behavior in the races where the candidates held different abortion positions.

Not all Senate races are contests between pro-choice Democrats and pro-life Republicans. In nearly half of the campaigns, both candidates held similar positions regarding abortion policy. If voters respond to the candidates' positions, then the effect of their abortion policy preferences will be smaller, perhaps nonexistent, in those races where the candidates' positions were similar. On the other hand, if voters do not respond to the candidates, and instead those more and less supportive of restrictive abortion laws habitually favor Republicans and Democrats, respectively, then the effect of abortion policy preferences will not vary across campaign contexts. A similar lack of variation will be observed if voters respond to the national parties' abortion positions rather than those of the Senate candidates, because the parties' positions are constant across election contexts.

The findings reported in table 2 address these issues. The voting models were estimated over the entire set of Senate elections. The first two columns of the table report the estimates from a model that constrains the effects of the parameters to be identical across campaign types. The third and fourth columns display the estimates of a model that permits the effects of the independent variables to vary across election contexts.[18] The results suggest that there is variation in voting behavior associated with whether the candidates held similar or different positions regarding abortion policy. Comparing the log-likelihoods of the two models, one finds an improvement in fit to the data with the unconstrained model that would probably not be evident if the determinants of vote choice were identical in both types of elections ($p < .01$).

Notice the pattern of differences in parameter estimates between races where the candidates held similar abortion positions and those where the candidates' positions were different. The unconstrained model estimates indicate that, in contrast to the substantial effect of abortion opinions in races where the candidates held different positions, there was virtually no effect of voters' abortion views in races where the candidates' positions were similar. This finding suggests that the initial observed relationship between abortion policy preferences and Senate voting behavior

TABLE 2. Logit Parameter Estimates of Voting for the Democratic Senate Candidate (multiple races design)

	Constrained Model		Unconstrained Model	
	Parameter Estimate	Standard Error	Parameter Estimate	Standard Error
Abortion views	.46	.14	−.02	.21
Abortion views × candidates' positions	—	—	.88	.28
Party identification	2.04	.12	2.31	.19
Party identification × candidates' positions	—	—	−.47	.24
Ideological self-identification	.78	.15	.85	.23
Ideological self-identification × candidates' positions	—	—	−.08	.30
Policy liberalism	.66	.14	.77	.21
Policy liberalism × candidates' positions	—	—	−.20	.28
Incumbency	1.00	.06	1.29	.10
Incumbency × candidates' positions	—	—	−.48	.13
Candidates' positions	—	—	.01	.23
Number of observations: 2,416				
Log-likelihood of constrained model: −1,169.7				
Log-likelihood of unconstrained model: −1,156.9				
p-value for difference: .0003				

Source: Pooled Senate Election Studies and data collected by author.

Note: Candidates' positions is coded 0 for races in which both Senate candidates held similar abortion policy positions and 1 for races in which the candidates held different positions. Each of the other independent variables listed in the table is coded as a trichotomy ranging from 0 (least liberal/Democratic) to 1 (most liberal/Democratic). See essay and appendix for details. Although they are not reported, both models include constants and variables indicating age, education, family income, gender, race, and religion.

(table 1) cannot properly be explained by either the habit or national party responsiveness hypotheses.

The results displayed in table 2 also permit the rejection of another competing explanation. Westlye (1991) argues that campaign intensity causes a greater level of policy voting because voters are provided sufficient information in hard-fought races to base their decisions on policy considerations. The model estimates reported in table 2 do not provide a direct test of Westlye's hypothesis, but they do rule out the possibility that Westlye's theory explains the pattern of results. If the cause of the larger effect of abortion views in races where the candidates' positions were different was to be found in higher levels of campaign intensity in those races, then the magnitudes of the effects of the other independent variables would be larger too. This is decidedly not the case. With the exception of abortion policy preferences, in elections where the candidates held different abortion positions the parameter estimates of the effects of all the independent variables are *smaller*.

Comparing the effects of independent variables in different campaign settings falls under Brady, Johnston, and Sides's (this volume) rubric of a "multiple races design."[19] The design is more powerful than a simple cross-sectional design that investigates a single election, or a set of elections, in which no variation in the campaign variable of interest is observed. Its use has led to the rejection of three rival explanations for the initial finding of a substantial effect of abortion views on voting behavior. If these were the only competing hypotheses, then concluding in favor of the responsiveness hypothesis would be warranted. But there are additional explanations that cannot be tested with the multiple races design. Consequently, other research designs should be considered.

Stacked Elections/Judgments Designs

Recall again the counterfactual condition associated with the set of observed candidates with different abortion positions. If, instead, their positions were similar, the responsiveness hypothesis predicts that the effect of abortion views on voting behavior would be diminished. The multiple races design approximates a comparison between observed and counterfactual conditions to the extent that differences other than the candidates' positions are minimized between the two types of campaigns. If candidates' positions were randomly assigned, then the multiple races design would constitute a controlled experiment and further analysis would be unnecessary. With little reason to assume this to be true, prudence dictates either confirming the validity of this possibility or employing a research design that can distinguish selection effects from the causal effects of candidates' policy positions. Otherwise, one cannot confidently interpret the findings.

Although the multiple races design permitted the rejection of the hypothesis that candidates' positions were merely a proxy for campaign intensity, the possibility of a spurious relationship remains. Wright and Berkman (1986) introduce another rival hypothesis.

> If some states have political cultures more disposed to ideological politics than others, then we might observe a correlation between candidate polarization and ideological voting even if voters were not responding to specific candidates. From this perspective, candidate polarization measures an aspect of political culture rather than the specific stimuli affecting voters. (578)

Not only might some states have more ideological politics in general, but the nature of abortion politics might also vary by state. For example, several studies have emphasized state differences in interest group activity and mobilization (Cohen and Barrilleaux 1993; Hansen 1993; Meier and McFarlane 1993). My own analysis of election exit polls reveals varying levels of partisan polarization within states regarding abortion policy preferences.

The general point is that the relationship between candidates' positions and voting behavior revealed by the multiple races design might not be causal. Both the level of abortion policy voting and the Senate candidates' positions might be caused by relatively fixed state characteristics. If this is true, then candidates' positions are simply epiphenomenal, associated with, but not the cause of, the level of abortion policy voting.

To determine whether Senate candidates' abortion positions truly cause the level of abortion policy voting or are simply an indicator of states' political cultures, a design that controls for fixed state effects must be employed. One possibility entails directly measuring aspects of state political cultures and including them in a multiple races design along with the Senate candidates' positions. This approach entails several disadvantages that suggest that another alternative should be sought. First, measuring the various dimensions of state political culture is no easy task. Second, even if valid indicators could be constructed, including them in voting models might result in levels of multicollinearity that would substantially diminish the possibility of obtaining precise estimates of the myriad state- and election-level effects.

A different approach that can distinguish fixed state effects from those of the candidates' positions is referred to as a "stacked design" by Brady, Johnston, and Sides (this volume). If aspects of state political cultures cause the level of policy voting in Senate elections, then these same factors would lead people to rely more heavily on their abortion opinions when making other political judgments too. For example, if abortion politics are especially salient in a particular state, then residents of that state will rely on their opinions regarding abortion when voting for senator and making other political judgments, such as assessing the president. In contrast, if the greater effects of voters' opinions regarding abortion policy on Senate voting are caused by candidates' holding contrasting abortion positions, then Senate candidates' abortion positions will not be associated with larger effects of voters' abortion opinions on other political judgments.

Stacked designs include dependent variables other than the primary one of interest. If similar variation in the magnitudes of estimated effects are found for the additional dependent variables, then attributing the variation in the magnitudes of the estimated effects of the independent variables on the primary dependent variable to a campaign characteristic is unwarranted.

In the present case, two additional dependent variables are available, voting for the House of Representatives and presidential approval. If the responsiveness hypothesis is correct, then the Senate candidates' positions will not be associated with the magnitude of the relationship between abortion opinions and House voting and presidential approval. If the candidates' positions merely reflect an aspect of state political cultures, then the observed relationship between Senate candidates' positions and voting for the Senate will also be apparent if either House voting or presidential approval is substituted for Senate voting.[20]

Tables 3 and 4 report the model estimates of voting for the Democratic House candidate and disapproval of President Bush, respectively.[21] Neither provides evidence for the fixed state effects hypothesis. To the extent that differences do exist, the parameter estimates suggest a *smaller* effect of abortion policy preferences on House voting and presidential approval in the states where the Senate candidates held different abortion

TABLE 3. Logit Parameter Estimates of Voting for the Democratic House Candidate (stacked design)

	Constrained Model		Unconstrained Model	
	Parameter Estimate	Standard Error	Parameter Estimate	Standard Error
Abortion views	.28	.15	.39	.20
Abortion views × candidates' positions	—	—	−.24	.28
Party identification	2.04	.12	1.98	.17
Party identification × candidates' positions	—	—	.14	.24
Ideological self-identification	.74	.15	.53	.22
Ideological self-identification × candidates' positions	—	—	.43	.31
Policy liberalism	.33	.14	.25	.20
Policy liberalism × candidates' positions	—	—	.15	.28
Candidates' positions	—	—	−.27	.20
Number of observations: 2,091				
Log-likelihood of constrained model: −1,098.0				
Log-likelihood of unconstrained model: −1,095.2				
p-value for difference: .35				

Source: Pooled Senate Election Studies and data collected by author.
Note: Candidates' positions is coded 0 for races in which both Senate candidates held similar abortion policy positions and 1 for races in which the candidates held different positions. Each of the other independent variables listed in the table is coded as a trichotomy ranging from 0 (least liberal/Democratic) to 1 (most liberal/Democratic). See essay and appendix for details. Although they are not reported, both models include constants and variables indicating age, education, family income, gender, race, and religion.

TABLE 4. Logit Parameter Estimates of Disapproval of President Bush (stacked design)

	Constrained Model		Unconstrained Model	
	Parameter Estimate	Standard Error	Parameter Estimate	Standard Error
Abortion views	.65	.15	.76	.21
Abortion views × candidates' positions	—	—	−.22	.28
Party identification	1.83	.12	1.69	.18
Party identification × candidates' positions	—	—	.29	.24
Ideological self-identification	.81	.15	.90	.21
Ideological self-identification × candidates' positions	—	—	−.20	.29
Policy liberalism	.54	.14	.47	.21
Policy liberalism × candidates' positions	—	—	.15	.28
Candidates' positions	—	—	.27	.23
Number of observations: 2,251				
Log-likelihood of constrained model: −1,113.3				
Log-likelihood of unconstrained model: −1,107.3				
p-value for difference: .03				

Source: Pooled Senate Election Studies and data collected by author.
Note: Candidates' positions is coded 0 for races in which both Senate candidates held similar abortion policy positions and 1 for races in which the candidates held different positions. Each of the other independent variables listed in the table is coded as a trichotomy ranging from 0 (least liberal/Democratic) to 1 (most liberal/Democratic). See essay and appendix for details. Although they are not reported, both models include constants and variables indicating age, education, family income, gender, race, religion, and survey year (1992 versus 1990).

positions. Thus the possibility that fixed characteristics of the states explain the observed relationship between the level of abortion policy voting and Senate candidates appears less likely.

Controlled Constituencies/Multiple Races Designs

The stacked design helped to rule out the general hypothesis of fixed state effects. However, there remains a more narrow version of the hypothesis. There may be fixed state effects with respect to particular election types or constituencies. For example, within states, consistent patterns of voting behavior may be apparent in statewide elections generally or Senate elections in particular. Analyzing presidential approval and House voting would not pick up this sort of effect. Another approach is necessary.

One conceptual possibility entails analyzing multiple Senate elections in the same state. Consider, for example, the California Senate races in 1992. In that year, two Senate elections were held, one for a regular six-year term and another for the remaining two years of a vacated seat. In one of these races, the candidates held opposing abortion positions.[22] In the other, both candidates were pro-choice.[23] The responsiveness hypothesis predicts that individuals' preferences regarding abortion policy would be more strongly related to voting behavior in the former race compared to the latter. In contrast, if the California political culture determines the level of abortion policy voting in Senate elections, then one would not observe differences across the races.

Although concurrent Senate elections are a rarity, a research design based on the logic of analyzing them may be developed and implemented. The Senate studies include data from Senate elections in 1990 and 1992. As a result, there is some overlap between races and states. Sixteen states held elections in both years. In four, both candidates were pro-life in each election. In five others, both were pro-choice in each election. In seven states, however, one of the elections pitted candidates who held different abortion positions, while in the other race the candidates held similar abortion positions. This latter group of states provides some variation in candidate positions that is independent of any fixed state characteristics. Consequently, if candidates' positions cause the degree to which voters' abortion opinions affect their votes, then the effect of abortion opinions should be greater in the seven races where the candidates held different positions. I term this a "controlled constituency multiple races design."

Table 5 presents model estimates that appear to further rule out the fixed state characteristics hypothesis. Overall the unconstrained model fits the data better and provides a considerable degree of confidence that the improvement in fit is not merely due to chance ($p < .01$). In addition, the pattern of coefficients is remarkably similar to those from the simple multiple races design. The estimated effect of voters' abortion policy preferences increases in the races where the candidates held different abortion positions, whereas the estimated effects of all the other independent variables are diminished in this campaign context.[24]

Summary and Conclusion

Moving beyond the basic research design that analyzes voting behavior in races where the Senate candidates held contrasting abortion positions has proven to be a valuable strategy. Each subsequent design helped rule out plausible explanations for the initial observed relationship between voters'

TABLE 5. Logit Parameter Estimates of Voting for the Democratic Senate Candidate (multiple race controlled constituency design)

	Constrained Model		Unconstrained Model	
	Parameter Estimate	Standard Error	Parameter Estimate	Standard Error
Abortion views	.75	.30	.54	.47
Abortion views × candidates' positions	—	—	.44	.60
Party identification	2.13	.28	2.32	.45
Party identification × candidates' positions	—	—	−.42	.57
Ideological self-identification	.80	.31	1.02	.53
Ideological self-identification × candidate's positions	—	—	−.15	.66
Policy liberalism	.60	.31	.76	.51
Policy liberalism × candidates' positions	—	—	−.39	.65
Incumbency	1.61	.17	2.34	.27
Incumbency × candidates' positions	—	—	−1.32	.35
Candidates' positions	—	—	.50	.48
Number of observations: 580				
Log-likelihood of constrained model: −261.8				
Log-likelihood of unconstrained model: −250.1				
p-value for difference: .0007				

Source: Pooled Senate Election Studies and data collected by author.

Note: Candidates' positions is coded 0 for races in which both Senate candidates held similar abortion policy positions and 1 for races in which the candidates held different positions. Each of the other independent variables listed in the table is coded as a trichotomy ranging from 0 (least liberal/Democratic) to 1 (most liberal/Democratic). See essay and appendix for details. Although they are not reported, both models include constants and variables indicating age, education, family income, gender, race, and religion.

abortion policy preferences and their ballot choices. Of course, there are always more possibilities. Consequently, concluding with absolute certainty that voters respond to the Senate candidates' abortion policy positions would be going too far. Nevertheless, as a result of employing the varied research designs discussed in this essay, confidence in the validity of the responsiveness hypothesis has been substantially enhanced; it is the only one of the considered hypotheses left standing.

More generally, none of the designs discussed in this essay are limited in their applicability to U.S. Senate elections. Nor are they exclusively limited to situations where there are numerous elections. Consider a concrete example regarding presidential elections. In their analysis of the 1988 election between George Bush and Michael Dukakis, Shanks and Miller (1991) found a substantial effect of voters' opinions regarding the death penalty on ballot choices. Those more supportive of using the death penalty were more likely to vote for Bush. In contrast, their analysis of the 1992 presidential election (Miller and Shanks 1996) revealed that voters' opinions regarding the death penalty were unrelated to ballot choices. Comparing the effect of the death penalty opinions in these two campaigns constitutes a "controlled constituency design" and lends support to the notion that voters respond to presidential candidates' policy positions.

To be sure, the research designs discussed in this essay do have a weakness. They are better at identifying a causal factor than revealing the causal process by which voters eventually respond to it. That is, the findings reported here have suggested that voters respond to Senate candidates' policy positions without illuminating exactly how this happens. However, the somewhat lengthy list of plausible hypotheses that have been falsified attests to the value of the approaches employed in this essay.

APPENDIX: Coding and Univariate Statistics

A. Measurement

Voters' preferences regarding abortion policy were measured using responses to three questions:

> 1. Do you think abortion should be legal under all circumstances, only legal under certain circumstances, or never legal under any circumstance?

2. Would you favor or oppose a state law that would require parental consent before a teenager under eighteen could have an abortion?
3. Would you favor or oppose a law in your state that would allow the use of government funds to help pay for the costs of abortion for women who cannot afford them?

Questions 2 and 3 included follow-ups to ascertain whether individuals' support or opposition was "strong" or "not strong." Answers to each of the three questions were coded to range from 0 (favoring more restrictive abortion policies) to 1 (favoring less restrictive abortion policies) and averaged to produce a single scale of abortion support. The average inter-item Pearson's correlation of the scale components is .35, and the coefficient of reliability (Cronbach's alpha) of the scale is .62.

A trichotomized version of the scale was constructed by placing roughly equal numbers of respondents into each of three categories. Simplifying the scale in this manner substantially eases the interpretation of the multivariate model estimates without altering the pattern of results. The one-third of the sample least supportive of minimal abortion restrictions are coded 0; those most supportive are coded 1; the remaining one-third are coded .5.

The policy liberalism scale is based on answers to ten questions. Eight of the items are from a battery of questions in which respondents were asked the following: "If you had a say in making up the federal budget this year, for which of the following programs would you like to see spending increased and for which would you like to see spending decreased?" The programs included in the scale are the environment, public schools, food stamps, fighting the disease AIDS, child care, defense spending, medical care, and government assistance for the homeless. Responses to two additional questions regarding the death penalty and government assistance for blacks were also included in the scale of policy liberalism. To construct the scale, each variable was coded to range from 0 (least liberal) to 1 (most liberal). Respondents' average responses were used to indicate their general level of policy liberalism. (Those with missing data for an item were assigned its mean value. Respondents who answered less than half the items, fewer than 1 percent of the voters in the Senate studies, were excluded from the analysis.) Like the abortion scale, a trichotomous indicator with an equal number of respondents in each category is used in the multivariate analyses. Those respondents with the least and most liberal policy preferences receive codes of 0 and 1, respectively. The middle one-third of the respondents are coded .5.

The measure of ideological self-identification is based on voters' answers to a set of questions about their political ideology. Respondents were asked to place themselves on a seven-point scale ranging from very liberal to very conservative. Those who did not provide an answer either because they had not "thought much about it" or "did not know" were then asked, "If you had to choose, would you consider yourself a liberal or a conservative?" Respondents who placed themselves on the conservative side of the seven-point scale or answered "conservative" in the follow-up question are coded as conservatives and receive a value of 0 on the ideological self-identification scale. Respondents who placed themselves on the liberal side of the seven-point scale or answered "liberal" in the follow-up question are coded as liberals and receive a value of 1 on the scale. The remaining respondents are classified as moderates and coded .5.

B. Univariate Statistics

The distributions, means, and standard deviations of the variables used in the multivariate analyses are reported in the following table.

Variable	Categories	Distribution (%)	Mean	Std. Dev.
Abortion policy preferences	Less supportive of liberal abortion laws (0)	30	.49	.38
	Mixed opinions (.5)	42		
	More supportive of liberal abortion laws (1)	29		
Party identification	Republican (0)	40	.52	.46
	Pure independent (.5)	15		
	Democrat (1)	45		
Ideological self-identification	Conservative (0)	48	.38	.40
	Moderate (.5)	29		
	Liberal (1)	23		
Policy liberalism	Less liberal (0)	33	.50	.41
	Mixed (.5)	34		
	More liberal (1)	33		
Incumbency	Republican incumbent (0)	36	.56	.45
	Open seat race (.5)	16		
	Democratic incumbent (1)	48		

NOTES

1. Westlye (1991) explains the inadequacies of the traditional National Election Studies for analyzing voting behavior in Senate elections.

2. Of course, other elections, namely those for the House, share these characteristics of Senate elections. In principle, the research designs employed here could be used for the analysis of House elections too. In practice, the task is more complicated because measuring the primary election-level variable, discussed in detail later, proves rather difficult.

3. All the research designs discussed in this essay depend on this feature of Senate elections.

4. For example, there is a stark contrast between the two parties' 1992 platforms. The Republican platform read, in part, "We therefore reaffirm our support for a human life amendment to the Constitution, and we endorse legislation to make clear that the 14th Amendment's protections apply to unborn children." Democrats, on the other hand, stood "behind the right of every woman to choose, consistent with *Roe v. Wade*, regardless of ability to pay, and support a national law to protect that right."

5. In other words, a pro-life voter is unlikely to change her views about abortion because a candidate who she likes for other reasons is pro-choice.

6. It is important to note that, although the substantive focus in this essay is policy voting, the research designs are applicable to a wide variety of possible campaign effects.

7. Data limitations largely determined the selection of races to analyze. The Senate Election Studies were conducted in 1988, 1990, and 1992. However, the items tapping abortion policy preferences were not asked in 1988. In addition, *The Abortion Report*, one of the primary sources of campaign information, was not published in 1988.

8. Although a more nuanced election-level variable might be desirable, reliably and validly constructing one on the basis of the available data is not feasible.

9. In all but two of these races, the Democratic candidate was pro-choice and the Republican candidate was pro-life. The two exceptions occurred in the 1990 campaigns in Alaska and Wyoming, where the Republican candidates were pro-choice and the Democratic candidates were pro-life. Although it would be worthwhile to analyze this type of race where the candidates hold positions at odds with the national parties, the source of individual-level data, the Senate Election Studies, provides less than one hundred cases from these elections, too few to permit any meaningful analysis of them.

10. Wright and Berkman (1986) attempted to analyze policy voting in Senate elections but due to data limitations were unable to employ any measures that tapped voters' policy preferences about particular issues. Instead, they operationalize policy voting as "the propensity of voters to use general policy liberalism-conservatism and evaluations of the president and his handling of the economy in their senatorial voting decisions" (575).

11. The details behind the construction of this measure are described in the appendix.

12. This statement reflects the view that voters' abortion policy preferences do

not determine their other policy preferences and their ideological and partisan identifications. This view is not without its critics. Miller and Shanks (1996) carefully review the issue and provide both a theoretical and methodological defense of the approach adopted here.

13. Republicans, pure independents, and Democrats receive codes of 0, .5, and 1, respectively. Independent leaners are coded as partisans of the party toward which they lean. The empirical results are virtually identical if they are coded as independents.

14. The constructions of these scales are described in the appendix.

15. The corresponding probabilities for party identification, ideological self-identification, policy liberalism, and incumbency are .43, .20, .13, and .20, respectively.

16. To put it another way, the independent variable (a campaign characteristic) must be correlated with the dependent variable (voting behavior.) Of course, observing a correlation between variables does not automatically imply causation. Additional tests are necessary.

17. Campbell and Cook (1979) classify this type of design as "one-group posttest-only" and argue that "if this were all the information we had about the variable [in this case candidates' positions] and the population, the design would be totally uninformative" (96).

18. The estimates in table 1 are not identically replicated (though they are nearly so) by the estimates of the unconstrained model reported in table 2 because the effects of the social and demographic characteristics were assumed to be identical across election types.

19. This is the approach that Cook, Jelen, and Wilcox (1994) employ in their analysis of abortion policy voting in the 1990 Senate elections.

20. Note that "stacked" designs may be used even if one has separate cross-sections, one for each race or judgment. When the respondents are the same, then controlling for individual fixed effects becomes possible, a topic not pursued in this essay.

21. Because Democratic votes were coded 1 and Republican votes coded 0 for both the Senate and House voting models, presidential approval was coded 1 for disapproval of Bush and 0 for approval.

22. This race pitted Barbara Boxer (D) against Bruce Herschensohn (R).

23. In this special election, Dianne Feinstein (D) faced John Seymour (R), the incumbent who had been appointed after Pete Wilson was elected governor.

24. Some caution is warranted because of the comparatively less precision of the effect estimates compared to the simple multiple races design.

REFERENCES

Alvarez, R. Michael, and Jonathan Nagler. 1995. "Economics, Issues, and the Perot Candidacy: Voter Choice in the 1992 Presidential Election." *American Journal of Political Science* 39:714–44.

Bendyna, Mary E., and Celinda C. Lake. 1994. "Gender and Voting in the 1992 Presidential Election." In *The Year of the Woman: Myths and Realities*, ed. Elizabeth Adell Cook, Sue Thomas, and Clyde Wilcox. Boulder: Westview.

Campbell, Donald T., and Thomas D. Cook. 1979. *Quasi-Experimentation: Design and Analysis Issues for Field Settings*. Chicago: Rand McNally.

Cohen, Jeffrey E., and Charles Barrilleaux. 1993. "Public Opinion, Interest Groups, and Public Policy Making: Abortion Policy in the American States." In *Understanding the New Politics of Abortion*, ed. Malcolm L. Goggin. Newbury Park, CA: Sage.

Cook, Elizabeth Adell, Ted G. Jelen, and Clyde Wilcox. 1994. "Issue Voting in U.S. Senate Elections: The Abortion Issue in 1990." *Congress and the Presidency* 21: 99–111.

Hansen, Susan B. 1993. "Differences in Public Policies toward Abortion: Electoral and Policy Context." In *Understanding the New Politics of Abortion*, ed. Malcolm L. Goggin. Newbury Park, CA: Sage.

Holland, Paul. 1986. "Statistics and Causal Inference." *Journal of the American Statistical Association* 81:945–60.

Jacobson, Gary C., and Raymond E. Wolfinger. 1989. "Information and Voting in California Senate Elections." *Legislative Studies Quarterly* 14:509–27.

Meier, Kenneth J., and Deborah R. McFarlane. 1993. "Abortion Politics and Abortion Funding Policy." In *Understanding the New Politics of Abortion*, ed. Malcolm L. Goggin. Newbury Park, CA: Sage.

Miller, Warren E., Donald R. Kinder, Steven J. Rosenstone, and the National Election Studies. 1993. *American National Election Study: Pooled Senate Election Study, 1988, 1990, 1992*. Computer file. 3d release. Ann Arbor: University of Michigan, Center for Political Studies (producer), Inter-university Consortium for Political and Social Research (distributor).

Miller, Warren E., and J. Merrill Shanks. 1996. *The New American Voter*. Cambridge, MA: Harvard University Press.

Shanks, J. Merrill, and Warren E. Miller. 1991. "Partisanship, Policy and Performance: The Reagan Legacy in the 1988 Election." *British Journal of Political Science* 21:129–97.

Westlye, Mark C. 1991. *Senate Elections and Campaign Intensity*. Baltimore: Johns Hopkins University Press.

Wright, Gerald C., Jr., and Michael Berkman. 1986. "Candidates and Policy in United States Senate Elections." *American Political Science Review* 80:567–88.

IV The Rules of the Game and Election Results

Do Polls Influence the Vote?

André Blais, Elisabeth Gidengil, and Neil Nevitte

POLLS PROVIDE INFORMATION ABOUT how well the parties are doing in a campaign. That information may affect voters' perceptions of the various parties' chances of winning in a first past the post (FPP) system such as Canada or the chances of being part of a coalition government in a proportional representation (PR) system. By affecting voters' expectations about the outcome of the election, polls may affect the vote. How and why could expectations affect voting choice? The literature suggests two key reasons: strategic voting and a contagion effect.

A strategic (or sophisticated or tactical) vote is a vote cast for a party that is not the preferred one, motivated by the intention to affect the outcome of the election (Blais and Nadeau 1996; Cox 1997; Blais et al., 2001). Typically, a strategic vote in a FPP election takes the form of supporting a second choice party that is perceived to have better chances of winning than the most preferred one. It appears that around 5 percent of voters cast a strategic vote in such elections (see Alvarez and Nagler 2000; Blais et al., 2001). Polls may affect strategic considerations because the latter are based on expectations about the outcome of the election. Polls may lead people not to vote for a given party because that party is perceived to be unlikely to win. Note that under such a scenario polls influence perceptions of the race, not preferences or evaluations of the parties.

A second possibility is that polls affect expectations about the outcome and that these expectations, in turn, affect preferences or evaluations. In this case, voters come to evaluate parties more positively if their chances of winning appear to be good and to evaluate parties more negatively if their chances seem to be slim. This is the classical contagion effect: voters rally to the parties that are doing well in the polls.[1]

Whether there are contagion (or bandwagon) effects remains a contentious issue. Some experimental studies have documented a bandwagon effect in the opinion formation process (Nadeau, Cloutier, and Guay 1993), but others insist that the effects of representations of public opinion on attitudes are much more complex (Mutz 1992). Conflicting results are also reported with respect to the vote. Ansolabehere and Iyengar's (1994) experimental research indicated a contagion effect on preferences but not on voting intentions. And Skalaban (1988) detected bandwagon effects in the 1980 and 1984 American presidential elections. Bartels (1985) identifies the presence of a momentum effect in the early but not in the late primaries. In our view, the existence of contagion effects in elections is not well established, but it would be imprudent to rule out the possibility of such effects.

Our objective, therefore, is not only to determine whether polls influence the vote but also to understand how and why. More specifically, our goal is to determine whether polls merely affect perceptions of the race, which would suggest strategic voting, or whether they also affect how voters evaluate the parties, which would suggest a contagion effect.

We examine the impact of polls in the 1988 Canadian election. We would expect polls to be particularly important in a FPP system such as Canada's because they can provide crucial information for supporters of weak parties who may consider voting strategically for their second choice. Strategic considerations are relevant in PR systems as well (Cox 1997; Blais and Massicotte 1996), but they are likely to be less powerful.

The impact of polls depends to a great extent on their visibility. A total of twenty-two polls were published during the 1988 Canadian election campaign. This is slightly more than usual in a Canadian election[2] but certainly less than in the United States or Britain.[3] Most of these polls were reported in the nightly TV news and made the headlines (Blais and Bastien 2001). Polls may not be as visible in Canada as in some countries where "readers and viewers have a continuous diet of polls, often with four or five surveys hitting the front pages every week" (Butler 1996, 248), but there is no doubt that they are an integral part of the campaign. And indeed three-quarters of voters indicated during the 1988 campaign that they had read or heard of a poll in the last seven days (Johnston et al. 1992, 206).

Methodology

The data are taken from the 1988 Canadian Election Study (CES). We rely on three approaches to assess the impact of polls. The first two are based on campaign survey data. The campaign pooled data analysis entails examining the vote intentions, expectations, and preferences of our respondents and relating these to the information conveyed by the polls at the time respondents were interviewed, whereas the time-series analysis involves analyzing daily patterns in aggregate vote intentions, expectations, and preferences and relating these to the nature of poll information that was available every day of the campaign.

The third approach, the panel analysis, uses both the campaign and the postelection surveys. It examines change (or absence of change) between the vote intention indicated during the campaign and the actual vote reported after the election, and it relates this to change between the poll information available at the time the individual was interviewed during the campaign and the information available by Election Day.

Each of these approaches has strengths and weaknesses. Perhaps the most logical approach for assessing the impact of campaign events, such as polls, is time-series analysis (Blais and Boyer 1996). This approach allows us to determine whether vote intentions for a party go up after the publication of a poll indicating support for it is on the rise. Time-series analysis has at least three limitations, however. First, one can never be certain that shifts in vote intentions should not be attributable to other campaign events. This limitation is a serious one, but this problem arises whatever the approach. The second problem concerns the small number of observations (about forty-five days), which makes it difficult for small effects to reach standard levels of significance. This problem is specific to time-series analysis. The third drawback flows from the fact that the aggregate daily data are based on small samples (typically eighty respondents), which yield large sampling errors. This problem holds whatever the approach but is aggravated in the case of time-series by the small number of observations.[4]

The campaign pooled data analysis is based on the same data as the time-series analysis, the only difference being that we look at individuals rather than at aggregate daily patterns. Because it is an individual-level analysis, it has two main advantages. First, more control variables, especially sociodemographic characteristics, can be included. Theoretically, the socioeconomic profiles of our daily samples should be similar, but we should have greater confidence in our findings if these variables are explicitly controlled for. Second, we can distinguish voters according to their exposure to polls. We can directly check whether polls have a greater impact on those who have seen them.

The panel data analysis has the great virtue of allowing us to look at concrete individual change in the campaign. If polls affect the vote, some individuals must vote differently from how they intended before the poll was published. Panel data allow us to determine whether those interviewed before the publication of a poll showing a party to be improving were more likely to shift to that party and/or less likely to abandon it.

Throughout the analysis, we focus on two races, the race between the Conservatives and the Liberals (to determine who would form the government) and the race between the Liberals and the New Democratic Party (NDP) (to determine who would form the official opposition).

Did Polls Affect Expectations?

Figure 1 presents the twenty-two national polls published in the media during the election campaign. Eight polls were released before the French and English debates that took place on October 24 and 25; they all gave the Conservatives a comfortable lead and had the Liberals and the NDP practically tied for second place. The polls published after the debates revealed that the Liberals had made substantial gains and were fighting with the Conservatives for first place. Until November 19, it was not clear from the polls which party was ahead. It was only with the publication of the final three polls, released two days before Election Day, that it became obvious that the Conservatives had regained the lead. Finally, each and every poll published after the debates confirmed that the Liberals had established a clear lead over the NDP.

The question is whether voters' expectations about the outcome of the election were influenced by the polls. Panel A in table 1 presents the findings of the campaign pooled data analysis. The dependent variable represents how much better, or worse, the respondent perceives the Conservatives' chances of winning to be compared to the Liberals' chances.[5] The key independent variable indicates by how much the Conservatives were ahead of (or trailing) the Liberals in the most recent poll published at the time the respondent was interviewed.

The campaign pooled model includes three types of control variables. First there is a debate variable, which is a dummy variable that takes the value of 1 from October 26, the day after the English debate, till the end of the campaign. Previous work has shown that the debates had a substantial impact on the vote (Blais and Boyer 1996). Debates may also have had

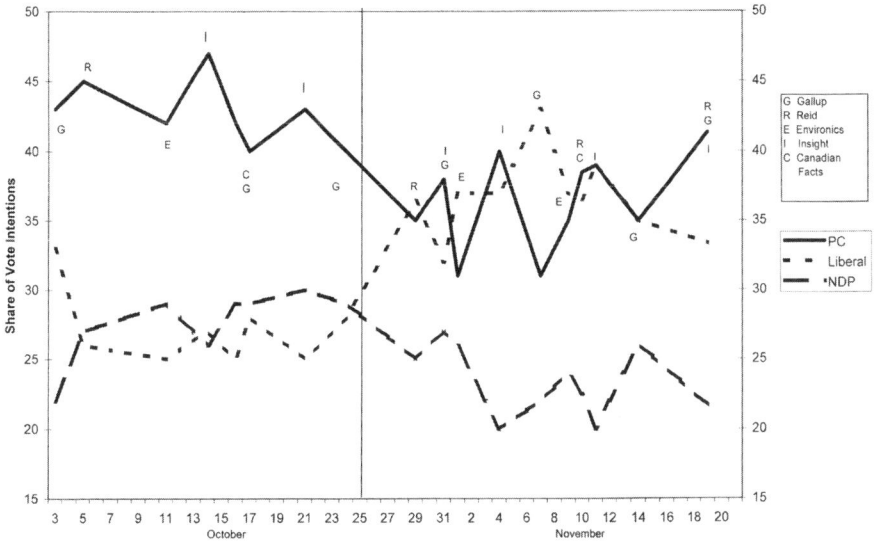

Fig. 1. Party positions in the 1988 polls

an effect on perceptions of the race, and it is important to isolate the specific impact of the polls, independent of the debates. Second, there is party identification. Those who identify with a party are inclined to overestimate its appeal (Uhlaner and Grofman 1986; Johnston et al. 1992). Finally, the model includes a set of sociodemographic factors (region, religion, education, gender, and union membership) that are usually considered to be salient in Canada.

The results shown in panel A of table 1 confirm that voters did respond to the information provided by the polls. The greater the Conservative lead over the Liberals in the most recent poll, the more inclined voters were to believe that the Conservatives had better chances of winning

TABLE 1. Impact of Polls on Expectation

	Conservative/Liberal B (s.e.)	Liberal/NDP B (s.e.)
A. Campaign pooled data Last poll	+.44 (.09)*** ($N = 3,584$)	+.54 (.08)*** ($N = 3,588$)
B. Time-series Last poll	+.25 (.12)** ($N = 41$)	−.01 (.14) ($N = 41$)

*Significant at the 0.10 level   **significant at the 0.05 level   ***significant at the 0.01 level

than did the Liberals. The same pattern held with respect to the Liberal versus NDP race.

Panel B in table 1 examines the same relationship, using time-series analysis. The dependent variable is average expectations on a given day of the campaign, and the key independent variable is the Conservative lead over the Liberals in the most recent poll. We wish to determine whether the publication of polls changes perceptions of the race. We include as a control variable average expectations as measured in our rolling cross-section survey during the days when the commercial poll in question was in the field.[6] This allows us to determine what expectations were after the publication of the poll and to compare them to expectations at the time the poll was conducted. The analysis also includes debate and party identification as control variables. The last poll variable comes up significant with respect to the Conservative versus Liberal race but not in the case of the Liberal versus NDP race.

Looking at the results in table 1, the poll coefficient is significant in three out of four equations.[7] Moreover, as expected, polls have a greater impact among those who actually see or read them. About 70 percent of respondents told us they had seen or read a poll in the last week. It turns out that polls appear to have affected perceptions only among these respondents (result not shown).[8]

There is thus relatively strong support for the view that polls affected voters' expectations about the outcome of the election. The next question to be addressed is whether polls also influenced the vote.

Did Polls Affect the Vote?

We start again with the campaign pooled data analysis. The setup is exactly the same as that used in table 1, the only difference being that the dependent variable is vote intention rather than expectation. Panel A in table 2 presents the findings. The poll coefficient is significant in the Liberal/NDP equation but not in the Conservative/Liberal one.

A similar pattern emerges out of the time-series analysis (panel B). Here the distribution of vote intentions on a given day is regressed on the results of the most recent poll, controlling for the distribution of vote intentions at the time the poll was conducted (as well as the distribution of party identification on a given day and whether the debates had been held or not). Again, the poll coefficient is significant in the Liberal/NDP equation but not the Conservative/Liberal one. Note, however, that the coefficient in the latter case is quite substantial even though it does not reach statistical significance.

Panel C of table 2 presents the panel data evidence. In this instance, the dependent variable is not vote intention but the vote as reported in the postelection survey. The logic here is to see whether a party gained (compared to vote intention) among those initially interviewed before that party's standing in the poll improved. The poll variable corresponds to the change in the parties' standing between the day the person was interviewed and Election Day.[9] Because the goal is to determine whether people were led to change their vote, we control for their initial vote intention and evaluations of the leaders, as well as for party identification and standard sociodemographic variables. Finally, we take into account whether the respondent was interviewed before or after the debates. Here, again, only one of the two poll coefficients is significant, but this time it is the one concerning the Conservative versus Liberal race.

Looking at the results in table 2, the poll variable is significant three times out of six, but the coefficient is positive six times out of six. And the median coefficient in these equations is a hefty .40.

Did the polls affect the vote only of those who had read or seen them? As with the analysis of expectations, we checked (with the campaign data) whether there was an interaction effect between polls and exposure to them. The findings are ambiguous.

There is evidence of an interactive effect in the case of the Conservative/Liberal equation: it seems that among poll watchers, and only among them, the propensity to vote Conservative rather than Liberal was related to the gap between the two parties in the most recent poll. There

TABLE 2. Impact of Polls on the Vote

	Conservative/Liberal B (s.e.)	Liberal/NDP B (s.e.)
A. Campaign pooled data	+.14 (.15)	+.37 (.19)**
Last poll	(N = 2,051)	(N = 1,490)
B. Time-series	+.52 (.36)	+.77 (.38)**
Last poll	(N = 41)	(N = 41)
C. Panel data	+.48 (.15)**	+.17 (.22)
Last poll (panel)	(N = 1,712)	(N = 1,113)

*Significant at the 0.10 level   **significant at the 0.05 level   ***significant at the 0.01 level

is no trace of an interaction effect with respect to the choice between the Liberals and the NDP.

All in all, there are good reasons to believe that the polls had an impact on the vote in the Canadian 1988 election. We have estimated their effect through six different regressions, based on three different approaches. Even though only three of the poll coefficients achieved statistical significance, all six of them had the expected positive sign. But did the polls affect the vote through strategic voting or via a contagion effect?

How Did the Polls Affect the Vote?

We have shown that polls had an impact on expectations about the outcome of the election and on the vote. It remains to specify the mechanism through which they influence the vote. We identified at the outset two potential mechanisms. The first is strategic voting. Under strategic voting, people are led not to vote for a party that they prefer because its chances of winning appear to be slim. In this scheme of things, the polls do not affect preferences—strategic voters still prefer the weak party but have an independent impact on the vote. Everything else (including preferences) being equal, voters are less inclined to support a party that is doing less well in the polls. If all of the polls' effect on the vote is accounted for by strategic voting, we should find that polls had no impact on how voters evaluated the parties and the leaders and that they influenced vote choice even after controlling for voters' preferences among the parties and the leaders.

The second potential mechanism through which polls may affect the vote is a contagion effect. If there is a contagion effect, voters should come to evaluate the parties and the leaders who are doing well in the polls more positively and those who are not doing well more negatively. If all of the polls' effect is accounted for by contagion, we should find that polls had an impact on ratings of parties and of leaders and that it is only because of these evaluations that they affected the vote, that is, the polls had no independent effect on the vote once preferences were taken into account.

Table 3 presents the evidence on the impact of polls on preferences as such. Here the dependent variable is relative evaluations of leaders and parties. The setup for the campaign pooled data, the time-series, and the panel data analysis is the same as in table 2, the only difference being that the dependent variable is relative preferences rather than voting intention or reported vote. In this instance, it turns out that the poll variable is not significant in any of the six equations. There is no evidence of a contagion effect. However, we should not rule out the possibility of a contagion effect since five of the six coefficients have the right positive sign. In each and every case, though, the poll coefficient is very small. We are led to conclude that the hypothesis that voters come to like the parties and the leaders who are doing well in the polls is not borne out by the data.

Table 4 is designed to detect the presence of strategic voting. The dependent variable is vote intention or reported vote, as in table 2, but we have additional control variables: evaluation of the parties and of the leaders and opinions on free trade.[10] Table 4 enables us to determine whether the polls affected vote intentions independently of how voters felt about the parties, the leaders, and free trade. There is evidence of such an independent effect. The poll variable comes out significant in four of the six equations and has the expected positive sign in a fifth case. This supports the view that the polls affected the vote because some voters were reluctant to support a party that was not doing well in the polls, whatever their feelings toward the parties and the leaders.

Strategic voting appears to have been the basic reason why the polls influenced vote choice. This is best illustrated by comparing the coefficients of the poll variable in the equations designed to measure the overall impact of the polls on vote choice (table 2) with those in the equations intended to estimate their impact on strategic voting as such, that is, controlling for voters' preferences (table 4). The median coefficients are respectively .40 and .35. The implication is that the polls influenced the vote

TABLE 3. Impact of Polls on Preferences

	Conservative/Liberal B (s.e.)	Liberal/NDP B (s.e.)
A. Campaign pooled data	+.11 (.07)	+.07 (.07)
Last poll	($N = 3,559$)	($N = 3,560$)
B. Time-series	+.17 (.19)	−.17 (.20)
Last poll	($N = 41$)	($N = 41$)
C. Panel data	+.08 (.07)	+.04 (.07)
Last poll	($N = 2,649$)	($N = 2,530$)

*Significant at the 0.10 level   **significant at the 0.05 level   ***significant at the 0.01 level

independently of preferences, and this is consistent with the view that strategic considerations were the key factor.

Conclusion

We have assessed the impact of polls in the 1988 Canadian election through three different approaches: first, a campaign pooled data analysis in which we have related individual respondents, expectations, vote intentions, and evaluations of the parties and leaders to the information conveyed by the polls (about how well each party was doing) at the time they were interviewed; second, a time-series analysis in which daily variations in aggregate expectations, vote intentions, and evaluations were correlated with variations in information provided by the polls; and third, a panel analysis in which changes in vote intentions and evaluations between the day individual respondents were interviewed during the campaign and Election Day were related to changes in the poll information coming out in the media during the same period.

The findings emerging from these three sets of analyses converge on four main conclusions about the 1988 Canadian election:

1. Polls affected voters' perceptions of the various parties' chances of winning.
2. Polls affected the vote.
3. Polls affected strategic voting as some voters became less inclined to support a party whose chances of winning appeared slim.
4. Polls did not have a contagion effect, since voters did not come to evaluate the parties and leaders who were doing well in the polls more positively.

TABLE 4. Impact of Polls on the Vote, Controlling for Preferences

	Conservative/Liberal B (s.e.)	Liberal/NDP B (s.e.)
A. Campaign pooled data	−.01 (.127)	+.37 (.17)**
Last poll	($N = 2,021$)	($N = 1,460$)
B. Time-series	+.61 (.31)*	+.96 (.36)**
Last poll	($N = 41$)	($N = 41$)
C. Panel data	+.32 (.13)**	+.11 (.21)
Last poll	($N = 1,554$)	($N = 964$)

*Significant at the 0.10 level   **significant at the 0.05 level   ***significant at the 0.01 level

Do Polls Influence the Vote? 273

These findings are limited to a specific election. More studies are needed to determine whether polls have similar effects in different settings. We have indicated at the outset that polls may play a more powerful role in a FPP system such as Canada. It would be very interesting to see if polls have a smaller impact in PR systems. We have also indicated that the effect of polls may depend on their visibility. It would also be interesting to compare their impact on the vote in countries where they are more or less visible than in Canada. We have also assumed that voters were reacting to the most recent poll, whatever its visibility. Another logical avenue of research would be to distinguish types of polls, most and least visible ones, and to determine whether the former have a greater influence on voters.

Whatever the context, however, a design such as that of the CES is particularly fruitful for assessing the impact of polls. The rolling cross-section component of the campaign survey allows us to see whether vote intentions move after the publication of a poll, while the campaign and postelection panel component allows us to see whether individual respondents vote differently from what they intended subsequent to the publication of a poll.

APPENDIX

Variables Included in the Regressions

Tables 1A, 2A, 3A: Last poll. Party identification, Debate, Female, High education, Quebec, West, Union member, and Catholic.

Table 1B: Last poll. Party identification, Debate, and Expectations.

Table 2B: Last poll. Party identification, Debate, and Vote intention (fieldwork).

Tables 2C, 3C: Last poll (panel). Party identification, Debate, Leaders, Voting intention, Female, High education, Quebec, West, Union member, and Catholic.

Table 3B: Last poll. Party identification, Debate, and Preferences (fieldwork).

Table 4A: Last poll. Party identification, Debate, Preferences, Free trade, Female, High education, Quebec, West, Union member, and Catholic.

Table 4B: Last poll. Party identification, Debate, Preferences, Free trade, and Vote intention (fieldwork).

Table 4C: Last poll (panel). Party identification, Debate, Leaders, Voting intention, Preferences (panel), Free trade (panel), Female, High education, Quebec, West, Union member, and Catholic.

Description of Variables

EXPECTATIONS

The following questions have been used:
—We will be using a scale which runs from 0 to 100, where 0 represents no chance for the party, 50 represents an even chance, and 100 represents certain victory. (Using the 0 to 100 scale), what do you think the Conservative/Liberal/New Democratic Party's chances are of winning the election in the whole country? (f2a/b/c).

Each party's score is standardized, that is, divided by the sum of the scores received by all the parties. The variable corresponds to the difference between the standardized scores given to two parties. The variable goes from -1 to 1.

VOTE INTENTION

The following questions have been used:
—Which party do you think you will vote for: the Conservative Party, the Liberal Party, the New Democratic Party, or another party? (b2)
—Perhaps you have not yet made up your mind. But which party are you leaning toward now? (b3)

The value of 1 is given to respondents who intended to vote Conservative (Conservative/Liberal) or Liberal (Liberal/ NDP), -1 to respondents who intended to vote Liberal (Conservative/ Liberal) or NDP (Liberal/NDP), and 0 to all others.

VOTE (PANEL)

The following question has been used:
—Which party did you vote for: the Conservative Party, the Liberal Party, the New Democratic Party, or another party? (xb2)

The value of 1 is given to respondents who voted Conservative (Conservative/Liberal) or Liberal (Liberal/NDP) and 0 to respondents who voted Liberal (Conservative/ Liberal) or NDP (Liberal/NDP).

LAST POLL

Difference in vote intentions for the two parties (Conservative-Liberal, Liberal-NDP) in the most recent poll. In the case of polls published in the morning newspapers, we used the same date. In the case of polls presented on evening television newscasts (CBC—Canadian Facts, CTV—Insight), we used the next day's date. In the case when two polls are published on the same day we used the two ratings' mean.

LAST POLL (PANEL)
Difference between the difference in vote intentions for the two parties (Conservative-Liberal, Liberal-NDP) in the last poll of the campaign and the difference in vote intentions for the two parties (Conservative-Liberal, Liberal-NDP) in the last poll published before the respondent was interviewed during the campaign.

LEADERS
The following questions have been used:
—How would you rate Brian Mulroney? (d2a), John Turner? (d2b), Ed Broadbent? (d2c) (on a scale from 0 to 100, where 0 represents a very negative feeling and 100 a very positive feeling).
The variable corresponds to the difference between ratings of the two party leaders (divided by 100) (Mulroney-Turner, Turner-Broadbent). The scale goes from -1 to 1.

PARTY IDENTIFICATION
The following question has been used:
—Thinking of federal politics, do you usually think of yourself as a Liberal, Conservative, NDP, or none of these? (i1)
The value of 1 is given to respondents who identify with the Conservatives (Conservative/Liberal) or the Liberals (Liberal/NDP), -1 to respondents who identify with the Liberals (Conservative/Liberal) or NDP (Liberal/NDP), and 0 to all others.

DEBATE
0 before October 26 and 1 on and after October 26.

PREFERENCE
The variable is an index made up of two questions. The following questions have been used:
—How would you rate Brian Mulroney? (d2a), John Turner? (d2b), Ed Broadbent? (d2c) (on a scale from 0 to 100, where 0 represents a very negative feeling and 100 a very positive feeling).
—How would you rate the Conservative Party? (d2d), the Liberal Party? (d2e), the New Democratic Party? (d2f) (on a scale from 0 to 100, where 0 represents a very negative feeling and 100 a very positive feeling).
Both ratings are divided by 100. The index is the sum of the two scores divided by 2. The variable corresponds to the difference between the two indexes (Conservative/Liberal, Liberal/NDP). The scale goes from -1 to 1.

PREFERENCE (PANEL)

The following questions have been used:

—How would you rate Brian Mulroney? (xe2a), John Turner? (xe2b), Ed Broadbent? (xe2c) (on a scale from 0 to 100, where 0 represents a very negative feeling and 100 a very positive feeling).

—How would you rate the Conservative Party? (xe2d), the Liberal Party? (xe2e) the New Democrat Party? (xe2f) (on a scale from 0 to 100, where 0 represents a very negative feeling and 100 a very positive feeling).

Both ratings are divided by 100. The index is the sum of the two scores divided by 2. The variable corresponds to the difference between the two indexes (Conservative/Liberal, Liberal/NDP). The scale goes from -1 to 1.

FREE TRADE

The following question has been used:

—As you know (Canada/the Mulroney government) has reached a Free Trade Agreement with the United States. All things considered, do you support the agreement or do you oppose it? (12)

The value of 1 was given to respondents who support the agreement, 0.5 to respondents who neither support nor oppose it, and 0 to respondents who oppose it.

FREE TRADE (PANEL)

The variable is an index made up of three questions;

—And now, a few questions about the Free Trade Agreement with the United States. All things considered do you support the agreement or do you oppose it? (x1la)

—How strongly do you (support/oppose) the agreement? Would you say very strongly, somewhat strongly or not very strongly? (x1lb)

— If you had to choose would you support or oppose the agreement? (x1lc)

The index goes from 0 to 8, where 0 represents very strong opposition and 8 represents very strong support. The value of 3 is given to respondents who said that they neither supported nor opposed the agreement but that if they had to choose they would oppose it, 5 is given to those who said that if they had to choose they would support it, and 4 is given to those who could not make a choice. The results are then divided by 8, and the scale goes from 0 to 1.

FEMALE
1 for women, 0 for men.

HIGH EDUCATION
The value of 1 is given when the respondent has some university education and 0 otherwise.

QUEBEC
The value of 1 is given when the respondent lives in Quebec and 0 otherwise.

WEST
The value of 1 is given when the respondent lives in British Columbia, Alberta, Saskatchewan, or Manitoba and 0 otherwise.

UNION MEMBER
The value of 1 is given when the respondent or a member of the household belongs to a labor union and 0 otherwise.

CATHOLIC
The value of 1 is given when the respondent's religion is Catholic and 0 otherwise.

NOTES

We thank Martin Turcotte, Annie Sabourin, Mathieu Turgeon, and Frederick C. Bastien for their research assistance; the Social Sciences and Humanities Research Council of Canada for its financial support; and Henry Brady and Richard Johnston for comments on previous drafts of this essay. The data are drawn from the 1988 CES. The CES included a rolling cross-section campaign period survey with a representative sample of 3,609 respondents and a postelection survey with 2,922 of the campaign survey respondents. The fieldwork was conducted by the Institute for Social Research at York University. The response rate for the campaign survey was 57 percent. The study was funded by the Social Sciences and Humanities Research Council of Canada. The coinvestigators were Richard Johnston (research director), André Blais, Henry Brady, and Jean Crête. Further information on the study can be found in Johnston et al. 1992.

1. Bartels (1988, 108–19) distinguishes four potential effects: strategic, supporting a winner, cue taking, and contagion. In our terminology, the first two are direct and the latter two indirect (expectations affect the vote through preferences). When contagion or cue taking occurs, voters come to like the party that is expected to win. The only difference is that the latter has a "rational" component (the voter reasons that people are not fools and that, since a given party has so much support, it must

be good). We are in no position to assess the "rationality" of voters' cognitive processes here. What matters, from our point of view, is that in both cases the outcome is the same: voters come to like the party that they expect to win. Suffice it to say that in our view contagion (or bandwagon) is not necessarily irrational and that it encompasses cue taking. We also associate a direct effect, independent of preferences, with a strategic calculus. Bartels suggests that some voters might vote for the party that they expect to win simply because they enjoy the pleasure of being on the winning side. We acknowledge that this is a theoretical possibility, but it is not clear how this could be tested, and a detailed analysis of vote for the second preferred party in the 1988 Canadian election is entirely consistent with a strategic calculus interpretation (Blais and Nadeau 1996). It seems to us that our distinction between a direct strategic effect and indirect contagion one is simple and clear and is sufficient for providing an overall account of the impact of polls on the vote.

2. There were fourteen polls in the 1993 election, for instance.

3. Butler and Kavanagh (1988, 125) indicate that there were seventy-three public polls in the 1987 British election.

4. More specifically, statistical tests are more sensitive to deviant cases with an n of 40 than with an n of 3,000.

5. See the appendix for a description of variables. All explanations of approaches and variables refer to the Conservative versus Liberal race. The same logic applies to the Liberal versus NDP race.

6. This is why we start on October 11. Fieldwork for the first two polls was completed before the start of the CES fieldwork.

7. It does not make sense to tap expectations about the outcome of the election after the election, and we cannot therefore proceed to a panel data analysis in the case of expectations.

8. We obtain this result by adding to the equations in panel A of table 1 LAST POLL × EXPOSED. When we do so, the interactive variable is highly significant, but LAST POLL is not.

9. For instance, for a respondent interviewed on October 6, the most recent poll indicated a nineteen-point Conservative lead over the Liberals. The last poll gave a lead of only eleven points. The Conservative lead had thus declined by eight points between October 6 and October 20.

10. Because free trade was the dominant issue of the campaign (see Johnston et al. 1992), opinions on this issue may be construed as an additional indicator of preferences.

REFERENCES

Alvarez, Michael, and Jonathan Nagler. 2000. "A New Approach for Modelling Strategic Voting in Multiparty Elections." *British Journal of Political Science* 30: 57–75.

Ansolabehere, Stephen, and Shanto Iyengar. 1994. "Of Horseshoes and Horse Races: Experimental Studies of the Impact of Poll Results on Electoral Behaviour." *Political Communication* 11:413–30.

Bartels, Larry. 1985. "Expectations and Preferences in Presidential Nominating Campaigns." *American Political Science Review* 79:804–15.

———. 1988. *Presidential Primaries and the Dynamics of Public Choice.* Princeton: Princeton University Press.

Blais, André, and Frederick Bastien. 2001. "Which Polls Matter Most?" Manuscript.

Blais, André, and Martin Boyer. 1996. "Assessing the Impact of Televised Debates: The Case of the 1988 Canadian Election." *British Journal of Political Science* 26: 143–64.

Blais, André, and Louis Massicotte. 1996. "Electoral Systems." In *Comparing Democracies: Elections and Voting in Global Perspective,* ed. Lawrence LeDuc, Richard G. Niemi, and Pippa Norris. Thousand Oaks, CA: Sage.

Blais, André, and Richard Nadeau. 1996. "Measuring Strategic Voting: A Two-Step Procedure." *Electoral Studies* 15:39–52.

Blais, André, Richard Nadeau, Elisabeth Gidengil, and Neil Nevitte. 2001. "Measuring Strategic Voting in Multiparty Plurality Elections." *Electoral Studies* 20:343–52.

Butler, David. 1996. "Polls and Elections." In *Comparing Democracies: Elections and Voting in Global Perspective,* ed. Lawrence LeDuc, Richard G. Niemi, and Pippa Norris. Thousand Oaks, CA: Sage.

Butler, David, and Dennis Kavanagh. 1988. *The British General Election of 1987.* London: Macmillan.

Cox, Gary W. 1997. *Making Votes Count: Strategic Coordination in the World's Electoral Systems.* New York: Cambridge University Press.

Johnston, Richard, André Blais, Henry E. Brady, and Jean Crête. 1992. *Letting the People Decide: Dynamics of a Canadian Election.* Montreal: McGill-Queen's University Press.

Mutz, Diana. 1992. "Impersonal Influence: Effects of Representations of Public Opinion on Political Attitudes." *Political Behavior* 14:89–122.

Nadeau, Richard, Édouard Cloutier, and Jean H. Guay. 1993. "New Evidence about the Existence of a Bandwagon Effect in the Opinion Formation Process." *International Political Science Review* 14:203–13.

Skalaban, Andrew. 1988. "Do the Polls Affect Elections? Some 1980 Evidence." *Political Behavior* 10:136–50.

Uhlaner, Carole Jean, and Bernard Grofman. 1986. "The Race May Be Close but My Horse Is Going to Win: Wish Fulfilment in the 1980 Presidential Election." *Political Behavior* 8:101–28.

Strategic Learning in Campaigns with Proportional Representation

Evidence from New Zealand

Richard Johnston and Jack Vowles

A CAMPAIGN IS LIKELY TO MATTER if strategic questions remain open when it starts. But the strategic possibilities of campaigns seem most obvious for single-member plurality or first past the post (FPP) systems. What of proportional representation (PR) systems? This essay explores the possibilities for strategic dynamics in New Zealand, once the ideal type of Westminster parliamentarism (Lijphart 1984) but now a thoroughly proportional system with coalition governments. The 1996 New Zealand election was the first fought under PR.

In the 1996 campaign, the strategic environment shifted with respect to two arenas:

> the "threshold" for very small parties, especially parties that were potentially *pivotal* to the subsequent parliamentary coalition game;
> "strategic sequencing," votes cast with a mind to which one of two major or *nucleus* parties will get priority in forming a government.

We show that the environment shifted, how and the extent to which voters became aware of these shifts, and what difference updated expectations made to vote intentions.

Possibilities

On strategic possibilities in campaigns, the analytic literature now seems clear. All electoral systems harbor a "Duvergerian" equilibrium, in which the number of viable candidates or parties is never more than $M + 1$, where M is the district magnitude. Under certain highly restrictive conditions there may also exist a "non-Duvergerian" equilibrium, where candidates or parties may number $M + 2$. In either case, poll information should be vital. At the beginning of a campaign it may not be clear which contestants will be winnowed out in the move to a Duvergerian outcome. The non-Duvergerian case can turn even more on poll information: imagine an early campaign situation in which the margin between the second- and third-place parties is less than the 95 percent confidence interval for differences of proportions in the typical opinion poll.[1]

These propositions seem most compelling in their implications for campaign effects under *strong* electoral systems (Cox 1997, 11), where the penalty for coordination failure is high. Strongest of all is the plurality formula. Voters in such systems should be highly attentive and responsive to poll information, a proposition borne out experimentally by Forsythe et al. (1993) and in the field by Johnston et al. (1992).

What about *weaker* systems? In general the more proportional the formula, the lower the penalty for failure. This implies that *strategically induced* movement in a campaign should be less marked under PR than under FPP.[2] But strategic incentives related to "wastage" of votes do remain under PR, even if they are weaker than under FPP, and other strategic considerations may take on greater force (Leys 1959; Sartori 1968).

The 1996 New Zealand election was conducted under a Mixed Member Proportional (MMP) electoral system, closely modeled on that of Germany. Citizens cast two votes, an "electorate" vote in a single member constituency and a "party" vote. The party vote is the critical one, for it alone determines the numerical allocation of seats. A party's electorate seats are banked toward its total entitlement, but the electorate vote plays no role in calculation of that entitlement (Blais and Massicotte 1996). The balance of seats is allocated from a national list according to the national popular vote. Compared to FPP, then, "wastage" should be small.

The idea of a wasted vote is still relevant at a *threshold*, another element New Zealand has borrowed from Germany. To enter the seat allocation, a party must clear one or the other of two hurdles. If the party receives at least 5 percent of the party vote it is entitled to a proportional share of all seats allocated. If it wins at least one electorate, it will be similarly entitled to enter the calculation. It is thus possible for a party with close to 5 percent of the party vote but with little geographic concentration to get no seats even as another party with a smaller share but with enough concentration to win one seat wins at least that seat and possibly more. Parties around the threshold may be very relevant to the prospective coalition game, and their chances may be widely reported. Elite cues and voter response could evolve with the campaign.

The payoff for surmounting the threshold may be particularly high where the success or failure of a very small ally hovering at the threshold margin may mean the difference between a parliamentary majority or minority for a potential coalition or at least for an "ideological family" of the left or right. In this case, voters who would otherwise choose their most favored nucleus party may instead vote for the marginal pivotal party to assist it over the threshold (Cox 1997, 81–83). In New Zealand, as in Germany, such a vote may be cast either as a national party vote or in a strategic electorate that the pivotal party may be placed to win and so cross the threshold by that means.

For parties clearly above the threshold, expectations may also matter, although not for reasons of wastage. Here the issue is *strategic sequencing* (Cox 1997, 194). Some systems explicitly give first crack at forming a coalition to the nucleus party with the largest seat share. In these circumstances voters whose first preference lies with a small potentially pivotal party might vote strategically for a larger ally to ensure that that ally becomes the nucleus of a government coalition.[3] Otherwise the coalition-formation sequence could be initiated by a party more hostile to the first mentioned small party. Strategic choice like this occurs in Israel, for instance (Felsenthal and Brichta 1985). The New Zealand situation, still tied in 1996 to Westminster assumptions, is more loosely defined, but the logic still holds. The existing government party, even if reduced to a minority, has a right to meet Parliament and try its luck. But that presumption must be conditional on the old government's continuing strength; not just any seat total will do. And the presumptive nucleus for an alternative coalition will almost certainly be a large party. In the alternative ideological "family" there thus may be pressure toward consolidation, if only to buttress one of its members' moral presumption. But which one? To the extent that the history of recent elections does not point to the likely leader, the "family" has a potentially severe coordination problem. Early polls and elite indications could be critical.

The Strategic Context for 1996

From 1935 to 1951, an almost pure two-party system prevailed in New Zealand. The center-right National Party competed against the center-left Labour Party across class and urban-rural cleavages. But pressure for change was evident in the 1950s, accelerated in the late 1970s, and went into a new gear in the late 1980s (Vowles 1994, 1997a, 1997b). By 1996, the party system was in an advanced state of breakdown.

The 1993 election marked a new peak in the system's fractionalization, with votes for the two largest parties falling just below 70 percent for the first time since 1928. Table 1 illustrates the main features of the 1993 and 1996 elections. It divides the parties into left and right blocs, with one center party. At the 1993 election, two new parties gained representation, with two members each. One, the left-leaning Alliance, had formed as a coalition of minor parties, including New Labour (with one member elected in 1990), the Greens, and the Liberals (a post-1990 election splinter from the National Party). The other, New Zealand First (NZF), was formed by dissident National member of Parliament (MP) Winston Peters in June 1993.

TABLE 1. Seat and Vote Shares in 1993 and 1996 (in percentages)

	Left, Right, or Center	1993 Election		1996 Preelection	1996 Postelection	
		Votes	Seats	Seats	Party Votes	Seats
ACT[a]	R	—	—	0	6.1	6.7
National	R	35.1	50.5	41.4	33.8	36.7
Christians[b]	R	2.0	0	1.0	4.3	0
Conservative	R	—	—	1.0	0.1	0
United	R	—	—	7.1	0.9	0.8
NZ First	C	8.4	2.0	4.0	13.4	14.2
Labour	L	34.7	45.4	41.4	28.2	30.8
Alliance	L	18.2	2.0	2.0	10.1	10.8
Legalize cannabis		—	—	—	1.7	0
Independent		—	—	1.0	—	0
N		100	99	98 (1 vacant)	100	120

[a]Association of Consumers and Taxpayers.
[b]Christian Heritage 1993; Christian Coalition 1996 (Christian Heritage and Christian Democrats).

Between 1993 and 1996, four other significant parties were formed, three in Parliament. Both major parties lost members to smaller parties, each time in anticipation of the transition to MMP. The Christian Coalition had as one component the Christian Heritage Party, which gained 2 percent of the vote in 1993 but no seats. The other component was a sitting MP who had defected from National. The Conservatives and United were purely parliamentary creations, intended as potential coalition partners for a major party and also in part as a means of rescuing the careers of politicians unlikely to be selected for winnable seats or positions by their former parties.[4] The Association of Consumers and Taxpayers (ACT) was set up outside Parliament as a neoliberal party to advance the views of Roger Douglas, the Labour minister of finance who had driven the market liberalization of the 1980s. Although led by a former Labour cabinet colleague of Douglas, Richard Prebble, ACT positioned itself on the ideological right.

Between the two elections of 1993 and 1996 a National government remained uneasily in power. Having won in 1993 with only a one-seat majority over all other parties, over the next three years National progressed through almost all possible parliamentary arrangements: single-party majority, majority coalition, minority single-party government, back to majority coalition on a different basis, and reverting to a minority coalition in the months before the 1996 election.

Over the same period, public support for the parties shifted dramatically. Support for the two left parties steadily fell, most strikingly when NZF rose steeply early in 1996, after Winston Peters's attacks on immigration and increased foreign ownership of New Zealand assets. On the eve of the 1996 campaign, the strategic implication of vote shares was uncertain, and their stability was problematic. National was the most popular party, but without enough support to form a single-party government and with no guarantee of a coalition partner to provide a majority. United, despite seven members in the house, was making no impression in the polls. National helped United out by declining to contest the electorate (Ohariu-Belmont) of the best-known United MP, Peter Dunne, virtually assuring United a single seat and opening up the possibility of United's gaining further list seats. The Christian Coalition and ACT were in sight of the 5 percent party-vote threshold, but not necessarily above it.

Meanwhile NZF and Labour, and, at times, even the Alliance, took turns as the most popular opposition party. It was assumed by almost all observers that NZF sought to defeat the government and that the most

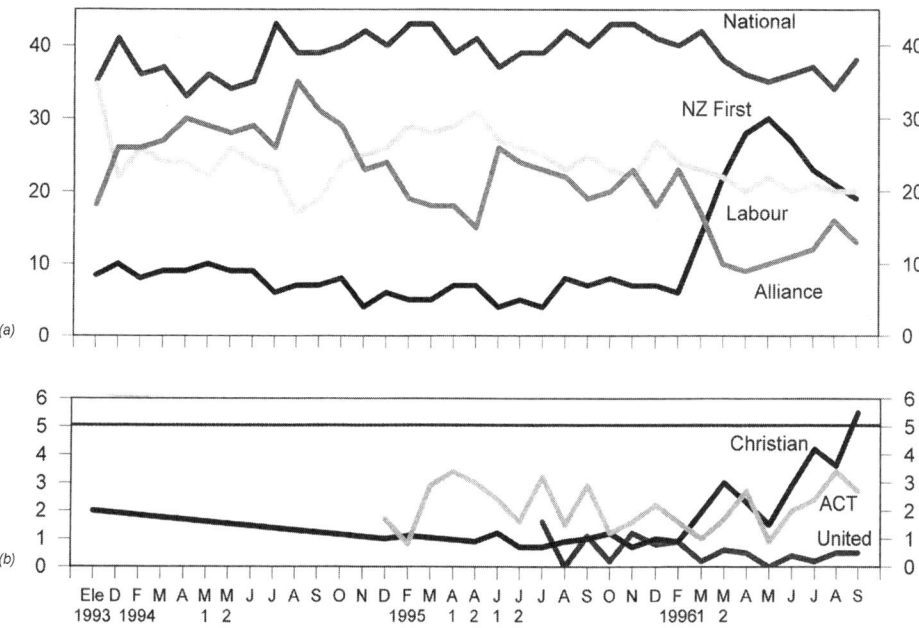

Fig. 1. Vote intentions, 1993–96: a, major parties; b, threshold parties. (Note: In some months there were two polls. Data from UMR-Insight, *National Business Review*.)

likely opposition coalition outcome would be a partnership of Labour and NZF. The Alliance indicated that in the absence of a preelection agreement it would not enter a coalition but would probably provide parliamentary support on confidence and supply for a non-National government.

This strategic environment defined the 1996 New Zealand election campaign as one of extreme uncertainty, fed by the volatility of the opposition vote and the electoral marginality of possible center-right coalition partners. National sought to reduce the marginality of United by effectively guaranteeing it representation in the new Parliament. But the prospects for the Christian Coalition and ACT appeared highly uncertain. In the best possible circumstances for the right, National, ACT, the Christian Coalition, and United might together gain enough seats for a parliamentary majority, but such a scenario was highly optimistic. On the other hand, although the three opposition parties were all certain to cross the threshold and might together command a parliamentary majority, their ability and willingness to sustain such a government were suspect. Labour's leader, Helen Clark, was unpopular among voters, and a vocal minority of

Labour MPs had been working against her since she displaced her predecessor, Mike Moore, just after the 1993 election. Although the experience of its parliamentary team and the residues of historical support for Labour should have been working in its favor, Labour entered the campaign limping and at a tactical disadvantage.

Figure 2 shows that the campaign eventually generated a Labour revival, but the opposition picture remained clouded until late September, when Labour finally pulled away from the others. Labour appears to have surged twice and fallen back once. Even with the late slump, Labour ended the campaign as the presumptive rival to National.

For the small parties, the prospect of clearing the 5 percent threshold was uncertain all along. United clearly was not going to, but retained the local advantage in Ohariu-Belmont (see previous discussion). Both the Christians and ACT toyed with the threshold all along. Until late September neither seemed more likely than the other to clear it. Then ACT surged and cleared the hurdle comfortably, but the Christians fell short.

Clearing the Threshold

For small parties, the question is whether the party will win *any* seats. As mentioned, under MMP a party becomes eligible for parliamentary seats either by winning at least 5 percent of the nationwide party vote or by winning at least one electorate seat. ACT eventually cleared both thresholds, but for much of the campaign its prospects seemed very much in doubt. United missed the 5 percent threshold by a wide margin but was virtually guaranteed an electorate seat by National's decision not to contest Ohariu-Belmont. The Christian Coalition flirted with the 5 percent threshold but had no realistic chance of winning any electorate seat.

According to figure 3, the campaign moved expectations toward the reality just described, but did so rather late and still left many respondents in the dark. For much of the campaign voters perceived ACT as hardly more viable than the Christians, with United seen as much the least viable of the three. In fact, a precampaign electorate poll had already indicated United on course to win Ohariu-Belmont, but most voters either did not have this information or, if they did, failed to absorb its threshold implications. Certainly, down to September 29, no enduring shift in threshold expectations occurred. Expectations seemed to drift: all three parties sagged around September 23–24 and then recovered, more or less. We have no explanation for

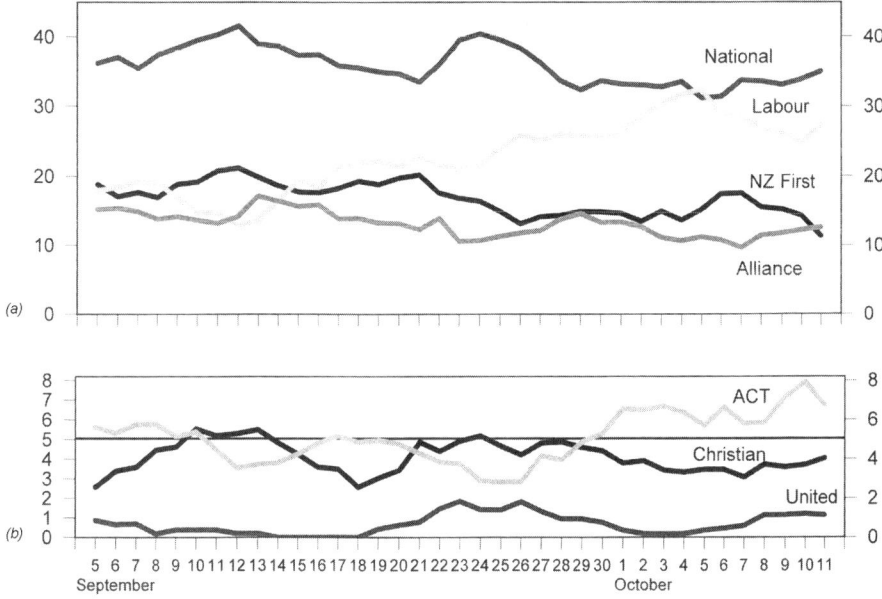

Fig. 2. Vote intentions in the 1996 campaign: *a*, major parties; *b*, threshold parties (five-day moving average)

the September 23–24 sag, but the general pattern is consistent with an electorate making straight party-vote calculations from national polls. Before September 28 the national numbers gave small parties little cause for optimism, and none suggested that either ACT or United had an advantage over the Christian Coalition. In four of the six polls published before September 28, the Christians outpolled ACT and in three, the Christians cleared the threshold. Only in the very first campaign-period poll (published September 14) did ACT's share exceed 5 percent.

Starting September 28, the informational situation shifted. That day saw the first electorate poll in Wellington Central, a seat contested by Richard Prebble, the ACT leader. This revealed a three-way race, with Prebble a close third. Essentially the same result was published on October 3, but the results of both of these polls had little circulation outside the lower North Island. On October 9 a Wellington Central electorate poll released on the most popular national TV news program gave Prebble a small plurality. On September 29 and 30, national polls suggested that ACT was at or above 5 percent. In four more national polls, ACT cleared the threshold twice and fell just short twice. Even where it fell short ACT outpolled

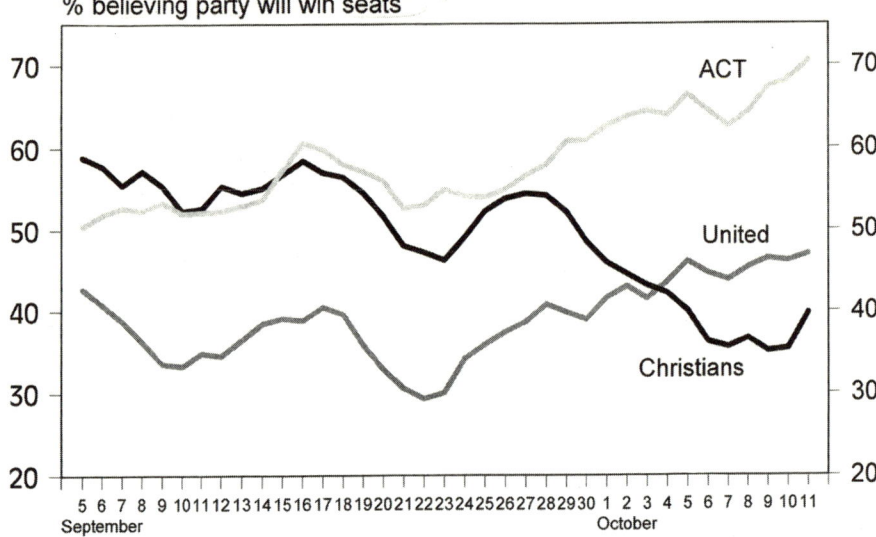

Fig. 3. Expectations for threshold parties (five-day moving average)

the Christians. The latter fell short of 5 percent in all six late polls. United's position also became very clear, as a September 30 poll in Ohariu-Belmont indicated that Peter Dunne was likely to receive an absolute majority.

Expectations moved toward reality, according to figure 3, as ACT and United moved up and the Christians dropped. For all the reality testing, however, perceptions still varied greatly at the end. To what extent did expectations reflect wish fulfilment, and did the campaign banish misperception?

Table 2 gives an account of factors governing expectations. Cross-sectional elements in the estimation are intended to do one or both of the following: stabilize other results or control for wish fulfilment bias. The two demographic variables, gender and age,[5] appear to be sources of bias. Males expressed systematically higher expectations than females for the threshold parties. Older voters were more skeptical than younger voters of ACT's and the Christians' chances. Also seeming to impart bias was the ideological camp of party identification, "left" for Alliance and Labour identifiers and "right" for National, Christian, ACT, and United identifiers. The clearest pattern was for ACT expectations, where the left-right gap in belief that ACT would clear the threshold was about nine points. Christian Coalition expectations also evoked a pale reflection of this pattern. Claiming that the party in question was closest on the most important policy also boosted the party's perceived chances. Was this really bias? This is a matter we return to in a moment.

The other terms in the table are longitudinal. Each party's standing in the most recently published national poll is entered.[6] For ACT and United, dummy variables corresponding to release of electorate polls also appear, scored 0 for respondents interviewed before the publication of the poll and scored 1 for respondents interviewed on any later day. One poll gave the Ohariu-Belmont results for Peter Dunne of United, but there the race was not even close. As mentioned previously, three polls briefed voters on Wellington Central, and only the third indicated that Prebble of ACT held a plurality. National poll information had its greatest effect on the Christian Coalition, reflecting the deterioration in that party's standing. For ACT and United national polls had no effect. In United's case this is exactly as it should be, for the national polls were not relevant given the Ohariu-Belmont facts. It was the publication of the local poll that shifted expectations for United. For ACT, the key was the cumulation of information that Richard Prebble was on the rise in Wellington Central. This is indicated by the succession of positive coefficients on successive polls. These coefficients should be read cumulatively, later ones added to earlier ones. Over half the total rise in ACT expectations was attributable to the third electorate poll reported on national television.

TABLE 2. Factors in Threshold Expectations

	Expectations for Winning a Seat By					
	ACT		Christians		United	
Party % in last poll	0.01	(0.01)	0.06	(0.01)***	0.05	(0.03)
Electorate poll						
1	0.06	(0.03)	—		0.08	(0.02)***
2	0.02	(0.04)	—		—	
3	0.08	(0.04)	—		—	
Left identification—general	−0.02	(0.02)	−0.01	(0.02)	−0.01	(0.02)
Right identification—general	0.07	(0.02)***	0.03	(0.02)	−0.01	(0.02)
Threshold party closest on issue	0.27	(0.5)***	0.47	(0.07)***	—	
Male	0.05	(0.02)**	0.03	(0.02)	0.09	(0.02)***
Age (−18)	−0.17	(0.04)***	−0.06	(0.04)	0.07	(0.04)
Intercept	0.52	(0.06)	0.21	(0.05)	0.274	(0.025)
R^2-adjusted	0.04		0.03		0.02	
s_u	0.48		0.49		0.48	
N	2,927		2,927		2,939	

Note: Entries in parentheses are standard errors.
*$p < 0.05$ **$p < 0.01$ ***$p < 0.001$

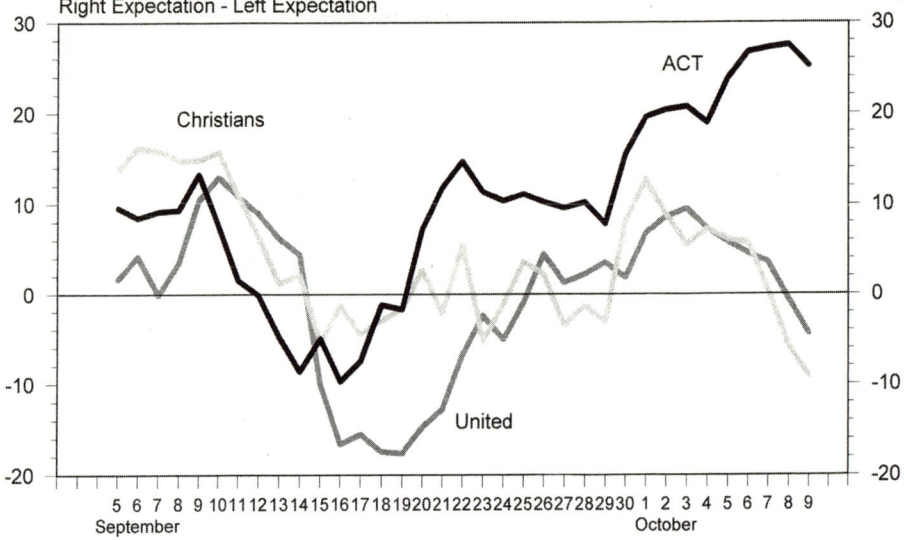

Fig. 4. Ideological differences in threshold expectations (seven-day moving average)

All longitudinal variables in table 2 are vulnerable to being styled as nothing more than time relabeled. For ACT and the Christians the national poll variable crudely divides the campaign into early and late, with only modest variation within halves of the campaign. The electorate poll variables, as dummies, divide the campaign even more crudely. But they derive credibility both from inspection of figure 3 and from common sense. The coefficient on the third Wellington Central result is not significant by the conventional test and criterion, but it is nearly so. More to the point, the null hypothesis refers to the difference between this poll and the immediately preceding one, a very stringent test, not between this poll and the period before any poll was published. By the latter criterion, the impact of the third poll is highly significant.

Ideological differences in strategic reckoning warrant closer attention. This could be just wish fulfilment, with no real motivational relevance. Or it could be that voters on the right have more incentive to weigh the prospects of small right and center-right parties with care. Time of campaign is relevant to distinguishing these processes and is controlled in figure 4, which presents week-by-week left-right differences in the percentage claiming that a small party will win a seat. The pattern is basically consistent with motivationally differentiated reality testing, although with a wrinkle. Most striking is the contrast between ACT and the other two parties. For the Christian Coalition and United, the left-right difference was large early and essentially null late. This is consistent with the spread of common knowledge, in this case, knowledge of weakness. For ACT, the left-right difference widened as the campaign progressed. In fact, *only* right-party identifiers saw ACT gain viability.[7] It is hard to fault their perceptions, as late polls and accounts of the race in Wellington Central all pointed to the party's strength. If this was bias, it was bias on the left, but there, bias was irrelevant; nothing hinged on it.[8]

This brings us to implications for the vote. Table 3 presents estimations for right-party identifiers only, as they had the clearest incentive to take strategic action at the threshold. Two strategic factors enter the estimation, the threshold expectation for the small party in question and the expectation for the National Party share of parliamentary seats.[9] For prediction to the impact of threshold expectations, strategic reasoning arguably cuts both ways. On the one hand, there is little point wasting a vote for a party with little chance of winning so much as one seat; the vote is better given to a more viable ideological ally. On the other hand, the greater the small party's chance of winning, the less necessary is any strategic action. Strategic action is most necessary when the ally is right at the threshold: if it falls below, the ideological family's combined seat share may

TABLE 3. Threshold Expectations and the Vote, Right Identifiers Only ($N = 586$)

	Party					
	ACT		Christians		United	
Expectation for the threshold party						
Expectation	0.07	(0.02)***	0.02	(0.01)*	0.01	(0.006)
Expectation for the National Party						
"Time-series"	−0.008	(0.006)	−0.004	(0.003)	0.000	(0.002)
"Cross-section"	0.006	(0.006)	−0.003	(0.003)	0.001	(0.002)
Threshold party closest	0.39	(0.05)***	0.33	(0.04)***	—	—
Threshold party ID	0.57	(0.09)***	0.68	(0.04)***	—	—
Male	0.04	(0.02)*	−0.02	(0.01)*	0.01	(0.01)
Age (−18)	−0.07	(0.005)	0.04	(0.03)	0.03	(0.02)*
Intercept	0.13	(0.34)	0.12	(0.12)	−0.04	(0.07)
R^2-adjusted	0.26		0.63		0.01	
s_u	0.25		0.12		0.07	

Note: Entries in parentheses are standard errors.
*$p < 0.05$ **$p < 0.01$ ***$p < 0.001$

be less than that available were the votes properly coordinated.[10] The National Party expectation carries a clearer indication: the greater the National share, the less the need for bolstering by small allies.

Expectations are broken into cross-sectional and time-series parts. We cannot assume as a matter of principle that the longitudinal and cross-sectional elements in expectations (or in many other factors, for that matter) operate the same way. At any given time there may be a strong positive relationship between expectation and intention. The overall surface of expectations may shift with no or little concomitant shift in intentions or vice versa. If we estimated a single coefficient for impact of expectation on intention we might capture a mainly cross-sectional effect. Using this coefficient to calculate the impact of the net shift in expectations would almost certainly yield an overestimate. Where possible, then, we separate longitudinal from cross-sectional variation as follows:

> First we derive a normalized seat expectation. For the National Party this is just the number of seats the respondent expects National to win divided by the total number the respondent expects for the four largest parties.
>
> The mean seat expectation for the respondent's interview date is subtracted from his or her normalized expectation.

This sequence has the following effect. The second variable retains cross-sectional information but is purged of longitudinal variance. With both variables in the estimation, the second captures only cross-sectional impact, leaving the first to capture only longitudinal impact. The coefficient on the first is the estimated dynamic effect, and the sum of the two coefficients captures the cross-sectional effect. In principle, this is not the best way to separate time-series from cross-sectional variance, but it is the only way available for expectational data.[11] For the threshold expectation itself, measured as a simple dummy variable, this method asks too much of the data, so we make no distinction between longitudinal and cross-sectional. Also in the estimation are two demographic variables, gender and age, together with two obvious substantive motives for choosing a party, whether or not it is the closest party on policy and whether or not the respondent identifies with it.

In actual results, threshold expectations play a simple role: the greater the expectation, the greater the likelihood of support for the party in question. One reading is this: no one is deluded that small-party success is so certain that strategic vigilance need not be kept; the effective range of the distribution is from subjective certainty of failure to diffident optimism, with the latter being a necessary minimum condition to unlock the vote. This was true for both ACT and the Christians but was most forcefully true for ACT. Threshold expectations had no impact on the United vote. But then, United, alone among these parties, never needed help.

Expectations for the National Party seat total may have mattered for the ACT vote and the Christian vote, but the estimation is unstable. For these parties, expectations coefficients are about the same size as or slightly larger than their respective standard errors, with the time-series coefficients slightly more so. Most noteworthy is the time-series coefficient in the ACT estimation. It indicates that, as expectations for National's seat total weaken, the likelihood of supporting ACT increases and vice versa. The coefficient suggests that a one-point drop in the expected National share yields an eight-tenths of a percent increase in the ACT vote, other things being equal. The indication is similar but weaker for the Christian vote. The estimates further indicate that the impact on the ACT vote is entirely longitudinal.[12]

Expectations and "Strategic Sequencing"

"Strategic sequencing" takes place where votes are cast with a mind to which putative nucleus party gets priority in attempting to form a government. Before they could think in those terms, voters had to resolve a prior question: which party would be the opposition nucleus, Labour or NZF?

Why not Alliance? It is true that, in the aftermath of the 1993 election, the Alliance share surged, such that that party seemed like National's chief rival for some months (fig. 1), and as recently as February 1996 the Alliance rivaled Labour. But the Alliance declined sharply before the campaign, and only for a few early days did Labour's share fall below the Alliance one. In these circumstances, the Alliance was reduced to being a pivot, and even that role was diminished twice over: first, by the Alliance's unequivocal preference for Labour over National, and, second, by its commitment only to support a Labour government, not to join it.[13]

The main beneficiary of the Alliance's 1996 decline, seemingly, was NZF, whose share grew three- to fivefold between February and May 1996. Although NZF fell back, it was level with Labour on the eve of the campaign (fig. 1) and outpolled Labour for some of the campaign's early days (fig. 2). Winston Peters made his prime ministerial ambitions clear and, like Labour, rejected a preelection coalition agreement. Up to the campaign, and often during it, Peters reserved his main attacks for the National government, giving the clear impression that NZF intended to participate in, and preferably form, an alternative government. Toward the end of the campaign, as his party stalled, he began to sound more like a pivot than a nucleus. For much of the period under study, however, NZF could be seen as locked in a struggle for primacy with Labour.

If Labour naturally presented itself as a traditional party of government, there was serious question at the start if this pretense was sustainable. Helen Clark's credibility was also clearly tied to her ability to draw votes, at the start much in doubt. The biggest story of the campaign was her personal rehabilitation, which was linked to her ability to clarify Labour's position on key issues (Johnston 1998). This story will inevitably poke through this essay's analysis and narrative, especially in the guise of control factors in multivariate estimations, treated subsequently.

Here, though, the factor of interest is voters' expectations for Labour and NZF, as described in figure 5, and what lay behind them. From the beginning, expectations for Labour were high, while expectations for NZF were realistically low, possibly even discounted. Respondents never projected a Labour seat share below 25 percent, even when fewer than 20 percent of those same respondents declared a Labour vote intention. As Labour's vote share rose, so did expectations. The two lines met at about 30 percent, accompanied each other into the low 30s, and then parted company. Where Labour's own vote fell back in the last week, expectations continued to drift up. Expectations for NZF drifted down over the campaign but were always fairly close to reality. The party was arguably discounted at the start and finish. In between, though, NZF expectations slightly outran intentions.

Some voters were more clear-headed in their expectations than others. For both Labour and NZF, partisans of the left and right got the race in clearer focus than did centrists. Centrists had the rank order of Labour and NZF roughly correct but updated their evaluations hardly at all. In the end, they discriminated the parties much less than did noncentrists; the image is of a random draw, somewhat modified by historical fact. The critical link is between left identifiers and expectations for Labour. At the start, left- and right-wing voters expected Labour to get between 25 percent and 30 percent of the seats. Starting in mid-September, however, left identifiers—and

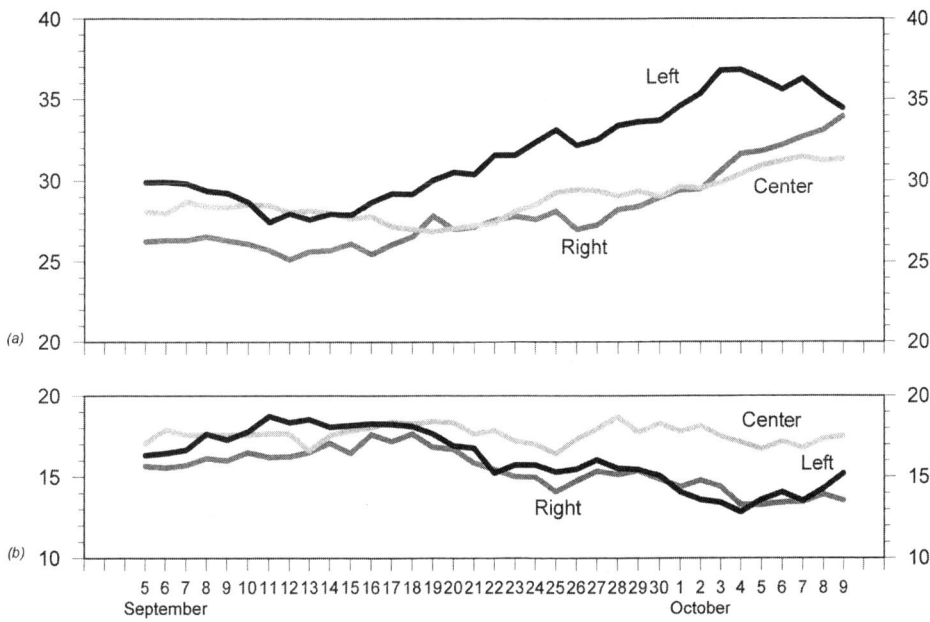

Fig. 5. Nucleus-party expectations by "ideological family": a, Labour; b, NZF (seven-day moving average)

only this group—began a rapid reevaluation of Labour's chances. There was a further acceleration of expectations after the first debate. Right identifiers also began upgrading their expectations at this point. But it will prove critical to the argument later in this essay that expectations on the left were already going up before the debate.

Table 4 attempts to account for expectations, with a mix of cross-sectional and longitudinal elements. Party identification terms are almost purely cross-sectional, as little systematic movement in the distribution occurred over the sample period. Issue and leader ratings tap both kinds of variation. The percentage choosing Helen Clark as the best prime minister surged at midcampaign, as did the percentage saying Labour was closest on the most important issue.[14] Poll information, of course, is purely longitudinal.

Expectations were clearly colored by predispositions, as indicated by party identification coefficients. For each of Labour and NZF, the most sharply contrasted identification groups were about 4.5 points apart, most optimistic being those identified with the party in question. Leader and issue evaluations also affected expectations, especially for NZF. Although we feel uncomfortable trying to separate longitudinal from cross-sectional,[15] longitudinal shifts in these evaluations must be a big part of the story. As large numbers of voters made a substantive reevaluation of Clark and her party, so must they—with good reason—have reevaluated the party's prospects.

This brings us once more to the truly independent strategic information, from polls. Polls did have an effect for each party, much stronger for Labour than for NZF. For the latter the effect is truly weak: a percentage-point shift in polls induced a 0.13 shift in expectations, both variables measured on the same scale. And the distance traversed by NZF's published poll standing over the campaign—the range from the last precampaign to the last preelection poll—was only 7 points. For Labour both things were greater: the unit shift in polls induced a 0.43 shift in seat expectations, other things being equal, and total range in Labour shares spanned 13 points.[16]

Expectations did respond to campaign cues, including polls. No less striking, though, is the weight of history. From the beginning, Labour was forecast as closer in seats to National and closer to its own previous history

TABLE 4. Factors in Labour and New Zealand First Expectations ($N = 2,412$)

	Labour		New Zealand First	
Identification				
Alliance	−2.1	(0.99)*	1.0	(1.0)
Labour	1.9	(0.5)***	−0.9	(0.5)
National	−0.3	(0.5)	−0.5	(0.5)
NZ First	−2.6	(1.0)**	3.7	(1.1)***
Best prime minister				
Bolger	1.5	(0.5)***	−0.7	(0.5)
Clark	1.2	(0.6)*	0.1	(0.6)
Peters	−2.3	(0.6)***	6.8	(0.6)***
Closest party on issue				
Alliance	−1.2	(0.6)*	−0.9	(0.6)
Labour	1.8	(0.5)***	−0.3	(−0.6)
National	−1.6	(0.5)**	0.1	(0.5)
NZ First	−3.1	(0.7)***	7.0	(0.7)***
Party % in last poll	0.43	(0.06)***	0.13	(0.07)
Intercept	21.4	(1.2)	13.1	(1.3)
R^2-adjusted	0.12		0.20	
s_u	8.4		8.8	

Note: Entries in parentheses are standard errors.
*$p < 0.05$ **$p < 0.01$ ***$p < 0.001$

than to its principal opposition rival, NZF. Events vindicated this early perception, but was it merely self-fulfilling? Had Clark not performed so well in the first debate, perhaps Labour expectations would have converged on predebate reality rather than the reverse.[17] That early perceptions mirrored history should not be surprising, however. The same was true in the early stages of the 1988 Canadian campaign, even though the historically central Liberal Party struggled to stay ahead of the New Democratic Party (Johnston et al. 1992, chap. 7). It also mirrors experimental findings on equilibrium dynamics in the absence of polls (Forsythe et al. 1993), and poll information was sparse early on. The sluggishness of expectational updating also parallels both the Canadian survey pattern and experimental evidence (Edwards 1982).

Table 5 examines the impact of expectations on the vote. One estimation covers the whole campaign, maximizing both number of cases and longitudinal variance. But treating the whole campaign as a homogeneous time period may do violence to the logic of the event. Certain kinds of

TABLE 5. Expectations, Coalitions, and the Labour Vote (respondents identified with right-wing parties excluded)

	Whole Campaign		Predebate		Postdebate	
Labour expectation						
"Time-series"	0.003	(0.003)	0.018^a	(0.010)	−0.002	(0.009)
"Cross-section"	0.004	(0.003)	−0.012	(0.010)	0.010	(0.009)
Identification						
Alliance	−0.01	(0.04)	−0.04	(0.05)	0.02	(0.06)
Labour	0.21	(0.02)***	0.19	(0.03)***	0.22	(0.03)***
NZ First	−0.007	(0.04)	−0.04	(0.05)	0.04	(0.06)
Best prime minister						
Bolger	−0.13	(0.03)***	−0.13	(0.03)***	−0.14	(0.04)***
Clark	0.22	(0.03)***	0.26	(0.04)***	0.19	(0.03)***
Peters	−0.10	(0.03)***	−0.14	(0.03)***	−0.04	(0.04)
Closest party on issue						
Alliance	−0.10	(0.03)***	−0.11	(0.04)**	−0.09	(0.04)*
Labour	0.39	(0.03)***	0.38	(0.03)***	0.40	(0.04)***
National	−0.07	(0.03)*	−0.07	(0.04)*	−0.06	(0.04)
NZ First	−0.08	(0.03)*	−0.03	(0.04)	−0.15	(0.05)**
Intercept	0.20	(0.20)	−0.32	(0.27)	0.23	(0.19)
R^2-adjusted	0.55		0.51		0.58	
s_u	0.31		0.31		0.31	
N	1,456		802		654	

Note: Entries in parentheses are standard errors.
$^a p < 0.10$ $*p < 0.05$ $**p < 0.01$ $***p < 0.001$

information may be more powerful early than late, or vice versa, and certain considerations may be primed. The table addresses these possibilities in a crude way by breaking the campaign in two at the first debate, the event that rehabilitated Helen Clark. The estimation includes identification, leader, and issue terms, parallel to table 4. Expectational variance is separated into time-series and cross-sectional components, on the logic and by the means described previously.

Basically, expectations are hypothesized to have a monotonic positive impact. One condition that justifies this is that neither nucleus party is far ahead of its rival. This cuts both ways, of course: the weaker the Labour expectation, the less likely the Labour vote, and vice versa. This condition held before the first debate but ceased to hold shortly after the debate, as Labour pulled away. As this happened, the expectation might have become less important. A second condition is that no pivot party be in peril at the threshold. This condition also held throughout the campaign, as the obvious pivot, the Alliance, always had a vote-intention share above 10 percent. Had this condition not held, then above some threshold, the impact from the Labour expectation might even reverse sign: the more comfortable Labour's apparent position, the more readily can effort shift to bolstering the Alliance.[18]

Although most of the power in the estimations derives from substantive factors, expectations seem pretty clearly to matter. In the whole-campaign estimation, a 1-point shift in the Labour seat expectation produced a Labour vote increment of about 0.3 points, other things being equal. The time-series coefficient is barely larger than its standard error, however. The real story is from the first half of the campaign. Here the coefficient implies an effect closer to two-to-one; that is, a one percentage point gain in perceived seat share was worth almost a 2-point gain in vote likelihood. In this period, the Labour vote-intention share did go up, if only gradually. Nothing else was breaking Labour's way, as the reevaluation of Helen Clark and the concomitant clarification of Labour's positions on key issues lay in the future. As figure 5 indicates, respondents on the left were the most sensitive to Labour's evolving situation: their expectation for Labour's share grew some 6 points before the debate. Voters in the center reevaluated Labour's chances hardly at all (indeed, they were quite unresponsive throughout the campaign). Still, in the pool of potential Labour voters, expectational impact was hardly trivial. Once substantive considerations accelerated Labour's rise, however, expectations played no further role, as indicated by the feeble postdebate coefficient.[19]

Discussion

On the eve of the 1996 campaign, the system presented voters with considerable strategic uncertainty. The campaign largely resolved the uncertainty, and published polls were critical to this resolution. In one sense, the polls were self-fulfilling. In another sense, they facilitated efficient behavior on the part of critical subsets of the electorate and, arguably, brought the result *closer* to the electorate's sincere preferences.

The campaign moved perception around the MMP threshold: ACT and United came to seem more viable and the Christian Coalition less so. These shifts accorded with reality and did so as reality itself moved, especially as polls put reality on the public record. The polls that moved perceptions were truly relevant to the choice. For ACT and United, only local polls were critical. Polls from Wellington Central confirmed that Richard Prebble was seriously in contention to win the seat, which would also ensure that ACT votes be translated into seats. For United, the one Ohariu-Belmont poll indicating victory for Peter Dunne shifted expectations dramatically. For the Christian Coalition, only nationwide polls mattered. Those were the only polls that *should* have mattered as the party had no realistic local stronghold, even as it flirted with the countrywide threshold. And shifts in expectation helped shift vote intentions for two of the three parties. Cross-sectionally, threshold perceptions exhibited bias, although some of what might look like bias was arguably motivationally appropriate attentiveness. Also relevant may have been expectations for the National Party. The weaker National was seen to be, the higher the probability of support for both ACT and the Christians.

The campaign also shifted expectations for potential nucleus parties, notably for Labour. The gradual upward drift in Labour intentions registered in upwardly revised expectations, even before Helen Clark's breakthrough in the first debate. Only voters on the left of the ideological spectrum recognized this drift, however. But only they were really prepared to act on it, so their alertness seems to complement that for right-wing voters in relation to ACT at the threshold. Both domains exhibited motivationally appropriate reality testing. Voters who ignored the information were unlikely to act on it.

Expectations were also subject to bias from history. At the outset, respondents projected Labour to win about as many seats as the party ultimately did win. This was true long before Labour's share of vote intentions actually reached that level. Evidently, voters felt the weight of history and discounted the more recent information. NZF did not so obviously have history on its side. Even under MMP, then, historically large parties may be advantaged, in that they can benefit from self-fulfilling expectations. Why should voters exhibit self-fulfilling expectations and behavior? The answer seems to lie in Cox's (1997) notion of "strategic sequencing." If big parties jockey for priority in forming the government, voters may factor expectations into their choice.

But, then, this evidence is for 1996, the first MMP election. The year's strategic confusion may only reflect the novelty of the situation. The rules were new, as was the level of electoral fragmentation. Some of that fragmentation was the result of attempts by parliamentary players to survive the transition. They too were operating in an unusually hazy context. As the system settles in, uncertainty may diminish. Ironically, this need not reduce the role of expectations. Expectations may just be more stable and even more self-fulfilling.

APPENDIX: The 1996 New Zealand Election Study

The New Zealand Election Study (NZES) Campaign Survey was conducted between September 5 and October 11, 1996, by the Survey Research Unit in the Department of Political Science and Public Policy at the University of Waikato. We gratefully acknowledge the work of Dr. Gabriel Dekel, director of the unit.

Respondents were selected by random digit dialing from a national sampling frame of telephone numbers, weighted to ensure that the sample would be balanced by region. Respondents were also weighted according to household size, so that responses from persons in larger households were properly balanced against those in smaller households. No quotas or weights were applied by age and gender, as checks early in the interviewing indicated random sampling was producing a demographically representative sample within expected sampling error. Interviews were conducted on computer. Callbacks were essentially unrestricted, and numbers for which there was no reply were called up to twenty times.

The total sample size was 4,448, of which 3,091 were NZES-funded seven-minute interviews and 1,357 were three-minute media-funded interviews. Most estimations and exhibits in this essay are based on the NZES-funded interviews. The response rate for this part of the sample was about 50 percent, on the assumption that numbers called twenty times or more with no reply were nonresidential.

The campaign survey was funded from a variety of sources, with some assistance from the budget of the 1996 Election Study, which was funded by New Zealand taxpayers through the Foundation for Research, Science, and Technology (FRST). Most of the support for the campaign survey came from the University of Waikato School of Social Sciences Research Committee and the University of Waikato and University of Auckland Research Committees. Further financial assistance also came from the *New Zealand Herald* and Television New Zealand.

NOTES

1. This is a stylization of Palfrey 1989; Fey 1997; and Cox 1997. We deliberately finesse considerations of local versus national equilibriation and of the measurement of M, as neither matters much to our argument.

2. Other kinds of movement may be greater, however. For example, the typically greater fractionalization of systems under PR may multiply the number of acceptable parties for any given voter, and this may facilitate shifts within blocs (Bartolini and Mair 1990).

3. In the use of the term *nucleus* to denote parties at the center of a coalition, we follow Laver and Schofield 1991, 206.

4. With the shift to MMP the number of electorates was cut almost in half, from ninety-five non-Maori seats to sixty. Many incumbents would thus be forced into head-to-head contests for reselection.

5. Ideally more demographic variables would be entered, but severe time constraints on the telephone wave made age and gender the only two available. We reestimated all the tables in this essay with a full inventory of postelection variables, but because this cut the total sample size in half, it contributed little to the stabilization of coefficients.

6. The poll variable was simply updated on each day. National polls appeared in a morning newspaper, the *New Zealand Herald*, which circulates in the upper North Island, where about half the country's population lives. Most electorate polls appeared in Wellington's *Evening Post*, which is read mainly in the lower North Island. The polls with most exposure were the Colmar-Brunton efforts featured on TV One's Network News at 6:00 p.m., and these included the final Wellington Central electorate poll. Polls conducted by CM Research appeared on the TV3 National News, also at 6:00 p.m. A single national poll early in the campaign was published in the *National Business Review*, conducted by UMR-Insight.

7. In the first week of fieldwork, 51.2 percent of left identifiers thought ACT would win a seat, as compared with 50.0 percent of right identifiers; corresponding percentages for the last week were 54.2 and 78.2.

8. The wrinkle is that the United pattern did not match the ACT one. United was viable at the end and came increasingly to be seen as such (fig. 3). The key may be that United was not really on the right, notwithstanding its coalitional commitment.

9. Respondents were asked the actual number of seats they thought a major party would win and were told not to worry about the total implied for the four clearly viable parties. The attribution was then normalized by that total, so that the expectation for a party is expressed as its percentage of the four-party seat total.

10. See the discussion in Cox 1997, 197–98.

11. For a formal discussion of alternative ways to capture time-series effects in rolling cross-section survey data, see Johnston and Brady 2002. This method corresponds to their equation (11).

12. The cross-sectional effect is the sum of the coefficients, which is close to zero. Tellingly, when only the normalized expectation is entered, the estimated coefficient is also close to zero.

13. Strictly speaking, any party is pivotal if its withdrawal from a proto-coalition deprives that body of a majority. In this sense, nucleus parties are also pivots. Our use applies to parties that are unlikely to lead a government, to supply the prime minister. The pivot image works best for a party of the center, potentially available for coalition with either nucleus party; here pivotal conveys the sense of an axis. But it also works for a party ideologically more extreme than its relevant nucleus; here pivotal conveys the sense of a hinge. Awkwardly, NZF was initially a potential nucleus but ultimately only a pivot.

14. All along, the most frequently cited issues, in descending order, were health care, education, and the economy. The percentage unable to name a party as closest on the most important issue dropped in step with the rise in the percentage naming Labour. It was not, then, that Labour took a space on which all party positions were known and fixed and shifted salience weights to its advantage. Rather, Labour clarified its own position in a space whose axes all along bore the same relationship to each other. For more detail, see Johnston 1998.

15. In addition to being dummy variables, the closeness measures are constructed from relative, rather than absolute, preference data.

16. Arguably the polls with only truly nationwide audience were the four Colmar-Brunton ones broadcast on TV One. In an alternative estimation we substituted the Comar-Brunton series for the all-poll series reported in table 4 and, reassuringly, extracted larger coefficients. We were anxious about a series with only four values, however, and so feel more comfortable reporting the coefficient on the more densely populated series.

17. As further grist for this mill, reevaluation of Clark and of her party's issue positions came primarily on the left, among voters for whom the new information was reinforcing (Johnston 1998).

18. Consistent with this discussion, we also estimated more complicated setups. One step was to include NZF and Alliance expectations, where Alliance expectations capture threshold concerns directly. Another step was to make the Labour (and possibly NZF) expectational terms curvilinear, such that the sign could reverse above some "comfort" level for strategic sequencing. These moves asked a lot

of our data and yielded no empirical gain. The NZF expectation is quite collinear with the Labour one, with unfortunate effects on standard errors. On the curvilinearity issue, our sense is that the overwhelming majority of respondents saw no relevant party near the threshold, much less below it, and never saw Labour as threatening to run away with the election, indeed always struggling to catch National. We capture some curvilinearity, however, simply by splitting analysis at the first debate.

19. Throughout the campaign, the cross-sectional impact of expectations was roughly constant, about 0.007 points. This can be calculated by adding the expectations coefficients. The whole-campaign, predebate, and postdebate sums are 0.007, 0.006, and 0.008, respectively.

REFERENCES

Bartolini, S., and P. Mair. 1990. *Identity, Competition and Electoral Availability: The Stabilisation of European Electorates, 1885–1985.* Cambridge: Cambridge University Press.

Blais, A., and L. Massicotte. 1996. "Electoral Systems." In *Comparing Democracies: Elections and Voting in Global Perspective,* ed. L. LeDuc et al. Thousand Oaks, CA: Sage.

Cox, G. W. 1997. *Making Votes Count: Strategic Coordination in the World's Electoral Systems.* Cambridge: Cambridge University Press.

Edwards, W. 1982. "Conservatism in Human Information Processing." In *Judgment under Uncertainty: Heuristics and Biases,* ed. D. Kahneman, P. Slovic, and A. Tversky. Cambridge: Cambridge University Press.

Felsenthal, D. S., and A. Brichta. 1985. "Sincere and Strategic Voters: An Israeli Study." *Political Behavior* 7:311–23.

Fey, M. 1997. "Stability and Coordination in Duverger's Law: A Formal Model of Preelection Polls and Strategic Voting." *American Political Science Review* 91: 135–47.

Forsythe, R., R. Myerson, T. A. Rietz, and R. Weber. 1993. "An Experiment on Coordination in Multi-Candidate Elections: The Importance of Polls and Election Histories." *Social Choice and Welfare* 10:223–47.

Johnston, R. 1998. "Issues, Leaders, and the Campaign." In *Voters' Victory? New Zealand's First Election under Proportional Representation,* ed. J. Vowles, P. Aimer, S. Banducci, and J. Karp. Auckland: Auckland University Press.

Johnston, R., A. Blais, H. E. Brady, and J. Crête. 1992. *Letting the People Decide: Dynamics of a Canadian Election.* Montreal: McGill-Queens University Press.

Johnston, R., and H. E. Brady. 2002. "The Rolling Cross-Section Design." *Electoral Studies* 21:283–95.

Laver, M., and N. Schofield. 1991. *Multiparty Government: The Politics of Coalition in Europe.* Oxford: Oxford University Press.

Leys, C. 1959. "Models, Theories and the Theory of Political Parties." *Political Studies* 7:127–46.

Lijphart, A. 1984. *Democracies: Patterns of Majoritarian and Consensus Government in Twenty-One Countries.* New Haven: Yale University Press.

Mair, P. 1996. "Party Systems and Structures of Competition." In *Comparing Democracies: Elections and Voting in Global Perspective,* ed. L. LeDuc et al. Thousand Oaks, CA: Sage.

Palfrey, T. R. 1989. "A Mathematical Proof of Duverger's Law." In *Models of Strategic Choice in Politics*, ed. Peter C. Ordeshook, 69–92. Ann Arbor: University of Michigan Press.

Sartori, G. 1968. "Political Development and Political Engineering." In *Public Policy*, ed. John D. Montgomery and Albert O. Hirschman. Cambridge: Cambridge University Press.

Vowles, J. 1994. "Dealignment and Demobilization: Nonvoting in New Zealand 1938–1990." *Australian Journal of Political Science* 28:96–114.

———. 1997a. "Waiting for the Realignment? The New Zealand Party System 1972–1993." *Political Science* 48:184–209.

———. 1997b. "Voters and Elections." In *New Zealand Politics in Transition*, ed. R. Miller, 199–211. Auckland: Oxford University Press.

V The Role of the Mass Media

Studying Statewide Political Campaigns

R. Michael Alvarez and Alexandra Shankster

THERE IS LITTLE IN THE ACADEMIC literature about the dynamics of campaign advertising strategies and their effects on candidate electoral success. While there have been theoretical and empirical studies of campaign strategy (Ferejohn and Noll 1978; Skarpedas and Grofman 1995; Glazer 1990) and scattered treatments of candidate advertising strategies (Roddy and Garramone 1988; Merritt 1984), our lack of understanding of the dynamics of advertising strategies has led some to wonder how much "campaigns matter" (Finkel 1993).

The difficulty in examining campaign dynamics stems from the lack of consistent data on candidate advertisements (West 1993). What little is known about campaign advertisements comes from selective sampling of television advertisements from presidential campaigns (West 1993) or from experimental studies (Ansolabehere et al. 1994; Ansolabehere and Iyengar 1995; Garramone 1985; Garramone et al. 1990). Presidential campaigns, however, have several characteristics that make them ill-suited for studying the effects of advertising strategies. As Lau and Pomper note, presidential campaigns feature the most prominent political figures, who are less likely to be "redefined" by an opponent's attack advertisement. Further, presidential candidates enjoy much more media exposure than do Senate or gubernatorial candidates (Lau and Pomper 2002). Most important, there is little variation in advertising strategies and the intensity of advertising across presidential campaigns. Finally, there is a very limited sample of presidential elections.

In this essay, we concentrate our analysis on two statewide races held in California. There recently has been some interest in studying statewide campaigns, largely because they do provide an important new resource for studying political campaigns (Lau and Pomper 2002; Dalager 1996; Freedman and Goldstein 1999; Sellers 1998; West 1993). In campaigns for offices such as state governor, U.S. Senate, and other statewide seats, there exists a great variety of campaigns and advertising strategies. The intensity of statewide races varies enormously, both within states and over time. By studying the advertising strategies of statewide campaigns, the quasi-experimental setting produces a natural experiment in which we may, in effect, study both dosage and treatment effects of campaign advertising.

In this essay we analyze data collected during the final eight weeks of two statewide campaigns in California during 1994: the races for governor and Senate. The campaigns were hard fought in that year and provide an interesting laboratory in which to study intense campaigns over time and to compare the advertising strategies between races. We first begin by presenting data from the television advertisements from these two races. This database of television advertisements from the last eight weeks of these races provides a unique opportunity to examine the strategies used in each campaign as candidates tried to get their messages through to the same voters. Next, we turn to the politically relevant questions: Did these advertisements matter? Did the messages the candidates sent through their television advertisements influence the electorate? To answer these questions, we use two sets of polling data from this election to see whether these television advertisements effectively communicated the messages of each candidate to the intended audience. We conclude with ways to improve the analysis of political campaigns by concentrating on suggestions for studying voter response to multiple campaign stimuli in one election year.

Data and Methods

We draw upon two sources of data in this essay. Both are taken from an intensive analysis of campaign television advertising. The first set contains advertisements from the 1994 California Senate race and the second, from the 1994 California governor's race. During the final eight weeks of the 1994 general election campaign, we videotaped prime-time television (6:00 p.m.–midnight) from the two most highly rated television channels in Los Angeles—KABC and KNBC. From these tapes, we obtained a day-by-day time-series of all television advertisements aired during this period by the four major party candidates for these offices: Pete Wilson and Kathleen Brown in the governor's race and Dianne Feinstein and Michael Huffington in the Senate race.[1]

In total, there were 682 advertisements aired during these weeks on these two stations, 340 from KABC and 342 from KNBC. This database is organized by individual advertisements, as we know both the day and the evening program during which each advertisement was aired. In total, 177 advertisements were aired by Wilson, 77 by Brown, 212 by Huffington, and 216 by Feinstein.

Importantly, candidate advertising is a method whereby a candidate tries to convey his or her message to an audience. Because a contested political campaign necessarily involves two or more candidates, an advertisement always focuses on one of the following: the candidate sponsoring the advertisement, the sponsoring candidate's opponent, or both the sponsoring candidate and the opponent in a comparative advertisement. As we shall show, the nature of the advertisement's focus often determines the tone: positive, negative, or a contrast of the candidates.[2] Thus, each advertisement in this database was analyzed by content to determine the sponsoring candidate, the tone (positive, attack, or contrast), the focus (whether it was primarily focused on the sponsoring candidate, the opponent, or a comparative advertisement), and the general theme of the advertisement (policy issues, personality and background, or policy record).[3]

This coding scheme provides an excellent analytical tool with which to understand the motivations of the candidates during their campaigns. In particular, by studying the tone and focus of television advertisements, we can better understand the strategies candidates use at different points in their campaigns. Positive statements about oneself are used by a candidate to sell his or her candidacy to an uncertain or skeptical electorate. Attack advertisements focus on the mistakes of one's opponent and can induce uncertainty or reduce the electorate's affect for the opponent. Comparative advertisements, designed to draw contrasts between the candidate and the opponent, are used to accomplish the goals of both positive and attack advertisements simultaneously.

Furthermore, as we shall see subsequently, there are repeatedly observed dynamics involved in candidate advertising. Candidates generally start the campaign using positive strategies, especially when they are introducing themselves to an uncertain or skeptical electorate. Positive advertisements help develop positive effect and rapport between the electorate and the candidate, help the candidate in building his or her electorate base, and, finally, help attract swing voters. Negative advertisements, on the other hand, tend to be used later in the campaign. These advertisements can have unpredictable consequences, as candidates who are perceived to have crossed some threshold of negativity in the attack may suffer a backlash. Therefore, negative advertisements are used when the potential of backlash can be minimized, generally late in the race and quite often only when a candidate is falling behind in the polls. Comparative advertisements, which combine aspects of positive and attack strategies, are used throughout the race.

To match the campaign strategies determined using this database with voter responses, we use polling data from this election to probe the two ways in which television advertisements might influence voters. First, they may influence the weights that voters place on various issues. We use an exit poll conducted by the *Los Angeles Times* to examine how voters weighted issues in their voting behavior in this election. While this exit poll covered the entire state on Election Day, it contained a large oversampling of voters in the Los Angeles area. One important note of caution, however, in interpreting our results is the absence of any data on the viewing habits of respondents. As noted in a study by Freedman and Goldstein, exposure to any particular campaign advertisement is a function of both the frequency with which the advertisement was aired and the amount of television watched by the respondent (Freedman and Goldstein 1999). Ideally, we would have access to the latter and be able to incorporate it into our analysis. However, as this data was not available at that time, we instead estimate our results using only the frequency with which an advertisement was aired. We believe this is partially justified, as, regardless of who actually viewed the advertisement, candidates employed specific campaign strategies, acting *as if* voters were watching them.

Further, in their study, Freedman and Goldstein used the Polaris Ad Detector, a tracking system that monitors political activity throughout the year. They found that, during the 1997 Virginia gubernatorial election, candidates were most likely to air advertisements during the daytime and early evening hours, concentrating most heavily on the half hour leading up to prime-time television (Freedman and Goldstein 1999). Therefore, we feel our analysis is likely to accurately capture the campaign tactics employed by candidates, because, as noted earlier, we analyzed advertisements aired between 6:00 p.m. and midnight.

Second, advertisements may influence voter evaluations of candidates over the course of the campaign season. We use three Field Polls from the general election campaign in 1994. These are telephone polls conducted statewide in July, September, and October 1994. As they are statewide samples, they provide an opportunity to examine the ways in which voters evaluated the candidates throughout the 1994 general election in California. Further, we may use these polls to determine whether changes in candidate evaluations correspond to changes in the media strategies of the candidates.

The Advertising Strategies in the 1994 Campaign

Cumulative Results

We begin by examining the general tone of candidate television advertisements in this election—whether the advertisements were primarily positive or negative or contrasted the candidates. We define a positive advertisement as one in which a candidate mentions factual information in a nonderogatory manner. Positive television advertisements, then, are primarily by one candidate about his or her own issue position, record, or personal background. We used the Surlin and Gordon (1977) operationalization of negative advertisements: a negative advertisement attacks the opponent's personality, policy platform, or party. To define contrast advertisements, we used Merritt's (1984) operationalization. Here, comparative advertisements highlight differences between candidates in order to highlight the superior qualities of the sponsor; these differ from negative advertisements that highlight the inferiority of the opponent.

Table 1 summarizes the relative frequencies of advertisement focus for each candidate (the gubernatorial candidates are in the left panels; the Senate candidates are in the right panels). These results provide mixed support for the common wisdom about the strategic interaction between incumbents and challengers. Jacobson (1992) summarizes the common types of advertising strategies for challengers as attempts "to convince people of their own virtues—at a minimum, that they are qualified for the office— but they are not likely to get far without directly undermining support for the incumbent" (87). Incumbents, however, are commonly believed to ignore opponents when they feel safe but may strike preemptively at the challenger if feeling vulnerable (96).

It is apparent that the focus strategies within each race are quite similar. In contrast, the focus strategies across races are quite distinct. It is possible that the vast difference observed in patterns is candidate driven or context specific. Feinstein went negative early in the race; Huffington then tried to protect himself by retaliating in kind. This tit-for-tat advertising strategy grew quite ugly, and by the end of the campaign, both candidates were primarily airing attack advertisement after attack advertisement.

In contrast, the gubernatorial campaign followed a more typical pattern. Wilson, the incumbent, aired more advertisements than did Brown (Wilson aired 177 advertisements during this period while Brown aired 77); however, both Brown and Wilson aired more positive than negative advertisements, thus conducting mainly positive campaigns (61 percent of Wilson's 177 advertisements and 68 percent of Brown's 77 advertisements were coded as positive in tone). For Brown, this might have been a suboptimal strategy, as the literature repeatedly finds that positive advertisements are less effective than negative advertisements. According to Guskind and Hangstrom (1988), it takes between five and ten viewings of a positive advertisement before the information sinks in. In contrast, it only takes one to two viewings of a negative advertisement for the message to have an impact on viewers.

Again, the Senate race differed greatly from the gubernatorial race.

TABLE 1. Candidates, Advertisement Type, and Content

	Wilson	Brown	Feinstein	Huffington
Advertisement type				
Positive	108 (61)	52 (68)	6 (3)	24 (11)
Attack	63 (36)	23 (30)	158 (73)	108 (51)
Contrast	6 (3)	2 (2)	52 (24)	80 (38)
Advertisement content				
Issue	128 (72)	52 (68)	0 (0)	28 (13)
Personal	7 (4)	0 (0)	206 (95)	28 (13)
Record	42 (24)	25 (32)	10 (5)	156 (74)
Issues				
Taxes	13 (7)	0 (0)	0 (0)	15 (10)
Education	0 (0)	14 (18)	0 (0)	0 (0)
Crime	56 (32)	0 (0)	6 (3)	28 (19)
Immigration	66 (37)	0 (0)	0 (0)	19 (13)
Ethics	0 (0)	0 (0)	39 (18)	89 (59)
Morality	0 (0)	0 (0)	171 (79)	0 (0)
Budget	0 (0)	23 (30)	0 (0)	0 (0)
Economy	42 (24)	40 (52)	0 (0)	0 (0)

Note: Entries are the number of advertisements in each category, followed by the percentage of each type for the specific candidate.

Michael Huffington, the Republican challenger, aired attack advertisements about his opponent and comparative advertisements with almost equal frequency. He aired relatively few positive advertisements about himself. Dianne Feinstein, the Democratic incumbent, focused her advertisements almost exclusively on attacking Huffington.

In contrast to Jacobson's findings, Wilson and Brown aired advertisement types in roughly equal proportions. Wilson, in airing mainly positive advertisements, followed the strategy normally associated with strong, secure incumbents. What makes this strategy an odd choice is that Wilson should have been anything but secure about his reelection prospects—sixteen months before the general election, he was losing by at least 20 percent in many polls! As late as July 1994, Wilson was in a statistical dead heat with Brown (38.5 percent for Wilson, 42.7 percent for Brown, in the July 1994 Field Poll). That the race was this close in the middle of the summer, moreover, should have led Brown to attempt to undermine support for Wilson through negative advertising. However, Brown seems to have tried to win the race through primarily positive advertising, in the face of conventional wisdom.

Feinstein, the other incumbent, should have felt more secure, as she had a slight lead over Huffington before the general election heated up (44.4 percent for Feinstein, 39.0 percent for Huffington). But in an environment characterized by uncertainty, Feinstein seems to have taken the risk averse strategy, mainly airing attack advertisements about her opponent. Furthermore, the challengers in both races seem to have followed the common wisdom outlined by Jacobson (1992); Wilson predominately attacked Brown, while Huffington used both attack and comparative advertisements in roughly equal proportions.

However, it is critical that we understand the content of these advertisements to better examine candidate advertising strategies. Table 1 also presents the breakdown of advertisement content into three general categories—whether the advertisement was primarily issue based, personality based, or record based—for each candidate. Both Wilson and Brown (left panels of table 1) focused heavily on issues in this race. Brown, however, sought to focus attention on both Wilson's record as governor and her own record as state treasurer. However, while the data in table 1 indicate that issues were a primary focus of advertising by these two candidates, it is not clear how informative these issue advertisements were.

During the Senate race, Huffington targeted Feinstein's record as incumbent senator, focusing mainly on her actions in office. There was a small amount of advertising by Huffington, however, focusing on both issues and personalities. But Feinstein's advertising strategy stands in clear contrast to Huffington's—she poured almost all of her advertising into attacks about Huffington's personal background.

Next, we examined the specific issues raised by the candidates in their advertising. We categorized all advertisements as having up to four specific themes. We then coded eight individual issues—taxes, education, crime, immigration, personal ethics, personal morality, state budget, and state economy. We present the frequencies of issue mention across the four campaigns at the bottom of table 1.

The governor's race focused on salient statewide issues. Wilson campaigned on the issues of illegal immigration, the state economy, crime, and taxes, while Brown focused most of her issue discussion on the state budget and economy. Wilson employed what the literature calls a "resonance strategy" (Johnson-Cartee and Copeland 1991; Combs 1979). This involves a series of persuasive messages that are "harmonious" with the experiences of the audience. In other words, political consultants search for hot buttons that they can exploit in the campaign (Combs 1979). In 1994, the major hot buttons were illegal immigration and crime, evidenced by the overwhelming passage of the controversial initiative Proposition 187.

The Senate race, however, was much more personal in nature than the governor's race. Huffington spent most of his television advertisement time discussing Feinstein's personal ethics. To a much lesser degree, he brought forward the more substantive issues of crime, illegal immigration, and taxes. Feinstein's strategy was quite clear: She devoted an overwhelming proportion of her advertising time on Huffington's personal morality and ethics. The more substantive issues received little attention in Feinstein's television advertisements.

These tables produce a revealing portrait of the candidate strategies in the 1994 California elections. A composite sketch of the cumulative evidence for each campaign's strategy shows the following:

> Wilson aired mostly positive television advertisements, focusing on his own positions on issues. The issues he discussed most generally were illegal immigration, the state economy, crime, and the state budget. When Wilson went negative, it was strategically successful. Brown ran attack advertisements, which did not focus on salient issues. She also ran advertisements personally attacking Wilson,

which, according to the literature, does win the favor of the electorate. She focused on the state economy and budget in her advertisements.

Feinstein relied almost exclusively on attack advertisements aimed at Huffington's personal morality and ethics.

Huffington ran mainly attack advertisements against Feinstein; however, he also aired some comparative advertisements. In general, Huffington focused mainly on Feinstein's personal ethics, but he also discussed crime, illegal immigration, and taxes.

By examining the cumulative evidence on the content and type of television advertisements used by each candidate in this race, a composite sketch of each candidate's advertisement strategy can easily be drawn.

In conclusion, the dramatic differences we observe in candidate strategies by these four different statewide campaigns lead to an important point: Despite the fact that each of these candidates was campaigning within exactly the same constituency, it is clear that each candidate believed different issues needed to be emphasized. This is true even when we look at the issue focused within each race, especially Wilson's and Brown's. While there might be many explanations for these dramatic differences in campaign issue focus, it is important to note that the candidates were issuing different appeals to the same electorate.

The key question, then, is, Did the voters receive these messages? That is, did the candidates' issue strategies connect with the electorate in ways the candidates intended? Did voters realize that the candidates emphasized different issues from each other? We return to these points later.

Dynamic Results

The analysis thus far has ignored the dynamic nature of our database of candidate television advertisements, which allows for an examination of the changing composition of each candidate's television advertisement strategy over the last eight weeks of the 1994 general election. In table 2 we give the weekly frequency of advertisements by the four campaigns. For the two gubernatorial candidates, Wilson maintained a consistent level of advertising throughout the last two months of the election. While Brown employed a similar strategy, surprisingly for a challenger, she aired few advertisements in the final, critical days of the election.

The Senate race stands in sharp contrast. There, Huffington was on the air consistently throughout the general election race, with an increase in advertising frequency in the last weeks of the election. Feinstein was not on the air in Los Angeles for the first week of the sample but advertised heavily in the last week of the race.

In addition to examining the frequency of advertisements, we may also observe *when* the candidates "went negative" and at what points in the campaign they were airing advertisements that were issue or personality based. In tables 3 and 4 we examine the weekly proportions of advertisements in each campaign by type (attack or positive in table 3) and by content (issue, personality, or record in table 4).

In table 3 we uncover more details about the advertising strategies of the candidates in this election year. In the first three weeks of this critical period of the election year, Wilson's advertisements were overwhelm-

TABLE 2. Candidate Advertising Share

Candidate	Campaign Week							
	1	2	3	4	5	6	7	8
Wilson	12	11	9	11	11	8	13	24
Brown	13	13	5	16	18	12	18	5
Huffington	6	8	8	8	17	13	16	24
Feinstein	0	1	14	16	13	13	15	28

Note: Entries are the percentage of advertisements aired by each candidate, in the respective week, of all advertisements aired by the candidate.

TABLE 3. Candidate Advertising Type

Candidate	Campaign Week							
	1	2	3	4	5	6	7	8
Wilson								
Positive	100	75	63	5	60	67	57	60
Attack	0	25	37	95	40	33	43	26
Brown								
Positive	100	70	0	0	93	100	93	0
Attack	0	30	100	100	7	0	0	75
Huffington								
Positive	0	6	100	33	0	0	0	0
Attack	0	0	0	67	64	57	58	74
Feinstein								
Positive	0	0	0	0	0	0	6	7
Attack	0	100	100	100	100	96	36	40

Note: Entries are the percentage of positive or attack advertisements aired each week by the candidate. Numbers do not sum to 100 due to the omission from this table of contrast advertisements.

ingly positive. But in the fourth week Wilson "went negative." Wilson's strategy shifts again in the next week, when his advertisements again become positive heading into Election Day.

Brown's strategy was quite different from Wilson's. In the first two weeks Brown aired positive advertisements more frequently than negative ones. In the third and fourth weeks Brown's strategy turned totally negative. This strategy dramatically shifts in the fifth week of the general election campaign, when Brown aired mainly positive advertisements for the next three weeks. Only in the last week did she return to negative advertisements.

The Senate race shows the use of different strategies in the types of messages communicated by the candidates in their television advertisement strategies. Huffington aired, almost exclusively, comparative advertisements in the first two weeks and then turned to positive advertisements in the third week. In the fourth week, Huffington "went negative," and his drumbeat of negative messages continued throughout the end of the race.

Feinstein "went negative" earlier than did Huffington. Recall from table 2 that Feinstein aired few television advertisements in the first two weeks of this race—the few she aired in the second week were negative. All of her advertisements contained negative attack messages in the third

TABLE 4. Candidate Advertising Content

Candidate	Campaign Week							
	1	2	3	4	5	6	7	8
Wilson								
Issue	5	45	69	100	100	100	83	79
Person	0	0	0	0	0	0	17	7
Record	95	55	31	0	0	0	0	14
Brown								
Issue	100	70	0	0	92	100	93	0
Person	0	0	0	0	0	0	0	0
Record	0	30	100	100	7	0	7	100
Huffington								
Issue	46	56	0	0	0	0	0	26
Person	0	6	35	17	0	0	0	36
Record	54	38	65	83	100	100	100	38
Feinstein								
Issue	0	0	0	0	0	0	0	0
Person	0	100	100	100	100	100	94	87
Record	0	0	0	0	0	0	6	13

Note: Entries are the percentage of issue, person, or record advertisements aired by each candidate during the respective weeks.

through fifth weeks of this time period. In the seventh and eighth weeks, however, Feinstein reduced the frequency of her negative advertisements and used a slightly higher frequency of comparative advertisements.

What seems to be happening in these races? The amount of heterogeneity across candidates, races, and time makes this a complicated set of campaigns to examine. However, some general patterns stand out. In the governor's race, Wilson began with positive advertisements, as we might expect from an incumbent who is ignoring his opponent. But when Brown "went negative" in the third and fourth weeks, Wilson responded with his own series of negative advertisements. While Brown returned to negative attacks at the end of the campaign, Wilson resumed his positive messages at the end—and easily won the election.

Table 4 breaks down the content of the candidate advertisements by week of the campaign. Again, Wilson's advertisements were primarily focused on his issue positions and his record, so there were few advertisements attacking Brown's record and personal background. Early in this campaign period, Wilson talked about Brown's record; but for most of this time Wilson stressed issues. Brown also discussed mainly issues and Wilson's record. Early in the race (the first two weeks) Brown talked mainly about issues in her television advertisements. She then moved mainly to a discussion of Wilson's record. Then she shifted back to issues, and, finally, in the last week of the race she aired record-oriented advertisements.

In the Senate race, Huffington focused his early comparison-based advertising strategy on emphasizing the distinction between his and Feinstein's records in office and issue emphases. Then, Huffington began to attack, and these attacks were predominately aimed at Feinstein's record as an incumbent. In the last week, though, Huffington mixed his message considerably by airing advertisements about issues, personalities, and the record, all in roughly equal proportions. Feinstein's message content was clear—she attacked Huffington's personal background almost exclusively. In the final weeks, her use of contrast advertisements contained some mention of their respective records but was primarily focused on personal backgrounds.

Strategy, Advertisements, and Voter Response

The primary question still remains to be answered: Did the various advertising strategies used by the candidates during these campaigns influence the electorate? In other words, were these advertising strategies effective?

For television advertisements about a particular issue to "matter" in an election campaign, a number of initial conditions must be satisfied. First, there must be voters in the electorate who feel that this issue is important or salient. Second, one or both of the candidates must have taken a position on the issue that is perceived with some degree of clarity by the electorate. Third, voters must receive the message about the issue.

Once these conditions are met, there are two distinct ways in which advertisements about an issue might influence voter decision making. The first is that these advertisements might influence the criteria upon which voters evaluate the candidates. For example, the fact that Brown attacked Wilson's record as incumbent governor might have influenced the way in which voters evaluated Wilson—voters might have focused on Wilson's record in office as an important factor in determining whether to vote for him rather than on the issues that Wilson raised in his advertisements. The second is that the advertisement strategies might influence the evaluations of the candidates directly, and, hence, the advertisements might persuade voters to change their preferences from one candidate to another. For example, Feinstein's predominately negative attack advertisements against Huffington might have led voters to evaluate Huffington more negatively and to then vote against him on Election Day.

Advertisements and Voter Decisions

Recall from the previous section that candidates tailored their messages to the electorate quite differently. Wilson and Brown stuck largely to issues, while Huffington and Feinstein focused on personal factors. This leads us to expect, first, that *issues of crime, illegal immigration, taxes, and the state economy ought to be more important to voters in their evaluations of the gubernatorial candidates, while personal ethics and morality ought to play a greater role in voter evaluations of the Senate candidates.* This expectation is a direct consequence of the patterns observed in table 1. There we showed that Wilson and Brown discussed crime, illegal immigration, taxes, and the state economy in their television advertisements, while Feinstein and Huffington discussed almost solely personal issues. Second, we expect that voters who are *more exposed to television advertisements ought to be more likely to use the information stressed in the advertisements of the candidates in their decisions.* Third, we predict that *since issues were discussed to a much greater extent in the gubernatorial race than in the Senate race, we should find that issues "matter more" in governor voting than in Senate voting.*

In table 5 we give the percentages of Los Angeles–area voters for each candidate who mentioned one of eight possible issues as important in their voting decisions: taxes, education, crime, immigration, ethics, morality, the state budget, or the economy and jobs.[4] In table 5 the percentages are given first, followed by the number of voters in the sample mentioning the issue as important.[5]

Immigration was an overwhelmingly important issue for Los Angeles–area voters in 1994. From 30 to 45 percent of the supporters of each candidate mentioned immigration as an important issue in their decision making. The variance that exists in these percentages is largely partisan, with 30 to 35 percent of Brown and Feinstein supporters interested primarily in immigration. In contrast, roughly 45 percent of Wilson and Huffington supporters were concerned with immigration.

Closer examination of the other issues shows that the supporters of different candidates in each race did not appear to benefit much from differential issue appeals. In the governor's race, supporters of Brown and Wilson both placed immigration and crime as the top two issues in their voting decisions. Brown's supporters saw education as the third most important

TABLE 5. Important Issues among Southern California Voters

	Voters Supporting			
	Brown	Wilson	Feinstein	Huffington
Taxes	2.6	4.2	2.3	4.4
	(30)	(72)	(30)	(62)
Education	14.1	7.1	12.1	7.6
	(161)	(123)	(159)	(107)
Crime	17.5	16.9	18.4	15.6
	(201)	(292)	(241)	(219)
Immigration	32.4	44.7	35.4	44.6
	(371)	(771)	(465)	(625)
Ethics	12.7	7.6	11.7	7.2
	(145)	(131)	(154)	(101)
Morality	5.6	9.0	5.1	10.4
	(64)	(155)	(67)	(146)
State budget	3.3	2.8	3.3	2.6
	(38)	(49)	(43)	(37)
Economy, jobs	11.9	7.7	11.7	7.4
	(136)	(133)	(154)	(103)
Total sample	1,146	1,726	1,313	1,400

Note: Data from the 1994 *Los Angeles Times* Exit Poll, Southern California voters. Entries give the percentage of voters for each candidate who said the particular issue was of importance to them, followed by the number of respondents in parentheses.

issue, closely followed by personal ethics and the economy. Wilson's supporters, though, saw four issues in a rough tie for third place in importance: education, ethics, morality, and the economy. Notice also that more Brown supporters saw crime as an important issue than Wilson supporters, and Wilson tapped the crime hot button, whereas Brown did not.

A similar pattern holds in the Senate race. Again, immigration and crime are the two most important issues for both Feinstein and Huffington supporters. Feinstein's supporters show the same issue ordering as Brown's (education followed by ethics and the economy). Huffington's supporters have the same issue rankings as Wilson: morality, education, the economy, and ethics in a four-way tie).

While interesting, the simple results in table 5 give only the bivariate relationships between issue preferences and candidate support. To examine the multivariate impact of issue preferences on candidate choice, we estimated three bivariate probit models. In each set of bivariate probit models, one dependent variable is coded 1 for a Republican vote and 0 for a Democratic vote in the gubernatorial race. The second dependent variable is coded likewise for the Senate race. We use bivariate probit in this case, as there is strong reason to believe that a voter's choice in one race might impact his or her choice in the other race and that this mutual dependence of voter choice might be motivated by the information he or she receives from the candidate's advertisement strategies. The bivariate probit model controls for this type of mutual dependence by estimating the correlation between the error term of each vote choice model, and it will allow us to examine the joint impact of issue importance on voting in each race simultaneously.

We include seven dummy variables for issue preferences in each bivariate probit model, with each being coded 1 if the voter said that a particular issue was important to them and 0 otherwise (the economy and jobs is the excluded category, so all the coefficients we estimate for issue preferences in our probit models are interpreted as the effect of mentioning the particular issue *relative* to mentioning the economy and jobs as an important issue). As control variables, we include dummy variables for gender (1 for women, 0 for men) and minority status (1 for ethnic minorities, 0 for non–ethnic minorities). There also are controls for pocketbook voting, party identification, and ideology (personal finances is coded with the high category representing voters who felt they were better off, the middle category the same, and the lower category worse off; partisanship with Democratic identification is coded with the low category, independence the middle, and Republican identification the high category; ideology is coded as liberals with the low category and conservatives the high category, with moderates in the middle category).

To examine how the different issues impacted voter decision making, we estimate three different bivariate probit models. All of the estimation results are presented in table 6. The first two columns of table 6 give the bivariate probit results for the full sample of Southern California voters, with one column presenting estimation results for gubernatorial voting and the other, Senate voting. The next four columns of table 6 provide two

TABLE 6. Probit Estimates

Independent Variables	All SC Voters		High Education		Low Education	
	Governor	Senate	Governor	Senate	Governor	Senate
Constant	−2.8*	−2.9*	−2.8*	−3.1*	−2.8*	−2.6*
	.16	.16	.21	.21	.26	.24
Taxes	.38*	.36*	.36*	.44*	.39*	.23*
	.08	.08	.11	.11	.13	.12
Education	−.32*	−.05	−.44*	−.06	−.11	−.04
	.09	.09	.11	.12	.14	.14
Crime	.28*	.02	.34*	.06	.19*	−.09
	.07	.07	.10	.09	.11	.10
Immigration	.42*	.35*	.36*	.44*	.52*	.20*
	.07	.07	.10	.10	.12	.11
Ethics	.06	.06	.13	.23*	−.02	−.14
	.11	.11	.14	.14	.18	.18
Morality	.39*	.51*	.56*	.65*	.23	.35*
	.14	.14	.19	.18	.23	.22
State budget	.06	.08	−.17	−.18	.39*	.43*
	.18	.18	.24	.24	.28	.28
Gender	.08	−.08	.05	−.09	.10	−.11
	.07	.06	.09	.09	.10	.01
Minority	−.58*	−.26*	−.28*	−.31*	−.93*	−.34*
	.09	.09	.13	.15	.13	.13
Personal Finances	−.05	−.14*	−.10*	−.12*	.05	−.14*
	.04	.04	.06	.05	.07	.07
Party ID	.89*	.89*	.94*	.88*	.86*	.91*
	.04	.04	.06	.06	.06	.06
Ideology	.51*	.50*	.51*	.53*	.51*	.49*
	.05	.05	.07	.07	.08	.08
ρ	.68*		.71*		.64*	
	.03		.04		.05	
Sample	2,581		1,437		1,123	
Log-likelihood ratio	−1,803.6		−971.0		−787.5	

Note: Entries are bivariate probit estimates from the 1994 Los Angeles Times Exit Poll.
*Statistically significant at the $p = .05$ level, one-tailed tests

reestimations of this full bivariate probit model, first for high education voters and then for low education voters. These latter two sets of bivariate probit results examine how media awareness influences the impact of candidate issue advertisements on voter decision making.[6]

In the full sample of Southern California voters, the coefficient estimates of primary interest are those for the issue preference variables. It is important to note that a number of these variables have statistically significant estimates. In the governor's race, taxes, education, crime, immigration, and morality all have statistically significant effects. The positive signs on these four parameters indicate that voters who thought that taxes, crime, immigration, or morality were important issues were significantly more likely to vote for Wilson, while voters who prioritized education were more likely to vote for Brown. Next, in the third column of table 6 are the results for Senate voting. Here, only three issue priorities have statistically significant effects on voting: taxes, immigration, and morality.

Do the results in table 3 demonstrate that candidate television advertisements had an impact on candidate choice? Perhaps. Recall table 1, where we gave the relative frequencies of candidate television advertisements on these same issues. We found that in the governor's race the candidates advertised mainly on crime, immigration, education, and the economy. In table 6 we present results that indicate that all of these issues were important to voters in this race. Furthermore, by stressing immigration, crime, and the economy, Wilson increased his support. Brown, on the other hand, obtained support for her emphasis on education.

In contrast, the candidates in the Senate race advertised much more frequently on issues of personal ethics and morality; they also advertised, but to a much lesser extent, about crime and immigration. Again, the Senate results in table 6 show that immigration appears to have been an important determinant of Senate voting. Also, morality was a strong influence on Senate voting.

The next issue we addressed was that of media awareness and its impact on voters' decisions. Ideally, we would use responses to questions directly measuring the voters' media exposure or campaign interest.[7] However, as the *Los Angeles Times* Exit Poll did not include questions of this sort, we instead used information gathered on the education level of the voters as a proxy for media exposure (Alvarez 1997). Thus, we stratified the sample into low and high education groups, with the basic criterion of classification being whether the voter had completed a college education. We estimated the bivariate probit models separately for each of the two groups, and the results are presented in the last four columns of table 6.

In table 6 four issues—taxes, crime, immigration, and the state budget—are statistically significant in gubernatorial voting for low education respondents. Of these, immigration seems to have the strongest influence on the likelihood of voting for Wilson, with taxes and crime well behind in estimated impact. But the high education voters, who we assume are more exposed to campaign advertisements, used more issue information in their voting: taxes, education, crime, immigration, and morality all are statistically significant predictors of their gubernatorial votes. For the high education voters, morality and education seem to have the strongest effects, with crime, taxes, and immigration slightly behind. The main difference between high and low education voters, then, lies in the emphasis that high education voters placed on education and morality and that low education voters placed on immigration. Since one of these issues (education) was emphasized in Brown's television advertisements, we conclude that exposure to television advertisements appears to enhance the importance of the issues stressed in the campaign in voter decisions.

The same analysis is repeated for Senate voting in table 6. Taxes, immigration, morality, and the state budget were again the important issues to low education Senate voters. But for high education Senate voters, who we argue are more exposed to candidate television advertisements, taxes, immigration, ethics, and morality are statistically significant. Thus, as in the gubernatorial race, candidate television advertisements reached more exposed individuals. Notice that there are two differences between high and low education Senate voters: for high education voters both ethics and morality were important components of their decisions and the state budget was not. Given the intense focus in the Senate race on both ethics and morality, and the understandable lack of focus on the state budgetary outlook, we conclude that more exposed voters may have been affected by the advertisements in the Senate race.

Another way to examine the impact of these different issues on voter choice and to see the degree of influence by candidate advertising focus is to use the bivariate probit results to make specific predictions about voter decisions under different "counterfactual" conditions. Using the bivariate probit results in table 6, we produce predicted probabilities that a hypothetical modal voter would cast ballots for Wilson and Huffington (a straight Republican ticket), for Brown and Huffington (a divided ticket), for Wilson and Feinstein (another divided ticket), or for Brown and Feinsten (a straight Democratic ticket) (these are called the "baseline" probabilities).[8] We then produce another set of predicted probabilities under the condition that only one of the issues was important for the hypothetical voter (these are called the "counterfactual" probabilities). Last, we subtract the "counterfactual" from the "baseline" probabilities and present these values in table 7. There, the top panel gives these counterfactual probability predictions for the full sample of Southern California voters; the middle panel, the high education subsample; and the bottom panel, the low education subsample. An entry in this table, then, gives the change in probability of casting a particular pair of votes, if the hypothetical voter thought the issues were important.

In terms of issues leading this hypothetical voter to cast a straight-ticket Republican vote, it is clear that taxes, immigration, and morality

TABLE 7. Issue Effects

	Change in Probability of Voting			
	Wilson-Huffington	Brown-Huffington	Wilson-Feinstein	Brown-Feinstein
Southern California voter				
Taxes	14	0	1	−15
Education	−5	4	−7	8
Crime	4	−2	7	−8
Immigration	14	0	2	−16
Ethics	2	1	0	3
Morality	18	2	−3	−17
State budget	3	1	0	−3
High education Southern California voter				
Taxes	13	−4	3	−12
Education	−3	1	−1	3
Crime	2	−5	7	−3
Immigration	14	−6	6	−14
Ethics	−3	−3	3	3
Morality	12	1	−3	−11
State budget	17	−1	−2	−15
Low education Southern California voter				
Taxes	15	1	−1	−16
Education	−7	5	−10	12
Crime	4	−2	9	−11
Immigration	15	1	−1	−16
Ethics	7	2	−2	−7
Morality	24	1	−2	−23
State budget	−6	0	−1	7

Note: Entries are the difference in the "counterfactual" and "baseline" probabilities computed from the bivariate probit estimates.

were winning issues for Wilson and Huffington. As shown in the first column of table 7, the salience of these issues for this hypothetical Los Angeles voter would lead her to be fourteen (taxes), fourteen (immigration), or eighteen (morality) points more likely to vote for Wilson and Huffington on the basis of each issue alone. Returning to table 1, taxes and immigration were issues that were presented exclusively by Wilson and Huffington in their television advertising.

As for issues leading to a straight-ticket Democratic vote, it is clear by table 7 that only one issue worked for the Democrats—education. In the full sample results, if the hypothetical voter thought education was an important issue, she would be eight points more likely to vote for Brown and Feinstein. However, only Brown focused advertising on this issue.

For the Democrats, especially Dianne Feinstein, the issue of personal morality was clearly a loser. In the full sample results in the top panel of table 7, we see that, if the hypothetical voter thought this was an important issue, she would be seventeen points less likely to vote for Brown and Feinstein. This was the issue, though, that formed much of the basis for Feinstein's attack advertising against Huffington, and from our results, it does not appear that Feinstein was successful in gaining voter support through her attacks on Huffington's morality. Finally, there is one issue that seemed to lead this hypothetical voter to split her ticket: the issue of crime. In the full sample results, a voter who felt crime was an important issue was eight points less likely to cast a straight Democratic ticket but was seven points more likely to cast a vote for Pete Wilson and Dianne Feinstein. In table 1 we showed that crime formed much of the basis of Wilson's advertising, and it was one of the issues that both Huffington and Feinstein used in their advertising. The results in table 6 show that crime was an issue on which Pete Wilson and Dianne Feinstein were viewed as successful.

Our third expectation was that issues, in general, ought to have a greater impact in voting for governor than for Senator, since the governor's race generally was more issue focused than the Senate race (which was much more character oriented). We used the bivariate probit results from table 6 to test this hypothesis. We reestimated the same probit models, after excluding the issue variables in one of the vote choice equations. This produced a statistical test for the joint significance of issues in these voting models.[9] The relevant χ^2 statistics for testing the joint effects of issues in each model are presented in table 8.

In table 8 there is clear support for this expectation. First, notice that the χ^2 statistic for issue voting in the governor's race is much greater than the same χ^2 for issue voting in the Senate race. Further, the χ^2 statistics for issue voting in the governor's race in both the high and low education subsamples are much greater than in the Senate models. Both of these results provide strong support for the claim that with more issue discussion in the governor's race issues became more important to voters' decisions in that race. We also see in table 8 another important result: issues had the largest effect for highly educated voters in the governor's race. This verifies both our second and third expectations, since the voters most exposed to the media were the most reliant on issue voting in the race dominated by discussion of issues.[10]

Advertisements and Candidate Evaluations

In this section we explore the hypothesis that candidate television advertisements change the general opinions voters have about the candidates or persuade people to vote for one candidate over the other. To test this, we use survey data from a different source: the Field Polls conducted during the general election among California voters. We use the July 12–17, September 13–18, and October 21–30 Field Polls.[11]

These three Field Polls are useful since each poll asked registered voters two important types of questions. The first were the general "positive-negative" evaluations of each candidate. The second were trial heats in each race, in which voters were asked to state which candidate they would vote for were the election to be held on the day of the interview.

In table 9 we give the "positive-negative" evaluations of each candidate in these three Field Polls. We present the percentages giving each evaluative response, and we calculate the net change over the general election period in the last column. Recall that Wilson ran mostly positive advertisements about himself; the negative attack advertisements he ran were mainly about Brown's stand on issues, three to four weeks before the election.

TABLE 8. Tests for Issue Voting

Race	Full Sample	Low Education	High Education
Governor	92.1*	33.4*	62.1*
Senate	48.7*	12.8	45.1*

Note: Entries are χ^2 statistics testing for the importance of issue voting in the probit results. Each test has seven degrees of freedom, and statistically significant entries are denoted by *.

Brown, on the other hand, ran attack advertisements in the middle of the race, mainly using positive advertisements at the end of the campaign. Therefore, if voters are being influenced by negative advertisements, their evaluations of either candidate could change; Brown's support could decrease if voters penalized her for running negative advertisements. On the other hand, Wilson's support could decrease if voters took Brown's attacks seriously.

The Senate race was primarily focused on negative attack advertisements. Huffington relied upon an advertising strategy that attacked Feinstein increasingly as the race progressed. Feinstein, on the other hand, al-

TABLE 9. Changes in Candidate Positive-Negative Evaluation

	July	Sept.	Oct.	Net Change
Brown				
Positive	53.5	46.0	40.2	−13.3
	(167)	(264)	(411)	
Negative	23.4	37.1	44.2	+20.8
	(73)	(213)	(452)	
No opinion	23.1	16.9	15.6	−7.5
	(72)	(97)	(160)	
Wilson				
Positive	41.6	50.3	49.0	+7.4
	(123)	(289)	(501)	
Negative	51.7	44.1	45.8	−5.9
	(153)	(253)	(469)	
No opinion	6.8	5.6	5.2	−1.6
	(20)	(32)	(53)	
Huffington				
Positive	29.5	31.9	26.4	−3.1
	(92)	(183)	(270)	
Negative	21.5	28.7	45.1	+23.6
	(67)	(165)	(461)	
No opinion	49.0	39.4	28.5	−20.5
	(153)	(226)	(292)	
Feinstein				
Positive	47.0	47.0	39.5	−7.5
	(139)	(270)	(404)	
Negative	42.6	44.8	50.4	+7.8
	(126)	(257)	(516)	
No opinion	10.5	8.2	10.1	−.4
	(31)	(47)	(103)	

Note: Entries are percentages, followed by sample sizes. These figures are from the July, September, and October Field Polls.

most exclusively relied upon attack advertisements. Therefore, one should expect either of two possible dynamics in candidate evaluations: if negative advertisements against the opponent are successful, negative evaluations should rise and positive evaluations should fall during the campaigns; the other possible effect is that negative advertisements "backfire" and negatively influence the evaluations of their sponsor. Given that both candidates used mainly negative advertisements, it will be difficult to discern between these two explanations.

In table 9 it appears that Wilson might have won the battle of the airwaves. During the general election, his positive evaluations increased by 7 percent, his negative evaluations decreased by 6 percent, and the number of people who have no opinion about his evaluation decreased slightly. By running mainly positive television advertisements about his own positions and a few advertisements against Brown's character at the end of the campaign, Wilson seems to have led California voters toward more positive (and less negative) evaluations of himself. Kathleen Brown, on the other hand, seems to have been the loser of the television advertising battle. Her positive evaluations fell considerably (13 percent), while her negative evaluations rose greatly (by 21 percent). The fact that Brown's positive evaluations fell and her negative evaluations rose indicates that her mainly positive message did not resonate with the electorate—or that it did not get through to most voters.

To some extent, the same dynamic was observed in the Senate race. There, Huffington's positive evaluations fell slightly during the general election (3 percent), while his negative evaluations skyrocketed upward (24 percent). Notice for Huffington, though, that the percentages of voters who said they had no opinion about Huffington fell considerably, from 49 percent in July to 29 percent in October. This indicates that Huffington was doing what challengers need to do—inform voters about their candidacy. The unfortunate problem for Huffington, though, was that, as the campaign wore on, the drop in the percentage of voters who had no opinion about Huffington was matched by the rise in the percentage of voters who had a negative evaluation of Huffington.

Feinstein's positive evaluations fell during the general election by 7 percent, and her negative evaluations rose by 8 percent. Feinstein began the general election with relatively high positive and negative evaluations (47 percent and 43 percent, respectively). The campaign produced a slight drop in her positive evaluations and a slight rise in her negative evaluations. The evidence from the Senate race, then, indicates that attack advertising influenced the electorate in this election: As the intensity of attack advertisements increased, so did the negative evaluations of both candidates. Attacks were focused on the opponent's character, similar to Brown's attack advertisements. Huffington, who aired considerably fewer attack advertisements in the final weeks of the campaign than did Feinstein, seems to have been the loser in terms of voter evaluations.

The next pressing question concerns whether these changes in candidate evaluations, which seem to track the television advertising strategies of the candidates, influenced the basic preferences of voters in each race. In table 10 we present the changes in the percentages of voters who supported the candidates in each race, in the same three Field Polls.

In the top panel of table 10 we present the results for the governor's race. For Wilson, the changes appear dramatic. In July, about 39 percent of California voters supported Wilson, which put him slightly behind Brown in the polls. But by October, almost 51 percent of voters said they preferred Wilson, which gave him a lead in the polls of almost 10 percent, with only days to go before the election. This is a 12 percent increase in Wilson support, coming mainly from the ranks of undecided voters. This indicates that Wilson's positive advertisements—and the rise in his positive evaluations—led to a large change in support for Wilson among California's most important voters: those who were undecided in the early months of the general election.

TABLE 10. Changes in Candidate Projected Votes

	July	Sept.	Oct.	Net Change
Brown	42.7	41.0	41.5	−1.2
	(265)	(233)	(388)	
Wilson	38.5	48.8	50.5	+12.0
	(241)	(277)	(473)	
Undecided	16.3	10.2	8.0	−8.3
	(102)	(58)	(75)	
Huffington	39.0	44.5	41.0	+2.0
	(237)	(252)	(366)	
Feinstein	44.4	40.6	46.5	+2.1
	(270)	(230)	(415)	
Undecided	16.6	14.8	12.5	−4.1
	(101)	(84)	(112)	

Note: Entries are percentages, followed by sample sizes. These figures are from the July, September, and October Field Polls.

In the lower panel of table 10 we give the same figures for the Senate race. The dynamics of candidate preference in this race are remarkable. In July, Feinstein had a 5.5 percent lead over Huffington. Though Feinstein fell behind Huffington in September, she regained her 5.5 percent lead over her opponent by October. The slight increase in support for both candidates (roughly 2 percent over the general election) was obtained from the ranks of the undecided voters, who split evenly for the two candidates by October. This shows that, while the attack strategies used by both candidates led to increased negative evaluations for the two candidates, the attack advertisements allowed Feinstein to keep Huffington's advances in the polls to a minimum.

Conclusions

In this essay we have undertaken a careful case study of the television advertisement strategies used by four separate campaigns in two statewide races in California during the 1994 election. We have shown that in this particular set of campaigns there was dramatic heterogeneity in candidate television advertisements, which we argue was due to different strategies employed by each candidate.

We also showed that the advertising strategies used by the candidates did influence the target audience. We presented data from both exit polls taken on Election Day and from telephone polls taken throughout the general election period, which demonstrated the effect of campaigns on which issues mattered in candidate choices on Election Day and also showed the correlation of attack advertisement strategies and changes in general candidate evaluations. Finally, we presented evidence that advertisements did shape changes in candidate preferences over the course of the general election.

Obviously we examined only four individual campaigns, in a particular election year, occurring in a state in which candidates for statewide office are forced to rely heavily on television advertising. The fact that this is a case study does limit the generalizability of the results here regarding candidate television strategies and voter responses to those strategies. But we feel that this study does show that more work of this sort is desperately needed.

Political campaigns in general, and television advertisement campaigns in particular, are not well understood in the academic political science literature. In fact, there is still some debate as to whether campaigns "matter"—whether they influence the electorate in substantial ways (e.g., Finkel 1993). Unfortunately, there have been few systematic studies of campaigns, and those that have been undertaken have been primarily concerned with presidential election campaigns. While presidential elections are important to study, presidential elections have characteristics that make them poor cases for our exclusive analytical focus. First, there is little variation in the media coverage and intensity of presidential campaigns, at least in recent years (Alvarez 1997; Graber 1983; Patterson 1980). Without much variation across campaigns in coverage or intensity, it is difficult to imagine how presidential elections can shed much light on these important campaign variables. Second, the sample of presidential elections is quite limited. Obviously presidential elections occur every four years, so in the time for which we have reliable survey data, we only have a handful or so of cases of presidential elections.

In this essay we have focused on subnational races—in particular, statewide races for office. Moving our analytic focus from the national level to the state level should serve to enhance our ability to understand how campaigns operate and what effects they have on the electorate. In each four-year presidential election cycle, there are roughly one thousand races in congressional and gubernatorial elections, with dramatic variation in campaign intensity, resource utilization, television advertising, media coverage, and the number of candidate debates and appearances. It is clear that this is a laboratory well suited to the study of political campaigns in America that is underutilized.

Therefore, by studying how four different candidates in two different races in the same election year tried to target voters in the same geographic area, we can get a clear sense of how voters respond to campaign messages. Thus, when one campaign focuses on a particular issue but the other campaigns do not, and we find that voters become concerned about that particular issue over the election cycle, we may provide clear evidence of the effect of a campaign message. To this effect, it is clear that statewide campaigns provide a much better laboratory for studying campaigns than do presidential campaigns.

NOTES

We thank the John Randolph Haynes and Dora Haynes Foundation for its support of this research project and the John M. Olin Foundation for its support of our research through a Faculty Fellowship. Kin Chang assisted with the collection of the data presented in this essay, and Reginald Roberts assisted with early analysis. Henry Brady and Richard Johnston provided invaluable comments on an earlier draft.

1. In the governor's race, Pete Wilson was the Republican incumbent and Kathleen Brown was his Democratic challenger. In the U.S. Senate race, Dianne Feinstein was the Democratic incumbent and Michael Huffington was her Republican challenger.

2. See Bartels and Vavreck 2000; and Jamieson, Waldman, and Sher 1998 for further explanation of these three categories.

3. Advertising focus and tone are often closely interrelated. Most advertisements targeting the opposing candidate are attacking or contrasting, while most advertisements about the candidate himself or herself are positive or contrasting. In the analysis that follows we concentrate on the tone of advertising in these campaigns.

4. The focus on only Los Angeles or Southern California voters in the survey data is to match up as closely as possible the survey data with the television advertisement data. It is obviously possible that the candidates ran different types or different mixes of advertisements in different parts of the state; this would only complicate and obfuscate the analysis of the television and survey data.

5. The question posed by the survey was, "Which issues—if any—were most important to you in deciding how to vote today? (Check up to two boxes)." The issues, in the order they appeared on the survey form, were taxes, education, crime, immigration, ethics, morality, business, environment, health care, state budget, economy, and none. The issues of business, environment, and health care were not used in this analysis since less than 1 percent of voters thought they were important and since they were not issues that the candidates discussed in their advertisements.

6. The interested reader will note that all of the estimates for each of the three bivariate probit models are statistically significant, indicating that indeed there is a substantial amount of unmeasured and correlated factors driving voters to make joint decisions in these two races.

7. Druckman (2002), for instance, designed an exit poll that asked respondents to which local newspapers they subscribed and how often they read the front page of their subscriptions. This, of course, is a superior way to measure exposure to news coverage of campaign messages, but it does not measure exposure and/or attention to actual campaign advertisements themselves.

8. The baseline probabilities for the full sample are .27 (Wilson-Huffington), .07 (Brown-Huffington), .20 (Wilson-Feinstein), and .46 (Brown-Feinstein); for the high education sample, .25 (Wilson-Huffington), .05 (Brown-Huffington), .22 (Wilson-Brown), and .48 (Brown-Feinstein); and for the low education sample, .37 (Wilson-Huffington), .14 (Brown-Huffington), .14 (Wilson-Feinstein), and .35 (Brown-Feinstein).

9. This is the standard test for joint significance in discrete choice models, where twice the difference between the log-likelihoods of the restricted and unrestricted models has a χ^2 distribution, with the degrees of freedom being equal to the number of restrictions being tested.

10. Recall that higher education was used as a proxy for media awareness.

11. The Field Institute conducts the California Poll at various times throughout each year. They are telephone surveys of the adult population of California.

REFERENCES

Allsop, D., and H. F. Weisberg. 1988. "Measuring Change in Party Identification in Election Campaigns." *American Journal of Political Science* 32:996–1017.

Alvarez, R. M. 1997. *Information and Elections.* Ann Arbor: University of Michigan Press.

Ansolabehere, S., and S. Iyengar. 1995. *Going Negative.* New York: Free Press.

Ansolabehere, S., S. Iyengar, A. Simon, and N. Valentino. 1994. "Does Attack Advertising Demobilize the Electorate?" *American Political Science Review* 88:829–38.

Bartels, L. M., and L. Vavreck. 2000. *Campaign Reform: Insights and Evidence.* Ann Arbor: University of Michigan Press.

Basil, M., C. Schooler, and B. Reeves. 1991. "Positive and Negative Advertising: Effectiveness of Ads and Perceptions of Candidates." In *Television and Political Advertising—Volume I: Psychological Processes, Communication and Society*, ed. F. Biocca. Hillsdale, NJ: Lawrence Erlbaum.

Berelson, B., P. F. Lazarsfeld, and W. McPhee. 1954. *Voting: A Study of Opinion Formation in a Presidential Campaign.* Chicago: University of Chicago Press.

Brians, C. L., and M. P. Wattenberg. 1996. "Campaign Issue Knowledge and Salience: Comparing Reception from TV Commercials, TV News and Newspapers." *American Journal of Political Science* 40:145–71.

Campbell, A., P. E. Converse, W. E. Miller, and D. E. Stokes. 1960. *The American Voter.* New York: Wiley.

Combs, J. E. 1979. "Political Advertising as a Popular Myth-Making Form." *Journal of American Culture* 2:331–40.

Dalager, Jon K. 1996. "Voters, Issues, and Elections: Are the Candidates' Messages Getting Through?" *Journal of Politics* 58:486–515.

Druckman, J. 2002. "Priming the Vote: Campaign Effects in a U.S. Senate Election." Working Paper, University of Minnesota, Minneapolis.

Faber, R. J., and M. C. Storey. 1984. "Recall of Information from Political Advertisements." *Journal of Advertising* 13:39–44.

Ferejohn, J. A., and R. G. Noll. 1978. "Uncertainty and the Formal Theory of Political Campaigns." *American Political Science Review* 72:492–505.

Finkel, S. E. 1993. "Reexamining the 'Minimal Effects' Model in Recent Presidential Campaigns." *Journal of Politics* 55:1–21.

Fiorina, M. P. 1981. *Retrospective Voting in American National Elections.* New Haven: Yale University Press.

Freedman, P., and K. Goldstein. 1999. "Measuring Media Exposure and the Effects of Negative Campaign Ads." *American Journal of Political Science* 43:1189–208.

Fridkin Kahn, K., and P. J. Kenney. 2002. "The Slant of the News: How Editorial Endorsements Influence Campaign Coverage and Citizens' Views of Candidates." *American Political Science Review* 96:381–94.

Garramone, G. M. 1984. "Voter Responses to Negative Political Ads." *Journalism Quarterly* 61:250–59.

———. 1985. "Effects of Negative Political Advertising: The Roles of Sponsor and Rebuttal." *Journal of Broadcasting and Electronic Media* 29:147–59.

Garramone, G. M., C. K. Atkin, B. E. Pinkleton, and R. T. Cole. 1990. "Effects of Negative Advertising on the Political Process." *Journal of Broadcasting and Electronic Media* 34:299–311.

Glazer, A. 1990. "Voting and Campaigning under Incomplete Information." *European Journal of Political Economy* 6:89–98.

Graber, Doris A. 1983. "Hoopla and Horse-Race in 1980 Campaign Coverage: A Closer Look." In *Mass Media and Elections: International Research Perspectives*, ed. W. Schulz and K. Schoenbach. Munich, Germany: Oelschlaeger.

Guskind, R., and J. Hagstrom. 1988. "In the Gutter." *National Journal* 20:2782–90.

Jacobson, G. C. 1992. *The Politics of Congressional Elections*. New York: Harper Collins.

Jamieson, K. H., P. Waldman, and S. Sher. 1998. "Eliminate the Negative? Defining and Refining Categories of Analysis for Political Advertisements." Paper presented at the Conference on Political Advertising in Election Campaigns, Washington, DC.

Johnson-Cartee, Karen S., and Gary A. Copeland. 1991. *Negative Political Advertising: Coming of Age*. Hillsdale, NJ: Erlbaum.

Just, M., A. Crigler, and L. Wallach. 1990. "Thirty Seconds or Thirty Minutes: What Viewers Learn from Spot Advertisements and Candidate Debates." *Journal of Communication* 40:120–33.

Kern, M. 1989. *30-Second Politics: Political Advertising in the Eighties*. New York: Praeger.

Lau R., and G. Pomper. 2002. "Effectiveness of Negative Campaigning in U.S. Senate Elections." *American Journal of Political Science* 46:47–66.

Lazarsfeld, P., B. Berelson, and H. Gaudet. 1944. *The People's Choice*. New York: Columbia University Press.

MacKuen, M. B., R. S. Erikson, and J. Stimson. 1992. "Peasants or Bankers? The American Electorate and the U.S. Economy." *American Political Science Review* 86:597–611.

Merritt, S. 1984. "Political Advertising: Some Empirical Findings." *Journal of Advertising* 13:27–38.

Patterson, T. C. 1980. *The Mass Media Election*. New York: Praeger.

Patterson, T. C., and R. D. McClure. 1976. *The Unseeing Eye*. New York: Putnam.

Roddy, B. L., and G. M. Garramone. 1988. "Appeals and Strategies of Negative Political Advertising." *Journal of Broadcasting and Electronic Media* 32:415–27.

Sellers, Patrick J. 1998. "Strategy and Background in Congressional Campaigns." *American Political Science Review* 92:159–71.

Skarpedas, S., and B. Grofman. 1995. "Modeling Negative Campaigning." *American Political Science Review* 89:49–60.

Surlin, S. H., and T. F. Gordon. 1977. "How Values Affect Attitudes toward Direct Reference Political Advertising." *Journalism Quarterly* 54:89–98.

Wattenberg, M. P. 1991. *The Rise of Candidate-Centered Politics*. Cambridge, MA: Harvard University Press.

West, D. M. 1993. *Air Wars*. Washington, DC: Congressional Quarterly.

Gender, Media Coverage, and the Dynamics of Leader Evaluations

The Case of the 1993 Canadian Election

Elisabeth Gidengil and Joanna Everitt

DOES GENDER CONDITION acceptance of media messages about male and female candidates? Drawing on insights from the media effects literature and the gender identity literature we argue that it does. This argument is tested using data from the 1993 Canadian election. With a high-profile woman running for the country's top executive office, this election offers an all too rare opportunity to examine sex-of-leader effects in a real-world setting. The truly propitious circumstance of this election (for scholars, at least) is that the woman in question was leading the Conservative Party in a fight for the Canadian right against a rival right-wing party led by a man. This means that the leaders' basic ideological orientation is effectively controlled in our analyses. Moreover, the rolling cross-section design of the campaign wave of the 1993 Canadian Election Study[1] enables us to assess the impact of media messages in real time by combining individual-level survey data with daily media quantities. Our study thus approximates a kind of natural experiment with the daily news coverage representing the introduced treatment. Few other countries and election campaigns have offered such an opportunity to explore the interaction between gender, media coverage, and leadership evaluations.

The Conservative Party leader was Kim Campbell, Canada's first female prime minister (albeit briefly). During the 1993 election her party suffered a massive hemorrhaging of support to Preston Manning's Reform

Party. The Conservatives had begun the campaign almost neck and neck with the Liberals, only to see their support collapse. They ended the campaign with a mere 16 percent of the popular vote. There is no shortage of explanations for this stunning defeat, not least an inept campaign, the massive unpopularity of the Conservative government under former leader Brian Mulroney, and the emergence of not one but two new regional parties.[2] Campbell, though, blamed her electoral woes squarely on the media. As the party's first female leader, she explained, she had been determined to do politics differently. The media, in her view, were just not ready for this: "new politics, old media."[3]

There was certainly evidence of sex-differentiated media coverage during the 1993 campaign (Gidengil and Everitt 1999, 2000, 2003a, 2003b). Indeed, it became the stuff of editorial comment.[4] The coverage was not simply asymmetrical but gendered. Television coverage of the leaders' debates, for example, focused disproportionately on confrontational displays of behavior on Campbell's part. This was apparent in metaphorical reconstructions of the debates (Gidengil and Everitt 1999, 2003a), in the selection of sound bites (Gidengil and Everitt 2000), and in the reporting of speech (Gidengil and Everitt 2003b). And there is evidence that negative media coverage damaged Campbell's image as a leader (Mendelsohn and Nadeau 1999). What interests us is whether negative media coverage of Campbell had more effect on men than on women.

Our argument that gender conditions the impact of media messages puts a gender spin on John Zaller's resistance axiom (1992). According to this axiom, viewers can be expected to resist messages that are at odds with their own predispositions. Gender identity could provide one such source of resistance. Like ethnic or regional identity, gender identity is a form of social identity. Tajfel (1981, 255) defines social identity as "that part of an individual's self-concept which derives from his [sic] knowledge of his membership of a social group (or groups) together with the value and emotional significance attached to that membership." Social identity theory focuses on the impact of that identity on social perceptions and attitudes. The central idea is that people seek a positive social identity by comparing their group to relevant out-groups. This process of social comparison, and the need for positive differentiation that motivates it, serves to heighten perceived in-group–out-group differences. Thus, Greene (1999, 2002, 2004), for example, reports that partisan social identity increases the perceived differences between parties and candidates and leads people to behave in a more partisan manner. Turner (1987) emphasizes that "the functioning of the social self-concept is situation-specific," becoming salient "as a function of an interaction between the characteristics of the perceiver and the situation" (43). Social identity will become particularly relevant when both in-group and out-group members are included in the comparison. In the context of an election, then, gender identity is most likely to come into play and have an effect on perceptions when the campaign features both male and female candidates.

A number of experimental studies have examined whether men show a pro-male bias and women show a pro-female bias in evaluating candidates for office. While sex differences have been apparent in reactions to male and female candidates in simulated races (Sigelman and Sigelman 1982; Sigelman et al. 1986; Lewis and Bierly 1990; Sanbonmatsu 2002), the empirical results have proved inconclusive and inconsistent when it comes to which sex is biased against which. It is not clear, however, that the experimental results necessarily generalize to real-world settings. It is one thing to evaluate a fictitious candidate on the basis of a written speech and quite another to react to real candidates in an actual campaign.

There are relatively few studies that have examined the interaction between the sex of the candidate and the sex of the voter in the real world of electoral politics. The strongest evidence of sex-of-voter effects in actual elections comes from Plutzer and Zipp (1996) and Banducci and Karp (2000).[5] Plutzer and Zipp (1996) found that the sex of the voter had a significant impact on voting for women candidates in statewide races in the United States, even controlling for party identification, previous presidential vote, race, and family income (Plutzer and Zipp 1996; cf. Cook 1994). They attributed this effect to gender identity, inferring that a sense of group solidarity creates a tendency for women to vote for women and men to vote for men. Banducci and Karp (2000) went on to test the gender identity hypothesis in parliamentary elections in Australia, Britain, Canada, and New Zealand. They found that in most cases the parties with female leaders tended to do better among female voters than among male voters. And, except for Margaret Thatcher in Britain, women rated female leaders more positively on average than men did. Consistent with the gender identity hypothesis, the effects of gender were mediated by leadership evaluations in every case but one for the women leaders.[6] Finally, in Canada, O'Neill (1998) has demonstrated that women rated the two female leaders[7] more favorably than men did in the 1993 Canadian Election and that this was a factor in drawing some female recruits to both parties. Similarly, Erickson (2003) has shown that women ranked the lone female leader higher than men did in the 1997 Canadian election, though they still ranked her behind two of the male leaders.

If gender identity also conditions acceptance of media messages about male and female leaders, women will be less likely to accept negative messages about a female leader or positive messages about a male leader, while the reverse will be true for men. Analyzing relative evaluations of Campbell and Manning enables us to provide a strong test of this hypothesis about the interaction between gender, media coverage, and leader evaluations. While one is a woman and the other a man, both led parties of the right. This permits some control of confounding factors like ideology and issue positions and thus makes it easier to disentangle any sex-of-leader effect. If the gender identity/resistance hypothesis is valid, we would expect negative media coverage of Campbell to have had more effect on men than on women because women would be more resistant than men to negative messages about a leader who is a woman. Conversely, we would expect positive coverage of Manning to have less effect on women than on men because women would be more resistant to positive messages about a leader who is a man.

Method

The data on leader evaluations are taken from the 1993 Canadian Election Study. The campaign wave of this study was based on a rolling cross-section design that enables us to link daily media coverage to leader evaluations. Leader evaluations were measured using a scale of 0 to 100, where 100 represented a very positive feeling toward the leader and 0 reflected a very negative feeling. Respondents who answered "not at all" when asked how well informed they felt about the leader were not asked to provide a rating. The Reform Party did not have a serious electoral presence in Canada's predominantly French-speaking province and so Quebec respondents were not asked to rate Preston Manning. Accordingly, the analysis is restricted to Canada outside Quebec.

The data on media coverage are derived from a content analysis of nightly newscasts on CBC, Canada's public broadcasting network. This follows conventional practice in studies of television news coverage in Canada (Johnston et al. 1992; Taras 1993; Mendelsohn 1993, 1996;

Mendelsohn and Nadeau 1999). It reflects CBC's dominant share among those who report watching any national television news (Johnston et al. 1992, 114–15)[8] and the fact that analyses that have compared the CBC with other networks and/or types of media have typically found similar trends in coverage (Wagenberg et al. 1988; Frizzell and Westell 1989; Nevitte et al. 2000). The content analysis was conducted by the National Media Archive at the Fraser Institute in Vancouver.[9]

The actual media quantities are based on the balance of positive and negative horse-race coverage. Horse-race coverage focuses on "who is ahead, who is behind, who is gaining, who is losing, what campaign strategy is being followed, and what the impact of campaign activities is on the candidate's chances of winning" (Joslyn 1984, 133). In Canada, as elsewhere, television news coverage is preoccupied with the horse-race in general and with the leaders' abilities as campaigners in particular. Indeed, the "leaders and the horse-race become interchangeable" (Mendelsohn 1993, 160). An analysis of news frames used in the first week's coverage of the 1993 campaign confirmed this pattern: the focus was "on what leaders did, what their tactical motivations were for doing it, and on understanding their actions and statements as a reaction to their standings in the polls" (Mendelsohn 1996, 18; cf. Mendelsohn and Nadeau 1999). Studies in the United States have found that media coverage of women candidates is even more likely to focus on the horse-race aspect (Kahn 1992; Kahn and Goldenberg 1991, 1997; but see Smith 1997), with the women often being held up to harsher media standards than their male counterparts (Kahn and Goldenberg 1991; Robinson and Saint-Jean 1991).

Research on priming would lead us to expect horse-race coverage to have a significant impact on evaluations of party leaders (Ansolabehere, Behr, and Iyengar 1991). The more the media focus on the viability of the leader's party, the more accessible—and hence more relevant—that information will be in voters' summary evaluations of the leader. Both experimental (Brady 1984) and survey-based (Bartels 1985, 1988) studies have demonstrated the link between the nature of media coverage and perceptions of candidate viability. And Brady and Johnston (1987) and Bartels (1988) have gone on to show that voters' evaluations of candidates are indeed closely tied to the candidates' viability. Viability seems to serve as an information shortcut for voters. As Mendelsohn (1996) writes with respect to media frames, "Whether campaign events go well . . . provides a simple, though questionable, metaphor: how well a leader can run the campaign indicates how well he or she will be able to run the government" (13).

This leaves the question of how to operationalize the media variables. We repeat the analysis with two different operationalizations. The first is simply the preceding day's value (in other words, the amount of positive horse-race coverage minus the amount of negative horse-race coverage).[10] However, based on a modeling of the impact of media messages, Fan (1988) concludes that "the impact of a mass media message decreases exponentially with a half-life of only one day" (5) and that most such messages will have minimal effects. He argues that "it is more useful to think of a series of persuasive messages having a powerful cumulative effect" (133). This is intuitively plausible. If the tone of coverage varies between positive and negative from night to night, we would expect the impact on leader evaluations to be minimal, certainly less than a few successive nights of consistently negative or consistently positive coverage. Accordingly, our second measure is a cumulative one that involves aggregating days of coverage.[11] Lacking a priori reasons to favor any particular aggregation, we experiment with different aggregations, beginning with the two preceding days, then the three preceding days, and so on, ending with the preceding six days.[12]

Results

Figures 1a and 1b track evaluations of Campbell and Manning across the entire campaign. The tracking employs a five-day moving average in order to smooth out the random "noise" caused by the small daily samples sizes (see Johnston and Brady 2002). In order to ease interpretation, the leader ratings have been rescaled to run from −50 to +50, with 0 indicating neutral feelings about the leader. As figure 1a shows, Campbell's popularity ebbed among women and men alike, but it is apparent that men's ratings of Campbell—and Manning—shifted much more than women's did as the campaign evolved. Men came to like Campbell much less and Manning much more than they did at the start of the campaign. Indeed, men's evaluations of Campbell went from favorable to unfavorable, while their evaluations of Manning did just the reverse (though his popularity among men was beginning to fall by the end of the campaign). Figure 1c highlights the contrasting dynamic in women's and men's relative evaluations of the two leaders. The moving averages now track the difference between Campbell's

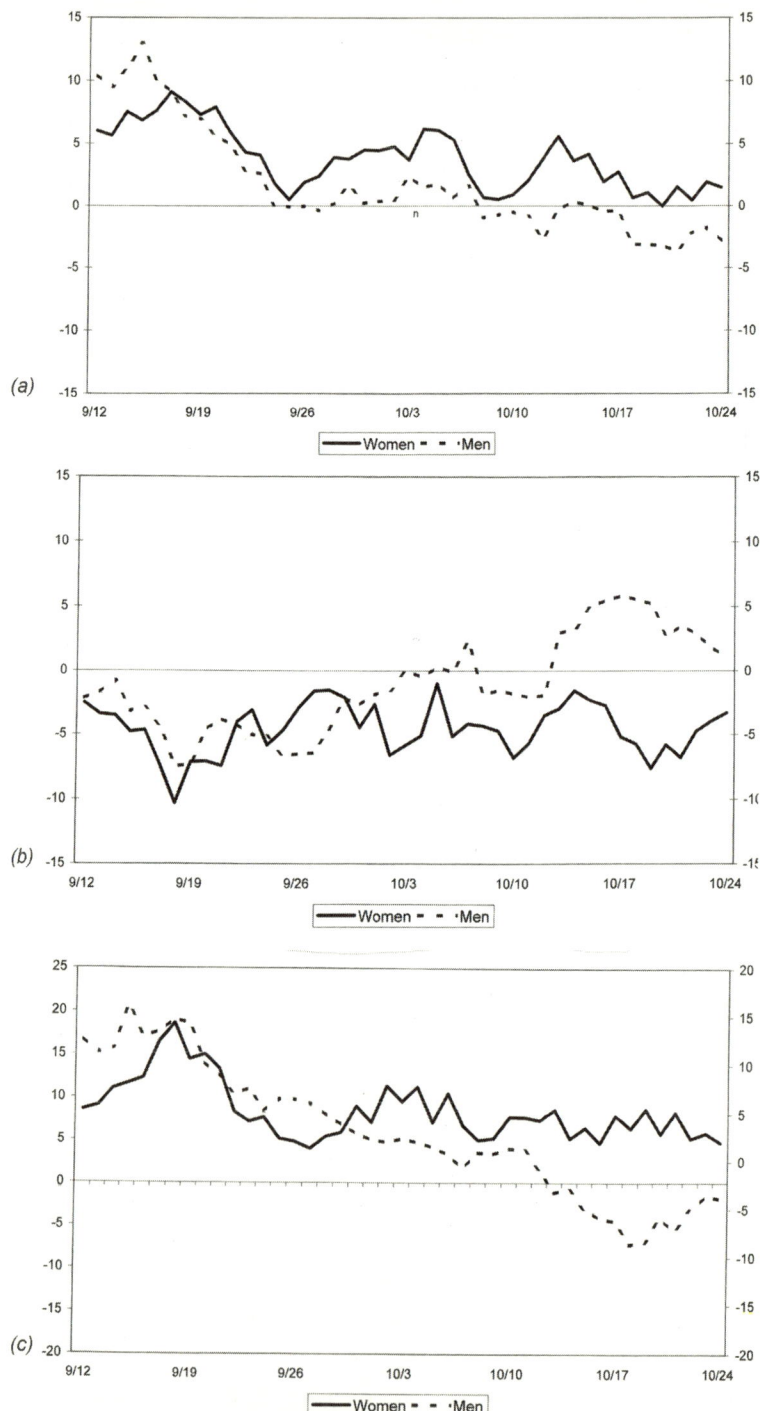

Fig. 1. *a*, Ratings of Campbell by sex; *b*, ratings of Manning by sex; *c*, Campbell-Manning ratings spread by sex

and Manning's ratings for women and men, respectively. The campaign started with women and men both evaluating Campbell more favorably than Manning, and when Campbell began losing ground to Manning over the opening two weeks, she did so among both groups, but then the gap between women and men began to widen. By the final two weeks of the campaign, Manning had overtaken Campbell in popularity among men but always lagged behind Campbell among women.

Such a graphic divergence in relative evaluations suggests that the sex of the voter did indeed matter. But what role did media coverage play in this process? We begin to answer this question by tracking the balance of horse-race coverage across the campaign. This is done by subtracting the amount of negative coverage each party received from the amount of positive coverage. Figures 2a and 2b show the five-day moving averages for both leaders' parties across the campaign, along with the daily values. Coverage of the Campbell campaign was consistently negative in tone.[13] Indeed, there was only a single day (September 28) of demonstrably positive coverage. Coverage of the Manning campaign, on the other hand, was almost always positive, with only two days (September 20 and October 13) of clearly negative coverage.

In order to assess whether this differential media coverage had an impact on leader evaluations, we regressed evaluations on the daily coverage quantities. Our two dependent variables were ratings of Campbell and Manning on a 100-point scale. The analyses were repeated using first the preceding day's balance of media coverage and then each of the cumulative measures. Controls were included for party identification, education, and region. It could be that voters were evaluating the two leaders not on the basis of their sex but on the basis of their partisanship (see Zipp and Plutzer 1985; Plutzer and Zipp 1996; Dolan 2004). In other words, men may have reacted more positively toward Manning and more negatively toward Campbell as the campaign progressed, not because one is a man and the other a woman but simply because of the parties they were leading. Accordingly, we controlled for the respondents' partisanship in order to avoid confounding the effects of sex and party and to determine whether media coverage had an impact net of partisan predispositions.[14] It is also important to assess whether media coverage had an effect independent of education. To the extent that media attention is related to education, there is a risk of confounding the effects of the media with social background unless education is controlled for (Joslyn and Ceccoli 1996). Finally, given the strong Western

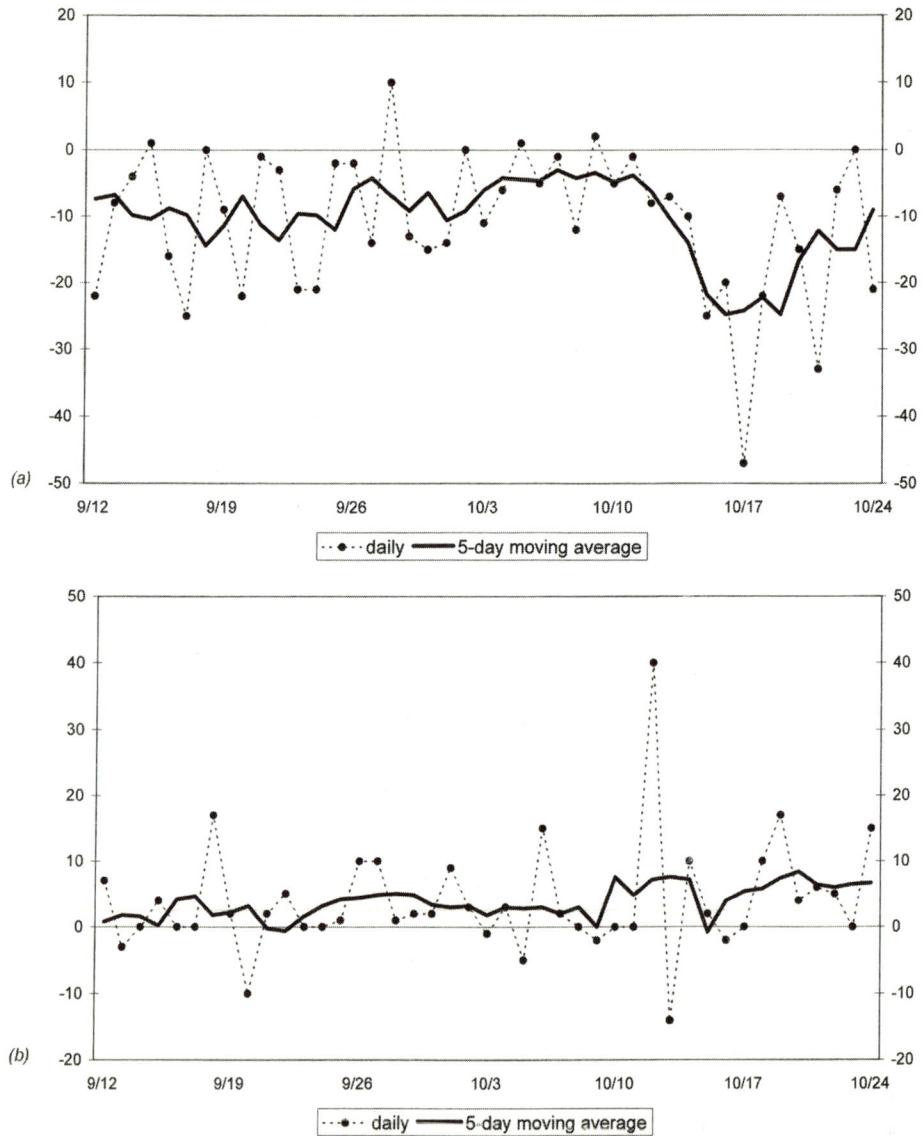

Fig. 2. Balance of horse-race coverage: *a*, Campbell campaign; *b*, Manning campaign

Canadian dimension to Reform's appeal, we have included a control for region. All of the controls took the form of dummy variables.[15]

The results are presented in table 1. As predicted, negative horse-race coverage has a stronger effect on men's evaluations of Campbell than on women's evaluations. The more negative the coverage of Campbell's campaign, the less favorably men rated her. The impact of coverage is clearly cumulative. It takes at least two days of coverage to have a significant effect on ratings. While coverage has a greater effect for men, women were not impervious to negative coverage of the Campbell campaign. In the women's case, though, only one of the media effects reaches conventional levels of statistical significance. The results for Manning are even more clear-cut. There is no indication that media coverage had an effect on women's evaluations of Manning. More positive coverage did little or nothing to persuade women to rate Manning more favorably. For men, on the other hand, successive days of positive coverage induced a significant shift in their evaluations of Manning. It took more days of coverage to have this impact on Manning's ratings than was the case for Campbell's ratings, a difference that may be attributable to the fact that coverage of the Manning campaign was less intense. The Manning campaign averaged seventeen horse-race statements per day of the campaign, compared with thirty for the Campbell campaign.

The media effects are not trivial. The cumulative scores for the balance of coverage are sufficiently large that their observed effects could make for appreciable shifts in leader evaluations. For Campbell, the average for

TABLE 1. Impact of Horse-Race Coverage on Leader Evaluations

	Campbell		Manning	
	Women	Men	Women	Men
Previous day	.08 (.06)	.06 (.05)	−.06 (.09)	.04 (.08)
Previous 2 days	.05 (.04)	.08 (.03)**	.02 (.08)	.08 (.07)
Previous 3 days	.07 (.03)*	.08 (.03)**	−.00 (.07)	.02 (.06)
Previous 4 days	.04 (.02)	.07 (.02)**	.04 (.06)	.09 (.05)
Previous 5 days	.03 (.02)	.05 (.02)**	.00 (.06)	.13 (.05)**
Previous 6 days	.03 (.02)	.05 (.02)**	.03 (.06)	.16 (.05)**
N	1,151	1,317	835	1,141

Note: The column entries are unstandardized OLS coefficients, with the standard errors shown in parentheses. Controls were included for education, region, and party identification. Leader evaluations were measured on a scale of 0 to 100.
*$p < .05$ **$p < .01$

the preceding three days of coverage (the period that had the greatest effect on her evaluations) was −30, while the average for the preceding six days for Manning was +19. Clearly, Campbell was handicapped by the negative coverage of her campaign, especially when it came to appealing to male voters, while Manning was helped by the positive tone of his campaign coverage, at least among men. The asymmetry of these effects supports the argument that gender identity conditions acceptance of media messages. Women resisted positive messages about the male leader and proved to be less accepting of negative messages about the female leader. Men, by contrast, were more accepting of negative messages about the female leader and positive messages about her male counterpart.

This leaves the questions of what it was about Campbell that men—and, to some extent, women—came to like less and what it was about Manning that men came to like more. The rationale for linking horse-race coverage to leader evaluations (see previous discussion) suggests that perceptions of the quality of leadership may play a mediating role. According to this line of reasoning, negative horse-race coverage (in other words, negative viability assessments) leads voters to see the leader as providing weak leadership and this, in turn, leads to a less favorable overall evaluation. Positive coverage would have the reverse effect. Testing for this causal link involves first examining the dynamic impact of trait ratings on overall leader evaluations in order to determine which traits were critical in voters' changing evaluations of the leaders and then entering those traits into the equations reported in table 1. If the traits do indeed mediate the relationship between horse-race coverage and overall evaluations, then the media coefficients should shrink.

Simply regressing overall evaluations on trait ratings would confound the across-time variation produced by the campaign with the cross-sectional variance resulting from differences in voters' social background characteristics, partisan attachments, and issue positions. Accordingly, we split trait ratings into their time-series and cross-sectional components (Johnston et al. 1992; Johnston and Brady 2002). The time-series component is simply the respondent's trait rating for the day of interview, while the cross-sectional component is the difference between the respondent's trait rating and the mean value for the day of interview for all respondents (Johnston and Brady 2002).[16] The two dependent variables are, again, leader ratings on a scale of 0 to 100, while the traits are measured on a scale of 0 to 3, where 3 means the trait described the leader very well and 0 means the trait did not describe the leader at all well. Controls were again included for education, region, and party identification (see previous discussion).

What matters most for the purpose of assessing the impact of campaign coverage are the dynamic effects of trait ratings. As table 2 shows, changing perceptions of leader traits during the course of the campaign did indeed affect overall evaluations of the leaders. Interestingly, the trait that had the greatest dynamic impact on reevaluations of Campbell was not her leadership ability but the growing perception that she was untrustworthy. Among women and men alike, a one-point increase in her perceived untrustworthiness diminished her overall evaluation by eleven or twelve points. This finding is interesting on two counts. First, media reports had been rife with charges of lack of candor and evasiveness surrounding Campbell's supposed secret plan to cut social programs. Second, experimental studies have found trustworthiness to be one of the stereotypically feminine traits ascribed to hypothetical female candidates (see, for example, Golebiowska 2001; Huddy and Terkildsen 1993a, 1993b; King and Matland 2003; Leeper 1991; Sapiro 1981–82). Gender stereotyping is most likely to occur when information is sparse (Kahn 1992; McDermott

TABLE 2. Dynamic Impact of Trait Perceptions on Leader Ratings

	Women	Men
1. Campbell		
Arrogance	−1.56 (2.88)	−8.40 (2.66)**
Compassion	3.53 (3.59)	−0.68 (3.85)
Intelligence	−3.11 (4.20)	1.88 (4.00)
Leadership	8.55 (4.10)*	4.82 (3.12)
Trustworthy	12.52 (3.97)**	11.54 (3.43)***
Speaks for women	−2.27 (4.49)	4.15 (2.94)
N	912	1,090
2. Manning		
Arrogance	−2.36 (4.30)	−8.46 (3.23)**
Compassion	4.70 (5.64)	4.06 (4.67)
Intelligence	−1.15 (5.73)	4.12 (4.54)
Leadership	3.22 (5.94)	2.15 (4.24)
Trustworthy	6.70 (5.67)	4.09 (4.52)
Speaks for women	5.04 (4.16)	0.69 (3.39)
N	558	844

Note: The column entries are unstandardized OLS coefficients, with the standard errors shown in parentheses. Controls were included for education, region, party identification, and cross-sectional variation in trait perceptions (the respondent's score minus the average for the day of interview). Leader evaluations were measured on a scale of 0 to 100, while traits were measured on a scale of 0 to 3.
*$p < .05$ **$p < .01$ ***$p < .001$

1997, 1998; Sapiro 1981–82). It may be that such judgments are particularly likely to be revised as voters are exposed to more information over the course of the election campaign.

Changing perceptions of Campbell's trustworthiness figured in both women's and men's reassessments of her. Where women and men parted company was in what else mattered. For women, reevaluations of Campbell's leadership qualities were also a factor, albeit a weaker one, in their overall reassessments. As women's evaluations of Campbell's leadership ability decreased, they came to rate her less favorably overall. For men, on the other hand, changing perceptions of Campbell's leadership ability did not play a significant role. While we should not overinterpret this difference, it is in line with studies in hypothetical settings that have indicated that women are more likely than men to base their judgments of female candidates on the stereotypically masculine quality of mastery (Mueller 1986; Huddy and Terkildsen 1993b). For men, the other critical trait was perceived arrogance. As men's perceptions of Campbell's arrogance increased, their overall rating of her decreased. Tellingly, there is no hint of this trait playing any role at all in women's reevaluations of Campbell. This same asymmetry is also evident in the evaluative dynamics for Manning. Changing perceptions of Manning on the arrogance dimension help account for fluctuations in men's overall evaluations of Manning but were simply not a factor for women. In fact, all of the dynamic effects were weak and unstable for women. This is not surprising. As we saw in figure 1b, women's overall ratings of Manning showed much less movement across the campaign than men's.

This still leaves the question of whether the impact of horse-race coverage was mediated via these changing trait assessments. To answer this, we regressed leader evaluations on both the daily media quantities and the traits identified as significant in table 2. We selected the media quantities on the basis of the results reported in table 1, choosing the cumulative measure that had the strongest impact on leader evaluations.[17] In order to control for cross-sectional variation in the trait ratings, we included a measure of the difference between the respondent's rating and the mean rating for the day of interview, as before. Controls were also included for education, region, and party identification. Table 3 reports both the original media effects and the media effects when trait ratings are added to the model. Comparing the two sets of effects enables us to assess the extent to which the impact of media coverage was mediated via a reassessment of leader traits.

As table 3 shows, the expectation that the effects of horse-race coverage would be mediated via reassessments of key traits is only supported in the case of men's reevaluations of Campbell. The critical trait turns out to be perceived arrogance. Adding dynamic evaluations of arrogance to the equation reduces the cumulative impact of horse-race coverage to insignificance. Indeed, the coefficient is now smaller than its standard error. Reassessments of Campbell's trustworthiness, on the other hand, do nothing to diminish the impact of horse-race coverage. This finding is repeated for women's evaluations of Campbell and men's evaluations of Manning. If negative horse-race coverage led women to like Campbell somewhat less, it was apparently not because that coverage led them to rate her leadership abilities or trustworthiness less favorably. Similarly, if positive horse-race coverage caused men to like Manning more it was not because that coverage led

TABLE 3. Dynamic Impact of Traits on the Relationship between Horse-Race Coverage and Leader Evaluations

	Horse-Race Coefficient
Campbell	
1. Men	
Previous 2 days' coverage	.08 (.03)**
Controlling for	
Arrogance	.02 (.03)
Trustworthiness	.09 (.03)**
2. Women	
Previous 3 days' coverage	.07 (.03)*
Controlling for	
Leadership	.06 (.03)*
Trustworthiness	.07 (.03)*
Manning	
1. Men	
Previous 5 days' coverage	.13 (.05)**
Controlling for	
Arrogance	.11 (.05)*

Note: The column entries are unstandardized OLS coefficients, with the standard errors shown in parentheses. Controls were included for education, region, party identification, and cross-sectional variation in trait perceptions (the respondent's score minus the average for the day of interview). Leader evaluations were measured on a scale of 0 to 100, while traits were measured on a scale of 0 to 3.

$*p < .05$ $**p < .01$

them to see him as lacking in arrogance. One inference from these findings is that the effects of horse-race coverage were direct.[18] In other words, negative horse-race coverage, in and of itself, led women to like Campbell somewhat less, while positive coverage led men to like Manning more. A fuller understanding of the relationship among media coverage, trait perceptions, and leader ratings requires a content analysis that focuses on media references to leader traits. What does seem clear from this analysis of the dynamic impact of trait perceptions is that changing perceptions of leadership abilities are not a critical factor in explaining the impact of horse-race coverage on overall evaluations.

Conclusion

Our central proposition about gender, media coverage, and leader evaluations was supported. As the 1993 Canadian election campaign progressed, men came to like Campbell less and Manning more. As predicted, these reevaluations of the two leaders could be linked to differences in the coverage of their respective campaigns. The more negative the coverage of Campbell's campaign, the less favorable men's ratings of Campbell became. Positive coverage of Manning's campaign had the reverse effect. The more positive the coverage, the more highly men rated Manning. Women, on the other hand, appeared to be more resistant to these media messages. Positive coverage had no effect on their ratings of Manning, and the effect of negative coverage of the Campbell campaign was much less in evidence than it was among men.

This pattern of results is consistent with the argument that gender identity conditions the acceptance of media messages about male and female political leaders. It suggests that women tend to resist negative messages about a female leader and positive messages about her male counterpart, whereas men are readier to accept these messages. Obviously, though, it is premature to generalize on the basis of a single experience. In particular, we need to know what happens when the pattern of gender-differentiated coverage is reversed: are women readier to accept positive messages about a female leader and negative messages about a male leader, and do men now prove the more resistant? What we can conclude at this point is that the use of a rolling cross-section in conjunction with daily media tracking provides a powerful design for assessing the dynamic impact of media coverage.

NOTES

We would like to thank Elizabeth Goodyear-Grant, Tim Sinke, and Matthew Hennigar for their research assistance. This research was supported by the Social Science and Humanities Research Council of Canada and the Fonds FCAR.

1. The total sample was broken up into forty-five replicates, one for each day of fieldwork. Release and clearance of replicates were controlled in order to make the day of interview effectively a random event. Differences between days of interview were thus solely the product of sampling error and of intervening events (including, potentially, shifts in media coverage). During the campaign 3,775 interviews were completed, for a response rate of 65 percent. The Institute for Social Research at York University conducted the fieldwork. The study was funded by the Social Sciences and Humanities Research Council of Canada and the principal investigators were Richard Johnston, André Blais, Henry Brady, Elisabeth Gidengil, and Neil Nevitte. Further information on the study may be found in Northrup and Oram 1994.

2. For an assessment of the impact of the party leaders' personalities in the 1993 election, see Johnston 2002.

3. "Campbell Not Making Many Personal Plans after Oct. 25 Election," *Gazette*, October 12, 1993, A8.

4. See "Liberals Go after 'Protest' Vote," *Globe and Mail*, October 9, 1993, A6.

5. See also Seltzer, Newman, and Leighton 1997 and Dolan 1998.

6. They found much more mixed support, though, for the hypothesis that evaluations of female leaders would have more impact on vote choice for women than for men.

7. The other female leader was Audrey McLaughlin of the left-leaning New Democratic Party.

8. During the 1988 campaign, less than one-third reported watching no CBC national news. Unfortunately, the question about television news sources was not repeated in the 1993 Canadian Election Study.

9. The reported intercoder reliability quotient (based on a random sample of 15 percent of the stories) for the content analysis of campaign coverage was 0.87 (National Media Archive 1993, 4). We are grateful to the National Media Archive for making the results of their content analysis available to us. The archive does not bear any responsibility for the analyses and interpretations presented here.

10. Mendelsohn and Nadeau (1999) report that the same day's coverage had a statistically significant, albeit weak, effect on Campbell's image as a strong leader in their time-series analysis. It seems counterintuitive that a 10:00 P.M. newscast would have an impact on respondents who would mostly have been interviewed earlier in the evening. Mendelsohn and Nadeau attribute the effect to the fact that the nightly newscast would partly pick up "old" news that had already been reported in the day's newspaper or on the 6:00 P.M. news. When we tested for same-day horse-race coverage, we found no effects on overall ratings of either Campbell or Manning.

11. In a similar vein, Dobrzynska, Blais, and Nadeau (2003) developed a measure of media coverage for the 1997 Canadian election campaign that identified periods during the campaign when the media coverage of a given party and/or its leader was particularly positive or particularly negative.

12. Mendelsohn and Nadeau (1999) report that negative shocks, defined as

coverage that was more negative than the average across the campaign, had more impact on ratings of Kim Campbell as a "strong leader" than did the same day's coverage. They reasoned that viewers are so used to seeing negative portrayals of political leaders that it takes unusually negative coverage to have an effect on opinion. However, we found no such effect when it came to overall ratings of Campbell and Manning. It should be noted that Mendelsohn and Nadeau used a time-series design, with data aggregated by day of interview.

13. The balance of horse-race coverage was negative on thirty-nine of the forty-seven days of the campaign. This is in line with Mendelsohn and Nadeau's (1999) finding, using their own content analysis, that the balance of coverage of Kim Campbell was negative on thirty-two days out of the forty-three coded. Previous studies have found that women are often held up to harsher media standards than their male counterparts (Kahn and Goldenberg 1991; Robinson and St.-Jean 1991). Since our comparison involves only two leaders, we are not in a position to assess whether coverage of Campbell's campaign was subject to such gender biases. It could simply be that she ran a singularly inept campaign and the media were merely reflecting that reality. It is worth noting, though, first, that coverage of the Campbell campaign was consistently negative even before the decline in the Conservative vote share became apparent and, second, that the media themselves remarked on the asymmetrical treatment. See "Liberals Go after 'Protest' Vote," *Globe and Mail*, October 9, 1993, A6.

14. Given the decline in Conservative partisanship between the 1988 and 1993 elections (Johnston et al. 1996), we repeated the analyses using voting in the previous federal election as an alternative measure of partisan predisposition. The results for the impact of media coverage were not materially affected, though the impact of the social background characteristics on leader evaluations was strengthened.

15. The dummy variables were party identifier; did not complete high school; university educated; and Western Canada resident.

16. There is, of course, potential collinearity between these two components (see Johnston and Brady 2002). To the extent that standard errors may be inflated, our test should be regarded as a conservative one.

17. Regardless of the chosen operationalization of horse-race coverage, taking account of the dynamic impact of perceived arrogance in the Campbell equation has more effect on the horse-race coefficient than does perceived trustworthiness. Similarly, the dynamic measure of perceived arrogance in the Manning equation has similar effects on the horse-race coefficient whether the previous five days' or the previous six days' coverage is used.

18. Two other inferences are, of course, possible, namely, error in the measurement of the traits and unmeasured traits.

REFERENCES

Ansolabehere, Stephen, Roy Behr, and Shanto Iyengar. 1991. "Mass Media and Elections." *American Politics Quarterly* 19:109–39.

Banducci, Susan A., and Jeffrey A. Karp. 2000. "Gender, Leadership and Choice in Multiparty Systems." *Political Research Quarterly* 53:815–48.

Bartels, Larry M. 1985. "Expectations and Preferences in Presidential Nominating Campaigns." *American Political Science Review* 79:804–15.

———. 1988. *Presidential Primaries and the Dynamics of Public Choice*. Princeton: Princeton University Press.
Brady, Henry E. 1984. "Chances, Utilities, and Voting in Presidential Primaries." Paper presented at the annual meeting of the Public Choice Society, San Francisco.
Brady, Henry E., and Richard Johnston. 1987. "What's the Primary Message: Horse Race or Issue Journalism?" In *Media and Momentum*, ed. Gary R. Orren and Nelson W. Polsby. Chatham, NJ: Chatham House.
Cook, Elizabeth Adell. 1994. "Voter Responses to Women Candidates." In *The Year of the Woman: Myths and Realities*, ed. Elizabeth Adell Cook, Sue Thomas, and Clyde Wilcox. Boulder: Westview.
Dobrzynska, Agnieszka, André Blais, and Richard Nadeau. 2003. "Do the Media Have a Direct Impact on the Vote? The Case of the 1997 Canadian Election." *International Journal of Public Opinion Research* 15:27–43.
Dolan, Kathleen. 1998. "Voting for Women in the 'Year of the Woman.'" *American Journal of Political Science* 42:272–93.
———. 2004. "The Impact of Candidate Sex on Evaluations of Candidates for the U.S. House of Representatives." *Social Science Quarterly* 85:206–17.
Erickson, Lynda. 2003. "In the Eyes of the Beholders: Gender and Leader Popularity in a Canadian Context." In *Women and Electoral Politics in Canada*, ed. Manon Tremblay and Linda Trimble, 160–76. Don Mills: Oxford University Press.
Fan, David P. 1988. *Predictions of Public Opinion from the Mass Media: Computer Content Analysis and Mathematical Modeling*. New York: Greenwood.
Frizzell, Alan, and Anthony Westell. 1989. "The Media and the Campaign." In *The Canadian General Election of 1988*, ed. Alan Frizzell, Jon H. Pammett, and Anthony Westell, 75–90. Ottawa: Carleton University Press.
Gidengil, Elisabeth, and Joanna Everitt. 1999. "Metaphors and Misrepresentation: Gendered Mediation in News Coverage of the 1993 Canadian Leaders' Debates." *Press/Politics* 4:48–65.
———. 2000. "Filtering the Female: Television News Coverage of the 1993 Canadian Leaders' Debates." *Women and Politics* 21:105–31.
———. 2003a. "Conventional Coverage/Unconventional Politicians: Gender and Media Coverage of Canadian Leaders' Debates, 1993, 1997, 2000." *Canadian Journal of Political Science* 36:559–77.
———. 2003b. "Talking Tough: Gender and Reported Speech in Campaign News Coverage." *Political Communication* 20:209–32.
Golebiowska, Ewa. 2001. "Group Stereotypes and Political Evaluation." *American Politics Research* 29:535–65.
Greene, Steven. 1999. "Understanding Party Identification: A Social Identity Approach." *Political Psychology* 20:393–403.
———. 2002. "The Social-Psychological Measurement of Partisanship." *Political Behavior* 24:171–97.
———. 2004. "Social Identity Theory and Party Identification." *Social Science Quarterly* 85:136–53.
Huddy, Leonie, and Nayda Terkildsen. 1993a. "Gender Stereotypes and the Perceptions of Male and Female Candidates." *American Journal of Political Science* 37: 119–47.

———. 1993b. "The Consequences of Gender Stereotypes for Women Candidates at Different Levels and Types of Office." *Political Research Quarterly* 46: 503–25.

Johnston, Richard. 2002. "Prime Ministerial Contenders in Canada." In *Leaders' Personalities and the Outcomes of Democratic Elections*, ed. Anthony King. Oxford: Oxford University Press.

Johnston, Richard, André Blais, Henry E. Brady, and Jean Crête. 1992. *Letting the People Decide: Dynamics of a Canadian Election*. Montreal: McGill-Queen's University Press.

Johnston, Richard, André Blais, Henry E. Brady, Elisabeth Gidengil, and Neil Nevitte. 1996. "The 1993 Canadian Election: Realignment, Dealignment, or Something Else?" Paper presented at the annual meeting of the American Political Science Association, San Francisco.

Johnston, Richard, and Henry E. Brady. 2002. "The Rolling Cross-Section Design." *Electoral Studies* 21:283–95.

Joslyn, Richard. 1984. *Mass Media and Elections*. Reading, MA: Addison-Wesley.

Joslyn, Richard, and Steve Ceccoli. 1996. "Attentiveness to Television News and Opinion Change in the Fall 1992 Presidential Campaign." *Political Behavior* 18: 141–70.

Kahn, Kim Fridkin. 1992. "Does Being Male Help? An Investigation of the Effects of Candidate Gender and Campaign Coverage on Evaluations of U.S. Senate Candidates." *Journal of Politics* 54:497–517.

Kahn, Kim Fridkin, and Edie N. Goldenberg. 1991. "Women Candidates in the News: An Examination of Gender Differences in U.S. Senate Campaign Coverage." *Public Opinion Quarterly* 55:180–99.

———. 1997. "The Media: Obstacle or Ally of Feminists?" In *Do the Media Govern? Politicians, Voters, and Reporters in America*, ed. Shanto Iyengar and Richard Reeves. Thousand Oaks, CA: Sage.

King, David C., and Richard E. Matland. 2003. "Sex and the Grand Ole Party: An Experimental Investigation of the Effect of Candidate Sex on Support for a Republican Candidate." *American Politics Research* 31:595–612.

Leeper, Mark Stephen. 1991. "The Impact of Prejudice on Female Candidates: An Experimental Look at Voter Inference." *American Politics Quarterly* 19:248–61.

Lewis, Kathryn E., and Margaret Bierly. 1990. "Toward a Profile of the Female Voter: Sex Differences in Perceived Physical Attractiveness and Competence of Political Candidates." *Sex Roles* 22:1–12.

McDermott, Monika L. 1997. "Voting Cues in Low-Information Elections: Candidate Gender as a Social Information Variable in Contemporary United States Elections." *American Journal of Political Science* 41:270–83.

———. 1998. "Race and Gender Cues in Low-Information Elections." *Political Research Quarterly* 51:895–918.

Mendelsohn, Matthew. 1993. "Television's Frames in the 1988 Canadian Election." *Canadian Journal of Communication* 18:149–71.

———. 1996. "Television News Frames in the 1993 Canadian Election." In *Seeing Ourselves: Media Power and Policy in Canada*, ed. Helen Holmes and Davis Taras, 8–22. 2d ed. Toronto: Harcourt Brace.

Mendelsohn, Matthew, and Richard Nadeau. 1999. "The Rise and Fall of Candidates in Canadian Election Campaigns." *Press/Politics* 4:63–76.

Mueller, Carol. 1986. "Nurturance and Mastery: Competing Qualifications for Women's Access to High Public Office?" *Research in Politics and Society* 2:211–32.

National Media Archive. 1993. "Election '93: What Role Did Television Play in the Outcome?" *On Balance* 6:1–8.

Nevitte, Neil, André Blais, Elisabeth Gidengil, and Richard Nadeau. 2000. *Unsteady State: The 1997 Canadian Federal Election.* Don Mills: Oxford University Press.

Northrup, David, and Anne Oram. 1994. *The 1993 Canadian Election Study, Incorporating the 1992 Referendum Survey on the Charlottetown Accord: Technical Documentation.* Toronto: Institute for Social Research, York University.

O'Neill, Brenda. 1998. "The Relevance of Leader Gender to Voting in the 1993 Canadian National Election." *International Journal of Canadian Studies* 17:105–30.

Plutzer, Eric, and John F. Zipp. 1996. "Identity Politics, Partisanship, and Voting for Women Candidates." *Public Opinion Quarterly* 60:30–57.

Robinson, Gertrude, and Armande Saint-Jean. 1991. "Women Politicians and Their Media Coverage." In *Women in Canadian Politics: Toward Equity in Representation,* ed. Kathy Megyery, 127–69. Toronto: Dundurn Press.

Sanbonmatsu, Kira. 2002. "Gender Stereotypes and Vote Choice." *American Journal of Political Science* 46:20–34.

Sapiro, Virginia. 1981–82. "If U.S. Senator Baker Were a Woman: An Experimental Study of Candidate Images." *Political Psychology* 2:61–83.

Seltzer, Richard A., Jody Newman, and Melissa V. Leighton. 1997. *Sex as a Political Variable: Women as Candidates and Voters in U.S. Elections.* Boulder: Lynne Rienner.

Sigelman, Carol K., Lee Sigelman, Dan B. Thomas, and Frederick D. Ribich. 1986. "Gender, Physical Attractiveness, and Electability: An Experimental Investigation of Voter Biases." *Journal of Applied Social Psychology* 16:229–48.

Sigelman, Lee, and Carol K. Sigelman. 1982. "Sexism, Racism, and Ageism in Voting Behavior: An Experimental Analysis." *Social Psychology Quarterly* 48:467–75.

Smith, Kevin B. 1997. "When All's Fair: Signs of Parity in Media Coverage of Female Candidates." *Political Communication* 14:71–82.

Tajfel, Henri. 1981. *Human Groups and Social Categories: Studies in Social Psychology.* Cambridge: Cambridge University Press.

Taras, David. 1993. "The Mass Media and Political Crisis: Reporting Canada's Constitutional Struggles." *Canadian Journal of Communication* 18:131–48.

Turner, John C. 1987. *Rediscovering the Social Group: A Self-Categorization Theory.* Oxford: Basil Blackwell.

Wagenberg, R. H., W. C. Soderlund, W. I. Romanow, and E. D. Briggs. 1988. "Campaigns, Images, and Polls: Mass Media Coverage of the 1984 Canadian Election." *Canadian Journal of Political Science* 21:117–28.

Zaller, John. 1992. *The Nature and Origins of Mass Opinion.* Cambridge: Cambridge University Press.

Zipp, John F., and Eric Plutzer. 1985. "Gender Differences in Voting for Female Candidates: Evidence from the 1982 Election." *Public Opinion Quarterly* 49:179–97.

Mass Media and Third-Party Insurgency

Richard Jenkins

ELECTION CAMPAIGNS ARE RARELY treated as decisive for election outcomes (Gelman and King 1993; Holbrook 1996; cf. Johnston et al. 1992). Instead, the information environment of campaigns is said to activate preexisting political predispositions within the electorate and thereby generate predictable outcomes. Although the "minimal effects" thesis has a strong hold on political science, this essay suggests that the focus on activation as the primary role of campaigns reflects a limited understanding of the potential power of campaigns. Information can change, and when it does, voters, especially those aware of the information change, can respond to the new information in meaningful ways. An analysis of the dramatic movement of Reform support during the 1993 election campaign in Canada reveals that campaigns can matter while providing an opportunity to unpack the relationship among voters, the media, and parties.

The 1993 Canadian election witnessed the successful insurgency of the Reform Party in English Canada.[1] While the emergence of Reform as the standard-bearer—at least temporarily—of the Canadian right could be partially explained ex post facto in terms of the conditions in place before the campaign, there is no way that such an outcome could have been predicted before the campaign began. Given that there were few voters who identified with the Reform Party or who knew much about Reform before the campaign began, Reform's success could not be the product of a simple activation process. More likely is that the campaign provided voters with information that allowed them to learn and thereby link their underlying attitudes, especially their attitudes on the welfare state, to the parties. This is consistent with the observation that "only as Reform's anti-deficit commitment became clear did the party break out of its ethno-religious base" (Johnston et al. 1996, 15).

If the campaign had an effect on the outcome by providing voters with information, then we would expect to find dynamics in the nature and amount of information available about Reform (Converse 1962; Zaller and Hunt 1995). The analysis begins with a consideration of the relative amount of news attention Reform received using daily television news readings of the density of Reform coverage. It is clear that independent decisions on the part of the news media changed the accessibility of Reform's key messages at different times during the campaign.

The next step is to consider whether voters who were interviewed when Reform was highly visible in the news were more likely to support the party by merging the media data with the rolling cross-section wave of the 1992–93 Canadian Election Study (Brady and Johnston 1996). The more coverage that Reform receives, the more accurate the perceptions of Reform's spatial location on the deficit issue should be and, therefore, the stronger the link between ideological predispositions and Reform vote intentions. While the information environment should induce temporal changes, Reform's growth should be constrained by the structure of awareness and ideological predispositions in the electorate. Not everyone will be aware of the change in news coverage of Reform (Price and Zaller 1993; Zaller 1992), and not everyone will be ideologically predisposed to agree with Reform policies. This suggests that the relationship between coverage and individual opinion should be thought of in terms of a two-mediator (awareness and welfare state predisposition) model of media effects (McGuire 1969, 1986; Zaller 1992, 1996).

The results confirm that the coverage-induced learning of Reform's fiscally conservative position on the welfare state was limited to respondents who were predisposed to both get and accept pro-Reform messages. Although coverage had more marginal direct effects on Reform support, there is clear evidence that changing credibility affected the likelihood of voting Reform. Before turning to the empirical evidence to support these claims, the claim that the main function of campaigns is to activate predispositions is considered. While the activation claim cannot be rejected outright, the applicability of the model is questioned. In its place, a dynamic model of campaign effects is considered.

Campaigns and the Media

Our ability to predict election outcomes with remarkable accuracy months before the campaign begins, especially in the United States, implies a minimal role for the campaign in structuring electoral choices (Gelman and King 1993). In a version of this argument, Holbrook (1996) argues that for every election there is an equilibrium outcome that the campaign moves toward. While there can be fluctuation during the campaign, the campaign will only result in a minimal amount of movement from that equilibrium point by Election Day. Campaigns, therefore, matter to the extent that they provide information necessary for voters to express their *enlightened preferences* (Gelman and King 1993). This is, of course, the basis for the idea that campaigns merely activate existing preference (Lazarsfeld, Berelson, and Gaudet 1948; Finkel 1993).

In contrast, Johnston et al. (1992, 1996) have championed the idea that the campaign can change people's minds or the dimension of choice, thus offering the possibility of multiple rather than unique equilibria. According to this argument, campaign events and issues offer strategic, dynamic opportunities for a new coalition or the reconstitution of long-term forces. The election context may powerfully shape the strategic landscape that parties face going into the campaign, but their own activities can be instrumental in shaping which of a number of outcomes emerges. From the multiple equilibria perspective, party strategy and events in the campaign can influence which equilibrium emerges, whereas from the single equilibrium perspective, the campaign brings voters to *the* equilibrium.

The activation hypothesis usually refers to the activation of party identification. The 1988 Canadian election could be viewed from this perspective because one of the main effects of the campaign was to bring Liberals to a Liberal vote intention (Johnston et al. 1992). Activation of party identification cannot, however, provide an explanation for the 1993 election. In 1993, the Reform Party had only about 4 percent of the identifiers but received almost 18 percent of the votes on Election Day. In contrast, the incumbent Conservative Party was unable to turn its historic level of underlying support into votes on Election Day. Party identification may serve or appear to serve as a basis for mobilization in some cases, but it cannot explain significant changes in party support.

An alternative is that the campaign serves to activate attitudes about incumbent performance. This approach is consistent with the fact that prediction models in the United States are based on variables such as economic growth and presidential popularity (Rosenstone 1983; Lewis-Beck and Rice 1992). The problem with this approach is that it assumes that there is a clear alternative to the incumbent. In multiparty contexts, reminding voters about the nature of economic conditions provides no information about where voters should cast their vote. Prediction models based on the expected Liberal share of the vote in Canada have been reasonably successful, but they presume that the Liberals are the natural party of government (Nadeau and Blais 1993, 1995). Voters who moved to Reform in the 1993 election were certainly abandoning the incumbent, but moving to Reform, which would not affect the composition of government, is not predictable within this framework.

The third possibility is that it is more basic predispositions that are activated by the campaign. According to Finkel, "what occurred during these [American] campaigns was not minimal in the sense of simple reinforcement of preferences, but predictable movement by the electorate toward casting votes in accordance with these underlying conditions and their accompanying political predispositions" (1993, 18). There are a number of problems with the notion of activating predispositions. The first is that predispositions in and of themselves are not linked to parties, so voters must also know or learn where the parties stand on the issues. Campaigns can matter, then, especially for insurgent parties that are by definition unknown, by providing that knowledge. The second problem is that people have more than one predisposition—being opposed to an accommodation with French Canada does not presuppose particular positions on the welfare state—so either some or all of a person's attitudes will be activated. If the issues cannot be predicted before the campaign begins, then there is scope for the campaign to matter by affecting which attitudes are activated.

The Media and Campaigns

The media are likely the key to unlocking the potential impact of election campaigns. The news media are fundamental for how voters come to make the link between their predispositions and the positions of the parties. Certainly voters penalize parties which they know little about (Bartels 1986; Brady and Ansolabehere 1989). Insurgent parties are particularly dependent on the news media because voters begin the campaign lacking information about the party (Zaller and Hunt 1994, 1995). In the same way, information can be critical for who emerges from the primaries in the United States (Bartels 1988). News coverage may also be critical for old parties, especially in multiparty systems where there is no clear government in waiting.

In effect, coverage measures are indicative of the likely penetration of information about the candidate in the mass public. Given that the Reform Party began the campaign with few partisans and considerable voter uncertainty about the party's stands, except perhaps on the question of an appropriate accommodation with Quebec, Reform support should be strongly associated with news treatment of the party. Since the party is relatively new to electoral competition, the boom and bust pattern of good followed by bad press may also apply.

A Model of Mass Media–Initiated Campaign Effects

While the mass media is the main source for information about politics, the effect of media messages will depend in part on characteristics of the individual. In particular, the influence of persuasive messages should be mediated by the person's likelihood of receiving a persuasive message and his or her likelihood of accepting it (McGuire 1968, 1986; Zaller 1992, 1996; Dalton, Beck, and Huckfeldt 1998). The flow of communication can be thought of as the content of the message, which must be received and then acted upon before one can observe persuasion.

One would not expect respondents who lack either the motivation to attend to or the cognitive abilities necessary to process the news to be influenced by the mass media. Dalton, Beck, and Huckfeldt (1998) found some support for differential reception of the evaluative content of newspapers and for the relationship between coverage and candidate preference. While there is some debate about the appropriate measure of news media consumption, it is clear that some respondents are more likely to consume and remember information they received from the mass media (Price and Zaller 1993; Rhee and Cappella 1997; Brians and Wattenberg 1996). Following Zaller, this essay makes use of a measure of awareness based on a series of factual questions and the interviewer rating of the respondent.[2]

Citizens are not simply ciphers responding to mass media inputs. Some messages are accepted and acted upon, while others are rejected or discounted. In part this reflects classical processes such as selective reception or cognitive dissonance (Festinger 1957). Joslyn and Ceccoli (1996) found that the effect of news attentiveness was dependent upon political predispositions. "Political predispositions, such as *affective partisan ties*, serve as filters, leading to patterns of selective exposure, attention and reception" (Schmitt-Beck 1996, 276). It is also true that people who have a store of information should be better able to counterargue new information, reducing the persuasive impact of any particular message.

Summary

The activation model of campaign effects that usually supports a minimal effects understanding of campaigns can, therefore, be the basis for a different understanding of campaigns, an understanding that allows for dynamic effects on subgroups of the population as the result of changes in the availability of political cues. An insurgent campaign is, of course, more likely to reveal this process.

The Path of the Vote, Coverage, and Credibility

The 1993 campaign began with the Conservative Party apparently in a close race with the Liberals (Johnston et al. 1994). That said, new parties—the Reform Party in the West and the Bloc Quebecois in Quebec—had emerged on the scene in the very regions that were central to the Conservative coalition since 1984. Reform, which combined a fiscally conservative agenda and a resistance to a substantive accommodation with Quebec, offered a clear right-wing alternative to the Conservative Party but, despite its positioning, entered the campaign with a small share of electoral support.

Reform did not, however, remain on the sidelines. Reform's share of vote intentions, the perceived credibility of Reform on the deficit, and news attention to Reform all underwent dramatic changes during the campaign. The close relationship between these variables suggests that Reform was able to overcome information deficiencies in the electorate so as to convince voters of its true deficit location in such a way as to increase its electoral support.

The dynamic movement of the campaign is clearly evident in the path of Reform intentions. There was almost no substantial change in Reform intentions over the first fourteen days of the campaign. From that point, intentions increased fairly gradually until they peaked about ten days before Election Day. In the last week, intentions then fell back. While the path of Reform intentions was gradual, it appears to have been precipitated by the drops in Conservative support, around day 11 and day 33 of the campaign (Johnston et al. 1994). Some of the early Conservative losses were absorbed by the Liberal Party, but Reform was a particular beneficiary, especially late in the campaign.

Accompanying the surge in Reform vote intentions were changes in the perceived credibility of Reform on deficit reduction. The surge in credibility is significant because it is the only party credibility or location measure that undergoes a dramatic change during the campaign. Credibility is measured by the following question: "Suppose the Reform Party wins the election, what do you think will happen to the deficit? Would a Reform government make the deficit: much bigger, somewhat bigger, about the same as now, somewhat smaller, or much smaller?" In fact, the question is both a party location and credibility question. For graphical purposes the "same as now" category was assigned the value of zero, so a positive value indicates that a Reform win would result in a smaller deficit while a negative value indicates the deficit would get larger. Those who lacked the information necessary to guess Reform's position were coded as zero. Figure 1 presents the daily mean, averaged over seven days, for the three major parties' perceived credibility on the deficit.

At the start of the campaign, the Reform Party was perceived to be as credible as the Conservative Party on deficit reduction. By the second week of the campaign, however, the Conservative Party had lost much of its early credibility on the deficit while Reform's credibility surged. The Liberal Party was never considered a credible party on the deficit, and the public's perception of its position never underwent a reevaluation. Much of Reform's early evaluation on the deficit was certainly susceptible to reevaluation. Twenty-eight percent of respondents interviewed in the first ten days of the campaign were unable to say what effect a Reform win would have on the size of the federal deficit. For comparison, the proportion who did not know what effect a Liberal or Conservative win would have was 10 and 9 percent, respectively. Early in the campaign, the question remained whether voters would have the combination of information and motivation to reevaluate Reform on this dimension. Such a reevaluation took place, but late in the campaign Reform's credibility declined. There is no obvious explanation for this decline. It may be that some of the early movement involved people giving Reform the benefit of the doubt. As information

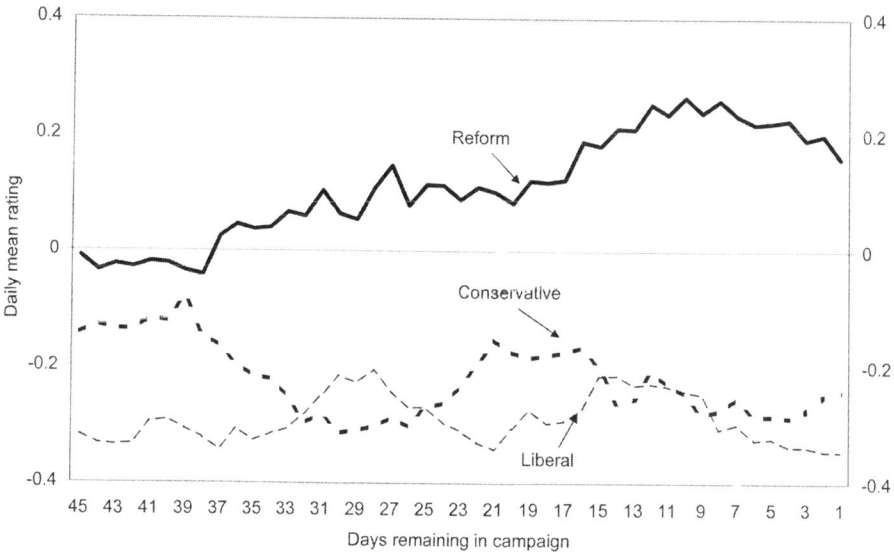

Fig. 1. Credibility of parties on deficit by day of campaign (seven-day moving average)

about Reform increased, voters had enough information to reevaluate Reform on this question.

The most likely source of information about the Reform Party's positions, including its one on the deficit, was the news media. During the first two weeks of the campaign Reform received a small proportion of coverage and was generally treated as a minor player in the campaign drama (fig. 2).[3] Before there were tangible indications that the Conservative vote share had collapsed or that Reform's share of support had increased, Reform began to receive more media attention, peaking at about 25 percent of coverage with twelve days remaining in the campaign. More sophisticated analyses using Granger causality confirm the visual impression that news media decisions were exogenous to changes in Reform support (Jenkins 1999a).[4] That is, the news began to give greater attention to Reform before Reform became more likely to be supported by the public. In fact, the increased news attention coincided with a greater emphasis on the deficit and social programs in the coverage of Reform. It was not simply more attention but rather attention that provided attentive voters with information about Reform's commitment to deficit reduction by way of spending cuts.

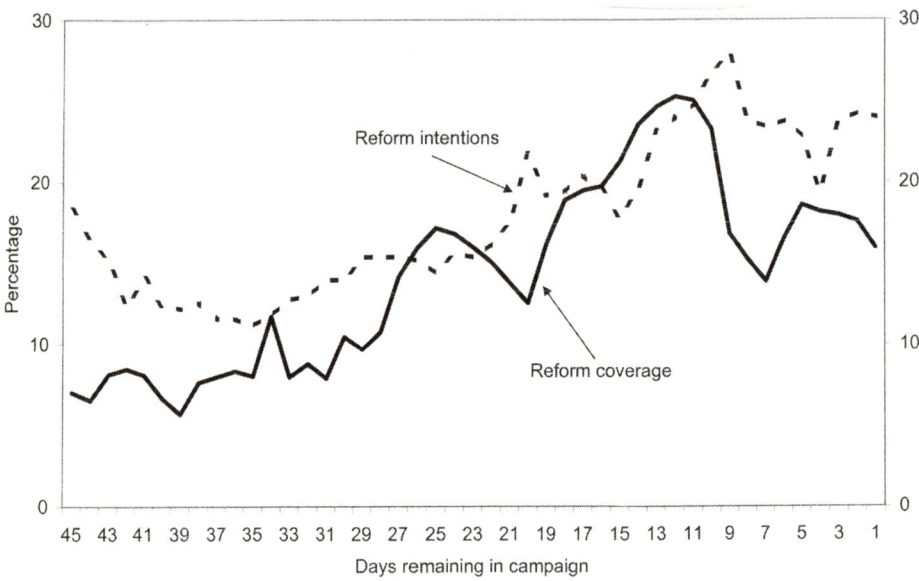

Fig. 2. News coverage and public support for Reform (five-day moving average)

Unpacking the Coverage, Credibility, and Intentions Relationship

While the three aggregate series appear to broadly coincide, the analysis that follows considers the relationship at the micro level rather than at the aggregate level. Consider the hypotheses as represented by the path diagram in figure 3. The theory expects that coverage will have an effect on perceptions of Reform's deficit credibility, which will in turn have an effect on the likelihood of supporting the Reform Party. In the following analysis each of the three paths is considered.

One of the potential problems with the path diagram is the assumption that a simplistic stimulus-response model of media effects is at work. Consequently, each hypothesis is modified to reflect the possibility that respondents who are more likely to receive messages and more likely to accept those messages will be influenced the greatest. These modifications produce the following equations that are estimated with both dependent variables: Reform's deficit credibility and Reform thermometer rating. Reform thermometer rating is used in place of a vote intention variable because it allows for the more straightforward use of ordinary least squares (OLS) regression. In fact, the vote intention and

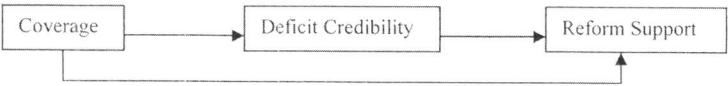

Fig. 3. Path diagram of key hypotheses

thermometer scores are closely related at both the aggregate and individual levels.

$$Y = \alpha + \beta_1 \text{Coverage} + \beta_2 \text{Welstate} + \beta_3 \text{Awareness}$$
$$+ \beta_4 \text{Demo} + \varepsilon \quad (1)$$

$$Y = \alpha + \beta_1 \text{Coverage} + \beta_2 (\text{Coverage} \times \text{Welstate})$$
$$+ \beta_3 (\text{Coverage} \times \text{Awareness}) + \beta_4 (\text{Coverage}$$
$$\times \text{Awareness} \times \text{Welstate}) + \beta_5 \text{Welstate} + \ldots + \varepsilon, \quad (2)$$

where

> Y is either respondent's position on Reform's credibility or respondent's Reform feeling thermometer score;
> *Coverage* is the absolute number of times Reform was coded as the object of television news coverage averaged over the previous five days;[5]
> *Welstate* is the respondent's position on an anti–welfare state index;
> *Awareness* is the respondent's level of political knowledge;
> *Demo* is a series of independent variables, including education, income, sex, and region.

The basic approach to both estimations is to regress the dependent variable—either Reform credibility or Reform thermometer score—on coverage, the respondent's ideological predispositions, awareness, and demographic characteristics. Table 1 provides a brief breakdown of the key independent variables used in the estimations. The only difference between the deficit credibility and Reform support models is the inclusion of a variable—attitudes toward French Canada—in the support estimations to control for the second dimension of political conflict in Canada, which would affect attitudes toward the party but is unlikely to affect perceptions of party location on a different issue.

The two-mediator model requires that there is an adequate means by which to identify individual predispositions. Since the growth in Reform support has been linked to the mobilization of fiscally conservative voters, an anti–welfare state index originally constructed by Johnston et al. (1996) is used as an indicator of underlying predispositions. A score of 1 on the index indicates an antipathy toward the welfare state and the costs associated with government spending. Since it undergoes no significant temporal change during the campaign, the index is a useful indicator of predispositions. To control for the second major cleavage dimension in Canada, which is dominated by the question of French Canada, attitudes toward French Canada are also included in the vote estimations (Brady and Johnston 1996; Johnston et al. 1992).[6]

The key difference between the two equations is the inclusion of interaction terms in equation (2). Equation (1) represents a baseline model in which coverage is presumed to have an impact on all respondents in the same manner. The three interaction terms in equation (2) allow for the possibility that coverage will have a larger impact if one of three conditions is true: the respondent is predisposed to accept the information (coverage × welstate); the respondent is likely to receive the information (coverage × awareness); or the respondent is both predisposed to accept and likely to receive the information (coverage × awareness × welstate). The two-mediator model expects that the coefficient on the last interaction will be the substantively important one in comparison.

In the pooled, cross-sectional estimations a number of demographic characteristics are controlled, but a decision was made not to control for a person's party identification. Demographic variables are entered because

TABLE 1. Distributions of Key Independent Variables

	Mean	Standard Deviation	Minimum	Maximum
Coverage (average of previous 5 days)	40.58	22.94	10.2	94.8
Anti–welfare state index	0.40	0.23	0	1
Anti–French Canada index	0.48	0.26	0	1
Awareness index	0.44	0.26	0	1
Education	6.11	2.06	1	11
Income	2.10	0.81	1	3

they capture proclivities for Reform that may not be captured by the ideological attitudes entered into the equation. For example, women could be less likely to support the Reform Party because of the presence of a female leader of the Conservative Party. The only potential problem with including the demographics is that variables like education might pick up some of the impact of awareness. The result of inclusion, however, is to make a conservative test of the role of awareness in mediating coverage.

Party identification is usually added to political science estimations, especially those involving party support, because it is thought to capture tendencies to support a party that are not captured by the other independent variables. It would be inappropriate, however, to enter party identification into the estimations here because party identification is not a stable attribute of respondents to the 1993 election study. The number of Reform identifiers increases from 4.1 percent of the week 1 sample to 6.9 percent of the week 6 sample (Johnston et al. 1996). Identification is, therefore, not exogenous. The most likely reason for the increase in the number of identifiers is learning about Reform, so it would be inappropriate to include identification in the estimations.[7]

Credibility on the Deficit

Reform's credibility gains during the campaign are potentially important in demonstrating the process by which welfare state attitudes became important to the Reform vote on Election Day because the credibility gains reflect a learning process. Did the credibility gains occur across the population, or were they largely from those who were aware of the message and predisposed to accept it? Did the accessibility of Reform messages, as indicated by the density of Reform coverage, provide the basis for the credibility gains?

We can get leverage on these possibilities by breaking down the evolution of credibility within subgroups of the population. The awareness and anti–welfare state scales were divided at the mean to create four groups. The two high aware groups are more likely to be aware of the changing news coverage and are therefore more likely to change across the campaign. Expectations about the role of anti–welfare state messages are more contested. On the one hand, we would expect that learning a party's position is simply a question of information or learning and not persuasion. This would mean that awareness would be the only mediator of

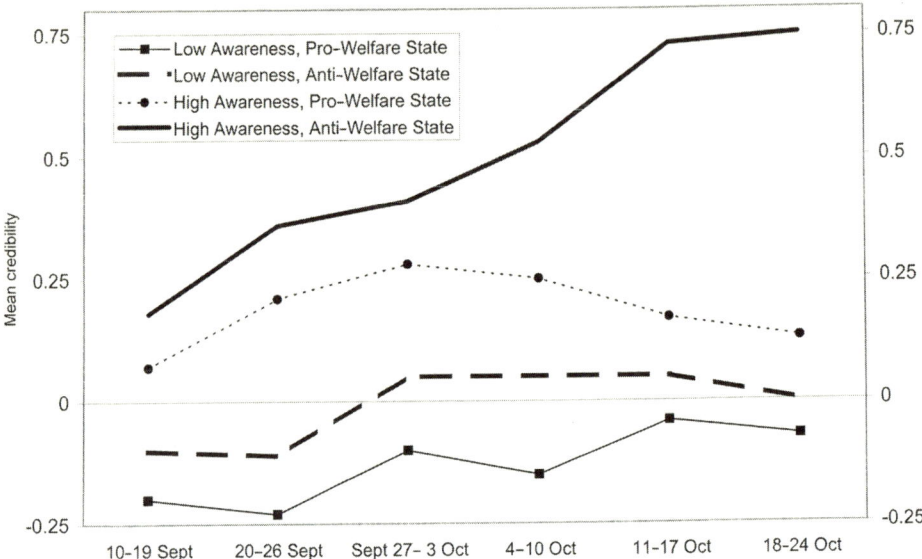

Fig. 4. Evolution of Reform credibility on the deficit by awareness and attitudes toward the welfare state. The awareness and welfare state scales were divided at their respective means to create the four groups ($n = 679, 409, 542, 647$).

the impact of coverage. On the other hand, the more one cares about an issue, the greater one perceives the differences between the parties (Krosnick 1988, 1990). In addition, the other parties certainly attacked the Reform Party's plan by emphasizing its unlikely success and the negative consequences of pursuing it. The contested nature of the plan makes it likely that underlying attitudes will be related to perceptions.

Figure 4 shows the movement in perceptions of Reform credibility within each of the groups. Almost all of the reevaluation of Reform takes place among the politically aware, anti–welfare state group. This confirms that predispositions mattered for being affected by the campaign communication. The weekly mean values for the low aware respondents, regardless of their ideological position, are stable across the campaign, which confirms the importance of awareness in mediating media effects. High aware, pro–welfare state respondents evaluate Reform's credibility to be higher on average than the low aware respondents, and there is a slight downward trend across the last couple weeks of the campaign—not coincidentally when other parties focused their attacks on Reform.

A Media Effects Model of Reform Credibility

The reevaluation of Reform's credibility by politically aware respondents who were ideologically predisposed to be concerned with or at least give priority to the deficit is prima facie evidence of a media-induced campaign effect. The next step is to test whether highly aware respondents responded to a quantifiable campaign stimuli. In this case, the surge and late campaign decline in the amount of Reform coverage is a likely candidate. While increased coverage should make Reform more visible and increase the information available to all respondents on which to make judgments, those who are unlikely to care about the issue or unlikely to receive the information should be less influenced.

The evidence presented in table 2 from the first estimation of the simple model (1) clearly establishes that respondents who were interviewed when Reform was the subject of more news coverage were more likely to view the party as credible on the deficit. The magnitude of the effect is, however, rather weak. A difference of thirty references to Reform in the average coverage of the previous five days is equivalent to only a 0.12 difference on a 5-point scale in perceived credibility. A difference of thirty provides a good benchmark for assessing the impact of coverage since it is substantial but not an unreasonable shift, given that there is a difference of eighty-four Reform mentions between the minimum and maximum averaged coverage variable.

When one considers the mediating factors, the impact of the same shift of coverage is magnified. Coverage has a stronger effect for respondents who score high on the anti–welfare state and awareness indices. The effect of the same change in coverage (30) would produce a 0.5 shift for a maximally aware respondent who scored a reasonable one standard deviation above the mean on the anti–welfare state index.[8] A respondent who was minimally aware would not be affected at all by the shift. When considered this way, the effect of the coverage appears to be stronger but more concentrated.

It is noteworthy that the decline in coverage predicts the drop in credibility at the end of the campaign, even if the drop is a small one relative to the earlier growth. Expanding coverage can be understood as the spreading of information about Reform so as to activate predispositions, but a subsequent drop in coverage should not itself produce a drop in credibility unless respondents are particularly short-memoried. One possibility is that, as Reform became more viable near the end, Reform and its deficit position were under increasing attack from the other parties. It does appear from figure 4 that it is pro–welfare state respondents who were viewing the party as less credible. Since the balance of good and bad press is not factored into the media values, it may be that the drop in credibility has more to do with the balance than the amount.

The Reform Party began the campaign about as credible on the

TABLE 2. News Media Coverage and Reform's Credibility on the Deficit

	Simple Coverage Model		Two-Mediator Model	
	b (s.e.)	Beta	b (s.e.)	Beta
Coverage of reform	0.004*** (0.001)	0.08	0.002 (0.004)	0.04
Coverage × anti–welfare state			−0.006 (0.008)	−0.08
Coverage × awareness			−0.003 (0.007)	−0.04
Coverage × awareness × anti–welfare state			0.028† (0.016)	0.25
Awareness × anti–welfare state	0.925** (0.348)	0.16	−0.164 (0.700)	−0.03
Awareness	0.654*** (0.167)	0.17	0.764* (0.328)	0.20
Anti–welfare state	−0.050 (0.189)	−0.01	0.182 (0.374)	0.04
Demographics				
Education	0.034** (0.011)	0.07	0.033** (0.011)	0.07
Income	−0.068* (0.029)	−0.05	−0.067* (0.029)	−0.05
Woman	0.025 (0.045)	0.01	0.028 (0.045)	0.01
Atlantic	0.100 (0.065)	0.04	0.100 (0.065)	0.04
Western	0.178*** (0.047)	0.09	0.182*** (0.047)	0.09
Intercept	−0.63*** (0.117)		−0.568** (0.176)	
Adj-R^2	0.11		0.11	
SEE	0.95		0.95	
N	2,045		2,045	

Note: Standard errors in parentheses; significant coefficients in boldface.
†$p < .10$ *$p < .05$ **$p < .01$ ***$p < .001$

deficit as its nearest rival, the Conservatives, but for all of that, a significant proportion of the public was not informed enough to say what effect a Reform win would have on the deficit. If Reform could get its message out, it could significantly improve its credibility. Two weeks into the campaign, the media began to devote increased attention to the Reform Party, and that coverage appears to be a plausible explanation for the surge in credibility at least among the politically aware and anti–welfare state respondents. Unfortunately for the Reform Party, a significant number of anti–welfare state respondents never reevaluated Reform on this question.

The Evolution of Reform Support

The campaign mattered for who reevaluated Reform's credibility, and there is good reason to believe that the information provided by news attention was important for that reevaluation. Did news attention to Reform have an effect on Reform support either directly or as a result of the reevaluation of Reform's credibility? In the next section, the relationship between coverage and Reform thermometer rating scores is examined before moving on to an analysis of the effect of credibility on Reform support.

As before, the analysis begins with a picture of the mean evaluation of Reform within the four groups identified earlier. Paralleling the earlier findings with respect to the evolution of credibility, almost all of the evolution of Reform support takes place among those respondents who are in both the high awareness and anti–welfare state groups. Similar results are evident if one uses the party's share of vote intentions rather than mean thermometer scores. Surprisingly, after peaking at a mean of over fifty-five in the fifth week of the campaign, the high aware and anti–welfare state group underwent a significant trend away from the Reform Party. The trend away from Reform among the high aware, anti–welfare state voters can largely be explained in terms of the increasing attacks on Reform and the priming of other noneconomic issues. The low awareness, anti–welfare state respondents become more supportive of Reform, but the magnitude of their increase is small. On Election Day, it appears that awareness only slightly differentiates the anti–welfare state respondents. While this confirms Fournier's (this volume) analysis of the campaign, it suggests that awareness mattered for how respondents got to their final vote.

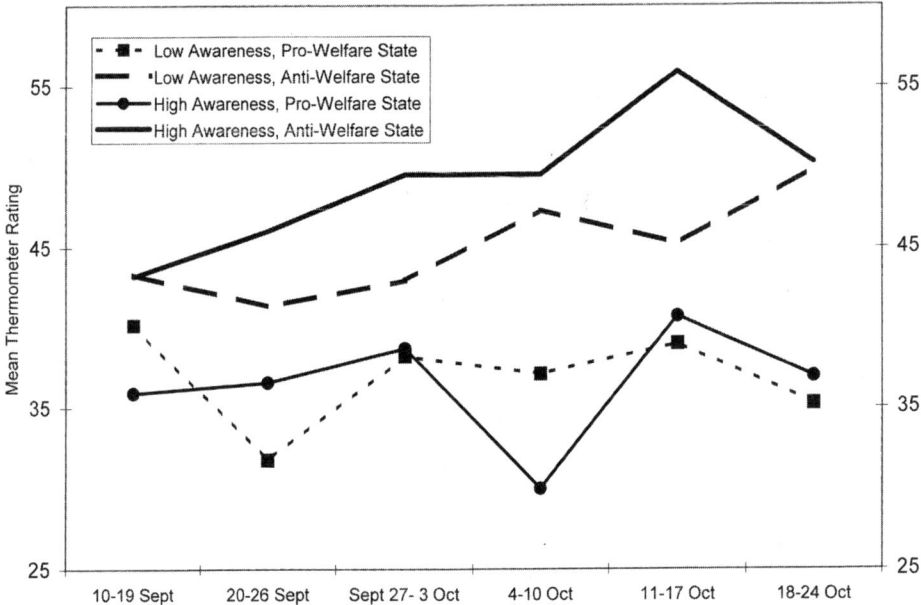

Fig. 5. Reform feeling thermometer by awareness and attitudes toward welfare state. The awareness and welfare state scales were divided at their respective means to create the four groups ($n = 681; n = 411; n = 545; n = 649$).

Coverage of Reform

As noted earlier, a visual inspection of the surges in both coverage and intentions leads us to expect that coverage will affect the path of Reform support. In addition, the evolution of Reform support among high aware, anti–welfare state respondents is evidence of a campaign effect. Of course, the previous analysis suggests that the effect of coverage will be mediated by reception and acceptance variables. The more predisposed an individual is to like Reform, the more he or she should respond to additional press since that press is likely to provide new and pro-Reform messages. The relationship between predispositions and coverage should be, however, dependent on the likelihood of receiving the media cues. The regression model used to estimate the relationship between coverage and credibility is reestimated here with some minor changes. The dependent variable is Reform thermometer rating and the model controls for attitudes toward French Canada.

Table 3 compares the simple coverage model, where coverage is presumed to have an equal impact on all respondents, with a fully specified two-mediator model. The effect of coverage is clearly evident even in the simple model, with each additional unit of coverage associated with a 0.075 change on the 100-point thermometer scale. This is a substantial effect, given that average coverage of Reform in the previous five days ranges between ten and ninety-five. A modest change of thirty translates into a 2.25 unit change on the thermometer rating.

TABLE 3. News Media Coverage and Changing Reform Thermometer Rating

	Simple Coverage Model		Two-Mediator Model	
	b (s.e.)	Beta	b (s.e.)	Beta
Coverage	0.075** (0.023)	0.07	−0.034 (0.089)	−0.03
Coverage × anti–welfare state			0.059 (0.205)	0.04
Coverage × awareness			0.062 (0.183)	0.04
Coverage × awareness × anti–welfare state			0.295 (0.389)	0.11
Awareness × anti–welfare state	30.501*** (8.719)	0.23	19.451 (17.526)	0.14
Awareness	−7.845 (4.202)	−0.08	−10.536 (8.303)	−0.11
Anti–welfare state attitudes	6.075 (4.802)	0.06	3.512 (9.520)	0.03
Anti–French Canada attitudes	11.677*** (2.064)	0.13	11.662*** (2.060)	0.13
Demographics				
Education	−0.118 (0.279)	−0.01	−0.125 (0.279)	−0.01
Income	−1.101 (0.711)	−0.04	−1.106 (0.710)	−0.04
Woman	−0.358 (1.121)	−0.01	−0.301 (1.119)	−0.01
Atlantic	−3.280* (1.665)	−0.05	−3.334* (1.662)	−0.05
Western	6.000*** (1.155)	0.13	6.020*** (1.154)	0.13
Intercept	29.086*** (3.203)		33.570*** (4.684)	
Adj-R^2		0.11		0.11
SEE		22.54		22.55
N		1,878		1,878

Note: Standard errors in parentheses; significant coefficients in boldface.
*$p < .05$ **$p < .01$ ***$p < .001$

The fully specified model reveals that a change in coverage is particularly strong among respondents who are both predisposed to support Reform on ideological grounds and likely to get the news coverage. Unfortunately, the high degree of collinearity that is introduced into the estimation by the interaction terms inflates the standard errors, producing coefficients that are not significant. While this makes hypothesis testing problematic, the coefficients can give us some leverage into the process of campaign change and the importance of individual-level mediators.

Coverage on its own does not have a positive impact on Reform support. The effect of coverage is stronger the higher the respondent's likely reception of the news and/or stronger if the respondent is ideologically compatible with the new information that coverage provides. Most important, being both likely to receive and likely to accept the new information is the most important contributor since the Beta coefficient for the three-way interaction is almost three times larger than either of the two-way interactions with coverage. One can get a feel for the more realistic estimation of the effect of coverage by simulating the impact of a thirty-unit change in coverage for the two-mediator model. Whereas a moderately (one standard deviation from the mean) anti–welfare state respondent who is perfectly informed will rate Reform five points higher if exposed to a thirty-unit change, the same respondent who is perfectly ignorant will rate Reform slightly lower than if coverage had not changed.

The relationship between coverage and intentions confirms the general finding of Zaller and Hunt (1994, 1995) with respect to the Reform Party. The size of the flow of communications about Reform provided a stimulus for an increased likelihood of supporting Reform. More specifically, coverage of Reform interacted with respondents' predispositions and likelihood of receiving political communication; high aware, anti–welfare state respondents responded to the surge in coverage during the middle of the campaign, producing a surge in Reform support (at least for this group).

Reform's Credibility on the Deficit

The two previous tests focused on the coverage-credibility and coverage-support relationships but did not directly test the relationship between credibility and support. To test this relationship a pooled, cross-sectional model of Reform support that incorporates the respondents' position on Reform's credibility (cross-section effect) as well as the mean credibility score for the party on the day the respondent was interviewed (longitudinal or campaign effect) is employed. Given that a pro–welfare state respondent should not be affected by either process, interaction terms are added.

The results in table 4 confirm these expectations. At any time during the campaign, the more credible an individual views the Reform Party, the more likely he or she is to support the party controlling for the aggregate evaluation of Reform. The main effect of credibility is small but significant, which suggests that Reform benefited from positive perceptions on

TABLE 4. Cross-Sectional and Longitudinal Effects of Changing Credibility

	Reform Support
Cross-sectional effect of credibility	
Credibility on deficit	2.655**
	(0.997)
Credibility on deficit × anti–welfare state	9.642***
	(1.987)
Longitudinal effect of credibility	
Daily mean credibility on deficit	−12.100*
	(5.977)
Daily mean credibility × anti–welfare state	33.605**
	(12.497)
Awareness	−3.159
	(2.298)
Anti–welfare state attitudes	13.444***
	(2.497)
Anti–French Canada attitudes	11.826***
	(1.945)
Demographics	
Education	−0.455
	(0.262)
Income	−0.469
	(0.666)
Woman	−0.663
	(1.050)
Atlantic	−4.385**
	(1.555)
Western	4.516***
	(1.090)
Intercept	33.178***
	(2.572)
Adj-R^2	0.91
SEE	21.51
N	1938

Note: Standard errors in parentheses; significant coefficients in boldface.
*$p < .05$ **$p < .01$ ***$p < .001$

this question even among those who were pro–welfare state. Being opposed to the welfare state attitude, however, strengthens the relationship between credibility and support as evident by the anti–welfare state–credibility interaction.

There is also evidence that the time of interview matters. That is, respondents who are interviewed when Reform is perceived by the public as a whole to be more credible are more likely to support the Reform Party. Again, the impact is dependent upon the respondents' underlying attitudes, with pro–welfare state respondents being immune from the trend toward public understanding of Reform's position. In fact, a pro-welfare respondent is likely to have a lower rating of Reform as public understanding of Reform's position increases. When the public as a whole understands Reform's *true* nature, pro–welfare state voters make fewer mistakes.[9]

While the link between credibility perceptions and support as demonstrated is clear, there is the possibility of individual projection effects where respondents perceive the party to be more credible because they intend to vote for that party. Since coverage plays a significant activation role for both dependent variables, projection effects only make it difficult to sort out the causal direction between credibility perceptions and Reform support. Projection effects do not change the argument that the campaign mattered for activation or that media coverage was an exogenous cause of the change in credibility and support.

Summary and Conclusion

The 1993 campaign clearly mattered for the distribution of political support on Election Day. In particular, coverage of Reform in the television news media was critical to the movement of Reform's support during the campaign. After the news media discovered Reform, the increased attention, combined with the emphasis on government spending and the deficit in the news coverage, contributed to more informed and positive judgments about Reform's credibility on the deficit. As a result, Reform was able to capture an increasing share of vote intentions. As information changed at least some voters were better able to link their underlying attitudes about the deficit to their choice.

Voters were, of course, motivated to support the Reform Party for more reasons than the party's position on the deficit and welfare state. Reform has traditionally appealed to those voters who share right-wing attitudes on cultural questions, such as the recognition of Quebec's place in Canada and the federal government's multiculturalism and immigration policies. Before the campaign began Canadians were aware of the party's position on this dimension, and the campaign did not encourage more learning. It is true, however, that a changing news discourse that featured a greater emphasis on multiculturalism and immigration in the last couple weeks did prime attitudes about minorities for voters (Jenkins 1999b). At the end of the campaign, both attitudes about the welfare state and attitudes about minorities in Canada were important.

If the analysis helps come to terms with the Reform success in 1993, it also provides important lessons for understanding the flow of communication in a campaign. It appears that, despite their intensity and the news coverage that they produce, campaigns do not reach everybody. The most knowledgeable are also the most likely to receive campaign communication. Reception is, however, only half of the story. The politically aware are not passive receptors. Instead, they tend to accept messages that are consistent with their predispositions. Those respondents who held pro–welfare state positions—positions inconsistent with Reform's location on the issue—were unaffected by the changing news environment.

While it appears that the 1993 campaign failed to reach those voters who are habitually unaware of political events, this is only part of the story. Setting aside the pro–welfare state voters who were unaffected by the campaign regardless of their awareness, the low aware voters who were predisposed to like Reform policies simply took longer to respond to campaign information. Of course, once they did the effect was smaller and they were no longer in step with the political discourse of the campaign. If low awareness voters learn anything during the campaign, it does not necessarily lead them to resemble those with higher levels of information (Bartels 1996; cf. Fournier, this volume). Low aware respondents did not figure out where Reform was located on the deficit. They were, however, just as likely to support the Reform Party at the end of the campaign. Low aware respondents gradually became more likely to support the Reform Party, while high aware respondents reduced their support over the final ten days paralleling the reduced coverage of Reform. High aware respondents brought their intentions in line with their welfare state position, leading to a significant shift toward Reform for most of the campaign and then away from the party at the end of the campaign. Low aware respondents gradually moved toward Reform.

These results suggest that campaigns can matter. Whenever the availability of political cues in the news media changes, there is the potential for campaign effects that are not by necessity ephemeral. News coverage allows voters, especially those attentive to the campaign, to locate parties and thereby figure out who to vote for given their underlying attitudes. The lack of information in the mass public about Reform set the stage for the campaign effects observed in 1993, and, more important, the shift in news coverage could not be predicted before the campaign started. These findings are consistent with Perot's campaign in 1992, but this does not mean that campaign effects will be restricted to elections that involve insurgents. In multiparty races, when there is more than one potential dimension of conflict or when a dramatic event changes the available cues about a party or its leader, there is the possibility of campaign effects of this kind. In fact, the notion that campaigns activate preexisting preferences assumes that voters only have one choice given their attitudes. It may only be in highly structured contests that this assumption will hold.

APPENDIX A: Awareness Scale

The scale was composed of seven items: six questions and the interviewer rating. The party position questions were all asked during the postelection wave of the survey, whereas the two questions about macroeconomic conditions—inflation and unemployment—were asked during the campaign. Responses to the macroeconomic condition questions are not related to time of interview, so using the campaign wave of the survey is unproblematic. Removing an item has almost no effect on the mean, variance, or alpha value of the scale. In addition to the six questions asked of respondents, the scale adds the interviewer rating of the respondent's political knowledge (Zaller 1992). The scale was standardized to vary between 0 and 1.

Question Wording

   pese17a: Do you happen to know which party promised do away with the North American Free Trade Agreement (NAFTA)? (1st response)

   pese18a: Do you happen to know which party promised to eliminate the deficit in three years? (1st response)

   pese19a: And do you happen to know which party promised to eliminate the deficit in five years? (1st response) pese20a: Do you happen to know which party promised to increase spending on public works? (1st response)

cpsh5: What would you say the inflation rate in Canada is these days, approximately? (correct response within ±2 percent)

cpsh4: What would you say the unemployment rate is these days, approximately? (correct response within 1.5 percent)

APPENDIX B: News Media Data

Data on television news media coverage were originally collected by the National Media Archive (Fraser Institute, Vancouver, British Columbia). The data were originally collected to serve the interests of the National Media Archive, which monitors media practices and is particularly concerned with questions of fairness in the coverage of different networks. The media archive transcribed election stories of the two major English language daily national news broadcasts (CBC and CTV).

Each transcript was then broken into codeable phrases that varied in length but captured a particular idea or reference. There are 14,327 coded bits contained in 531 election stories during the forty-five days of the campaign (September 8–October 24, 1993). Each bit was then assigned a code for who spoke the identified phrase and their partisan affiliation; the party that was discussed in or targeted by the phrase; the valence of the phrase (positive, neutral, or negative); and whether the phrase involved a discussion of the campaign (if so, what aspect?) or a particular issue (if so, what issue?). The coding was undertaken by two coders, and a random sample of the data was checked for intercoder reliability (0.87).

NOTES

1. Since Reform ran no candidates in Quebec and others have argued that Quebec represents a different electorate (Johnston et al. 1992), for the purposes of this essay all analysis refers to the electorate outside Quebec.

2. See appendix A for information about the construction of the awareness scale. While self-reported media use is on the surface a basis for distinguishing respondents in terms of reception, it does not perform as well as factual questions (Zaller 1992; Price and Zaller 1993). Knowledge distinguishes people on the basis of "attending to, comprehending, and retaining news" (Price and Zaller 1993, 134), and this is closer to the likelihood of receiving political communication.

3. See appendix B for discussion of media data.

4. A Granger causality test applied to the two series allowed the author to reject the null hypothesis that coverage did not Granger-cause intentions with six

different lag structures. In addition, an error-correction analysis of the two series found that a change in coverage had both an immediate and long-term effect on the amount of Reform support (Jenkins 1999a).

5. To allow for both recent coverage and some memory from recent days, the coverage variable is the amount of coverage of which the Reform Party was the object, averaged over the five days before the respondent was interviewed. This is generally consistent with the findings concerning the path of the aggregate series (Jenkins 1999a). The point of the coverage variable is to provide a representation of the media environment when the respondent was interviewed.

6. The French Canada index is different from the index used by Johnston et al. (1996) in that the postelection items have been dropped to increase the number of valid cases.

7. In fact, including party identification has only minor effects on the interaction coefficients.

8. This simulation is based on a hypothetical respondent who is high school educated, is middle income, and is a woman from Ontario.

9. Since some pro–welfare state voters will support Reform despite its position on social programs, not all of their support for Reform is the result of mistakes.

REFERENCES

Bartels, Larry M. 1988. *Presidential Primaries and the Dynamics of Public Choice.* Princeton: Princeton University Press.

———. 1996. "Uninformed Votes: Information Effects in Presidential Elections." *American Journal of Political Science* 40:194–230.

Brady, Henry E. 1993. "Knowledge, Strategy, and Momentum in Presidential Elections." *Political Analysis* 5:1–38.

Brady, Henry E., and Stephen Ansolabehere. 1989. "The Nature of Utility Functions in Mass Publics." *American Political Science Review* 83 (1): 143–63.

Brady, Henry E., and Richard Johnston. 1996. "Statistical Methods for Analyzing Rolling Cross-Sections with Examples from the 1988 and 1993 Canadian Election Studies." Paper presented at the annual meeting of the Midwest Political Science Association, Chicago, April 18–20.

Brians, Craig L., and Martin P. Wattenberg. 1996. "Campaign Issue Knowledge and Salience: Comparing Reception from TV Commercials, TV News, and Newspapers." *American Journal of Political Science* 40 (1): 172–93.

Converse, Philip E. 1962. "Information Flow and the Stability of Partisan Attitudes." *Public Opinion Quarterly* 26:578–99.

Dalton, Russell J., Paul A. Beck, and Robert Huckfeldt. 1998. "Partisan Cues and the Media: Information Flows in the 1992 Presidential Election." *American Political Science Review* 92 (1): 111–26.

Festinger, Leon. 1957. *A Theory of Cognitive Dissonance.* Stanford: Stanford University Press.

Finkel, Steven E. 1993. "Reexamining the 'Minimal Effects' Model in Recent Presidential Campaigns." *Journal of Politics* 55 (1): 1–21.

Gelman, Andrew, and Gary King. 1993. "Why Are American Presidential Election

Campaign Polls So Variable When Votes Are So Predictable?" *British Journal of Political Science* 23:409–51.

Holbrook, Thomas M. 1996. *Do Campaigns Matter?* Thousand Oaks, CA: Sage.

Jenkins, Richard W. 1999a. "How Much Is Too Much? Media Attention and Popular Support for an Insurgent Party." *Political Communication* 16:429–45.

———. 1999b. "Campaigns, the Media and Insurgent Success: The Reform Party and the 1993 Election." PhD diss., University of British Columbia, Vancouver.

Johnston, Richard, André Blais, Henry E. Brady, and Jean Crête. 1992. *Letting the People Decide: Dynamics of a Canadian Election.* Kingston: McGill-Queen's Press.

Johnston, Richard, André Blais, Henry E. Brady, Elisabeth Gidengil, and Neil Nevitte. 1996. "The 1993 Canadian Election Campaign: Realignment, Dealignment, or Something Else?" Paper presented at the annual meeting of the American Political Science Association, San Francisco.

Johnston, Richard, André Blais, Elisabeth Gidengil, Neil Nevitte, and Henry E. Brady. 1994. "The Collapse of a Party System? The 1993 Canadian General Election." Paper presented at the annual meeting of the American Political Science Association, New York, September.

Joslyn, Mark R., and Steve Ceccoli. 1996. "Attentiveness to Television News and Opinion Change in the Fall 1992 Presidential Campaign." *Political Behavior* 18 (2): 141–70.

Krosnick, Jon A. 1988. "The Role of Attitude Importance in Social Evaluation: A Study of Policy Preferences, Presidential Candidate Evaluations, and Voting Behaviour." *Journal of Personality and Social Psychology* 55 (2): 196–210.

———. 1990. "Government Policy and Citizen Passion: A Study of Issue Publics in Contemporary America." *Political Behavior* 12:59–92.

Lazarsfeld, Paul, Bernard Berelson, and Hazel Gaudet. 1948. *The People's Choice.* 2d ed. New York: Columbia University Press.

Lewis-Beck, Michael S., and Tom W. Rice. 1992. *Forecasting Elections.* Washington, DC: Congressional Quarterly.

McGuire, William J. 1968. "Personality and Susceptibility to Social Influence." In *Handbook of Personality Theory and Research*, ed. E. F. Borgatta and W. W. Lambert. Chicago: Rand-McNally.

———. 1969. "The Nature of Attitudes and Attitude Change." In *Handbook of Social Psychology*, ed. Gardner Lindzey and Elliott Aronson, vol. 3, 2d ed. Reading, MA: Addison-Wesley.

———. 1986. "The Myth of Mass Media Impact: Savagings and Salvagings." *Public Communication and Behavior* 1:173–257.

Nadeau, Richard, and André Blais. 1993. "Explaining Election Outcomes in Canada: Economy and Politics." *Canadian Journal of Political Science* 26 (4): 775–90.

———. 1995. "Economic Conditions, Leader Evaluations and Election Outcomes in Canada." *Canadian Public Policy* 21 (2): 212–18.

Price, Vincent, and John Zaller. 1993. "Measuring Individual Differences in Likelihood of News Reception." *Public Opinion Quarterly* 57:133–64.

Rhee, June W., and Joseph N. Cappella. 1997. "The Role of Political Sophistication in Learning From News." *Communication Research* 24 (3): 197–233.

Rosenstone, Steven J. 1983. *Forecasting Presidential Elections.* New Haven: Yale University Press.
Schmitt-Beck, Rüdiger. 1996. "Mass Media, the Electorate, and the Bandwagon: A Study of Communication Effects on Vote Choice in Germany." *International Journal of Public Opinion Research* 8 (32): 266–91.
Zaller, John. 1992. *The Nature and Origins of Mass Opinion.* New York: Cambridge University Press.
———. 1996. "The Myth of Mass Media Impact Revived: New Support for a Discredited Idea." In *Political Persuasion and Attitude Change,* ed. Diana C. Mutz, Paul M. Sniderman, and Richard Brody, 17–78. Ann Arbor: University of Michigan Press.
Zaller, John, and Mark Hunt. 1994. "The Rise and Fall of Candidate Perot: Unmediated versus Mediated Politics—Part I." *Political Communication* 11:357–90.
———. 1995. "The Rise and Fall of Candidate Perot: The Outsider versus the Political System—Part II." *Political Communication* 12:97–123.

Contributors

R. Michael Alvarez is professor of political science at the California Institute of Technology.

Stephen Ansolabehere is professor of political science at the Massachusetts Institute of Technology.

Larry M. Bartels is Donald E. Stokes Professor of Public and International Affairs and director of the Center for the Study of Democratic Politics at Princeton University.

André Blais holds the Canada Research Chair in Electoral Studies and is professeur titulaire of political science at the Université de Montréal.

Henry E. Brady is Class of 1941 Monroe Deutsch Professor of Political Science and Public Policy and director of the Survey Research Center and of UC DATA at the University of California, Berkeley.

Laurel Elms is a doctoral student at the University of California, Berkeley.

Joanna Everitt is associate professor of political science at the University of New Brunswick, St. John.

Patrick Fournier is professeur adjoint in political science at the Université de Montréal.

Elisabeth Gidengil is professor of political science at McGill University.

Benjamin Highton is associate professor of political science at the University of California, Davis.

Gary C. Jacobson is professor of political science at the University of California, San Diego.

Richard Jenkins is corporate director of public opinion research at TNS Canadian Facts.

Richard Johnston is professor of political science and Distinguished University Scholar at the University of British Columbia.

Neil Nevitte is professor of political science at the University of Toronto.

Alexandra Shankster is a doctoral student at the University of California, San Diego.

John Sides is assistant professor of political science at George Washington University.

Paul M. Sniderman is Fairleigh S. Dickinson Jr. Professor of Public Policy and professor of political science at Stanford University.

Jack Vowles is professor of political science at the University of Auckland, New Zealand.

Index

abortion, 55; and candidate issue positions and effect on voters, 9, 243–55; and Freedom of Choice Act, 243; and *Roe v. Wade*, 243; and *Webster v. Reproductive Health Services*, 243
Abramowitz, Alan I., 218n3, 222, 228
Abrams, Samuel, 90
acceptability bias, 31
Achen, Christopher, 129, 131, 137, 138, 140, 143, 153, 159
activation of preferences, 5, 50, 80, 92, 356; problem with model of, 357–59
advertising, 31, 116; and campaigns, 14, 98, 307–32; and candidate shares, 316; negative, 117, 309–11; positive, 309–11
agenda setting, 48, 70
Alesina, Alberto, 33
Allsop, Dee, 20n7
Allum, Nick, 49
Althaus, Scott L., 45, 47
Alvarez, R. Michael, 9, 10, 17, 21n21, 71, 94, 242, 247, 263, 323
Angrist, Joshua, 132n3
Ansolabehere, Stephen, on: campaign spending, 204, 206, 218n3, 236; minimal effects model, 9; negative advertising, 10, 13, 21n22, 29, 127, 128, 307; preference formation, 264, 359; priming, 340
attack advertising, 10, 30; effects of, 309–11, 329–31
Austen-Smith, David, 35, 36

"average causal effect" (in experiments), 120, 130
awareness. *See* political awareness

ballot, partisan and nonpartisan, 123–24
Banducci, Susan, 338
bandwagon voting, 127–28; 263–64. *See also* strategic considerations
bandwidth, 179–81, 182–85. *See also* graphical smoothing
Banks, Jeffrey, 35, 36
Barone, Michael, 225, 240n5
Barrilleaux, Charles, 250
Bartels, Larry M., on: advertising campaigns, 333n2; campaign spending, 21n22, 204; effects of media exposure, 29, 73n21, 129, 130, 131, 139, 146, 160n4, 340, 359; forecasting, 7, 20n9, 97; learning models, 35, 45, 80, 101; measurement error, 14, 50, 51, 52, 53, 141, 154, 218n3; panel design, 15, 68, 136, 143; political reasoning, 47, 54, 55, 72n3, 151, 377; polls, 277n1; primaries, 6, 81, 82, 83, 89, 94, 135, 164, 360; priming, 9, 11
Bartolini, S., 301n2
Bastien, Frederick, 264
Baumgartner, Frank R., 21n15
Beck, Nathaniel, 97, 160n14
Beck, Paul A., 360
Behr, Roy, 340

385

Berelson, Bernard R., 4, 5, 15, 19n4, 30, 49, 80, 81, 85, 92, 127, 135, 358
Berkman, Michael, 250, 258n10
Bernoulli trial, 36
Bierly, Margaret, 338
Blais, André, 11, 45, 71, 73n16, 158, 263, 264, 265, 278n1, 281, 351n11, 359
Bollen, Kenneth A., 141
Bos, Theodore, 160n14
Bowers, Jacob, 17
Boyer, Martin, 158, 265
Box-Steffensmeier, Janet M., 145, 204
Bradshaw, Joel, 21n13
Brady, Henry E., on: campaign effects, 11, 29; effects of media on perceptions of candidates, 340, 359; measurement error, 137; research design, 249, 251; rolling cross section, 16, 134, 160n11, 189, 190, 192n11, 193n17, 302n11, 341, 346, 352n16, 357, 366
Brannon, Laura R., 8, 48, 72n6
Brau, Shawn, 13, 21n14
Brehm, John, 153, 154
Breuning, Marijke, 68, 148
Brians, Craig Leonard, 21n22, 360
Brichta, A., 282
Brody, Richard A., 45, 46, 72n5, 125
Brown, James W., 49
Burkhart, Michael P., 218n3
Bush, George H.W., 21n17, 29, 30, 80, 95, 99, 100, 115
Butler, David, 264, 278n3

Caldeira, Gregory A., 10
Calvert, Randall, 35
campaign: activity, 6; advertising, 9, 199; advertising and effects on electoral success, 307–32; challenges to study of, 121–31; as context of deliberation, 50–51; definition of, 1–3; discourse, effect of, 4, 48; effectiveness of for incumbents, 230–34; effects of on voter perceptions, 45; effort, spending as indication of, 5; and enlightenment vs manipulation of voters, 19; as experiment, 115–32, 308; institutional conditions of, 1–2; intensity of, 2–3, 224, 249; and learning effects, 50, 62, 224, 359, 360–78; as mobilizer of voters, 30; negative, 10; orientations, 30; and policy voting, 242–55; and priming of the economy, 9; and priming of issue preferences, 94–95, 99–100; and reduction of heterogeneity in decision-making, 69–70; as reinforcer of existing political spending, 200–217, 234–37
Campbell, Angus, 5, 7, 21n16, 30, 92
Campbell, Donald T., 134, 259n17
Campbell, James E., 7, 9, 90, 193n17
Canadian Election Studies (CES), 55, 191n8; as field experiments, 14; and rolling cross-sections, 16, 135, 187–89, 224, 264, 273, 357
candidates, advertising by, 309; campaigns and voter perceptions of, 8, 45, 83, 95–97, 98, 116, 139–40, 145, 199; effects on voting behaviour, 242–57; as factor in intensity, 4; gendered perceptions of, 336–50; issue ownership by, 12; name recall and recognition of, 225–28; perceived competence and credibility of, 6, 33; polls and voter perceptions of, 271–72; spending by, 5; spending and recognition of, 208–17; viability of, 6. *See also* leaders
Cappella, Joseph N., 360
Carroll, R.J., 185
Carsey, Thomas M., 8, 21n20
Carter, Jimmy, 90, 91, 92, 95, 138, 145, 159n1
Ceccoli, Steve, 343, 360
Clawson, Rosalee A., 48, 50
cleavages, 9
Cleveland, William, 182, 240n2
Clinton, Bill, 73n15, 80, 91, 97, 100, 122, 182, 215, 218n14
Clinton, Joshua D., 21n22

Cloutier, Édouard, 73n21, 264
coalitional signal, as a strategic consideration, 11
Coates, Dennis, 204
cognitive dissonance, 31, 360
cognitive shortcuts, 31, 47; viability of candidate as, 340
Cohen, Jeffrey E., 250
Columbia School, 4, 5, 6, 20n5
Combs, J. E., 314
competence, perceived, of party leaders/candidates, 6, 33
competitiveness, factors in, 12
conditioning. *See* panel conditioning
Condorcet's jury theorem, 35, 36
congressional elections, 4, 5, 8; and campaign spending, 199–217; and incumbent candidates, 221–38
Conover, Pamela Johnston, 10, 94
contagion effect. *See* bandwagon effect
conventions, nominating, 3, 116, 122; as experimental treatments, 124
Converse, Philip E., 5, 137, 138, 143, 145, 356
Cook, Elizabeth Adell, 259n19, 338
Cook, Thomas D., 134, 259n17
Coombs, Steven L., 21n15
Copeland, Gary A., 314
counterfactual reasoning, value of, 242; research methods used to approximate, 243–55
Cox, Gary, 263, 264, 281, 282, 300, 301n1, 302n10
credibility, of leaders/candidates, 3; of parties, 361–78
Crewe, Ivor, 42
cross-sectional survey, 5; and measurement of campaign spending, 207

Dalager, Jon K., 10, 308
Dalton, Russell J., 360
Day, George S., 168
Deaton, Angus, 190
debates, 3, 6, 7, 14, 98, 116, 165, 187, 266–67; as experimental treatments, 124; media coverage of, 337; and perceptions of Al Gore's honesty, 165–68, 182–85
deliberative poll, 49
Delli Carpini, Michael X., 45, 47, 54, 56
Dilullio, John, 33
Dobrzynska, Agnieszka, 351n11
Dolan, Kathleen, 343, 351n5
Downs, Anthony, 31, 33
Druckman, J., 333n7
Dunkelberg, William C., 168

economic voting, 9; model of, 32–37
economy, 8, campaigns and perceptions of, 95–97; and effect on competitiveness, 12; and election outcomes, 32–42; and forecasting, 7, 9, 29, 78–79; and private information, 31
education, and issue voting, 323–27; and media exposure, 323
Edwards, W., 297
elections, forecasting, 7
Electoral College, 3
electoral systems, 37, 263, 273; and strategic voting, 280–300
Elms, Laurel, 14, 17, 39
Equal Rights Amendment (ERA), 246
Erbring, Lutz, 21n15
Erickson, Lynda, 339
Erikson, Robert S., 20n12, 32, 193n17, 204, 218n3
Ettema, James S., 49
events, 79, 80, 135, 156, 165; as experimental treatments, 124; and priming issues, 8
Everitt, Joanna, 12, 337
exit polls, 250, 310, 323. *See also* polls
expectations, and campaign spending, 204; and effect of party identification, 295–98; and influence on vote intention, 280–300; and polls, 263–73, 281–83, 286–91, 296–300; of voters, 11, 263
expenditure. *See* spending, candidate
experimental control, 118–20
experiments, 340; campaigns as, 115–32

Fair, Ray, 7
Fan, David P., 341
Fedderson, Timothy, 35
Federal Election Campaign Act (1971), 200
Federal Election Commission, 124, 218n13, 236, 240n6
Feldman, Stanley, 10, 94, 137, 143, 159n3
Felsenthal, D. S., 282
Ferejohn, J. A., 307
Festinger, Leon, 360
Fey, M., 301n1
field experiments, 14
Finkel, Steven E., 15, 19n3, 21n22, 50, 78, 81, 136, 307, 358, 359
Fiorina, Morris P., 31, 33, 34, 90
Fishkin, James, 45, 47, 50, 54, 55
Fiske, Susan, 56
focus groups, 117
forecasting models, 7, 35, 41, 78, 81, 90, 97. *See also* minimal effects model
Forsythe, R., 281, 297
Fournier, Patrick, 10, 45, 47, 371, 377
Framing, 31, 48, 70, 200, 340
Franklin, Charles H., 10, 22n27, 45, 94, 145, 159
Freedman, Paul, 21n22, 22n28, 308, 310
Freedom of Choice Act, 243
Freeman, John R., 160n9
Free Trade Agreement (FTA), 6, 21n25, 55, 187
Fritz, Sara, 236
Frizzell, Alan, 340
Fuller, Wayne A., 141

Gallup, George, 73n21
Garand, James C., 7
Garramone, G. M., 307
Gaudet, Hazel, 4, 5, 15, 49, 81, 135, 358
Geer, John, 21n22
Geertz, Clifford, 115
Gelman, Andrew, on: activation of preferences, 50; impact of the economy, 9, 20n5, 78–79, 85, 97, 237, 356, 358; polls and election outcomes, 80, 124; voter decision-making 30, 45
gender, in conditioning voter response, 12, 336–50; identity, 337, 338, 339; as information for voters, 123
Gerber, Alan S., 10, 14, 131, 218n3, 236
Gerbner, George, 49
Germond, Jack, 30, 80, 99
Gidengil, Elisabeth, 11, 12, 337
Glantz, Stanton A., 218n3
Glazer, A., 307
Goidel, Robert, 73n21, 204
Goldenberg, Edie N., 21n15, 340, 352n13
Goldstein, Ken, 21n22, 22n28, 308, 310
Golebiowska, Ewa, 347
Gordon, T. F., 311
Gore, Al, 21n18, 22n28; debates and perceptions of, 165–68, 174–79, 181, 182, 191n2; and failure to emphasize the economy, 90, 97; and forecasting models, 9
Goren, Paul, 72n2
"Granger causality" and cross-lag models in panel data, 160n9
graphical smoothing, by locally weighted scatterplot smoothing (LOWESS or LOESS), 182–85; by moving averages, 182–85; and rolling cross sections, 16, 165, 175–85; and splines, 182–85
Green, Donald P., 10, 14, 160n6, 204, 218n3
Green, P. J., 185
Greene, Steven, 337
Grier, Kevin B., 204
Grofman, Bernard, 267, 307
Gross, Donald A., 204
Groves, Robert M., 168
Guay, Jean H., 73n21, 264
gubernatorial elections, 148, 308–32
Guskind, R., 312

Hagen, Michael G., on campaign as natural experiment, 18; on evaluations of candidates, 21n18, 45, 165, 182; on party identification, 192n10; on rolling cross section, 16, 187
Hammond, Thomas H., 21n20
Hangstrom, J., 312
Hansen, John Mark, 10, 250
Hardle, Wolfgang, 179
Hawkins, Thomas M., 168
Heckman, James, 132n3, 153, 154
Heise, David R., 138
heterogeneity, of decision-making, 45–70
Hetherington, Marc J., 21n17
Hibbs, Douglas A. Jr., 7, 42n1
Highton, Benjamin, 9
Hill, David, 48
Hillygus, D. Sunshine, 15
Holbrook, Thomas, 7, 9, 10, 20n10, 21n16, 37, 49, 80, 84, 124, 174, 356, 358
Holland, Paul, 242
House of Representatives, elections as one-sided information flows, 39
Huckfeldt, Robert, 360
Huddy, Leonie, 347, 348
Humes, Brian D., 21n20
Hunt, Mark, 149, 357, 360, 374
Hurley, Norman L., 47
Hutchings, Vincent L., 8

Imbens, Guido, 132n3
incumbent candidates, 2; and activation model, 358; and campaign strategies, 311; in congressional elections, 221–38; and information, 67, 123; name recall and recognition of, 225–28; popularity of, administration and forecasting models, 7; and spending levels, 200–204; spending and recognition of, 208–17
independent voters, 40, 150–52
"information flow," 4
information and: campaign effects, 30, 47–48, 122–25, 200, 356–57; as experimental stimulus, 116; and gender stereotyping, 347–48; and incumbency, 67, 221–38; and knowledge gap hypothesis, 49, 62, 70; lack of, 47; low vs high levels, 30, 62–67; measurement of levels of, 56; one-sided and two-sided flows of, 39–41; private, 31, 33–34, 38–40; public, 31, 37–41; and reasoning 45–70; updating of, 34–35
informing, role of campaigns in, 10, 13
instrument effect, 15
intensity, of campaign 2–3, 224, 308; and policy voting, 249
interest, 10; and mobilization, 40; prior levels and campaign effects, 30; and reception of information, 38–41
issue, salience of, 5, 6; campaigns and impact on preferences, 94–95, 99; dimensionality of, context, 12; education and, voting, 323–27; novelty of, 12; television advertising and, voting, 319–27
issue positions, of voters, 8
Iyengar, Shanto, on: negative advertising, 10, 13, 21n22, 29, 39, 117, 127, 128, 307; preference formation, 264; priming, 8, 31, 72n6, 85, 116, 340

Jackman, Simon, 15, 159
Jacobson, Gary C., 5, 10, 17, 29, 39, 131, 199, 204, 205, 216, 218n3, 221, 224, 230, 231, 246, 311, 313
Jamieson, Kathleen Hall, on: advertising campaigns, 333n2; campaign as natural experiment, 18; evaluations of candidates, 21n18, 45, 165, 182; party identification, 192n10; rolling cross section, 16, 187
Jelen, Ted G., 259n19
Jenkins, Richard, 11, 71, 363, 377, 380n4
Jennings, M. Kent, 135
Johnson-Cartee, Karen S., 314
Johnston, J., 204

Johnston, Richard, on: campaign effects on individual voting behavior, 24, 45, 356, 358; campaign as natural experiment, 18; Canadian campaigns, 73n16, 81, 357, 361, 362, 366, 367, 379n1, 380n6; Canadian television news coverage, 339, 340; candidate evaluations, 165, 182, 294, 340, 351n2; party identification, 20n7, 192n10, 267, 352n14; political information, 47, 48, 50, 55, 66, 68, 72n7; polls, 11, 264, 281, 297; priming, 8, 21n18, 85; research design, 249, 251; rolling cross section, 6, 16, 134, 138, 158, 160n11, 187, 188, 190, 193n17, 224, 302n11, 341, 346, 357; strategic voting, 122, 128
Jones, Bryan D., 21n15
Joreskog, Karl G., 138
Joslyn, Richard, 340, 343, 360
Jowell, Roger, 45, 47, 50, 55
Just, Marion R., 81, 136

Kahn, Kim Fridkin, 4, 8, 19n2, 21n22, 108n2, 340, 347, 352n13
Karp, Jeffrey A., 338
Kavanagh, Dennis, 278n3
Keeter, Scott, 45, 47, 54, 56
Keith, Bruce E., 150, 152
Kelley, Stanley, 108
Kenney, Patrick J., 4, 8, 19n2, 21n22, 108n2
Kenny, Christopher, 204, 224
Kern, Montague, 99
Kernell, Samuel, 125, 224
kernel weights (graphical), 177, 178–79, 182
Key, V. O., 30, 31
Kinder, Donald, 8, 31, 72n6, 85, 116
King, David, 347
King, Gary, on: impact of the economy, 9, 20n5, 78–79, 85, 97, 237, 356, 358; voter decision-making, 30, 45; activation of preferences, 50; polls and election outcomes, 80, 124
knowledge, 199; and campaign spending, 200–217; measures of, 34, 56, 221, 223
knowledge gap hypothesis, 49, 70. See also under information
Kramer, Gerald, 33, 34, 37, 42n1
Krasno, Jonathan S., 204, 218n3
Krause, George A., 47
Krosnick, Jon A., 8, 48, 50, 68, 72n6, 85, 148
Kuklinski, James H., 47
Kwak, Nojin, 49

laboratory experiments, 13–14
Lahda, Krishna K., 47
Lapinski, John S., 21n22
Lau, Richard R., 21n22, 56, 307, 308
Laver, M., 301n3
Lazarsfeld, Paul F., 4, 5, 15, 19n4, 30, 49, 80, 85, 92, 127, 135, 358
leaders, 45; evaluations of, 46, 55; gender and evaluation of, 339–50. See also candidates
learning, 8, 35, 46, 62, 69; through campaigns, 50, 356; through deliberative poll, 49; media impact on, 360–78
Leeper, Mark Stephen, 347
Leighton, Melissa V., 351n5
Lenz, Gabriel, 85, 86, 108
Levitt, Steven, 204
Lewis, Kathryn E., 338
Lewis-Beck, Michael, 7, 37, 42n1, 78, 359
Leys, C., 281
Lijphart, Arend, 280
Lin, Tse-Min, 160n9
locally weighted scatterplot smoothing (LOWESS/LOESS), 182–85
Lodge, Milton, 13, 20n12, 21n14
LOESS. See locally weighted scatterplot smoothing
Londregan, John, 33
LOWESS. See locally weighted scatterplot smoothing
low information rationality, 47
Luepker, Russell V., 49

Lupia, Arthur, 47
Luskin, Robert, 45, 47, 50, 54, 56

MacKuen, Michael B., 21n15, 48
Magleby, David B., 217
Mair, P., 301n2
Mann, Thomas E., 221–24, 228, 230
Marcus, George E., 10, 21n19
Markko, Gregory A., 10
Markus, Gregory B., 15, 81, 136
Massicotte, Louis, 264, 281
mass media. *See* media
Matland, Richard E., 347
McBurnett, Michael, 204, 224
McClure, Robert D., 81, 136
McCombs, Maxwell E., 21n15
McDermott, Monika L., 347
McFarlane, Deborah R., 250
McGuire, William J., 21n24, 357, 360
McGraw, Kathleen M., 20n12
McKelvey, Richard, 116
McPhee, William N., 4, 5, 15, 19n4, 30, 49, 80, 81, 85, 92, 127, 135
measurement error, 129; and panel design, 15, 137–47; and party identification measure, 189; and rolling cross sections, 175–76; and survey data, 124
media, attention and intensity of campaign, 2–4, 6, 19, 357–58; cumulative impact of, coverage, 345; exposure to, 15, 138–39; "horse-race" coverage, 340, 349–50; mainstream effect of, on public opinion 49–50, 70; and name recognition and recall of incumbents, 232; polarization effect of, on public opinion, 49–50; political awareness and, message reception, 360–78; and priming, 8, 121, 340; and sex-differentiated coverage of campaign, 337; susceptibility of public influence from, 48; "two-mediator model" of, effects, 357, 366, 373
Meech Lake Accord (Canada), 6, 55
Meier, Kenneth J., 250

Mendelberg, Tali, 8, 13, 85
Mendelsohn, Matthew, 8, 21n18, 337, 339, 340, 351n10, 352n12
Menino, Thomas, 115
Merritt, S., 307, 311
Miller, Nicholas R., 47, 48, 50, 72n6
Miller, Warren E., 5, 131, 199, 228, 243, 255, 259n12
"minimal effects" model, 356; as based on Presidential elections, 8; explanation of, 4; factors leading to refutation of, 7, 13. *See also* forecasting models
mobilization, of voters, 3, 10, 13; campaigns' role in, 30; two-sided information flow and, 40
Moffitt, Robert, 190
Monson, J. Quin, 217
Moore, David W., 49
Morgan, Michael, 49
Morris, Dwight, 236
moving average. *See* graphical smoothing
Mueller, Carol, 348
multiple races design, 17, 247–49; controlled constituency and, 253–54, 255
Mutz, Diana, 264

Nadeau, Richard, 73n21, 263, 264, 278n1, 337, 340, 351n10, 352n12, 359
Nagler, Jonathan, 242, 247, 263
National Annenberg Election Studies (NAES), 110n13; and rolling cross-sections, 16, 165, 167, 169, 191n1
National Election Studies (NES), 5, 82, 83, 84, 86, 108n2, 117, 128, 131, 136, 138, 146, 149, 151, 153, 154, 155, 199, 207, 216, 245; and Continuous Monitoring Survey (1984), 135; Missouri Election Study, 222, 224; as prototype of "multiple races" design, 17; and Senate Election Studies, 17, 243, 244, 258n7
negative campaigning, 10
Nelson, Thomas E., 48, 50
Nevitte, Neil, 11, 45, 55, 68, 73n16

Neuman, W. Russell, 21n19
Newbold, Paul, 160n14
Newman, Jody, 351n5
Nie, Norman, 159
Niemi, Richard, 135
Nijman, T., 190
Noll, R. G., 307
Norris, Pippa, 15, 45
North American Free Trade Agreement (NAFTA), 3, 73n14, 122
Northrup, David, 191n7

O'Neill, Brenda, 338
opinion polls. *See* polls
Orren, Gary, 192n11
Oxley, Zoe M., 48, 50

Page, Benjamin I., 21n21, 47
Palfrey, Thomas, 116, 204, 218n3, 301n1
Palmquist, Bradley, 160n6
panel attrition, 68, 137, 153
panel conditioning, 68, 137, 153, 173; solutions to, 154
panel design, 14–15, 135–37, 185–87; advantages of, 136; and "cross-lag" models, 148; and measures of campaign spending, 207; and "pseudo-panels," 190
parabolic Epanechnikov kernel, 179. *See also* kernel weights
partisanship, and effect of campaign, 30, 92–93; and information levels, 30. *See also* party identification
party conventions, 7
party identification, 5, 6, 8, 46, 55, 83, 321; and activation hypothesis, 358; and evaluation of leaders/candidates, 343; and impact on expectations, 295–98; interaction with spending and voter recognition of candidates, 213–15; and measurement error, 189; and perceptions of elections, 267; and presidential votes, 151–52; and votes for Senate, 244; when not controlled for, 366–67

party label, as voter information, 123
Pessendorfer, Wolfgang, 35
Patterson, Samuel C., 10, 11, 15
Patterson, Thomas E., 20n6, 81, 136
persuasion, 7, 9, 46, 84, 94–97; defined, 82, 94; in typology of campaign effects, 8, 13
Petrocik, John R., 21n23, 85
Piazza, Thomas, 42n3
Plott, Charles, 116
Plutzer, Eric, 338, 343
pocketbook voting, 33–34, 37, 321. *See also* economic voting
Polaris Ad Detector, 310
polarization, position issues and, 9; of voters, 6
policy, voter assessment of, 33; voting, 243–55
political awareness, 12, 360, 367–78
political conditions, and effect on competitiveness, 12
political sophistication, of voters, 127. *See also under* information; knowledge
polls, 47, 78, 82, 117; deliberative, 49; exit, 250; and expectations, 263–73, 281–83, 286–91, 296–300; influence of, on vote, 263–73; and perceptions of candidates, 271–72; to test efficacy of campaign messaging, 308–32
Pomper, Gerald M., 21n22, 307, 308
Pope, Jeremy, 90
Popkin, Samuel L., 9, 20n5, 29, 31, 38
position issues, 9
post-election survey, 5
predispositions, 5, 8, 19, 50, 138–39, 357–59; and news attentiveness, 360–61
pre-election survey, 5
presidential campaigns, 4, 7, 82; as basis for minimal effects model, 8; and problems for understanding effect of advertising campaigns, 332
presidential primaries, 6, 11, 127, 360; and forecasting models, 7
Presser, Stanley, 128
Price, Vincent, 50, 357, 379n2

primary elections. *See* presidential primaries
priming, 5, 8, 9, 13, 69, 70, 84–92, 200; as cognitive shortcut, 31; defined, 82; of economic perceptions, 91; and effect of "horse-race" coverage, 340; and election outcomes, 9; and interpretation of elections, 10; and position issues, 9
proportional representation (PR), and affect on strategic considerations, 11

Quirk, Paul J., 47

race, as voter information, 123
Rae, Saul Forbes, 73n21
Rahn, Wendy, 68, 72n2, 148
randomization, in research design, 119, 129–30
research design, 13–18. *See also* field experiments; laboratory experiments; multiple races design; panel design; rolling cross-section
"resonance strategy," 314. *See also* campaign advertising
retrospective voting, 41, 123
Rhee, June W., 360
Rice, Tom, 37, 42n1, 78
Riker, William H., 21n20
Rivers, Douglas, 46, 48, 51
Roberts, Caroline, 49
Robinson, Gertrude, 340, 352n13
Roddy, B. L., 307
Roe v. Wade, 243, 258n4
rolling cross-section (RCS), 6, 15–16, 164–91; advantages of, 171–75; and measures of campaign spending, 207; and "replicates," 169; and sampling, 16, 164; and smoothing, 16; and U.S. House Elections, 221, 224; and utility for understanding effects of polls, 273; and understanding impact of media, 336, 357
rolling panel design, 155
Romer, Daniel, 110n13, 191n1
Rosenstiel, Tom, 80

Rosenstone, Steven, 7, 10, 42n1, 78, 159, 207, 359
Rosenthal, Howard, 33
Rubin, Donald, 119, 132n3
Ruppert, David, 185

Saint-Jean, Armande, 340, 352n13
salience, of politics 2–3; indicators of, 3; of issues, 5, 6, priming and, of issues, 8, 85–86
sampling: error, 175–76; noise, 16, 175; and rolling cross-sections, 16, 164, 191; size, 164
Sanbonmatsu, Kira, 338
Sanders, Mitch S., 108n1, 135
Sapiro, Virginia, 347, 348
Sartori, Giovanni, 281
senate elections, 3, 145, 224, 243–55, 308–32
Schickler, Eric, 160n6
Schofield, N., 301n3
Schrott, Peter R., 50, 81
Schuman, Howard, 128
Segal, Jeffrey A., 218n3
Sellers, Patrick J., 308
Seltzer, Richard A., 351n5
Shanks, J. Merrill, 255, 259n12
Shankster, Alexandra, 9, 17
Shapiro, Robert Y., 47
Shaw, Daron R., 4, 16, 20n10, 84, 174
Shaw, Donald L., 21n15
Shepsle, Kenneth A., 21n21
Sher, S., 333n2
Shields, Todd, 73n21
shortcuts. *See* cognitive shortcuts
Sides, John, 249, 251
Sigelman, Carol K., 338
Sigelman, Lee, 338
signals, reception of, 37–41
Signorielli, Nancy, 49
Silverman, B. W., 185
Simon, Adam F., 8, 21n22
Simon, Herbert, 73n21
Skalaban, Andrew, 264
Skarpedas, S., 307
Smith, Kevin B., 340

Smith, Richard, 56
smoothing. *See* graphical smoothing
Sniderman, Paul, on experimental research, 116; on House elections, 39; on message reception, 42n3, 45; on political reasoning, 46, 72n5; on rolling cross section, 14, 17
Snyder, James M. Jr., 204, 206
spending, candidate, 3, 5, 78, 200; changes in, over campaign, 207–17; differences between incumbents and challengers, 200–217, 234–37; different types, 236; and expectations of election outcomes, 204; and recognition of candidates, 208–17
stacked design, 249–53
Steenbergen, Marco R., 13, 21n14
Stimson, James A., 45
Stoker, Laura, 17
Stokes, Donald, 5, 33, 131, 199, 228
strategic considerations, of voters, 11, 122, 215, 358
strategic sequencing, defined, 282, 293; and expectations, 293–98; 300
strategic vote, defined, 263
Stroh, Patrick, 20n12
Sturgis, Patrick, 45, 47, 49
Surlin, S. H., 311

Tajfel, Henri, 337
Taras, David, 339
television advertising, 3, 5; and Bush vs. Clinton, 80; and campaign effects in statewide races, 308–32; and issue voting, 319–27; and laboratory experiments, 13
television ratings, as measure of reception, 124
Terkildsen, Nayda, 347, 348
Tetlock, Philip E., 45, 46, 72n5
threshold parties, defined, 286; and expectations, 286–93
Tichenor, P. J., 49
Tufte, Edward, 33, 37, 41, 42n1
Turner, John C., 338

"two-mediator model," 357, 366, 373. *See also* media

Uhlaner, Carole Jean, 267
Ujifusa, Grant, 225, 240n5
U.S. Presidential Debate Commission, 125

valence issues, 9
Valentino, Nicholas A., 8
Vavreck, Lynn, 85, 94, 108, 135, 333n2
Verbeek, M., 190
viability, of candidates, 6, as a strategic consideration, 11
voters, as factor in intensity, 4
voter turnout, campaign effects on, 10; economic voting and, 36–37; negative advertising and, 117–21
Vowles, Jack, 11, 122, 128, 283

Wagenberg, R. H., 340
Waldman, P., 333n2
Wand, M. P., 185
Wasted vote, 37, 127, 281–82. *See also* strategic considerations of voters
Wattenberg, Martin P., 21n22, 150, 360
Webster v. Reproductive Health Services, 243
Weisberg, Herbert F., 20n7
Welch, William P., 204
West, D. M., 307, 308
Westell, Anthony, 340
Westlye, Mark Christopher, 4, 17, 19n2, 224, 225, 249, 258n1
White, Ismail K., 8
Wilcox, Clyde, 259n19
Wiley, David E., 136, 138, 139, 159n3
Wiley, James A., 136, 138, 139, 159n3
Williams, John T., 160n9
Witcover, Jules, 30, 80, 99
Wlezien, Christopher, 20n12, 193n17
Wolfinger, Raymond E., 221, 223, 228, 246
Wright, Gerald C., 135, 250, 258n10

Zaller, John, on campaign effects, 8, 29, 110n13, 131, 149, 160n4, 189; on information reception, 4, 21n24, 30, 31, 38, 39, 42n3, 337, 357, 360, 374, 378, 379n2; on forecasting models, 7; on measuring campaign effects, 131, 137, 173; on political reasoning, 46, 50, 52, 56, 127, 130

Zipp, John F., 338, 343